Praise for *Lean Analytics*

"Your competition will use this book to outgrow you."
Mike Volpe—CMO, Hubspot

"Everyone has data, the key is figuring out what pieces will improve your learning and decision making. Everyone knows they need metrics, but finding ones that are specific, measurable, actionable, relevant, and timely is a huge challenge. In Lean Analytics, *Ben and Alistair have done a masterful job showing us how to use data and metrics to peer through the haze of uncertainty that surrounds creating new businesses and products. This book is a huge gift to our industry."*
Zach Nies—Chief Technologist, Rally Software

"Lean Analytics is the missing piece of Lean Startup, with practical and detailed research, advice and guidance that can help you succeed faster in a startup or large organization."
Dan Martell—CEO and Founder, Clarity

"Entrepreneurs need their own reality distortion field to tilt at improbable windmills. But that delusion can be their undoing if they start lying to themselves. This book is the antidote. Alistair and Ben have written a much-needed dose of reality, and entrepreneurs who ignore this data-driven approach do so at their peril."
Brad Feld—Managing Director, Foundry Group; Co-founder, TechStars; and Creator, the Startup Revolution series of books

"Lean Analytics will take you from Minimum Viable Product to Maximally Valuable Product. It's as useful for product managers at today's multi-billion dollar companies as it is for entrepreneurs who aspire to build those of tomorrow."
John Stormer—Senior Director of New Products, Salesforce

"The bad news is, there will always be people out there smarter than you. The good news is, Alistair and Ben are those guys. Using Lean Analytics *will give you the edge you need."*

Julien Smith—*New York Times* bestselling author of *Trust Agents* and *The Flinch*

"At Twitter, analytics has been key to understanding our users and growing our business. Smart startups need to embrace a data-driven approach if they're going to compete on a level playing field, and this book shows you how."

Kevin Weil—Director of Product, Revenue, Twitter

"A must-read on how to integrate analytics deep into an emerging product, and take the guesswork out of business success."

Peter Yared—CTO/CIO, CBS Interactive

"Lean Analytics is a detailed explanation of the data-driven approach to running a business. Thoughtfully composed by two experienced entrepreneurs, this is a book I will make part of my training materials at Sincerely, Inc., and all future companies."

Matt Brezina—Founder, Sincerely, Inc., and Xobni

"Pearson's Law states, 'That which is measured improves.' Croll and Yoskovitz extend our understanding of Lean management by bringing rigorous measurement techniques to a new frontier: the earliest stages of new product development and launch. If entrepreneurs apply their frameworks, they should see reduced waste and big improvements in startup success rates.

Thomas Eisenmann—Howard H. Stevenson Professor of Business Administration, Harvard Business School

"This isn't just a book about web analytics or business analytics—it's a book about what organizations should and shouldn't measure, and how to transform that data into actionable practices that will help them succeed. Alistair and Benjamin have compiled a robust set of case studies that illustrate the power of getting analytics right, and, if taken to heart, their tips and takeaways will make entrepreneurs, marketers, product and engineering folks better at what they do."

Rand Fishkin—CEO and Co-founder, Moz

"I bet you'd never imagined that success depends on your ability to fail. Fail faster, fail forward. And the secret to that success is your ability to learn and iterate quickly using data. Qualitative and quantitative. Let Alistair and Ben show you how to get to startup nirvana smarter!"

Avinash Kaushik—Author, *Web Analytics 2.0*

"Lean Analytics shows you how to move insanely fast by getting your metrics to tell you when you're failing and how to do something about it. Tons of honest, meaningful advice—a must-read for Founders who want to win."

Sean Kane—Co-founder, F6S and Springboard Accelerator

"There are only two skills that are guaranteed to reduce the chances of startup failure. One is clairvoyance; the other is in this book. Every entrepreneur should read it."

Dharmesh Shah—Founder and CTO, HubSpot

"First you need to build something people love. Then you need to attract and engage people to find and use it. Having a deep understanding of your data and metrics is fundamental in achieving this at scale. Lean Analytics is a detailed, hands-on approach to learning what it means to track the right metrics and use them to build the right products."

Josh Elman—VC, Greylock Partners

"Lean Analytics *is the natural evolution of the Lean Startup movement,*
which began as a humble blog and has blossomed into a global movement.
This book delivers concrete, hard-won insights spanning all business models
and company stages. It's a must-read for any business leader who's looking
to succeed in an increasingly data-driven world."

Mark MacLeod—Chief Corporate Development Officer, FreshBooks

"*A vital part of the founder's toolkit. If you're starting a*
company, you need to read this."

Mark Peter Davis—Venture Capitalist and Incubator

"Lean Analytics *is packed with practical, actionable advice and*
engaging case studies. You need to read this book to understand
how to use data to build a better business."

Paul Joyce—Co-founder and CEO, Geckoboard

"*Get this book now. Even if you're only thinking about starting something,*
Lean Analytics *will help. It's a dose of tough love that will greatly increase*
your chances of survival and success. Start off on the right foot and read
this book; you won't regret it."

Dan Debow—Co-CEO and Founder, Rypple; SVP, Work.com

"*Stop thinking and just buy this book. It's the secret sauce. If*
you're an entrepreneur, it's required reading."

Greg Isenberg—CEO, fiveby.tv; Venture Partner, Good People Ventures

"*This is a treasure for the Lean Startup movement—a dense collection*
of actionable advice, backed by real case studies. Lean concepts are easy
to understand but often difficult to put into practice, but Lean Analytics
makes the path clear and gives you the tools to measure your progress."

Jason Cohen—CEO, WP Engine

Lean Analytics

Use Data to Build a Better Startup Faster

Alistair Croll
Benjamin Yoskovitz

O'REILLY®

Beijing · Cambridge · Farnham · Köln · Sebastopol · Tokyo

Lean Analytics

by Alistair Croll and Benjamin Yoskovitz

Published by O'Reilly Media, Inc., 1005 Gravenstein Highway North, Sebastopol, CA 95472.

O'Reilly books may be purchased for educational, business, or sales promotional use. Online editions are also available for most titles (safari.oreilly.com). For more information, contact our corporate/institutional sales department: (800) 998-9938 or corporate@oreilly.com.

Editor: Mary Treseler

Production Editor: Holly Bauer

Copyeditor: Rachel Monaghan

Proofreader: Jilly Gagnon

Indexer: Lucie Haskins

Cover Designer: Mark Paglietti

Interior Designers: Ron Bilodeau and Monica Kamsvaag

Illustrator: Kara Ebrahim

March 2013: First Edition.

Revision History for the First Edition:

2013-02-19	First release
2013-03-13	Second release
2013-03-15	Third release
2013-08-16	Fourth release
2013-10-18	Fifth release
2014-03-14	Sixth release

See *http://oreilly.com/catalog/errata.csp?isbn=0636920026334* for release details.

ISBN: 978-1-449-33567-0

[CW]

For Riley, who's already mastered the art of asking "why" five times.
—Alistair

For my brother, Jacob, who passed away too soon, but inspires me still to challenge myself and take risks.
—Ben

Contents

PART ONE: STOP LYING TO YOURSELF

PART TWO: FINDING THE RIGHT METRIC FOR RIGHT NOW

PART THREE: LINES IN THE SAND

Foreword

For some reason, the Lean Startup movement has proven excellent at producing bumper stickers. Odds are, if you're reading this, you know some of our most popular additions to the business lexicon: pivot, minimum viable product, Build-Measure-Learn, continuous deployment, or Steve Blank's famous "get out of the building." Some of these you can already buy on a t-shirt.

Given that the past few years of my life have been dedicated to promoting these concepts, I am not now trying to diminish their importance. We are living through a transformation in the way work is done, and these concepts are key elements of that change. The Lean Series is dedicated to bringing this transformation to life by moving beyond the bumper stickers and diving deep into the details.

Lean Analytics takes this mission to a whole new level.

On the surface, this new world seems exciting and bold. Innovation, new sources of growth, the glory of product/market fit and the agony of failures and pivots all make for riveting drama. But all of this work rests on a foundation made of far more boring stuff: accounting, math, and metrics. And the traditional accounting metrics—when applied to the uncertainties of innovation—are surprisingly dangerous. We call them vanity metrics, the numbers that make you feel good but seriously mislead. Avoiding them requires a whole new accounting discipline, which I call "innovation accounting."

Trust me, as an entrepreneur, I had no interest in accounting as a subject. To be honest, in far too many of my companies, the accounting was incredibly simple anyway: revenue, margins, free cash flows—they were all zero.

But accounting is at the heart of our modern management techniques. Since the days of Frederick Winslow Taylor, we have assessed the skill of managers by comparing their results to the forecast. Beat the plan, get a promotion. Miss the plan, and your stock price declines. And for some kinds of products, this works just fine. Accurate forecasting requires a long and stable operating history from which to make the forecast. The longer and more stable, the more accurate.

And yet who really feels like the world is getting more and more stable every day? Whenever conditions change, or we attempt to change them by introducing a truly new product, accurate forecasting becomes nearly impossible. And without that yardstick, how do we evaluate if we're making progress? If we're busy building the wrong product, why should we be proud to be doing it on time and on budget? This is the reason we need a new understanding of how to measure progress, both for ourselves as entrepreneurs and managers, as investors in the companies we fund, and the teams under our purview.

That is why an accounting revolution is required if we're to succeed in this new era of work. And Ben and Alistair have done the incredibly hard work of surveying the best thinking on the metrics and analytics, gathering in-depth examples, and breaking new ground in presenting their own frameworks for figuring out which metrics matter, and when. Their work collecting industry-wide benchmarks to use for a variety of key metrics is worth the price of admission all by itself.

This is not a theoretical work, but a guide for all practitioners who seek new sources of growth. I wish you happy hunting.

Eric Ries
San Francisco
February 4, 2013

Preface

The Lean Startup movement is galvanizing a generation of entrepreneurs. It helps you identify the riskiest parts of your business plan, then finds ways to reduce those risks in a quick, iterative cycle of learning. Most of its insights boil down to one sentence: *Don't sell what you can make; make what you can sell.* And that means figuring out what people want to buy.

Unfortunately, it's hard to know what people really want. Many times, they don't know themselves. When they tell you, it's often what they think you want to hear.* What's worse, as a founder and entrepreneur, you have strong, almost overwhelming preconceptions about how other people think, and these color your decisions in subtle and insidious ways.

Analytics can help. Measuring something makes you accountable. You're forced to confront inconvenient truths. And you don't spend your life and your money building something nobody wants.

Lean Startup helps you structure your progress and identify the riskiest parts of your business, then learn about them quickly so you can adapt. *Lean Analytics* is used to measure that progress, helping you to ask the most important questions and get clear answers quickly.

---

* *http://www.forbes.com/sites/jerrymclaughlin/2012/05/01/would-you-do-this-to-boost-sales-by-20-or-more/*

In this book we show you how to figure out your business model and your stage of growth. We'll explain how to find the One Metric That Matters to you right now, and how to draw a line in the sand so you know when to step on the gas and when to slam on the brakes.

Lean Analytics is the dashboard for every stage of your business, from validating whether a problem is real, to identifying your customers, to deciding what to build, to positioning yourself favorably with a potential acquirer. It can't force you to act on data—but it can put that data front and center, making it harder for you to ignore, and preventing you from driving off the road entirely.

Who This Book Is For

This book is for the entrepreneur trying to build something innovative. We'll walk you through the analytical process, from idea generation to achieving product/market fit and beyond, so this book both is for those starting their entrepreneurial journey as well as those in the middle of it.

Web analysts and data scientists may also find this book useful, because it shows how to move beyond traditional "funnel visualizations" and connect their work to more meaningful business discussions. Similarly, business professionals involved in product development, product management, marketing, public relations, and investing will find much of the content relevant, as it will help them understand and assess startups.

Most of the tools and techniques we'll cover were first applied to consumer web applications. Today, however, they matter to a far broader audience: independent local businesses, election managers, business-to-business startups, rogue civil servants trying to change the system from within, and "intrapreneurs" innovating within big, established organizations.*

In that respect, *Lean Analytics* is for anyone trying to make his or her organization more effective. As we wrote this book, we talked with tiny family businesses, global corporations, fledgling startups, campaign organizers, charities, and even religious groups, all of whom were putting lean, analytical approaches to work in their organizations.

How This Book Works

There's lots of information in this book. We interviewed over a hundred founders, investors, intrapreneurs, and innovators, many of whom shared

---

* An intrapreneur is an entrepreneur within a large organization, often fighting political rather than financial battles and trying to promote change from within.

their stories with us, and we've included more than 30 case studies. We've also listed more than a dozen best-practice patterns you can apply right away. And we've broken the content into four big parts.

- Part I focuses on an understanding of Lean Startup and basic analytics, and the data-informed mindset you'll need to succeed. We review a number of existing frameworks for building your startup and introduce our own, analytics-focused one. This is your primer for the world of Lean Analytics. At the end of this section, you'll have a good understanding of fundamental analytics.

- Part II shows you how to apply Lean Analytics to your startup. We look at six sample business models and the five stages that every startup goes through as it discovers the right product and the best target market. We also talk about finding the One Metric That Matters to your business. When you're done, you'll know what business you're in, what stage you're at, and what to work on.

- Part III looks at what's normal. Unless you have a line in the sand, you don't know whether you're doing well or badly. By reading this section, you'll get some good baselines for key metrics and learn how to set your own targets.

- Part IV shows you how to apply Lean Analytics to your organization, changing the culture of consumer- and business-focused startups as well as established businesses. After all, data-driven approaches apply to more than just new companies.

At the end of most chapters, we've included questions you can answer to help you apply what you've read.

The Building Blocks

Lean Analytics doesn't exist in a vacuum. We're an extension of Lean Startup, heavily influenced by customer development and other concepts that have come before. It's important to understand those building blocks before diving in.

Customer Development

Customer development—a term coined by entrepreneur and professor Steve Blank—took direct aim at the outdated, "build it and they will come" waterfall method of building products and companies. Customer development is focused on collecting continuous feedback that will have a material impact on the direction of a product and business, every step of the way.

Blank first defined customer development in his book *The Four Steps to the Epiphany* (Cafepress.com) and refined his ideas with Bob Dorf in *The Startup Owner's Manual* (K & S Ranch). His definition of a startup is one of the most important concepts in his work:

> *A startup is an organization formed to search for a scalable and repeatable business model.*

Keep that definition in mind as you read the rest of this book.

Lean Startup

Eric Ries defined the Lean Startup process when he combined customer development, Agile software development methodologies, and Lean manufacturing practices into a framework for developing products and businesses quickly and efficiently.

First applied to new companies, Eric's work is now being used by organizations of all sizes to disrupt and innovate. After all, Lean isn't about being cheap or small, it's about eliminating waste and moving quickly, which is good for organizations of any size.

One of Lean Startup's core concepts is *build→measure→learn*—the process by which you do everything, from establishing a vision to building product features to developing channels and marketing strategies, as shown in Figure P-1. Within that cycle, *Lean Analytics* focuses on the *measure* stage. The faster your organization iterates through the cycle, the more quickly you'll find the right product and market. If you measure better, you're more likely to succeed.

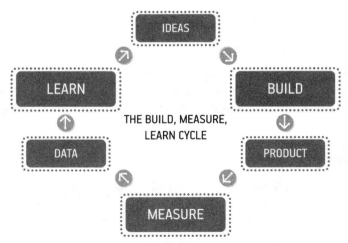

Figure P-1. The build→measure→learn cycle

The cycle isn't just a way of improving your product. It's also a good reality check. Building the minimum product necessary is part of what Eric calls *innovation accounting*, which helps you objectively measure how you're doing. Lean Analytics is a way of quantifying your innovation, getting you closer and closer to a continuous reality check—in other words, to reality itself.

We'd Like to Hear from You

Please address comments and questions concerning this book to the publisher:

O'Reilly Media, Inc.
1005 Gravenstein Highway North
Sebastopol, CA 95472
(800) 998-9938 (in the United States or Canada)
(707) 829-0515 (international or local)
(707) 829-0104 (fax)

We have a web page for this book where we list errata, examples, and any additional information. You can access this page at:

http://oreil.ly/lean_analytics

The authors also maintain a website for this book at:

http://leananalyticsbook.com/

To comment or ask technical questions about this book, send email to:

bookquestions@oreilly.com

For more information about our books, courses, conferences, and news, see our website at *http://www.oreilly.com*.

Find us on Facebook: *http://facebook.com/oreilly*

Follow us on Twitter: *http://twitter.com/oreillymedia*

Watch us on YouTube: *http://www.youtube.com/oreillymedia*

Safari® Books Online

Safari Books Online (*www.safaribooksonline.com*) is an on-demand digital library that delivers expert content in both book and video form from the world's leading authors in technology and business.

Technology professionals, software developers, web designers, and business and creative professionals use Safari Books Online as their primary resource for research, problem solving, learning, and certification training.

Safari Books Online offers a range of product mixes and pricing programs for organizations, government agencies, and individuals. Subscribers have access to thousands of books, training videos, and prepublication manuscripts in one fully searchable database from publishers like O'Reilly Media, Prentice Hall Professional, Addison-Wesley Professional, Microsoft Press, Sams, Que, Peachpit Press, Focal Press, Cisco Press, John Wiley & Sons, Syngress, Morgan Kaufmann, IBM Redbooks, Packt, Adobe Press, FT Press, Apress, Manning, New Riders, McGraw-Hill, Jones & Bartlett, Course Technology, and dozens more. For more information about Safari Books Online, please visit us online.

Thanks and Acknowledgments

This book took a year to write, but decades to learn. It was more of a team effort than most, with dozens of founders, investors, and innovators sharing their stories online and off. Our personal blog readers, as well as the hundreds of subscribers to our Lean Analytics blog who gave us feedback, deserve much of the credit for the clever parts; we deserve all of the blame for the bad bits.

Mary Treseler was the voice of our readers and called us out when we strayed too far into jargon. Our families stayed amazingly patient and helped with several rounds of reading and editing. We sent early copies of critical chapters to reviewers, who verified our assumptions and checked our math, and many of them contributed so much useful feedback that they're practically co-authors. Sonia Gaballa of Nudge Design did great work with our website, and the production team at O'Reilly put up with our unreasonable demands and constant changes. And folks at Totango, Price Intelligently, Chartbeat, Startup Compass, and others all dug into anonymized customer data to enlighten us on things like Software as a Service, pricing, engagement, and average metrics.

But most of all, we want to thank people who challenged us, shared with us, and opened their kimonos to tell us the good and bad parts of startups, often having to fight for approval to talk publicly. Some weren't able to, despite their best efforts, and we'll leave their stories for another day—but every piece of feedback helped shape this book and our understanding of how analytics and Lean Startup methods intertwine.

STOP LYING TO YOURSELF

In this part of the book, we'll look at why you need data to succeed. We'll tackle some basic analytical concepts like qualitative and quantitative data, vanity metrics, correlation, cohorts, segmentation, and leading indicators. We'll consider the perils of being too data-driven. And we'll even think a bit about what you should be doing with your life.

It depends on what the meaning of the word "is" is.

William Jefferson Clinton

CHAPTER 1

We're All Liars

Let's face it: you're delusional.

We're all delusional—some more than others. Entrepreneurs are the most delusional of all.

Entrepreneurs are particularly good at lying to themselves. Lying may even be a prerequisite for succeeding as an entrepreneur—after all, you need to convince others that something is true in the absence of good, hard evidence. You need believers to take a leap of faith with you. As an entrepreneur, you need to live in a semi-delusional state just to survive the inevitable rollercoaster ride of running your startup.

Small lies are essential. They create your reality distortion field. They are a necessary part of being an entrepreneur. But if you start believing your own hype, you won't survive. You'll go too far into the bubble you've created, and you won't come out until you hit the wall—hard—and that bubble bursts.

You need to lie to yourself, but not to the point where you're jeopardizing your business.

That's where data comes in.

Your delusions, no matter how convincing, will wither under the harsh light of data. Analytics is the necessary counterweight to lying, the yin to the yang of hyperbole. Moreover, data-driven learning is the cornerstone of success in startups. It's how you learn what's working and iterate toward the right product and market before the money runs out.

We're not suggesting that gut instinct is a bad thing. Instincts are inspiration, and you'll need to listen to your gut and rely on it throughout the startup journey. But don't disembowel yourself. Guts matter; you've just got to test them. *Instincts are experiments. Data is proof.*

The Lean Startup Movement

Innovation is hard work—harder than most people realize. This is true whether you're a lone startup trying to disrupt an industry or a rogue employee challenging the status quo, tilting at corporate windmills and steering around bureaucratic roadblocks. We get it. Entrepreneurship is crazy, bordering on absurd.

Lean Startup provides a framework by which you can more rigorously go about the business of creating something new. Lean Startup delivers a heavy dose of intellectual honesty. Follow the Lean model, and it becomes increasingly hard to lie, especially to yourself.

There's a reason the Lean Startup movement has taken off now. We're in the midst of a fundamental shift in how companies are built. It's vanishingly cheap to create the first version of something. Clouds are free. Social media is free. Competitive research is free. Even billing and transactions are free.* We live in a digital world, and the bits don't cost anything.

That means you can build something, measure its effect, and learn from it to build something better the next time. You can iterate quickly, deciding early on if you should double down on your idea or fold and move on to the next one. And that's where analytics comes in. Learning doesn't happen accidentally. It's an integral part of the Lean process.

Management guru and author Peter Drucker famously observed, "If you can't measure it, you can't manage it."† Nowhere is this truer than in the Lean model, where successful entrepreneurs build the product, the go-to-market strategy, and the systems by which to learn what customers want—simultaneously.

---

* When we say "free," we mean "free from significant upfront investment." Plenty of cloud and billing services cost money—sometimes more money than you'd spend doing it yourself—once your business is under way. But free, here, means free from outlay in advance of finding your product/market fit. You can use PayPal, or Google Wallet, or Eventbrite, or dozens of other payment and ticketing systems, and pass on the cost of the transaction to your consumers.

† In *Management: Tasks, Responsibilities, Practices* (HarperBusiness), Drucker wrote, "Without productivity objectives, a business does not have direction. Without productivity measurements, it does not have control."

Poking a Hole in Your Reality Distortion Field

Most entrepreneurs have been crushed, usually more than once. If you haven't been solidly trounced on a regular basis, you're probably doing it wrong, and aren't taking the risks you need to succeed in a big way.

But there's a moment on the startup rollercoaster where the whole thing comes right off the rails. It's truly failed. There's little more to do than turn off the website and close down the bank account. You're overwhelmed, the challenges are too great, and it's over. You've failed.

Long before the actual derailment, you knew this was going to happen. It wasn't working. But at the time, your reality distortion field was strong enough to keep you going on faith and fumes alone. As a result, you hit the wall at a million miles an hour, lying to yourself the whole time.

We're not arguing against the importance of the reality distortion field— but we do want to poke a few holes in it. Hopefully, as a result, you'll see the derailment in time to avoid it. We want you to rely less on your reality distortion field, and rely more on Lean Analytics.

CASE STUDY | **Airbnb Photography—Growth Within Growth**

Airbnb is an incredible success story. In just a few years, the company has become a powerhouse in the travel industry, providing travelers with an alternative to hotels, and providing individuals who have rooms, apartments, or homes to rent with a new source of income. In 2012, travelers booked over 5 million nights with Airbnb's service. But it started small, and its founders—adherents to the Lean Startup mindset—took a very methodical approach to their success.

At SXSW 2012, Joe Zadeh, Product Lead at Airbnb, shared part of the company's amazing story. He focused on one aspect of its business: *professional photography.*

It started with a hypothesis: "Hosts with professional photography will get more business. And hosts will sign up for professional photography as a service." This is where the founders' gut instincts came in: they had a sense that professional photography would help their business. But rather than implementing it outright, they built a *Concierge Minimum Viable Product* (MVP) to quickly test their hypothesis.

What Is a Concierge MVP?

The *Minimum Viable Product* is the smallest thing you can build that will create the value you've promised to your market. But nowhere in that definition does it say how much of that offering has to be real. If you're considering building a ride-sharing service, for example, you can try to connect drivers and passengers the old-fashioned way: by hand.

This is a concierge approach. It recognizes that sometimes, building a product—even a minimal one—isn't worth the investment. The risk you're investigating is, "Will people accept rides from others?" It's emphatically *not*, "Can I build software to match drivers and passengers?" A Concierge MVP won't scale, but it's fast and easy in the short term.

Now that it's cheap, even free, to launch a startup, the really scarce resource is attention. A concierge approach in which you run things behind the scenes for the first few customers lets you check whether the need is real; it also helps you understand which things people really use and refine your process before writing a line of code or hiring a single employee.

Initial tests of Airbnb's MVP showed that professionally photographed listings got *two to three times* more bookings than the market average. This validated the founders' first hypothesis. And it turned out that hosts were wildly enthusiastic about receiving an offer from Airbnb to take those photographs for them.

In mid-to-late 2011, Airbnb had 20 photographers in the field taking pictures for hosts—roughly the same time period where we see the proverbial "hockey stick" of growth in terms of nights booked, shown in Figure 1-1.

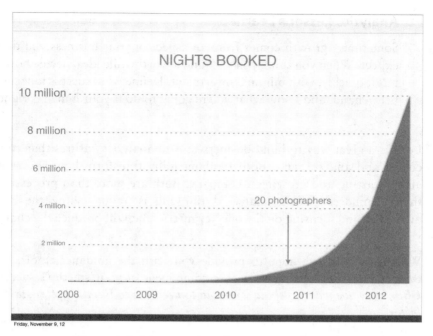

Figure 1-1. It's amazing what you can do with 20 photographers and people's apartments

Airbnb experimented further. It watermarked photos to add authenticity. It got customer service to offer professional photography as a service when renters or potential renters called in. It increased the requirements on photo quality. Each step of the way, the company measured the results and adjusted as necessary. The key metric Airbnb tracked was shoots per month, because it had already proven with its Concierge MVP that more professional photographs meant more bookings.

By February 2012, Airbnb was doing nearly 5,000 shoots per month and continuing to accelerate the growth of the professional photography program.

Summary

- Airbnb's team had a hunch that better photos would increase rentals.

- They tested the idea with a Concierge MVP, putting the least effort possible into a test that would give them valid results.

- When the experiment showed good results, they built the necessary components and rolled it out to all customers.

Analytics Lessons Learned

Sometimes, growth comes from an aspect of your business you don't expect. When you think you've found a worthwhile idea, decide how to test it quickly, with minimal investment. Define what success looks like beforehand, and know what you're going to do if your hunch is right.

Lean is a great way to build businesses. And analytics ensures that you'll collect and analyze data. Both fundamentally transform how you think about starting and growing a company. Both are more than processes—they're mindsets. Lean, analytical thinking is about asking the right questions, and focusing on the one key metric that will produce the change you're after.

With this book, we hope to provide you with the guidance, tools, and evidence to embrace data as a core component of your startup's success. *Ultimately, we want to show you how to use data to build a better startup faster.*

CHAPTER 2

How to Keep Score

Analytics is about tracking the metrics that are critical to your business. Usually, those metrics matter because they relate to your business model—where money comes from, how much things cost, how many customers you have, and the effectiveness of your customer acquisition strategies.

In a startup, you don't always know which metrics are key, because you're not entirely sure what business you're in. You're frequently changing the activity you analyze. You're still trying to find the right product, or the right target audience. In a startup, the purpose of analytics is *to find your way to the right product and market before the money runs out.*

What Makes a Good Metric?

Here are some rules of thumb for what makes a good metric—a number that will drive the changes you're looking for.

A good metric is comparative. Being able to compare a metric to other time periods, groups of users, or competitors helps you understand which way things are moving. "Increased conversion from last week" is more meaningful than "2% conversion."

A good metric is understandable. If people can't remember it and discuss it, it's much harder to turn a change in the data into a change in the culture.

A good metric is a ratio or a rate. Accountants and financial analysts have several ratios they look at to understand, at a glance, the fundamental health of a company.* You need some, too.

There are several reasons ratios tend to be the best metrics:

- **Ratios are easier to act on.** Think about driving a car. Distance travelled is informational. But speed—distance per hour—is something you can act on, because it tells you about your current state, and whether you need to go faster or slower to get to your destination on time.

- **Ratios are inherently comparative.** If you compare a daily metric to the same metric over a month, you'll see whether you're looking at a sudden spike or a long-term trend. In a car, speed is one metric, but speed right now over average speed this hour shows you a lot about whether you're accelerating or slowing down.

- **Ratios are also good for comparing factors that are somehow opposed, or for which there's an inherent tension.** In a car, this might be distance covered divided by traffic tickets. The faster you drive, the more distance you cover—but the more tickets you get. This ratio might suggest whether or not you should be breaking the speed limit.

Leaving our car analogy for a moment, consider a startup with free and paid versions of its software. The company has a choice to make: offer a rich set of features for free to acquire new users, or reserve those features for paying customers, so they will spend money to unlock them. Having a full-featured free product might reduce sales, but having a crippled product might reduce new users. You need a metric that combines the two, so you can understand how changes affect overall health. Otherwise, you might do something that increases sales revenue at the expense of growth.

A good metric changes the way you behave. This is by far the most important criterion for a metric: what will you do differently based on changes in the metric?

- "Accounting" metrics like daily sales revenue, when entered into your spreadsheet, need to make your predictions more accurate. These metrics form the basis of Lean Startup's *innovation accounting*, showing you how close you are to an ideal model and whether your actual results are converging on your business plan.

---

* This includes fundamentals such as the price-to-earnings ratio, sales margins, the cost of sales, revenue per employee, and so on.

- "Experimental" metrics, like the results of a test, help you to optimize the product, pricing, or market. Changes in these metrics will significantly change your behavior. Agree on what that change will be before you collect the data: if the pink website generates more revenue than the alternative, you're going pink; if more than half your respondents say they won't pay for a feature, don't build it; if your curated MVP doesn't increase order size by 30%, try something else.

Drawing a line in the sand is a great way to enforce a disciplined approach. A good metric changes the way you behave precisely *because* it's aligned to your goals of keeping users, encouraging word of mouth, acquiring customers efficiently, or generating revenue.

Unfortunately, that's not always how it happens.

Renowned author, entrepreneur, and public speaker Seth Godin cites several examples of this in a blog post entitled "Avoiding false metrics."[*] Funnily enough (or maybe not!), one of Seth's examples, which involves car salespeople, recently happened to Ben.

While finalizing the paperwork for his new car, the dealer said to Ben, "You'll get a call in the next week or so. They'll want to know about your experience at the dealership. It's a quick thing, won't take you more than a minute or two. It's on a scale from 1 to 5. You'll give us a 5, right? Nothing in the experience would warrant less, right? If so, I'm very, very sorry, but a 5 would be great."

Ben didn't give it a lot of thought (and strangely, no one ever did call). Seth would call this a *false metric*, because the car salesman spent more time asking for a good rating (which was clearly important to him) than he did providing a great experience, which was supposedly what the rating was for in the first place.

Misguided sales teams do this too. At one company, Alistair saw a sales executive tie quarterly compensation to the number of deals in the pipeline, rather than to the number of deals closed, or to margin on those sales. Salespeople are coin-operated, so they did what they always do: they followed the money. In this case, that meant a glut of junk leads that took two quarters to clean out of the pipeline—time that would have been far better spent closing qualified prospects.

Of course, customer satisfaction or pipeline flow is vital to a successful business. But if you want to change behavior, your metric must be tied to the behavioral change you want. If you measure something and it's not

---

[*] http://sethgodin.typepad.com/seths_blog/2012/05/avoiding-false-metrics.html

attached to a goal, in turn changing your behavior, you're wasting your time. Worse, you may be lying to yourself and fooling yourself into believing that everything is OK. That's no way to succeed.

One other thing you'll notice about metrics is that they often come in pairs. *Conversion rate* (the percentage of people who buy something) is tied to *time-to-purchase* (how long it takes someone to buy something). Together, they tell you a lot about your cash flow. Similarly, *viral coefficient* (the number of people a user successfully invites to your service) and *viral cycle time* (how long it takes them to invite others) drive your adoption rate. As you start to explore the numbers that underpin your business, you'll notice these pairs. Behind them lurks a fundamental metric like revenue, cash flow, or user adoption.

If you want to choose the right metrics, you need to keep five things in mind:

Qualitative versus quantitative metrics

Qualitative metrics are unstructured, anecdotal, revealing, and hard to aggregate; quantitative metrics involve numbers and statistics, and provide hard numbers but less insight.

Vanity versus actionable metrics

Vanity metrics might make you feel good, but they don't change how you act. Actionable metrics change your behavior by helping you pick a course of action.

Exploratory versus reporting metrics

Exploratory metrics are speculative and try to find unknown insights to give you the upper hand, while reporting metrics keep you abreast of normal, managerial, day-to-day operations.

Leading versus lagging metrics

Leading metrics give you a predictive understanding of the future; lagging metrics explain the past. Leading metrics are better because you still have time to act on them—the horse hasn't left the barn yet.

Correlated versus causal metrics

If two metrics change together, they're correlated, but if one metric *causes* another metric to change, they're causal. If you find a causal relationship between something you want (like revenue) and something you can control (like which ad you show), then you can change the future.

Analysts look at specific metrics that drive the business, called *key performance indicators* (KPIs). Every industry has KPIs—if you're a restaurant owner, it's the number of covers (tables) in a night; if you're an investor, it's the return on an investment; if you're a media website, it's ad clicks; and so on.

Qualitative Versus Quantitative Metrics

Quantitative data is easy to understand. It's the numbers we track and measure—for example, sports scores and movie ratings. As soon as something is ranked, counted, or put on a scale, it's quantified. Quantitative data is nice and scientific, and (assuming you do the math right) you can aggregate it, extrapolate it, and put it into a spreadsheet. But it's seldom enough to get a business started. You can't walk up to people, ask them what problems they're facing, and get a quantitative answer. For that, you need qualitative input.

Qualitative data is messy, subjective, and imprecise. It's the stuff of interviews and debates. It's hard to quantify. You can't measure qualitative data easily. If quantitative data answers "what" and "how much," qualitative data answers "why." *Quantitative data abhors emotion; qualitative data marinates in it.*

Initially, you're looking for qualitative data. You're not measuring results numerically. Instead, you're speaking to people—specifically, to people you think are potential customers in the right target market. You're exploring. *You're getting out of the building.*

Collecting good qualitative data takes preparation. You need to ask specific questions without leading potential customers or skewing their answers. You have to avoid letting your enthusiasm and reality distortion rub off on your interview subjects. Unprepared interviews yield misleading or meaningless results.

Vanity Versus Real Metrics

Many companies claim they're data-driven. Unfortunately, while they embrace the *data* part of that mantra, few focus on the second word: *driven*. If you have a piece of data on which you cannot act, it's a vanity metric. If all it does is stroke your ego, it won't help. You want your data to inform, to guide, to improve your business model, to help you decide on a course of action.

Whenever you look at a metric, ask yourself, "What will I do differently based on this information?" If you can't answer that question, you probably shouldn't worry about the metric too much. And if you don't know which metrics *would* change your organization's behavior, you aren't being data-driven. You're floundering in data quicksand.

Consider, for example, "total signups." This is a vanity metric. The number can only increase over time (a classic "up and to the right" graph). It tells us nothing about what those users are doing or whether they're valuable to us. They may have signed up for the application and vanished forever.

"Total active users" is a bit better—assuming that you've done a decent job of defining an active user—but it's still a vanity metric. It will gradually increase over time, too, unless you do something horribly wrong.

The real metric of interest—the *actionable* one—is "percent of users who are active." This is a critical metric because it tells us about the level of engagement your users have with your product. When you change something about the product, this metric should change, and if you change it in a good way, it should go up. That means you can experiment, learn, and iterate with it.

Another interesting metric to look at is "number of users acquired over a specific time period." Often, this will help you compare different marketing approaches—for example, a Facebook campaign in the first week, a reddit campaign in the second, a Google AdWords campaign in the third, and a LinkedIn campaign in the fourth. Segmenting experiments by time in this way isn't precise, but it's relatively easy.* And it's actionable: if Facebook works better than LinkedIn, you know where to spend your money.

Actionable metrics aren't magic. They won't tell you what to do—in the previous example, you could try changing your pricing, or your medium, or your wording. The point here is that you're doing *something* based on the data you collect.

PATTERN | # Eight Vanity Metrics to Watch Out For

It's easy to fall in love with numbers that go up and to the right. Here's a list of eight notorious vanity metrics you should avoid.

1. **Number of hits.** This is a metric from the early, foolish days of the Web. If you have a site with many objects on it, this will be a big number. Count people instead.

---

* A better way is to run the four campaigns concurrently, using analytics to group the users you acquire into distinct *segments*. You'll get your answer in one week rather than four, and control for other variables like seasonal variation. We'll get into more detail about segmentation and cohort analysis later.

PART ONE: STOP LYING TO YOURSELF

2. **Number of page views.** This is only slightly better than hits, since it counts the number of times someone requests a page. Unless your business model depends on page views (i.e., display advertising inventory), you should count people instead.

3. **Number of visits.** Is this one person who visits a hundred times, or are a hundred people visiting once? Fail.

4. **Number of unique visitors.** All this shows you is how many people saw your home page. It tells you nothing about what they did, why they stuck around, or if they left.

5. **Number of followers/friends/likes.** Counting followers and friends is nothing more than a popularity contest, unless you can get them to do something useful for you. Once you know how many followers will do your bidding when asked, you've got something.

6. **Time on site/number of pages.** These are a poor substitute for actual engagement or activity unless your business is tied to this behavior. If customers spend a lot of time on your support or complaints pages, that's probably a bad thing.

7. **Emails collected.** A big mailing list of people excited about your new startup is nice, but until you know how many will open your emails (and act on what's inside them), this isn't useful. Send test emails to some of your registered subscribers and see if they'll do what you tell them.

8. **Number of downloads.** While it sometimes affects your ranking in app stores, downloads alone don't lead to real value. Measure activations, account creations, or something else.

Exploratory Versus Reporting Metrics

Avinash Kaushik, author and Digital Marketing Evangelist at Google, says former US Secretary of Defense Donald Rumsfeld knew a thing or two about analytics. According to Rumsfeld:

> There are known knowns; there are things we know that we know. There are known unknowns; that is to say there are things that we now know we don't know. But there are also unknown unknowns—there are things we do not know, we don't know.

Figure 2-1 shows these four kinds of information.

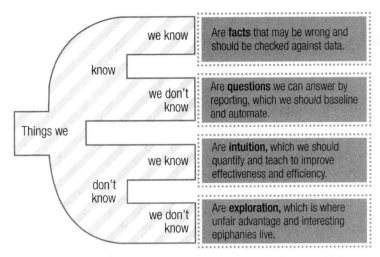

Figure 2-1. The hidden genius of Donald Rumsfeld

The "known unknowns" is a reporting posture—counting money, or users, or lines of code. We *know* we don't know the value of the metric, so we go find out. We may use these metrics for accounting ("How many widgets did we sell today?") or to measure the outcome of an experiment ("Did the green or the red widget sell more?"), but in both cases, we know the metric is needed.

The "unknown unknowns" are most relevant to startups: exploring to discover something new that will help you disrupt a market. As we'll see in the next case study, it's how Circle of Friends found out that moms were its best users. These "unknown unknowns" are where the magic lives. They lead down plenty of wrong paths, and hopefully toward some kind of "eureka!" moment when the idea falls into place. This fits what Steve Blank says a startup should spend its time doing: searching for a scalable, repeatable business model.

Analytics has a role to play in all four of Rumsfeld's quadrants:

- It can check our facts and assumptions—such as open rates or conversion rates—to be sure we're not kidding ourselves, and check that our business plans are accurate.

- It can test our intuitions, turning hypotheses into evidence.

- It can provide the data for our spreadsheets, waterfall charts, and board meetings.

- It can help us find the nugget of opportunity on which to build a business.

In the early stages of your startup, the unknown unknowns matter most, because they can become your secret weapons.

| CASE STUDY | ## Circle of Moms Explores Its Way to Success |

Circle of Friends was a simple idea: a Facebook application that allowed you to organize your friends into circles for targeted content sharing. Mike Greenfield and his co-founders started the company in September 2007, shortly after Facebook launched its developer platform. The timing was perfect: Facebook became an open, viral place to acquire users as quickly as possible and build a startup. There had never been a platform with so many users and that was so open (Facebook had about 50 million users at the time).

By mid-2008, Circle of Friends had 10 million users. Mike focused on growth above everything else. "It was a land grab," he says, and Circle of Friends was clearly viral. But there was a problem. Too few people were actually *using* the product.

According to Mike, less than 20% of circles had any activity whatsoever after their initial creation. "We had a few million monthly uniques from those 10 million users, but as a general social network we knew that wasn't good enough and monetization would likely be poor."

So Mike went digging.

He started looking through the database of users and what they were doing. The company didn't have an in-depth analytical dashboard at the time, but Mike could still do some exploratory analysis. And he found a segment of users—moms, to be precise—that bucked the poor engagement trend of most users. Here's what he found:

- Their messages to one another were on average 50% longer.

- They were 115% more likely to attach a picture to a post they wrote.

- They were 110% more likely to engage in a threaded (i.e., deep) conversation.

- They had friends who, once invited, were 50% more likely to become engaged users themselves.

- They were 75% more likely to click on Facebook notifications.

- They were 180% more likely to click on Facebook news feed items.

- They were 60% more likely to accept invitations to the app.

The numbers were so compelling that in June 2008, Mike and his team switched focus completely. They pivoted. And in October 2008, they launched Circle of Moms on Facebook.

Initially, numbers dropped as a result of the new focus, but by 2009, the team grew its community to 4.5 million users—and unlike the users who'd been lost in the change, these were actively engaged. The company went through some ups and downs after that, as Facebook limited applications' abilities to spread virally. Ultimately, the company moved off Facebook, grew independently, and sold to Sugar Inc. in early 2012.

Summary

- Circle of Friends was a social graph application in the right place at the right time—with the wrong market.

- By analyzing patterns of engagement and desirable behavior, then finding out what those users had in common, the company found the right market for its offering.

- Once the company had found its target, it focused—all the way to changing its name. Pivot hard or go home, and be prepared to burn some bridges.

Analytics Lessons Learned

The key to Mike's success with Circle of Moms was his ability to dig into the data and look for meaningful patterns and opportunities. Mike discovered an "unknown unknown" that led to a big, scary, gutsy bet (drop the generalized Circle of Friends to focus on a specific niche) that was a gamble—but one that was based on data.

There's a "critical mass" of engagement necessary for any community to take off. Mild success may not give you escape velocity. As a result, it's better to have fervent engagement with a smaller, more easily addressable target market. Virality requires focus.

Leading Versus Lagging Metrics

Both leading and lagging metrics are useful, but they serve different purposes.

A leading metric (sometimes called a *leading indicator*) tries to predict the future. For example, the current number of prospects in your sales funnel gives you a sense of how many new customers you'll acquire in the future.

If the current number of prospects is very small, you're not likely to add many new customers. You can increase the number of prospects and expect an increase in new customers.

On the other hand, a lagging metric, such as *churn* (which is the number of customers who leave in a given time period) gives you an indication that there's a problem—but by the time you're able to collect the data and identify the problem, it's too late. The customers who churned out aren't coming back. That doesn't mean you can't act on a lagging metric (i.e., work to improve churn and then measure it again), but it's akin to closing the barn door after the horses have left. New horses won't leave, but you've already lost a few.

In the early days of your startup, you won't have enough data to know how a current metric relates to one down the road, so measure lagging metrics at first. Lagging metrics are still useful and can provide a solid baseline of performance. For leading indicators to work, you need to be able to do cohort analysis and compare groups of customers over periods of time.

Consider, for example, the volume of customer complaints. You might track the number of support calls that happen in a day—once you've got a call volume to make that useful. Earlier on, you might track the number of customer complaints in a 90-day period. Both could be leading indicators of churn: if complaints are increasing, it's likely that more customers will stop using your product or service. As a leading indicator, customer complaints also give you ammunition to dig into what's going on, figure out why customers are complaining more, and address those issues.

Now consider account cancellation or product returns. Both are important metrics—but they measure after the fact. They pinpoint problems, but only after it's too late to avert the loss of a customer. Churn is important (and we discuss it at length throughout the book), but looking at it myopically won't let you iterate and adapt at the speed you need.

Indicators are everywhere. In an enterprise software company, quarterly new product bookings are a lagging metric of sales success. By contrast, new qualified leads are a leading indicator, because they let you predict sales success ahead of time. But as anyone who's ever worked in B2B (business-to-business) sales will tell you, in addition to qualified leads you need a good understanding of conversion rate and sales-cycle length. Only then can you make a realistic estimate of how much new business you'll book.

In some cases, a lagging metric for one group within a company is a leading metric for another. For example, we know that the number of quarterly bookings is a lagging metric for salespeople (the contracts are signed already), but for the finance department that's focused on collecting payment, they're a leading indicator of expected revenue (since the revenue hasn't yet been realized).

Ultimately, you need to decide whether the thing you're tracking helps you make better decisions sooner. As we've said, a real metric has to be actionable. Lagging and leading metrics can both be actionable, but leading indicators show you what *will* happen, reducing your cycle time and making you leaner.

Correlated Versus Causal Metrics

In Canada, the use of winter tires is correlated with a decrease in accidents. People put softer winter tires on their cars in cold weather, and there are more accidents in the summer.* Does that mean we should make drivers use winter tires year-round? Almost certainly not—softer tires stop poorly on warm summer roads, and accidents would increase.

Other factors, such as the number of hours driven and summer vacations, are likely responsible for the increased accident rates. But looking at a simple correlation without demanding causality leads to some bad decisions. There's a correlation between ice cream consumption and drowning. Does that mean we should ban ice cream to avert drowning deaths? Or measure ice cream consumption to predict the fortunes of funeral home stock prices? No: ice cream and drowning rates both happen *because of* summer weather.

Finding a correlation between two metrics is a good thing. Correlations can help you predict what will happen. But finding the *cause* of something means you can change it. Usually, causations aren't simple one-to-one relationships. Many factors conspire to cause something. In the case of summertime car crashes, we have to consider alcohol consumption, the number of inexperienced drivers on the road, the greater number of daylight hours, summer vacations, and so on. So you'll seldom get a 100% causal relationship. You'll get several independent metrics, each of which "explains" a portion of the behavior of the dependent metric. But even a degree of causality is valuable.

You prove causality by finding a correlation, then running an experiment in which you control the other variables and measure the difference. This is hard to do because no two users are identical; it's often impossible to subject a statistically significant number of people to a properly controlled experiment in the real world.

---

* *http://www.statcan.gc.ca/pub/82-003-x/2008003/article/10648/c-g/5202438-eng.htm*

If you have a big enough sample of users, you can run a reliable test without controlling all the other variables, because eventually the impact of the other variables is relatively unimportant. That's why Google can test subtle factors like the color of a hyperlink,* and why Microsoft knows exactly what effect a slower page load time has on search rates.† But for the average startup, you'll need to run simpler tests that experiment with only a few things, and then compare how that changed the business.

We'll look at different kinds of testing and segmentation shortly, but for now, recognize this: correlation is good. Causality is great. Sometimes, you may have to settle for the former—but you should always be trying to discover the latter.

Moving Targets

When picking a goal early on, you're drawing a line in the sand—not carving it in stone. You're chasing a moving target, because you really don't know how to define success.

Adjusting your goals and how you define your key metrics is acceptable, provided that you're being honest with yourself, recognizing the change this means for your business, and not just lowering expectations so that you can keep going in spite of the evidence.

When your initial offering—your minimum viable product—is in the market and you're acquiring early-adopter customers and testing their use of your product, you won't even know how they're going to use it (although you'll have assumptions). Sometimes there's a huge gulf between what you assume and what users actually do. You might think that people will play your multiplayer game, only to discover that they're using you as a photo upload service. Unlikely? That's how Flickr got started.

Sometimes, however, the differences are subtler. You might assume your product has to be used daily to succeed, only to find out that's not so. In these situations, it's reasonable to update your metrics accordingly, provided that you're able to prove the value created.

---

* *http://gigaom.com/2009/07/09/when-it-comes-to-links-color-matters/*

† *http://velocityconf.com/velocity2009/public/schedule/detail/8523*

| # HighScore House Defines an "Active User"

HighScore House started as a simple application that allowed parents to list chores and challenges for their children with point values. Kids could complete the tasks, collect points, and redeem the points for rewards they wanted.

When HighScore House launched its MVP, the company had several hundred families ready to test it. The founders drew a line in the sand: in order for the MVP to be considered successful, parents and kids would have to each use the application four times per week. These families would be considered "active." It was a high, but good, bar.

After a month or so, the percentage of active families was lower than this line in the sand. The founders were disappointed but determined to keep experimenting in an effort to improve engagement:

- They modified the sign-up flow (making it clearer and more educational to increase quality signups and to improve onboarding).

- They sent email notifications as daily reminders to parents.

- They sent transactional emails to parents based on actions their kids took in the system.

There was an incremental improvement each time, but nothing that moved the needle significantly enough to say that the MVP was a success.

Then co-founder and CEO Kyle Seaman did something critical: *he picked up the phone.* Kyle spoke with dozens of parents. He started calling parents who had signed up, but who weren't active. First he reached out to those that had abandoned HighScore House completely ("churned out"). For many of them, the application wasn't solving a big enough pain point. That's fine. The founders never assumed the market was "all parents"—that's just too broad a definition, particularly for a first version of a product. Kyle was looking for a smaller subset of families where HighScore House would resonate, to narrow the market segment and focus.

Kyle then called those families who *were* using HighScore House, but not using it enough to be defined as active. Many of these families responded positively: "We're using HighScore House. It's great. The kids are making their beds consistently for the first time ever!"

The response from parents was a surprise. Many of them were using HighScore House only once or twice a week, but they were getting value out of the product. From this, Kyle learned about segmentation and which types of families were more or less interested in what the company was offering. He began to understand that the initial baseline of usage the team had set wasn't consistent with how engaged customers were using the product.

That doesn't mean the team shouldn't have taken a guess. Without that initial line in the sand, they would have had no benchmark for learning, and Kyle might not have picked up the phone. But now he really understood his customers. The combination of quantitative and qualitative data was key.

As a result of this learning, the team redefined the "active user" threshold to more accurately reflect existing users' behavior. It was okay for them to adjust a key metric because they truly understood why they were doing it and could justify the change.

Summary

- HighScore House drew an early, audacious line in the sand—which it couldn't hit.

- The team experimented quickly to improve the number of active users but couldn't move the needle enough.

- They picked up the phone and spoke to customers, realizing that they were creating value for a segment of users with lower usage metrics.

Analytics Lessons Learned

First, know your customer. There's no substitute for engaging with customers and users directly. All the numbers in the world can't explain why something is happening. Pick up the phone right now and call a customer, even one who's disengaged.

Second, make early assumptions and set targets for what you think success looks like, but don't experiment yourself into oblivion. Lower the bar if necessary, but not for the sake of getting over it: that's just cheating. Use qualitative data to understand what value you're creating and adjust only if the new line in the sand reflects how customers (in specific segments) are using your product.

Segments, Cohorts, A/B Testing, and Multivariate Analysis

Testing is at the heart of Lean Analytics. Testing usually involves comparing two things against each other through segmentation, cohort analysis, or A/B testing. These are important concepts for anyone trying to perform the kind of scientific comparison needed to justify a change, so we'll explain them in some detail here.

Segmentation

A segment is simply a group that shares some common characteristic. It might be users who run Firefox, or restaurant patrons who make reservations rather than walking in, or passengers who buy first-class tickets, or parents who drive minivans.

On websites, you segment visitors according to a range of technical and demographic information, then compare one segment to another. If visitors using the Firefox browser have significantly fewer purchases, do additional testing to find out why. If a disproportionate number of engaged users are coming from Australia, survey them to discover why, and then try to replicate that success in other markets.

Segmentation works for any industry and any form of marketing, not just for websites. Direct mail marketers have been segmenting for decades with great success.

Cohort Analysis

A second kind of analysis, which compares similar groups over time, is cohort analysis. As you build and test your product, you'll iterate constantly. Users who join you in the first week will have a different experience from those who join later on. For example, all of your users might go through an initial free trial, usage, payment, and abandonment cycle. As this happens, you'll make changes to your business model. The users who experienced the trial in month one will have a different onboarding experience from those who experience it in month five. How did that affect their churn? To find out, we use cohort analysis.

Each group of users is a cohort—participants in an experiment across their lifecycle. You can compare cohorts against one another to see if, on the whole, key metrics are getting better over time. Here's an example of why cohort analysis is critical for startups.

Imagine that you're running an online retailer. Each month, you acquire a thousand new customers, and they spend some money. Table 2-1 shows your customers' average revenues from the first five months of the business.

	January	February	March	April	May
Total customers	1,000	2,000	3,000	4,000	5,000
Average revenue per customer	$5.00	$4.50	$4.33	$4.25	$4.50

Table 2-1. Average revenues for five months

From this table, you can't learn much. Are things getting better or worse? Since you aren't comparing recent customers to older ones—and because you're commingling the purchases of a customer who's been around for five months with those of a brand new one—it's hard to tell. All this data shows is a slight drop in revenues, then a recovery. But average revenue is pretty static.

Now consider the same data, broken out by the month in which that customer group started using the site. As Table 2-2 shows, something important is going on. Customers who arrived in month five are spending, on average, $9 in their first month—nearly double that of those who arrived in month one. That's huge growth!

	January	February	March	April	May
New users	1,000	1,000	1,000	1,000	1,000
Total users	1,000	2,000	3,000	4,000	5,000
Month 1	$5.00	$3.00	$2.00	$1.00	$0.50
Month 2		$6.00	$4.00	$2.00	$1.00
Month 3			$7.00	$6.00	$5.00
Month 4				$8.00	$7.00
Month 5					$9.00

Table 2-2. Comparing revenues by the month customers arrived

Another way to understand cohorts is to line up the data by the users' experience—in the case of Table 2-3, we've done this by the number of months they've used the system. This shows another critical metric: how quickly revenue declines after the first month.

Cohort	Month of use				
	1	2	3	4	5
January	$5.00	$3.00	$2.00	$1.00	$0.50
February	$6.00	$4.00	$2.00	$1.00	
March	$7.00	$6.00	$5.00		
April	$8.00	$7.00			
May	$9.00				
Averages	$7.00	$5.00	$3.00	$1.00	$0.50

Table 2-3. Cohort analysis of revenue data

A cohort analysis presents a *much* clearer perspective. In this example, poor monetization in early months was diluting the overall health of the metrics. The January cohort—the first row—spent $5 in its first month, then tapered off to only $0.50 in its fifth month. But first-month spending is growing dramatically, and the drop-off seems better, too: April's cohort spent $8 in its first month and $7 in its second month. A company that seemed stalled is in fact flourishing. And you know what metric to focus on: drop-off in sales after the first month.

This kind of reporting allows you to see patterns clearly against the lifecycle of a customer, rather than slicing across all customers blindly without accounting for the natural cycle a customer undergoes. Cohort analysis can be done for revenue, churn, viral word of mouth, support costs, or any other metric you care about.

A/B and Multivariate Testing

Cohort experiments that compare groups like the one in Table 2-2 are called *longitudinal* studies, since the data is collected *along* the natural lifespan of a customer group. By contrast, studies in which different groups of test subjects are given different experiences at the same time are called *cross-sectional* studies. Showing half of the visitors a blue link and half of them a green link in order to see which group is more likely to click that link is a cross-sectional study. When we're comparing one attribute of a subject's experience, such as link color, and assuming everything else is equal, we're doing A/B testing.

You can test everything about your product, but it's best to focus on the critical steps and assumptions. The results can pay off dramatically: Jay Parmar, co-founder of crowdfunded ticketing site Picatic, told us that simply changing the company's call to action from "Get started free" to "Try it out free" increased the number of people who clicked on an offer—known as the *click-through rate*—by 376% for a 10-day period.

A/B tests seem relatively simple, but they have a problem. Unless you're a huge web property—like Bing or Google—with enough traffic to run a test on a single factor like link color or page speed and get an answer quickly, you'll have more things to test than you have traffic. You might want to test the color of a web page, the text in a call to action, and the picture you're showing to visitors.

Rather than running a series of separate tests one after the other—which will delay your learning cycle—you can analyze them all at once using a technique called *multivariate analysis*. This relies on statistical analysis of the results to see which of many factors correlates strongly with an improvement in a key metric.

Figure 2-2 illustrates these four ways of slicing users into subgroups and analyzing or testing them.

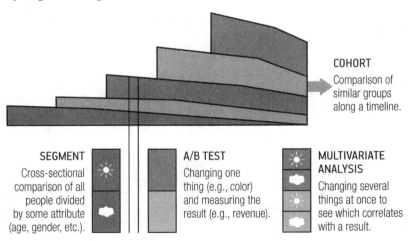

Figure 2-2. Cohorts, segments, A/B testing, and multivariate analysis, oh my

The Lean Analytics Cycle

Much of Lean Analytics is about finding a meaningful metric, then running experiments to improve it until that metric is good enough for you to move to the next problem or the next stage of your business, as shown in Figure 2-3.

Eventually, you'll find a business model that is sustainable, repeatable, and growing, and learn how to scale it.

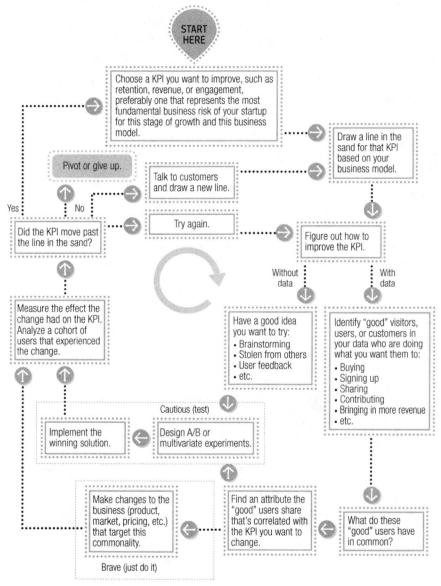

Figure 2-3. The circle of life for analytical startups

We've covered a lot of background on metrics and analytics in this chapter, and your head might be a bit full at this point. You've learned:

- What makes a good metric

- What vanity metrics are and how to avoid them

- The difference between qualitative and quantitative metrics, between exploratory and reporting metrics, between leading and lagging metrics, and between correlated and causal metrics

- What A/B testing is, and why multivariate testing is more common

- The difference between segments and cohorts

In the coming chapters, you'll put all of these dimensions to work on a variety of business models and stages of startup growth.

EXERCISE | Evaluating the Metrics You Track

Take a look at the top three to five metrics that you track religiously and review daily. Write them down. Now answer these questions about them:

- How many of those metrics are good metrics?

- How many do you use to make business decisions, and how many are just vanity metrics?

- Can you eliminate any that aren't adding value?

- Are there others that you're now thinking about that may be more meaningful?

Cross off the bad ones and add new ones to the bottom of your list, and let's keep going through the book.

CHAPTER 3

Deciding What to Do with Your Life

As a founder, you're trying to decide what to spend the next few years of your life working on. The reason you want to be lean and analytical about the process is so that you don't waste your life building something nobody wants. Or, as Netscape founder and venture capitalist Marc Andreesen puts it, *"Markets that don't exist don't care how smart you are."**

Hopefully, you have an idea of what you want to build. It's your blueprint, and it's what you'll test with analytics. You need a way of quickly and consistently articulating your hypotheses around that idea, so you can go and verify (or repudiate) them with real customers. To do this, we recommend Ash Maurya's Lean Canvas, which lays out a clear process for defining and adjusting a business model based on customer development. We'll discuss Ash's model later in this chapter.

But the canvas is only half of what you need. It's not just about finding a business that works—you also need to find a business that you want to work on. Strategic consultant, blogger, and designer Bud Caddell has three clear criteria for deciding what to spend your time on: something that you're good at, that you want to do, and that you can make money doing.

Let's look at the Lean Canvas and Bud's three criteria in more detail.

---

* *http://pmarca-archive.posterous.com/the-pmarca-guide-to-startups-part-4-the-only*

The Lean Canvas

The Lean Canvas is a one-page visual business plan that's ongoing and actionable. It was created by Ash Maurya, and inspired by Alex Osterwalder's Business Model Canvas.* As you can see in Figure 3-1, it consists of nine boxes organized on a single sheet of paper, designed to walk you through the most important aspects of any business.

PROBLEM	SOLUTION	UNIQUE VALUE PROPOSITION	UNFAIR ADVANTAGE	CUSTOMER SEGMENTS
List your top 1–3 problems **1**	Outline a possible solution for each problem **4**	Single, clear, compelling message that turns an unaware visitor into an interested prospect **3** HIGH-LEVEL CONCEPT List your X for Y analogy (e.g., YouTube = Flickr for videos)	Something that can't be easily copied or bought **9**	List your target customers and users **2**
EXISTING ALTERNATIVES List how these problems are solved today	KEY METRICS List the key numbers that tell you how your business is doing **8**		CHANNELS List your path to customers **5**	EARLY ADOPTERS List the characteristics of your ideal customers
COST STRUCTURE List your fixed and variable costs **7**			REVENUE STREAMS List your sources of revenue **6**	

Figure 3-1. You can describe your entire business in nine small boxes

The Lean Canvas is fantastic at identifying the areas of biggest risk and enforcing intellectual honesty. When you're trying to decide if you've got a real business opportunity, Ash says you should consider the following:

1. **Problem:** Have you identified real problems people know they have?

2. **Customer segments:** Do you know your target markets? Do you know how to target messages to them as distinct groups?

3. **Unique value proposition:** Have you found a clear, distinctive, memorable way to explain why you're better or different?

4. **Solution:** Can you solve the problems in the right way?

---

* *http://www.businessmodelgeneration.com/canvas*

5. **Channels:** How will you get your product or service to your customers, and their money back to you?

6. **Revenue streams:** Where will the money come from? Will it be one-time or recurring? The result of a direct transaction (e.g., buying a meal) or something indirect (magazine subscriptions)?

7. **Cost structure:** What are the direct, variable, and indirect costs you'll have to pay for when you run the business?

8. **Metrics:** Do you know what numbers to track to understand if you're making progress?

9. **Unfair advantage:** What is the "force multiplier" that will make your efforts have greater impact than your competitors?

We encourage every startup to use Lean Canvas. It's an enlightening experience, and well worth the effort.

What *Should* You Work On?

The Lean Canvas provides a formal framework to help you choose and steer your business. But there's another, more human, side to all of this.

Do you want to do it?

This doesn't get asked enough. Investors say they look for passionate founders who really care about solving a problem. But it's seldom called out as something to which you should devote much thought. If you're going to survive as a founder, you have to find the intersection of demand (for your product), ability (for you to make it), and desire (for you to care about it).

That trifecta is often overlooked, withering under the harsh light of data and a flood of customer feedback. But it shouldn't. *Don't start a business you're going to hate.* Life is too short, and your weariness will show.

Bud Caddell has an amazingly simple diagram of how people should choose what to work on, shown in Figure 3-2.

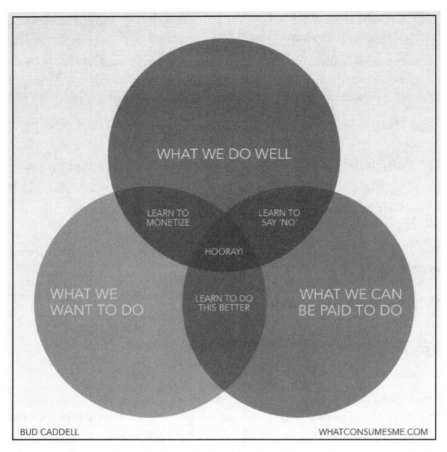

Figure 3-2. Bud Caddell's diagram belongs on every career counselor's wall

Bud's diagram shows three overlapping rings: what you *like* to do, what you're *good at*, and what you *can be paid* to do. For each intersection between rings, he suggests a course of action:

- If you want to do something and are good at it, but can't be paid to do it, *learn to monetize.*

- If you're good at something and can be paid to do it, but don't like doing it, *learn to say no.*

- If you like to do something and can be paid to do it, but aren't very good at it, *learn to do it well.*

This isn't just great advice for career counselors; when launching a new venture, you need to properly assess these three dimensions as well.

First, ask yourself: *can I do this thing I'm hoping to do, well?* This is about your ability to satisfy your market's need better than your competitors, and it's a combination of design skill, coding, branding, and myriad other factors. If you identify a real need, you won't be the only one satisfying it, and you'll need all the talent you can muster in order to succeed. Do you have a network of friends and contacts who can give you an unfair advantage that improves your odds? Do you have the talent to do the things that matter *really* well? *Never start a company on a level playing field— that's where everyone else is standing.*

These same rules apply to people working in larger organizations. Don't launch a new product or enter a new market unless your existing product and market affords you an unfair advantage. Young competitors with fewer legacies will be fighting you for market share, and your size should be an advantage, not a handicap.

Second, figure out *whether you like doing this thing*. Startups will consume your life, and they'll be a constant source of aggravation. Your business will compete with your friends, your partner, your children, and your hobbies. You need to believe in what you're doing so that you'll keep at it and ride through the good times and the bad. Would you work on it even if you weren't being paid? Is it a problem worth solving, that you'll brag about to others? Is it something that will take your career in the direction you want, and give you the right reputation within your existing organization? If not, maybe you should keep looking.

Finally, be sure *you can make money doing it.** This is about the market's need. You have to be able to extract enough money from customers for the value you'll deliver, and do so without spending a lot to acquire those customers—and the process of acquiring them and extracting their money has to scale independent of you as a founder.

For an intrapreneur, this question needs to be answered simply to get approval for the project, but remember that you're fighting the opportunity cost—whatever the organization could be doing instead, or the profitability of the existing business. If what you're doing isn't likely to have a material impact on the bottom line, maybe you should look elsewhere.

This is by far the most important of the three; the other two are easy, because they're up to you. But now you have to figure out if anyone will pay you for what you can and want to build.

---

* Not everyone is hoping to make money with his or her startup. Some people are doing it for attention, or to fix government, or to make the world a better place. If that's you, replace "money" with "produce the results I'm hoping to achieve" as you read this book.

In the early stages of a startup, you'll be dealing with a lot of data. You're awash in the tides of opinion, and buffeted by whatever feedback you've heard most recently.

Never forget that you're trying to answer three fundamental questions:

- Have I identified a problem worth solving?
- Is the solution I'm proposing the right one?
- Do I actually want to solve it?

Or, more succinctly: *should I go build this thing?*

EXERCISE | Create a Lean Canvas

Go to *http://leancanvas.com* to create your first canvas. Pick an idea or project you're working on now, or something you've been thinking about. Spend 20 minutes on the canvas and see what it looks like. Fill in the boxes based on the numbered order, but feel free to skip boxes that you can't fill out. We'll wait.

How did you do? Can you see what areas of your idea or business are the riskiest? Are you excited about tackling those areas of risk now that you see them described in the canvas? If you're confident, share your Lean Canvas with someone else (an investor, advisor, or colleague) and use it as a discussion starter.

CHAPTER 4

Data-Driven Versus Data-Informed

Data is a powerful thing. It can be addictive, making you overanalyze everything. But much of what we actually do is unconscious, based on past experience and pragmatism. And with good reason: relying on wisdom and experience, rather than rigid analysis, helps us get through our day. After all, you don't run A/B testing before deciding what pants to put on in the morning; if you did, you'd never get out the door.

One of the criticisms of Lean Startup is that it's too data-driven. Rather than be a slave to the data, these critics say, we should use it as a tool. We should be data-informed, not data-driven. Mostly, they're just being lazy, and looking for reasons not to do the hard work. But sometimes, they have a point: using data to optimize one part of your business, without stepping back and looking at the big picture, can be dangerous—even fatal.

Consider travel agency Orbitz and its discovery that Mac users were willing to reserve a more expensive hotel room. CTO Roger Liew told the *Wall Street Journal*, "We had the intuition [that Mac users are 40% more likely to book a four- or five-star hotel than PC users and to stay in more expensive rooms], and we were able to confirm it based on the data."[*]

On the one hand, an algorithm that ignores seemingly unrelated customer data (in this case, whether visitors were using a Mac) wouldn't have found this opportunity to increase revenues. On the other hand, an algorithm that

---

[*] *http://online.wsj.com/article/SB10001424052702304458604577488822667325882.html*

blindly optimizes based on customer data, regardless of its relationship to the sale, may have unintended consequences—like bad PR. Data-driven machine optimization, when not moderated by human judgment, can cause problems.

Years ago, Gail Ennis, then CMO of analytics giant Omniture, told one of us that users of the company's content optimization tools had to temper machine optimization with human judgment. Left to its own devices, the software quickly learned that scantily clad women generated a far higher click-through rate on web pages than other forms of content. But that click-through rate was a short-term gain, offset by damage to the brand of the company that relied on it. So Omniture's software works alongside curators who understand the bigger picture and provide suitable imagery for the machine to test. *Humans do inspiration; machines do validation.*

In mathematics, a local maximum is the largest value of a function within a given neighborhood.* That doesn't mean it's the largest *possible* value, just the largest one in a particular range. As an analogy, consider a lake on a mountainside. The water isn't at its lowest possible level—that would be sea level—but it's at the lowest possible level in the area surrounding the lake.

Optimization is all about finding the lowest or highest values of a particular function. A machine can find the optimal settings for something, but only within the constraints and problem space of which it's aware, in much the same way that the water in a mountainside lake can't find the lowest possible value, just the lowest value within the constraints provided.

To understand the problem with constrained optimization, imagine that you're given three wheels and asked to evolve the best, most stable vehicle. After many iterations of pitting different wheel layouts against one another, you come up with a tricycle-like configuration. It's the optimal three-wheeled configuration.

Data-driven optimization can perform this kind of iterative improvement. What it can't do, however, is say, "You know what? Four wheels would be way better!" Math is good at optimizing a known system; humans are good at finding a new one. Put another way, *change favors local maxima; innovation favors global disruption.*

In his book *River Out Of Eden* (Basic Books), Richard Dawkins uses the analogy of a flowing river to describe evolution. Evolution, he explains, can create the eye. In fact, it can create dozens of versions of it, for

---

* http://en.wikipedia.org/wiki/Maxima_and_minima

PART ONE: STOP LYING TO YOURSELF

wasps, octopods, humans, eagles, and whales. What it can't do well is go *backward*: once you have an eye that's useful, slight mutations don't usually yield improvements. A human won't evolve an eagle's eye, because the intermediate steps all result in bad eyesight.

Machine-only optimization suffers from similar limitations as evolution. If you're optimizing for local maxima, you might be missing a bigger, more important opportunity. It's your job to be the intelligent designer to data's evolution.

Many of the startup founders with whom we've spoken have a fundamental mistrust of leaving their businesses to numbers alone. They want to trust their guts. They're uneasy with their companies being optimized without a soul, and see the need to look at the bigger picture of the market, the problem they're solving, and their fundamental business models.

Ultimately, quantitative data is great for testing hypotheses, but it's lousy for generating new ones unless combined with human introspection.

PATTERN | How to Think Like a Data Scientist

Monica Rogati, a data scientist at LinkedIn, gave us the following 10 common pitfalls that entrepreneurs should avoid as they dig into the data their startups capture.

1. **Assuming the data is clean.** Cleaning the data you capture is often most of the work, and the simple act of cleaning it up can often reveal important patterns. "Is an instrumentation bug causing 30% of your numbers to be null?" asks Monica. "Do you really have that many users in the 90210 zip code?" Check your data at the door to be sure it's valid and useful.

2. **Not normalizing.** Let's say you're making a list of popular wedding destinations. You could count the number of people flying in for a wedding, but unless you consider the total number of air travellers coming to that city as well, you'll just get a list of cities with busy airports.

3. **Excluding outliers.** Those 21 people using your product more than a thousand times a day are either your biggest fans, or bots crawling your site for content. Whichever they are, ignoring them would be a mistake.

4. **Including outliers.** While those 21 people using your product a thousand times a day are interesting from a *qualitative* perspective, because they can show you things you didn't expect, they're not good for building a general model. "You probably want to exclude

them when building data products," cautions Monica. "Otherwise, the 'you may also like' feature on your site will have the same items everywhere—the ones your hardcore fans wanted."

5. **Ignoring seasonality.** "Whoa, is 'intern' the fastest-growing job of the year? Oh, wait, it's June." Failure to consider time of day, day of week, and monthly changes when looking at patterns leads to bad decision making.

6. **Ignoring size when reporting growth.** Context is critical. Or, as Monica puts it, "When you've just started, technically, your dad signing up does count as doubling your user base."

7. **Data vomit.** A dashboard isn't much use if you don't know where to look.

8. **Metrics that cry wolf.** You want to be responsive, so you set up alerts to let you know when something is awry in order to fix it quickly. But if your thresholds are too sensitive, they get "whiny"— and you'll start to ignore them.

9. **The "Not Collected Here" syndrome.** "Mashing up your data with data from other sources can lead to valuable insights," says Monica. "Do your best customers come from zip codes with a high concentration of sushi restaurants?" This might give you a few great ideas about what experiments to run next—or even influence your growth strategy.

10. **Focusing on noise.** "We're hardwired (and then programmed) to see patterns where there are none," Monica warns. "It helps to set aside the vanity metrics, step back, and look at the bigger picture."

Lean Startup and Big Vision

Some entrepreneurs are maniacally, almost compulsively, data-obsessed, but tend to get mired in analysis paralysis. Others are casual, shoot-from-the-hip intuitionists who ignore data unless it suits them, and pivot lazily from idea to idea without discipline. At the root of this divide is the fundamental challenge that Lean Startup advocates face: how do you have a minimum viable product and a hugely compelling vision at the same time?

Plenty of founders use Lean Startup as an excuse to start a company without a vision. "It's so easy to start a company these days." They reason, "the barriers are so low that everyone can do it, right?" Yet having a big vision is important: starting a company without one makes you susceptible to outside influences, be they from customers, investors, competition, press, or anything else. Without a big vision, you'll lack purpose, and over time you'll find yourself wandering aimlessly.

So if a big, hairy, audacious vision is important—one with a changing-the-world type goal—how does that reconcile with the step-by-step, always-questioning approach of Lean Startup?

The answer is actually pretty simple. You need to think of Lean Startup as the process you use to move toward and achieve your vision.

We sometimes remind early-stage founders that, in many ways, they aren't building a product. *They're building a tool to learn what product to build.* This helps separate the task at hand—finding a sustainable business model—from the screens, lines of code, and mailing lists they've carefully built along the way.

Lean Startup is focused on learning above everything else, and encourages broad thinking, exploration, and experimentation. It's not about mindlessly going through the motions of *build→measure→learn*—it's about really understanding what's going on and being open to new possibilities.

Be Lean. Don't be small. We've talked to founders who want to be the leading provider in their state or province. Why not the world? Even the Allies had to pick a beachhead, but landing in Normandy didn't mean they lacked a big vision. They just found a good place to start.

Some people believe Lean Startup encourages that smallness, but in fact, used properly, Lean Startup helps *expand* your vision, because you're encouraged to question everything. As you dig deeper and peel away more layers of what you're doing—whether you're looking at problems, solutions, customers, revenue, or anything else—you're likely to find a lot more than you expected. If you're opportunistic about it, you can expand your vision and understand how to get there faster, all at the same time.

FINDING THE RIGHT METRIC FOR RIGHT NOW

You now have an understanding of analytics fundamentals. So let's talk about the importance of focus, about specific business models, and about the stages every startup goes through as it discovers the right product and the best target market. Armed with this, you'll be able to find the metrics that matter to you.

It is the framework which changes with each new technology and not just the picture within the frame.

Marshall McLuhan

CHAPTER 5

Analytics Frameworks

Over the years we've seen a number of frameworks emerge that help us understand startups and the changes they undergo as they grow, find their markets, and help startups acquire customers and revenue. Each framework offers a different perspective on the startup lifecycle, and each suggests a set of metrics and areas on which to focus.

After comparing and contrasting a number of these frameworks, we've created our own way to think about startups, and in particular the metrics that you use to measure your progress. We'll use this new framework throughout the book—but first, let's take a look at some of the existing frameworks and how they fit into Lean Analytics.

Dave McClure's Pirate Metrics

Pirate Metrics—a term coined by venture capitalist Dave McClure—gets its name from the acronym for five distinct elements of building a successful business. McClure categorizes the metrics a startup needs to watch into acquisition, activation, retention, revenue, and referral—AARRR.[*]

Figure 5-1 shows our interpretation of his model, describing the five steps through which users, customers, or visitors must progress in order for your company to extract all the value from them. Value comes not only from a

---

[*] *http://www.slideshare.net/dmc500hats/startup-metrics-for-pirates-long-version*

transaction (revenue) but also from their role as marketers (referral) and content creators (retention).

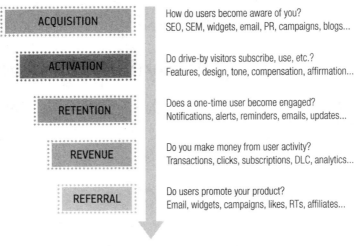

ACQUISITION — How do users become aware of you?
SEO, SEM, widgets, email, PR, campaigns, blogs...

ACTIVATION — Do drive-by visitors subscribe, use, etc.?
Features, design, tone, compensation, affirmation...

RETENTION — Does a one-time user become engaged?
Notifications, alerts, reminders, emails, updates...

REVENUE — Do you make money from user activity?
Transactions, clicks, subscriptions, DLC, analytics...

REFERRAL — Do users promote your product?
Email, widgets, campaigns, likes, RTs, affiliates...

Figure 5-1. Even pirates need metrics, says Dave McClure

These five elements don't necessarily follow a strict order—users may refer others before they spend money, for example, or may return several times before signing up—but the list is a good framework for thinking about how a business needs to grow (see Table 5-1).

Element	Function	Relevant metrics
Acquisition	Generate attention through a variety of means, both organic and inorganic	Traffic, mentions, cost per click, search results, cost of acquisition, open rate
Activation	Turn the resulting drive-by visitors into users who are somehow enrolled	Enrollments, signups, completed onboarding process, used the service at least once, subscriptions
Retention	Convince users to come back repeatedly, exhibiting sticky behavior	Engagement, time since last visit, daily and monthly active use, churns
Revenue	Business outcomes (which vary by your business model: purchases, ad clicks, content creation, subscriptions, etc.)	Customer lifetime value, conversion rate, shopping cart size, click-through revenue
Referral	Viral and word-of-mouth invitations to other potential users	Invites sent, viral coefficient, viral cycle time

Table 5-1. Pirate Metrics and what you should track

Eric Ries's Engines of Growth

In *Lean Startup*, Eric Ries talks about three engines that drive the growth of a startup. Each of these has associated *key performance indicators* (KPIs).

Sticky Engine

The sticky engine focuses on getting users to return, and to keep using your product. It's akin to Dave McClure's retention phase. If your users aren't sticky, churn will be high, and you won't have engagement. Engagement is one of the best predictors of success: Facebook's early user counts weren't huge, but the company could get nearly all students in a university to use the product, and to keep coming back, within a few months of launch. Facebook's stickiness was off the charts.

The fundamental KPI for stickiness is customer retention. Churn rates and usage frequency are other important metrics to track. Long-term stickiness often comes from the value users create for themselves as they use the service. It's hard for people to leave Gmail or Evernote, because, well, that's where they store all their stuff. Similarly, if a player deletes his account from a massively multiplayer online game (MMO), he loses all his status and in-game items, which he's worked hard to earn.

Stickiness isn't only about retention, it's also about frequency, which is why you also need to track metrics like time since last visit. If you have methods of driving return visits such as email notifications or updates, then email open rates and click-through rates matter, too.

Virality Engine

Virality is all about getting the word out. Virality is attractive because it compounds—if every user adds another 1.5 users, your user base will grow infinitely until you've saturated all users.*

The key metric for this engine is the *viral coefficient*—the number of new users that each user brings on. Because this is compounding (the users they bring, in turn, bring their own users), the metric measures how many users are brought in with each viral cycle. Growth comes from a viral coefficient of greater than one, but you also have to factor in churn and loss. The bigger the coefficient, the faster you grow.

---

* It's never really this simple; churn, competitors, and other factors mean it's not really infinite, of course.

Measuring viral coefficient isn't enough. You also need to measure the actions that make up the cycle. For example, when you join most social networks, you're asked to connect to your email account to find contacts, then you're given the option to invite them. They receive emails, which they might act upon. Those distinct stages all contribute to virality, so measuring actions is how you tweak the viral engine—by changing the message, simplifying the signup process, and so on.

There are other factors at play with virality as well, including the speed with which a user invites another (known as the *viral cycle time*) and the type of virality. We'll dive into these later in the book.

Paid Engine

The third engine of growth is payment. It's usually premature to turn this engine on before you know that your product is sticky and viral. Meteor Entertainment's *Hawken* is a multiplayer game that's free to play, but it makes money from in-game upgrades. Meteor is focusing on usage within a beta group first (stickiness), then working on virality (inviting your friends to play), and finally payment (players buying upgrades to become competitive or enhance the in-game experience).

Getting paid is, in some ways, the ultimate metric for identifying a sustainable business model. If you make more money from customers than it costs you to acquire them—and you do so consistently—you're sustainable. You don't need money from external investors, and you're growing shareholder equity every day.

But getting paid, on its own, isn't an engine of growth. It's just a way to put money in the bank. Revenue helps growth only when you funnel some of the money generated from revenue back into acquisition. Then you have a machine that you can tune to grow the business over time.

The two knobs on this machine are *customer lifetime value* (CLV) and *customer acquisition cost* (CAC). Making more money from customers than you spend acquiring them is good, but the equation for success isn't that simple. You still need to worry about cash flow and growth rate, which are driven by how long it takes a customer to pay off. One way to measure this is *time to customer breakeven*—that is, how much time it will take to recoup the acquisition cost of a customer.

Ash Maurya's Lean Canvas

We looked at the Lean Canvas in Chapter 3, when we talked about deciding what problem you should solve. See the sidebar "How to Use a Lean Canvas" for some tips on putting it into practice.

How to Use a Lean Canvas

Unlike a traditional business plan, you should use and update the Lean Canvas continuously. It's a "living, breathing" plan, not a hypothetical tome of nonsense that you throw out the minute you start actually working on your startup. Once you've filled out the Lean Canvas (or most of it), you start running experiments to validate or invalidate what you've hypothesized.

In its simplest form, think of each box as a "pass/fail": if your experiments fail, you don't go to the next box; rather, you keep experimenting until you hit a wall completely or get to the next step. The only exception is the "Key metrics" box, which is meant to keep a record of the most important metrics you're tracking. You don't run experiments on this box, but it's important to fill it out anyway because it's definitely open to debate and discussion.

Each of the boxes in Ash's canvas has relevant metrics you need to track, as outlined in Table 5-2 (the canvas actually has a box for metrics, which should get updated each time you focus on something different in the canvas). These metrics either tie your one-page business model to reality by confirming each box, or they send you back to the drawing board. The individual metrics may change depending on your type of business, but the guidelines are valuable just the same. We'll share more details later in the book on the key metrics that matter based on your type of business, as well as benchmarks you can aim for.

Lean Canvas box	Some relevant metrics
Problem	Respondents who have this need, respondents who are aware of having the need
Solution	Respondents who try the MVP, engagement, churn, most-used/least-used features, people willing to pay
Unique value proposition	Feedback scores, independent ratings, sentiment analysis, customer-worded descriptions, surveys, search, and competitive analysis
Customer segments	How easy it is to find groups of prospects, unique keyword segments, targeted funnel traffic from a particular source
Channels	Leads and customers per channel, viral coefficient and cycle, net promoter score, open rate, affiliate margins, click-through rate, PageRank, message reach

Lean Canvas box	Some relevant metrics
Unfair advantage	Respondents' understanding of the UVP (Unique Value Proposition), patents, brand equity, barriers to entry, number of new entrants, exclusivity of relationships
Revenue streams	Lifetime customer value, average revenue per user, conversion rate, shopping cart size, click-through rate
Cost structure	Fixed costs, cost of customer acquisition, cost of servicing the nth customer, support costs, keyword costs

Table 5-2. Lean Canvas and relevant metrics

Sean Ellis's Startup Growth Pyramid

Sean Ellis is a well-known entrepreneur and marketer. He coined the term *growth hacker* and has been heavily involved with a number of meteoric-growth startups, including Dropbox, Xobni, LogMeIn (IPO), and Uproar (IPO). His Startup Growth Pyramid, shown in Figure 5-2, focuses on what to do *after* you've achieved product/market fit.

Figure 5-2. Like building, real pyramid, startup growth is back-breaking labor

The question this poses a of course, is how do you know if you've achieved product/market fit? Sean devised a simple survey that you can send customers (available at *survey.io*) to determine if you're ready for accelerated growth. The most important question in the survey is "How would you feel if you could no longer use this product or service?" In Sean's experience, if 40% of people (or more) say they'd be very disappointed to lose the service, you've found a fit, and now it's time to scale.

The Long Funnel

In the early days of the Web, transactional websites had relatively simple conversion funnels. Visitors came to the home page, navigated to the product they wanted, entered payment information, and confirmed their order.

No more. Today's funnel extends well beyond the front door of a website, across myriad social networks, sharing platforms, affiliates, and price-comparison sites. Both offline and online factors influence a single purchase. Customers may make several tentative visits prior to a conversion.

We call this the Long Funnel. It's a way of understanding how you first come to someone's attention, and the journey she takes from that initial awareness through to a goal you want her to complete (such as making a purchase, creating content, or sharing a message). Often, measuring a long funnel involves injecting some kind of tracking into the initial signal, so you can follow the user as she winds up on your site, which many analytics packages can now report. Figure 5-3 shows the Social Visitors Flow report in Google Analytics, for example.

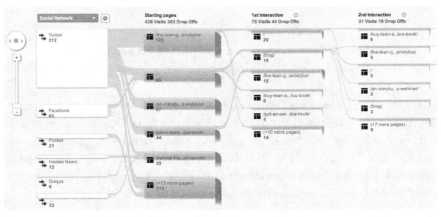

Figure 5-3. Where your paying customers waste most of their time before they buy from you

What's more, overlapping traffic sources can show how much a particular platform influenced conversions, as shown in Figure 5-4.

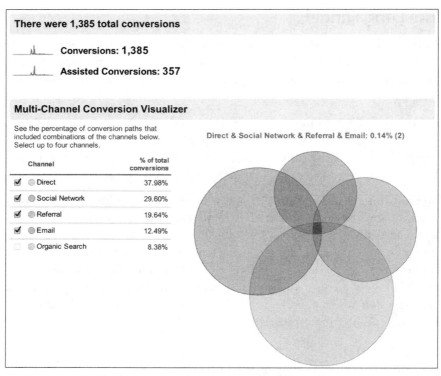

Figure 5-4. Sometimes it takes a lot of peer pressure to acquire a customer

We tracked our own long funnel during the process of launching the Lean Analytics Book website.[*] We didn't have a hard "goal" such as a purchase, but we did have a number of things we wanted visitors to do: sign up for our mailing list, click on the book cover, and take a survey. By creating custom URLs for our proponents to share, we injected a signal into the start of the Long Funnel, and were able to see how our message spread.

We learned, for example, that author and speaker Julien Smith's followers were less likely to fill out the survey than Eric Ries's and Avinash Kaushik's followers, unless they were returning visitors, in which case they were more likely to do so. This kind of insight can help us choose the right kind of proponent for future promotional efforts.

* http://leananalyticsbook.com/behind-the-scenes-of-a-book-launch/

The Lean Analytics Stages and Gates

Having reviewed these frameworks, we needed a model that identified the distinct stages a startup usually goes through, and what the "gating" metrics should be that indicate it's time to move to the next stage. The five stages we identified are Empathy, Stickiness, Virality, Revenue, and Scale. We believe most startups go through these stages, and in order to move from one to the next they need to achieve certain goals with respect to the metrics they're tracking.

Figure 5-5 shows the stages and gates of Lean Analytics, and how this model lines up with the other frameworks. A good portion of the book is structured by our stages, so it's important to understand how this works.

THE STAGES OF LEAN ANALYTICS

MAURYA LEAN CANVAS	LEAN STARTUP	MCCLURE PIRATE METRICS	SEAN ELLIS GROWTH PYRAMID	LEAN ANALYTICS STAGE	"GATE" NEEDED TO MOVE FORWARD
Problem	Problem validation	Acquisition (of testers, prospects, etc.)	Product/ market fit	Empathy	I've found a real, poorly met need a reachable market faces
Customer segments	Solution validation				
Unique value proposition	MVP building	Activation			I've figured out how to solve the problem in a way they will accept and pay for
	MVP iteration, sticky engine	Retention		Stickiness	
Solution			Stacking the odds		I've built the right product/features/ functionality that keeps users around
(Natural) channels	Organic growth, viral engine	Referral		Virality	
Revenue stream	Monetization, price engine	Revenue		Revenue	The users and features fuel growth organically and artificially
Cost structure					
(Formal) channels	Inorganic growth, beyond Lean	Attention (at scale, customers)	Scale growth	Scale	I've found a sustainable, scalable business with the right margins in a healthy ecosystem
Unfair advantage					
					I can achieve a successful exit for the right terms

STARTUP LIFECYCLE STAGE · *GROWTH RATE*

Figure 5-5. Frameworks, frameworks everywhere

Ultimately, there are a number of good frameworks that help you think about your business.

- Some, like Pirate Metrics and the Long Funnel, focus on the act of acquiring and converting customers.
- Others, like the Engines of Growth and the Startup Growth Pyramid, offer strategies for knowing when or how to grow.
- Some, like the Lean Canvas, help you map out the components of your business model so you can evaluate them independent of one another.

We're proposing a new model called the Lean Analytics Stages, which draws from the best of these models and puts an emphasis on metrics. It identifies five distinct stages startups go through as they grow.

While we believe the Lean Analytics Stages represent a fairly simple framework for understanding your startup's progress, we recognize that it can still look overwhelming. And even with our framework, you'll still use the other frameworks as well, so there's a lot to digest. That's why you should put all of this aside (for now!) and focus on the One Metric That Matters, which we'll cover in the next chapter.

CHAPTER 6

The Discipline of One Metric That Matters

Founders are magpies, chasing the shiniest new thing they see. They often use the pivot as an enabler for chronic ADD, rather than as a way to iterate through ideas in a methodical fashion.

But one of the keys to startup success is achieving real focus and having the discipline to maintain it. You may succeed if you're unfocused, but it'll be by accident. You'll spend a lot more time wandering aimlessly, and the lessons learned are more painful and harder-won. If there's any secret to success for a startup, it's focus.

Focus doesn't mean myopia. We're not saying that there's only one metric you care about from the day you wake up with an idea to the day you sell your company. We are, however, saying that at any given time, there's one metric you should care about above all else. Boiled down to its very essence, Lean Startup is really about getting you to focus on the right thing, at the right time, with the right mindset.

As noted in Chapter 5, Eric Ries talks about three engines that drive company growth: the sticky engine, the viral engine, and the paid engine. But he cautions that while all successful companies will ultimately use all three engines, it's better to focus on one engine at a time. For example, you might make your product sticky for its core users, then use that to grow virally, and then use the user base to grow revenue. That's focus.

In the world of analytics and data, this means picking a single metric that's incredibly important for the step you're currently working through in your startup. We call this the One Metric That Matters (OMTM).

The OMTM is the one number you're completely focused on above everything else for your current stage. Looking at CLV (customer lifetime value) isn't meaningful when you're validating a problem, but it might be the right metric to focus on as you're approaching product/market fit.

You'll always track and review multiple numbers. Some will be important: these are your key performance indicators (KPIs), which you'll track and report every day. Others will be stored away for future use, such as when it's time to tell the company history to an investor or to make an infographic. Setting up and managing instrumentation is fairly easy these days with tools like Geckoboard, Mixpanel, Kissmetrics, Totango, Chartbeat, and others. But don't let your ability to track so many things distract you. *Capture everything, but focus on what's important.*

CASE STUDY | ## Moz Tracks Fewer KPIs to Increase Focus

Moz (previously known as SEOmoz) is a successful *Software as a Service* (SaaS) vendor that helps companies monitor and improve their websites' search engine rankings. In May 2012, the company raised $18 million. Its CEO, Rand Fishkin, published a detailed post about the company's progress up to that point.[*] Rand's update did include a number of vanity metrics—when you have roughly 15 million visitors on your site each year, you have the right to a bit of vanity—but he also shared some very specific and interesting numbers related to conversions from free trials to paid subscriptions and churn.

We spoke with Joanna Lord, Vice President of Growth Marketing at Moz, to learn more about how the company handles metrics. "We are very metrics-driven," she says. "Every team reports to the entire company weekly on KPIs, movement, and summaries. We also have a huge screen up in the office pumping out customer counts and free trial counts. We believe that having company-wide transparency into the metrics keeps us all informed, and is a great reminder of the progress (as well as the challenges) we are seeing as a company."

For a company that's found product/market fit and is now focused on scaling, it becomes more challenging to focus on a single metric. This isn't surprising; there are multiple departments all growing quickly, and the business can tackle several different things simultaneously. But even with all these concurrent efforts, Joanna says that one metric

---

[*] *http://www.seomoz.org/blog/mozs-18-million-venture-financing-our-story-metrics-and-future*

stands above the rest: *Net Adds*. This metric is the total of new paid subscribers (either conversions from free trials or direct paid signups) minus the total who cancelled.

"Net Adds helps us quickly see high cancel days (and troubleshoot them) and helps us get a sense of how our free trial conversion rate is doing," Joanna says.

Moz tracks other related metrics including Total Paying, New Free Trials Yesterday, and 7-Day Net Add Average. All of these really bubble up into Net Adds per day.

Interestingly, when Moz raised its last round of financing, one of its lead investors, the Foundry Group's Brad Feld, suggested that it track fewer KPIs. "The main reason for this is that as a company, you can't simultaneously affect dozens of KPIs," Joanna says. "Brad reminded us that 'too much data' can be counterproductive. You can get lost in strange trends on numbers that aren't as big-picture as others. You can also lose a lot of time reporting and communicating about numbers that might not lead to action. By stripping our daily KPI reporting down to just a few metrics, it's clear what we're focused on as a company and how we're doing."

Summary

- Moz is metrics-driven—but that doesn't mean it's swimming in data. It relies on one metric above all others: Net Adds.

- One of its investors actually suggested *reducing* the number of metrics the company tracks to stay focused on the big picture.

Analytics Lessons Learned

While it's great to track many metrics, it's also a sure way to lose focus. Picking a minimal set of KPIs on which your business assumptions rely is the best way to get the entire organization moving in the same direction.

Four Reasons to Use the One Metric That Matters

The OMTM is of most importance early on. Later, as your startup scales, you will want to focus on more metrics, and you'll have the resources and experience to do so. Importantly, you'll also have a team to whom you can delegate metrics. Your operations person might care about uptime or latency, your call center might worry about average time on hold, and so on.

At Year One Labs, one of the litmus tests for us as advisors and investors was the clarity with which a team understood, and tracked, their OMTM. If it was on the tip of their tongues, and aligned with their current stage, that was a good thing. If they didn't know what it was, if it was the wrong metric for their stage, if they had several metrics, or if they didn't know what the current value was, we knew something was wrong.

Picking the OMTM lets you run more controlled experiments quickly and compare the results more effectively. Remember: the One Metric That Matters changes over time. When you're focused on acquiring users (and converting them into customers), your OMTM may be tied to which acquisition channels are working best or the conversion rate from signup to active user. When you're focused on retention, you may be looking at churn, and experimenting with pricing, features, improving customer support, and so on. The OMTM changes depending on your current stage, and in some cases it will change quickly.

Let's look at four reasons why you should use the One Metric That Matters.

- **It answers the most important question you have.** At any given time, you'll be trying to answer a hundred different questions and juggling a million things. You need to identify the riskiest areas of your business as quickly as possible, and that's where the most important question lies. When you know what the right question is, you'll know what metric to track in order to answer that question. That's the OMTM.

- **It forces you to draw a line in the sand** and have clear goals. After you've identified the key problem on which you want to focus, you need to set goals. You need a way of defining success.

- **It focuses the entire company.** Avinash Kaushik has a name for trying to report too many things: data puking.* Nobody likes puke. Use the OMTM as a way of focusing your entire company. Display your OMTM prominently through web dashboards, on TV screens, or in regular emails.

- **It inspires a culture of experimentation.** By now you should appreciate the importance of experimentation. It's critical to move through the *build→measure→learn* cycle as quickly and as frequently as possible. To succeed at that, you need to actively encourage experimentation. It will lead to small-*f* failures, but you can't punish that. Quite the opposite: failure that comes from planned, methodical testing is simply how you learn. It moves things forward in the end. It's how you avoid

---

* *http://www.kaushik.net/avinash/difference-web-reporting-web-analysis/*

big-*F* Failure. Everyone in your organization should be inspired and encouraged to experiment. When everyone rallies around the OMTM and is given the opportunity to experiment independently to improve it, it's a powerful force.

CASE STUDY | Solare Focuses on a Few Key Metrics

Solare Ristorante is an Italian restaurant in San Diego owned by serial entrepreneur Randy Smerik. Randy has a background in technology and data, once served as the general manager for business intelligence firm Teradata, and has five technology exits under his belt. It's no surprise that he's brought his data-driven mindset to the way he runs the business.

One evening at the restaurant, Randy's son Tommy—who manages the bar—yelled out, "24!" Since we're always looking for stories about business metrics, we asked him what the number meant. "Every day, my staff tells me the ratio of staff costs to gross revenues for the previous day," he explained. "This is a fairly well-known number in the restaurant industry. It's useful because it combines two things you have a degree of control over—per-diner revenues and staffing costs."

Randy explained when staffing costs exceed 30% of gross revenues, that's bad, because it means that you're either spending too much on staff or not deriving enough revenue per customer. A Michelin-starred restaurant can afford to have more staff, and pay them more, because it sells customers expensive wines and enjoys good per-customer revenue. At the other end of the spectrum, a low-margin casual dining restaurant has to keep staff costs down.

The ratio works because it's:

- **Simple:** It's a single number.

- **Immediate:** You can generate it every night.

- **Actionable:** You can change staffing, or encourage upselling, the very next day, whereas ingredient costs, menus, or leasing take longer to modify.

- **Comparable:** You can track it over time, and compare it to other restaurants in your category.

- **Fundamental:** It reflects two basic facets of the restaurant business model.

As it turns out, 24% is about right. Below 20%, there's a chance that you're under-serving customers and that their dining experience might suffer (Randy could experiment with different staffing levels and measure the tips diners leave, or comments on Yelp, if he wanted to be really analytical).

Randy also uses a second metric to predict how many customers he'll have. At 5 p.m. every day, his staff sends him the number of reservations that have currently been made for the evening. "If I get 50 reservations at 5 p.m., I know I'll have around 250 covers that night," he says. "We've learned that a 5-to-1 ratio is normal for Solare."

This number doesn't work across all restaurants—the in-demand Michelin-starred restaurant has a 1-to-1 ratio, since it's sold out, and a fast food restaurant that doesn't take reservations obviously can't use the metric. But for Solare reservations at 5 p.m., plus some experience, provides a good leading indicator of what the night will be like. It also allows the Solare team to make small adjustments to staffing or buy additional produce in time to ensure that the restaurant can handle the traffic.

Summary

- Restaurants know from experience that demand is tied to reservations, and what the right ratio of staffing to revenue should be.

- Good metrics help predict the future, giving you an opportunity to anticipate problems and correct them.

Analytics Lessons Learned

Even non-technical businesses need to find a few, simple metrics that relate to their core business model, then track them over time to predict what's going to happen and identify patterns or trends.

Drawing Lines in the Sand

Knowing which metric to focus on isn't enough. You need to draw a line in the sand as well. Let's say that you've decided "New Customers Per Week" is the right metric to focus on because you're testing out new ways of acquiring customers. That's fair, but it doesn't answer the real question: *How many new customers per week do you need?* Or more specifically: *How many new customers per week (per acquisition channel) do you think defines a level of success that enables you to double down on user acquisition and move to the next step in the process?*

You need to pick a number, set it as the target, and have enough confidence that if you hit it, you consider it success. And if you don't hit the target, you need to go back to the drawing board and try again.

Picking the target number for any given metric is extremely hard. We've seen many startups struggle with this. Often, they avoid picking a number altogether. Unfortunately, this means it's difficult to know what to do once an experiment is completed. If, in our example, the user acquisition experiment is a dismal failure, any number you had picked beforehand is probably immaterial; you'll know it's a failure. And if your efforts are insanely successful, you're going to know that as well. It'll be obvious. But most of the time, experiments end up right in the big fat middle. There was some success, but it wasn't out of this world. Was it enough success to keep going, or do you have to go back and run some new experiments? That's the trickiest spot to be in.

There are two right answers to the question of what success looks like. The first comes from your business model, which may tell you what a metric has to be. If you know that you need 10% of your users to sign up for the paid version of your site in order to meet your business targets, then that's your number.

In the early stages of your business, however, you're still figuring out what your business model should look like. It won't tell you precisely what you need. The second right answer is to look at what's normal or ideal. Knowing an industry baseline means you know what's likely to happen, and you can compare yourself to it. In the absence of any other information, this is a good place to start. We'll share some industry benchmarks that may be helpful to you later in the book.

The Squeeze Toy

There's another important aspect to the OMTM. And we can't really explain it better than with a squeeze toy.

If you optimize your business to maximize one metric, something important happens. Just like one of those bulging stress-relief squeeze toys, squeezing it in one place makes it bulge out in another. And that's a good thing. Optimizing your OMTM not only squeezes that metric so you get the most out of it, but it also reveals the next place you need to focus your efforts, which often happens at an inflection point for your business:

- Perhaps you've optimized the number of enrollments in your gym, and you've done all you can to maximize revenues—but now you need to focus on cost per customer so you turn a profit.

- Maybe you've increased traffic to your site—but now you need to maximize conversion.

- Perhaps you have the foot traffic in your coffee shop you've always wanted—but now you need to get people to buy several coffees rather than just stealing your Wi-Fi for hours.

Whatever your current OMTM, expect it to change. And expect that change to reveal the next piece of data you need to build a better business faster.

EXERCISE | Define Your OMTM

Can you pick the One Metric That Matters for your startup? Give it a try. If you did the exercise at the end of Chapter 2, you have a short list of good metrics you track; now pick the one you couldn't live without.

Could your entire company work exclusively on improving that metric? What might break if you did? Could you draw a line in the sand to measure results? If not, that's OK. For now, write down your One Metric That Matters and where it currently stands, and we'll come back to the line later.

CHAPTER 7

What Business Are You In?

How you get and make money drives what metrics you should care about. In the long term, the riskiest part of a business is often directly tied to how it makes money.

Many startups can build a product and solve technical issues, some can attract the right (and occasionally large) audiences, but few make money. Even giants like Twitter and Facebook have struggled with extracting money from their throngs of users.

There's no more iconic symbol of a startup than the lemonade stand, and with good reason—it's a simple, entrepreneurial, low-risk way to learn how businesses operate. And like a lemonade stand, while it might be reasonable and strategic to delay monetization—giving away lemonade for a while to build a clientele—you have to be planning your business model early on.

If we asked you to describe the business model of a lemonade stand, you'd probably say that it's about selling lemonade for more than it costs to make it. Pressed for more detail, you might say that costs include:

- Variable costs of materials (lemons, sugar, cups, water)

- One-time costs of marketing (stand, signage, cooler, bribing a younger sibling to stand in the street)

- Hourly costs of staffing (which, let's face it, are pretty negligible when you're a kid)

You might also say that revenue is a function of the price you charge, and the number of cups sold.

Now let's suppose that you're asked to identify the risky parts of the business. They include the variability of citrus futures, the weather, the foot traffic in your neighborhood, and so on.

One thing we've noticed about almost all successful founders we've met is their ability to work at both a very detailed, and a very abstracted, level within their business. They can worry about the layout of a page or the wording of an email subject one day, and consider the impact of one-time versus monthly recurring sales the next. That's partly because they're not only trying to run a business, they're also trying to discover the best business model.

To decide which metrics you should track, you need to be able to describe your business model in no more complex a manner than a lemonade stand's. You need to step back, ignore all the details, and just think about the really big components.

When you reduce things to their basic building blocks in this way, you come up with only a few fundamental business models on the Web. Interestingly, all of them share some common themes. First, their aim is to grow (in fact, Paul Graham says that a focus on growth is the one defining attribute of a startup).[*] And second, that growth is achieved by one of Eric Ries's fundamental Engines of Growth: an increase in stickiness, virality, or revenue.

Each business model needs to maximize the thrust from these three engines in order to flourish. Sergio Zyman, Coca-Cola's CMO, said marketing is about *selling more stuff to more people more often for more money more efficiently.*[†]

Business growth comes from improving one of these five "knobs":

- **More stuff** means adding products or services, preferably those you know your customers want so you don't waste time building things they won't use or buy. For intrapreneurs, this means applying Lean methods to new product development, rather than starting an entirely new company.

- **More people** means adding users, ideally through virality or word of mouth, but also through paid advertising. The best way to add users is when it's an integral part of product use—such as Dropbox, Skype, or a project management tool that invites outside users outsiders—

---

[*] *http://paulgraham.com/growth.html*

[†] *http://www.zibs.com/zyman.shtml*

since this happens automatically and implies an endorsement from the inviting user.

- **More often** means stickiness (so people come back), reduced churn (so they don't leave), and repeated use (so they use it more frequently). Early on, stickiness tends to be a key knob on which to focus, because until your core early adopters find your product superb, it's unlikely you can achieve good viral marketing.

- **More money** means upselling and maximizing the price users will pay, or the revenue from ad clicks, or the amount of content they create, or the number of in-game purchases they make.

- **More efficiently** means reducing the cost of delivering and supporting your service, but also lowering the cost of customer acquisition by doing less paid advertising and more word of mouth.

About Those People

Business models are about getting people to do what you want in return for something. *But not all people are equal.* The plain truth is that not every user is good for you.

- Some are good—but only in the long term. Evernote's freemium model works partly because users eventually sign up for paying accounts, but it can take them two years to do so.

- Some provide, at best, free marketing, and while they may never become paying users, they may amplify your message or invite someone who will pay.

- Some are downright bad—they distract you, consume resources, spam your site, or muddy your analytics.

When you get a wave of visibility, few of the resulting visitors will actually engage with your product. Many are just driving by. As Vinicius Vacanti, co-founder and CEO of Yipit, recalls in a blog post inspired by his company's 2010 launch:[*]

> Was that our big launch? Why didn't more people sign up? Why didn't people complete the sign-up flow? Why weren't people coming back? Now that people covered our startup, how are we supposed to get more press? Why aren't our users pushing their actions to Facebook and Twitter? We got some users to invite their friends but why aren't their friends accepting the invite?

---

[*] *http://viniciusvacanti.com/2012/11/19/the-depressing-day-after-you-get-techcrunched/*

The key here is analytics. You need to segment real, valuable users from drive-by, curious, or detrimental ones. Then you need to make changes that maximize the real users and weed out the bad ones. That may be as blunt as demanding a credit card up front—a sure way to reject curious users who don't have any intention of committing or paying. Or it may be a subtler approach, such as not trying to reactivate disengaged users once they've been gone for a while.

If you're a developer of a game that users play once, or an e-commerce site stocking rarely purchased items, that's fine—just get your money up front. If you're a SaaS provider with low incremental costs for additional users, freemium may work, as long as you clearly separate engaged from casual users. If you expect buyers to purchase from you often, you need to make them feel loved. You get the picture.*

Segmenting real users from casual ones also depends on how much effort your users have to put into using the application. Some products collect information passively: Fitbit logs walking steps; Siri notices when you've arrived somewhere; Writethatname analyzes your inbox for new contacts. Users don't have to do much, so it can be hard to tell if they've "checked out." It's easier to find disengaged users if they have to actively use the product.

Consider the aforementioned Fitbit, a tiny life-logging device that measures steps, from which it calculates calories burned, miles walked, stairs climbed, and overall activity.

Fitbit users can simply record their steps with a device in their pocket, they can use it to sync data to the company's hosted application, they can visit the portal to see their statistics and share them with friends, they can manually enter sleep and food data to augment what's collected passively, and they can buy the premium Fitbit offering to help them reach their health goals.

Each of these use models represents a different tier of engagement, and Fitbit could segment users across these five segments. And it should: it's perfectly acceptable for a Fitbit user to only use the clip-on device to record the number of steps taken per day, without ever uploading that information, but as a result the company won't be able to monetize that user beyond the initial purchase (through on-site ads, premium subscriptions, or selling aggregate user data, for example). The value of that user is significantly lower. Predicting revenues accurately relies on an understanding of how its different user segments employ the product.

As a startup, you have a wide range of payment and incentive models from which to choose: freemium, free trial, pay up-front, discount, ad-funded, and so on. Your choice needs to match the kind of segmentation you're doing, the time it takes for a user to become a paying customer, how easy it is to use your service, and how costly an additional drive-by user is to the business.

Not all customers are good. Don't fall victim to customer counting. Instead, optimize for *good* customers and segment your activities based on the kinds of customer those activities attract.

The Business Model Flipbook

A product is more than the thing you buy. It's the mix of service, branding, fame, street cred, support, packaging, and myriad other factors you pay for. When you purchase an iPhone, you're also getting a tiny piece of Steve Jobs's persona.

In the same way, a business model is a combination of things. It's what you sell, how you deliver it, how you acquire customers, and how you make money from them.

Many people blur these dimensions of a business model. We're guilty of it, too. Freemium isn't a business model—it's a marketing tactic. SaaS isn't a business model—it's a way of delivering software. The ads on a media site aren't a business model—they're a way of collecting revenue.

Later in the book we're going to outline six sample businesses. But before we do that, we want to talk about how we came up with them. Think of one of the flipbooks you had as a kid—the kind where you could combine different body parts on each page to make different characters.

You can build business models this way, but instead of heads, torsos, and feet, you have several aspects of a business: the acquisition channel, selling tactic, revenue source, product type, and delivery model.

- The **acquisition channel** is how people find out about you.

- The **selling tactic** is how you convince visitors to become users or users to become customers. Generally, you either ask for money or you provide some kind of scarcity or exclusivity—such as a time limit, a capacity limit, the removal of ads, additional functionality, or the desire to keep things to themselves—to convince them to act.

- The **revenue source** is simply how you make money. Money can come from your customers directly (through a payment) or indirectly (through advertising, referrals, analysis of their behavior, content creation, and so on). It can include transactions, subscriptions, consumption-based billing charges, ad revenue, resale of data, donations, and much more.

- The **product type** is what value your business offers in return for the revenue.

- The **delivery model** is how you get your product to the customer.

Figure 7-1 shows these five aspects, with a variety of models and examples for each one. Remember that this is only a set of examples—most businesses will rely on several acquisition channels, or experiment with different revenue models, or try various sales tactics.

ACQUISITION CHANNEL	How the visitor, customer, or user finds out about the startup	• Paid advertising • Search engine mgmt. • Social media outreach • Inherent virality • Artificial virality • Affiliate marketing • Public relations • App/ecosystem mkt.	• Banner on **Informationweek.com** • High pagerank for **ELC** in kids' toys • Active on Twitter (i.e., **Kissmetrics**) • Inviting team member to **Asana** • Rewarding **Dropbox** user for others' signups • Sharing a % of sales with a referring **blogger** • Speaker submission to **SXSW** • Placement in the **Android market**
SELLING TACTIC	What the startup does to convince the visitor or user to become a paying customer	• Simple purchase • Discounts & incentives • Free trial • Freemium • Pay-for-privacy • Free-to-play	• Buying a PC on **Dell.com** • **Black Friday** discount, loss leader, free ship • Time-limited trial such as **Fitbit** Premium • Free tier, relying on upgrades, like **Evernote** • Free account content is public, like **Slideshare** • Monetize in-app purchases, like **Airmech**
REVENUE MODEL	How the startup extracts money from its visitors, users, or customers	• One-time **transaction** • Recurring **subscription** • **Consumption** charges • **Advertising** clicks • Resale of **user data** • **Donation**	• Single purchase from **Fab** • Monthly charge from **Freshbooks** • Compute cycles from **Rackspace** • PPC revenue on **CNET.com** • **Twitter's** firehose license • **Wikipedia's** annual campaign
PRODUCT TYPE	What the startup does in return. May be a product or service; may be hardware or software; may be a mixture	• **Software** • **Platform** • **Merchandising** • **User-generated** content • **Marketplace** • **Media/content** • **Service**	• **Oracle's** accounting suite • Amazon's **EC2** cloud • **Thinkgeek's** retail store • **Facebook's** status update • **Airbnb's** list of house rentals • **CNN's** news page • A hairstylist
DELIVERY MODEL	How the product gets to the customer	• **Hosted** service • **Digital** delivery • **Physical** delivery	• **Salesforce.com's** CRM • **Valve** purchase of desktop game • Knife shipped from **Sur La Table**

Figure 7-1. Just like the flipbooks you had as a kid, with more words

Lots to Choose From

There is an abundance of "pages" you can put into the flipbook. The team at Startup Compass, a startup dedicated to helping companies make better business decisions with data, identifies 12 revenue models: advertising, consulting, data, lead generation, licensing fee, listing fee, ownership/hardware, rental, sponsorship, subscription, transaction fee, and virtual goods. Venture capitalist Fred Wilson has a document listing a vast number of web and mobile revenue models, many of which are variants on six basic ones we'll list later in the book.*

Startup Compass also suggests some "fundamental" financial models that combine several pages from the flipbook: search, gaming, social network, new media, marketplace, video, commerce, rental, subscription, audio, lead generation, hardware, and payments.

You can use these "pages" to create a back-of-the-napkin business model. For example, Figure 7-2 shows a sample business model flipbook for Dropbox.

BUSINESS ASPECT	FLIPBOOK PAGE(S)	DROPBOX EXAMPLE
ACQUISITION CHANNEL	• Inherent virality • Artificial virality	• Sharing files with others • Free storage when others sign up
SELLING TACTIC	• Freemium	• Limited-capacity accounts are free; subscribe when you need more
REVENUE MODEL	• Recurring subscription	• $99/year, monthly fees, enterprise tiers
PRODUCT TYPE	• Platform	• Storage-as-a-service with APIs, collaboration, synchronization tools
DELIVERY MODEL	• Hosted service • Digital delivery	• Cloud storage, web interface • Desktop client software

Figure 7-2. Turning the flipbook pages to Dropbox

There's another advantage of stating business models in a flipbook structure like this: it encourages lateral thinking. Each turn of a "page" is a pivot: what would it mean to offer Dropbox as a physical delivery? Or to charge up front for it? Or to rely on paid advertising?

Six Business Models

In the coming chapters, we're going to look at six business models. Each model is a blend of these aspects, and we've tried to mix them up enough to give you a taste of some common examples. But just like a kid's flipbook, there's a huge variety: from the aforementioned list, there are over 6,000 permutations, and our list of aspects isn't by any means exhaustive.

---

* *https://hackpad.com/Ch2paBpUyIU#Web-and-Mobile-Revenue-Models*

As if that weren't confusing enough, you can employ several at once: Amazon is a transactional, physical-delivery, SEM (search engine marketing), simple-purchase retailer, but it's also running sub-businesses such as user-generated content in the form of product reviews. So unlike those relatively simple children's books, your business can quite easily be a many-headed monster.

In the face of this complexity, we've decided to keep our six business models simple. We'll talk about several aspects of those businesses, and the metrics that matter most to companies of each sort. Think of it as opening the business model flipbook to a particular "page"—one in which you see elements of your own business.

- If you're running an e-commerce business where you sell things to customers, turn to Chapter 8.

- If you're delivering SaaS to users, turn to Chapter 9.

- If you're building a mobile application and using in-app purchases to generate revenue, head to Chapter 10.

- If you're creating content and making money from advertising, you'll find details on media sites in Chapter 11.

- If your primary focus is getting your users to generate content on your platform the way Twitter, Facebook, or reddit do, turn to Chapter 12.

- If you're building a two-sided marketplace where buyers and sellers can come together, check out Chapter 13.

Most businesses fall into one of these categories. Some won't, but they have close parallels in the real world. A restaurant is transactional, like e-commerce; an accounting business offers a recurring service, like a SaaS company, and so on. Hopefully, you'll find a model that's close enough for you to learn important lessons about analytics and apply them to your business, as we review the stages of growth in Chapter 14 and beyond.

EXERCISE | ## Pick Your Business Model

In the following chapters we go through six sample business models. Find yours and write it down, then list all the metrics we define in that business model and see how well that aligns with what you're tracking. For the metrics that you're tracking, put down the values as they stand today, if you haven't already. If your business overlaps on a couple of models (which isn't uncommon), then grab metrics from each of those models and include them in this exercise.

CHAPTER 8

Model One: E-commerce

In an e-commerce company, a visitor buys something from a web-based retailer. This is perhaps the most common kind of online business, and it's certainly the one that the majority of traditional analytics tools are aimed at. Big retailers like Amazon, Walmart.com, and Expedia are all e-commerce companies.

If the e-commerce model most closely matches your business, this chapter will show you some of the most important metrics you need to watch, as well as some "wrinkles" that make the analytics more complex.

Early e-commerce models consisted of a relatively simple "funnel": a visitor arrived at the site, navigated through a series of pages to get to a particular item, clicked "buy," provided some payment information, and completed a purchase. This is the traditional "conversion funnel" from which mainstream analytics packages like Omniture and Google Analytics emerged.

But modern e-commerce is seldom this simple:

- The majority of buyers find what they're looking for through search rather than by navigating across a series of pages. Shoppers start with an external search and then bounce back and forth from sites they visit to their search results, seeking the scent of what they're after. Once they find it, on-site navigation becomes more important. This means on-site funnels are somewhat outdated; keywords are more important.

- Retailers use recommendation engines to anticipate what else a buyer might want, basing their suggestions on past buyers and other users with similar profiles. Few visitors see the same pages as one another.

- Retailers are always optimizing performance, which means that they're segmenting traffic. Mid- to large-size retailers segment their funnel by several tests that are being run to find the right products, offers, and prices.

- Purchases begin far from the website itself, in social networks, email inboxes, and online communities, making the buying process harder to track.

E-commerce companies make money in a straightforward way: they charge for products, which they then deliver either electronically (e.g., digital downloads on iTunes) or physically (e.g., shipping shoes from Zappos). They spend money to acquire customers through advertising and affiliate referrals. Prices are set based on what the market will bear, or on expectations set by competitors. Some large retailers with the budget and time to invest in it will generate prices algorithmically based on supply, demand, and constant testing, which in some cases leads to absurd pricing[*] or recommendations based on factors such as browser type.

Loyalty-focused e-retailers like Amazon build a recurring relationship with their users. They have a wide variety of products to offer, and buyers return often, so they do everything they can to make purchasing simple and automatic (in Amazon's case, the company patented the one-click purchase model, which it now licenses to other retailers, including Apple).

These relationship-focused e-commerce companies encourage users to build wishlists and review products, which means that while their core business model is e-commerce, they care about other models, such as user-generated content (UGC), too—as long as those models act as an enabler for purchases. On the other hand, e-commerce retailers that don't expect frequent, repeat sales focus on getting as much from their buyer as they can and on getting the buyer to spread the word.

PATTERN | ## What Mode of E-commerce Are You?

Kevin Hillstrom of Mine That Data, a consultancy focused on helping companies understand how their customers interact with advertising,

---

[*] In his post "Amazon's $23,698,655.93 book about flies," UC Berkeley biologist Michael Eisen explains how algorithmic price wars between book merchants drove the price of a textbook on flies up to $23 million dollars (*http://www.michaeleisen.org/blog/?p=358*).

products, brands, and channels, works with a number of e-commerce companies. He says it's essential for online retailers to know what kind of relationship they have with their buyers, because this drives everything from marketing strategy to shopping cart size. To understand this, he calculates the *annual repurchase rate*: what percentage of people who bought something from you last year will do so this year?

Acquisition mode

If less than 40% of last year's buyers will buy this year, then the focus of the business is on new customer acquisition. Loyalty programs aren't good long-term investments for this kind of business. Kevin says that 70% of e-commerce businesses fall into this category when they're mature. Vendors of scuba or rock climbing equipment might be a great example of this: many of their customers buy gear once, and don't get so hooked on the hobby that they need to upgrade. That's not a bad thing—it just dictates marketing strategy. An online vendor of eyewear might put more of its marketing efforts into convincing past buyers to refer others, and less into convincing those buyers to purchase multiple pairs of glasses, for example.

Hybrid mode

If 40–60% of last year's buyers will buy this year, then the company will grow with a mix of new customers and returning customers. It needs to focus on acquisition as well as on increasing purchase frequency—the average customer will buy 2 to 2.5 times a year. Zappos is a hybrid model e-commerce company.

Loyalty mode

If 60% or more of last year's buyers will buy something this year, the company needs to focus on loyalty, encouraging loyal clients to buy more frequently. Loyalty programs work well only if the retailer has this kind of engagement, and only 10% of e-commerce businesses end up in this mode when mature. Amazon is a good example of a company in this mode.

The annual repurchase rate is an early indicator of how an e-commerce startup will succeed in the long term. Even before a year has elapsed, an e-commerce company can look at 90-day repurchase rates and get a sense of which model it's in.

- A 90-day repurchase rate of 1% to 15% means you're in acquisition mode.

- A 90-day repurchase rate of 15% to 30% means you're in hybrid mode.

- A 90-day repurchase rate of over 30% means you're in loyalty mode.

There's nothing particularly bad about any of these models. Kevin has clients where only 25% of this year's buyers will purchase something next year. These clients are successful because they know they need a large number of new customers at relatively low costs, and they concentrate all of their marketing efforts around reliable, affordable customer acquisition.

"It doesn't matter whatsoever what mode a business is in. But it means *everything* for the CEO to know what mode he or she is in," Kevin says. "I see too many leaders trying to increase loyalty. If you're in acquisition mode, you probably can't—and shouldn't try to—increase loyalty. The average customer only needs a couple of pairs of jeans a year, for instance. You can't force the customer to buy more! Knowing your customer and mode is really important."

Kevin says he frequently sees business leaders with seasonal e-commerce properties trying to convince customers to buy gifts off-season. "It doesn't work," he says. "They're in acquisition mode. They're better off creating awareness during the year so that they get new customers in November and December."

While it's important to optimize revenues, don't try to make your customers into something they're not. "I don't try to force my customer to do things my customer isn't pre-inclined to do. With Zappos, for example, I wouldn't necessarily try to push my customer from hybrid mode to loyalty mode. But I do try to improve customer service (free returns), and that brings in new customers (half of hybrid mode success) who feel comfortable with my business," says Kevin. "If I am in acquisition mode, then I will still try to improve service and merchandise and the like, but I know that my primary goal is to always get new customers, even once my business is mature."

Kevin says it's difficult to move the annual repurchase rate by more than 10%, despite a company's best efforts. "If the annual repurchase rate is 30%, it will vary between 27% and 33%," he says.

With the rise of social networks and sites like Facebook and Pinterest, which can refer visitors, e-commerce companies are increasingly interested in a long funnel that begins with a tweet, a video, or a link, and ends with a purchase. Online retailers need to understand what messages, on what platforms, generate the kinds of visitors who buy things. Once they're on the site, the emphasis is on maximizing the amount of stuff a buyer will purchase.

Getting pricing right is critical—particularly if you're an acquisition-mode e-commerce site that gets only one chance to extract revenue from a customer. A 1992 study on business optimization by management consulting firm McKinsey compared the impact of improving different aspects of the business on operating profit.[*]

As Figure 8-1 illustrates, getting pricing right has a huge impact on the overall profitability of a business. A later study conducted in 2003 suggested a smaller impact of only 8%—but one that still far outstripped other efforts.[†]

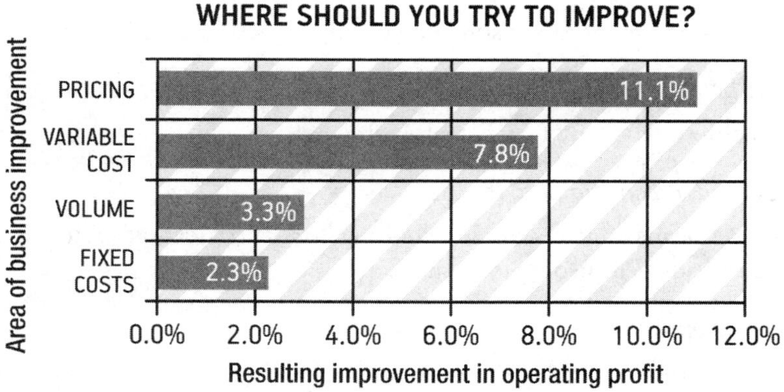

WHERE SHOULD YOU TRY TO IMPROVE?

Figure 8-1. Want to fix your business? Get the price right

A Practical Example

Consider an online luxury goods store. Subscribers to the site get exclusive deals at reduced prices for items that are curated by the site's operators. Visitors to the site can browse what's available, but must sign up to place an order or put something in a shopping cart; by signing up, they agree to receive a daily email update. Visitors can also tweet or like something they see on the site.

The company cares about several key metrics:

---

*   http://hbr.org/1992/09/managing-price-gaining-profit/ar/8

†   http://download.mckinseyquarterly.com/popr03.pdf

Conversion rate

The number of visitors who buy something.

Purchases per year

The number of purchases made by each customer per year.

Average shopping cart size

The amount of money spent on a purchase.

Abandonment

The percentage of people who begin to make a purchase, and then don't.

Cost of customer acquisition

The money spent to get someone to buy something.

Revenue per customer

The lifetime value of each customer.

Top keywords driving traffic to the site

Those terms that people are looking for, and associate with you—a clue to adjacent products or markets.

Top search terms

Both those that lead to revenue, and those that don't have any results.

Effectiveness of recommendation engines

How likely a visitor is to add a recommended product to the shopping cart.

Virality

Word of mouth, and sharing per visitor.

Mailing list effectiveness

Click-through rates and ability to make buyers return and buy.

More sophisticated retailers care about other metrics such as the number of reviews written or the number considered helpful, but this is really a secondary business within the organization, and we'll deal with these when we look at the user-generated content model in Chapter 12. For now, let's look at the preceding metrics in a bit more detail.

Conversion Rate

Conversion rate is simply the percentage of visitors to your site who buy something. It's one of the first metrics you use to assess how you're doing. It's simple to calculate and experiment with. You'll slice conversion rate in many ways—by demographics, by copy, by referral, and so on—to see what makes people more likely to buy.

Early on, conversion rate may even be more important than total revenue because your initial goal is to simply prove that someone will buy something (and it gives you that person's email address and data on what he purchases). But there's also a risk in focusing too intensely on conversion rate. Conversion rate is highly dependent on your type of e-commerce business, and whether your success will be driven by loyalty, new customer acquisition, or a hybrid of the two.

Purchases Per Year

While conversion rate is important, it doesn't tell the whole story. There are many examples of e-commerce sites with high or low conversion rates that are successful. It depends on the type of e-commerce site and how people buy. A store that sells coffins probably sells only one per lifetime; a grocery store sells to a customer several times a week.

If you look at the repurchase rate on a 90-day cycle, it becomes a very good leading indicator for what type of e-commerce site you have. There's no right or wrong answer, but it is important to know whether to focus more on loyalty or more on acquisition.

Shopping Cart Size

The other half of the conversion rate equation is the size of the shopping cart. Not only do you want to know what percentage of people bought something, you also want to know how much they spent. You may find that one campaign is more likely to make people buy, but another might make fewer people spend more money.

In practice, you'll compare the total revenue you're generating to the way in which you acquired that revenue, in order to identify the most lucrative segments of your reachable audience. But don't get too caught up in top-line revenue; profit is what really matters.

Bill D'Alessandro of Skyway Ventures, a private investment firm focused on e-commerce companies, says, "The key to successful e-commerce is in increasing shopping cart size; that's really where the money is made. I like to think of customer acquisition cost as a fixed cost, so any increase in order size is expanding your margin."

Abandonment

Not everyone buys something. At its simplest, abandonment rate is the opposite of conversion rate. But a purchasing process often has several steps—reviewing items in a shopping cart, providing shipping information, entering billing details, and so on. In some cases, the process may even involve a third-party site: Kickstarter sends users to Amazon to provide their credit card information, and Eventbrite links to PayPal so buyers can pay for tickets.

The number of people who abandon a funnel at each of these stages is the abandonment rate. It's important to analyze it for each step in order to see which parts of the process are hurting you the most. In some cases, this may be a particular form field—for example, asking people for their nationality could be alienating buyers. Tools like ClickTale perform abandonment analysis within the form itself, making it easier to pinpoint bottlenecks in the conversion process where you're losing customers.

Cost of Customer Acquisition

Once you know you can extract money from visitors, you'll want to drive traffic to the site. You may be using advertising, social media outreach, mailing lists, or affiliates. Whatever the case, you're going to need to add it up. E-commerce sites are simple math: make more from selling things than it costs you to find buyers and deliver the goods.

Accounting for the cost of acquisition in aggregate is fairly easy; it's more complicated when you have myriad channels driving traffic to your site. The good news is that analytics tools were literally built to do this for you. The reason Google has a free analytics product is because the company makes money from relevant advertising, and wants to make it as easy as possible for you to buy ads and measure their effectiveness.

Revenue Per Customer

Revenue per customer (or lifetime value) is important for all types of e-commerce businesses, regardless of whether you're focused on new customer acquisition or loyalty (or both). Even if your business doesn't engender loyalty (because you're selling something that's infrequently purchased), you want to maximize revenue per customer; you do so by increasing shopping cart size and conversion while reducing abandonment. Revenue per customer is really an aggregate metric of other key numbers, and represents a good, single measure of your e-commerce business's health.

CASE STUDY | WineExpress Increases Revenue by 41% Per Visitor

WineExpress.com is the exclusive wine shop partner of the Wine Enthusiast catalog and website, which have been providing quality wine accessories and storage for over 30 years. The company actively A/B tests and runs different experiments to improve sales conversions.

It decided to tackle one of the most highly trafficked pages on its site—the "Wine of the Day" page—which features a single wine option that ships for just 99 cents. The company drives traffic to the page through an opt-in email list and site navigation. The page's central focus, aside from the featured product, is a virtual wine-tasting video with the company's highly regarded wine director.

The "Wine of the Day" page already converted well, but WineExpress.com felt there was an opportunity to improve it. However, the team was well aware of the challenge which is faced by all e-commerce sites: striking a balance between optimizing sales transactions and optimizing overall revenues. Focusing too much on sales conversions may negatively impact the bottom line if the average order size drops in the process.

WineExpress.com engaged conversion optimization agency WiderFunnel Marketing to develop and execute a strategy for the "Wine of the Day" page. WiderFunnel developed and tested three design variations, aiming mostly at testing different layout approaches. Figure 8-2 shows the original layout.

In the end, one of the variations was a clear winner, leading to a 41% increase in revenue per visitor. "Conversion also went up," says Chris Goward, CEO of WiderFunnel, "but the key here is that revenue per visitor went up substantially. A lot of e-commerce vendors focus too much on conversion. For WineExpress.com the success is that people bought substantially more product."

Figure 8-2. The original WineExpress "Wine of the Day" page

The winning layout and design is shown in Figure 8-3.

Figure 8-3. How would 41% more revenue per visitor change your business?

"We found that placing the video above the fold was a key element in the success of the new page," says Chris. "The eyeflow of the new layout also improved clarity, with fewer distracting elements that could draw you away from purchasing."

Summary

- WineExpress.com used A/B testing to find a better-converting page.

- While conversion went up, the real gain was a 41% increase in revenue per visitor.

Analytics Lessons Learned

Page optimization is important. But be sure you're optimizing the right metric. You don't just want a high conversion rate—though that's good. You want high *revenue per visitor*, or *high customer lifetime value* (CLV), because that's what's really driving your business model.

Keywords and Search Terms

Most people find products by searching for them, whether that's in a web browser, on a search engine, or within a site. In each case, you want to know which keywords drive traffic that turns into money.

For paid search, you're going to be bidding against others for popular keywords in search engines like Google. Understanding which words are a comparatively good "value"—not too expensive, but still able to drive a reasonable amount of traffic—is what search engine marketing professionals do for a living.

For unpaid search, you'll be more focused on good, compelling content that improves your ranking with search engines, and on writing copy that includes the desirable search terms your paying customers tend to use (so you'll be featured in search results because of your relevance).

You also want to analyze search *within* your site. First, you want to be sure you have what people are after. If users are searching for something and not finding it—or searching, then pressing the back button—that's a sign that you don't have what they want. Second, if a significant chunk of searches fall into a particular category, that's a sign that you might want to alter your positioning, or add that category to the home page, to see if you can capture more of that market faster. Jason Billingsley, former VP of Innovation at Elastic Path, an enterprise e-commerce platform vendor, says, "Numbers vary by vertical and by site, but on-site search tools typically account for 5–15% of navigation."

We're not going to get into the details of search engine optimization and search engine marketing here—those are worlds unto themselves. For now, realize that search is a significant part of any e-commerce operation, and the old model of formal navigational steps toward a particular page is outdated (even though it remains in many analytics tools).

Recommendation Acceptance Rate

Big e-commerce companies use recommendation engines to suggest additional items to visitors. Today, these engines are becoming more widespread thanks to third-party recommendation services that work with smaller retailers. Even bloggers have this kind of algorithm, suggesting other articles similar to the one the visitor is currently reading.

There are many different approaches to recommendations. Some use what the buyer has purchased in the past; others try to predict purchases from visitor attributes like geography, referral, or what the visitor has clicked so far. Predictive analysis of visitors relies heavily on machine learning, and the metrics you'll track will vary from tool to tool, but they all boil down to one thing: *how much additional revenue am I generating through recommendations?*

When you make adjustments to the recommendation engine, you'll want to see if you moved the needle in the right direction.

Virality

For many e-commerce sites, virality is important, because referral and viral attention drives cheap, high-value traffic. It has the lowest cost of customer acquisition and the highest implied recommendation from someone the recipient trusts.

Mailing List Click-Through Rates

Email might not seem particularly sexy in a mobile, always-on world. But consider this: if you have the permission to reach out to your customers— and they do what you tell them to—you can keep them engaged far more effectively. Fred Wilson, partner at venture capital firm Union Square Ventures, calls email a secret weapon.[*]

Just a few years ago, many analysts and investors were wondering whether social media was going to lead to the end of email. In an ironic twist of fate, it turns out that social media adoption is driven by email. More and more social applications are leveraging the power of email to drive repeat usage and retention.

---

* *http://www.avc.com/a_vc/2011/05/social-medias-secret-weapon-email.html*

Every email you send can be blocked in many ways before a user does something you want, as shown in Figure 8-4.

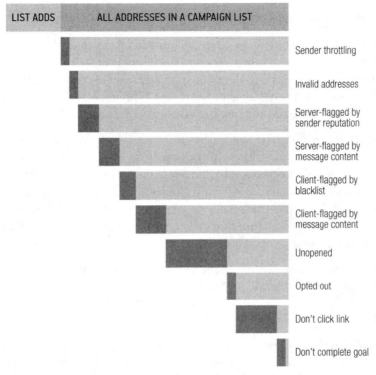

Figure 8-4. Every email runs this gauntlet; is it any wonder your click-throughs are low?

Even those who respond to the call to action within a message might not do something useful once they get to your website. In some cases, the unsubscribe rate caused by a bad email can overshadow any profit from the campaign, so email is a tool to use carefully.

You calculate the email click-through rate by dividing the number of visits you get from a campaign by the number of messages you've sent. A more sophisticated analysis of email click-through rate will include a breakdown of the various places where things can go wrong—for example, what percentage of email addresses didn't work anymore—and a look at the eventual outcome you're after (such as a purchase).

You also need to create a campaign contribution metric—basically, the added revenue from the campaign, minus the cost of the campaign and the loss due to unsubscribes. The good news is that most email platforms include this data with minimal effort.

Offline and Online Combinations

All e-commerce vendors have to deliver something to buyers. That delivery may be electronic, but in most cases, it means moving physical goods around. Not only do high shipping costs reduce conversion rates, but successful, timely delivery is also a huge factor in buyer satisfaction and repeat purchases. Offline components of any e-commerce business need to be analyzed carefully.

Shipping Time

Real-time delivery and next-day shipping are increasingly common, and buyers are becoming more demanding. Shipping time is key, and it's tightly linked to how effectively the retailer handles logistics. E-commerce companies can most likely achieve significant operational efficiencies just by optimizing their fulfillment and shipping processes. These efficiencies turn into a competitive advantage, because they let you sell to consumers who are more interested in faster, better-quality service than the cheapest price.

Stock Availability

"When items are out of stock, sales go down," says Jason Billingsley. "Of course that's obvious, but few e-commerce vendors do anything about it." Improving your inventory management can make a big difference to your bottom line. Jason recommends lowering out-of-stock items on product list or category pages, effectively hiding them from consumers. You can also hide these items from searches, or again, make sure they appear lower in the search results.

It's also interesting to analyze inventory versus sales. "A lot of e-commerce vendors hold too much inventory for things that don't sell well, and not enough for things that do sell well," says Jason. He recommends aligning product categories based on how much they make up of sales versus inventory. If you're not selling a lot in a product category, but that group of products makes up a high percentage of your inventory, things are out of balance.

Visualizing the E-commerce Business

Figure 8-5 represents a user's flow through an e-commerce business, along with the key metrics at each stage.

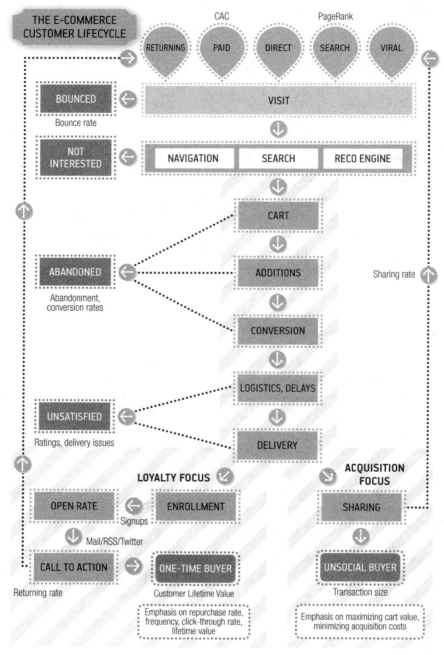

Figure 8-5. More than a typical funnel: how e-commerce businesses acquire customers

Wrinkles: Traditional E-commerce Versus Subscription E-commerce

So far, we've looked at a relatively simple e-commerce model involving a one-time purchase. Plenty of services, however, are subscription-based. This complicates things.

Subscription services bill the customer on a regular basis. Churn is easier to measure—the customer doesn't renew his account or cancels outright—but happens more dramatically. Rather than a gradual reduction in purchases over time, the customer's revenue simply stops. If this is you, check out the following business model—Software as a Service—because it applies to you as well.

Phone companies devote considerable effort to tackling this kind of churn. They build sophisticated models that predict when a subscriber is about to cancel her service, and then offer her a new phone or a discount on a renewed contract just before the cancellation happens.

Expired payment information is also a concern for subscriptions. If you try to charge a customer's credit card for his monthly renewal and the transaction fails, you have to convince him to re-enter payment details.

From an analytics perspective, this means tracking additional metrics for the rate of payment expiration, the effectiveness of renewal campaigns, and the factors that help (or hinder) renewal rates. These metrics matter later on as you're working to reduce churn, but as the total number of loyal users grows, renewal revenue represents a significant portion of total revenue.

Key Takeaways

- It's vital to know if you're focused on loyalty or acquisition. This drives your whole marketing strategy and many of the features you build.

- Searches, both off- and on-site, are an increasingly common way of finding something for purchase.

- While conversion rates, repeat purchases, and transaction sizes are important, the ultimate metric is the product of the three of them: revenue per customer.

- Don't overlook real-world considerations like shipping, warehouse logistics, and inventory.

There's another business model that's close to e-commerce: two-sided marketplaces. Both models are concerned with transactions between a buyer and a seller, and the loyalty of customers. If you want to learn more about marketplaces, head to Chapter 13. Otherwise, you can move on to Chapter 14 to understand how your current stage affects the metrics you watch.

CHAPTER 9

Model Two: Software as a Service (SaaS)

A SaaS company offers software on an on-demand basis, usually delivered through a website it operates. Salesforce, Gmail, Basecamp, and Asana are all examples of popular SaaS products. If you're running a SaaS business, here's what you need to know about metrics.

Most SaaS providers generate revenue from a monthly (or yearly) subscription that users pay. Some charge on a consumption basis—for storage, for bandwidth, or for compute cycles—although this is largely confined to Infrastructure as a Service (IaaS) and Platform as a Service (PaaS) cloud computing companies today.

Many SaaS providers offer a tiered model of their service, where the monthly fee varies depending on some dimension of the application. This might be the number of projects in a project management tool, or the number of customers in a customer relationship management application. Finding the best mix of these tiers and prices is a constant challenge, and SaaS companies invest considerable effort in finding ways to upsell a user to higher, more lucrative tiers.

Because the incremental cost of adding another customer to a SaaS service is negligible—think of how little it costs Skype to add a new user—many SaaS providers use a freemium model of customer acquisition.* Customers can start using a free version of the service that's constrained, in the hopes

---

* There are many ways to approach freemium, from free trials to crippled products to discount coupons, which we'll look at in more detail when we tackle revenue optimization.

that they'll consume all the free capacity and pay for more. Dropbox, for example, gives subscribers a few gigabytes of storage for free, then does everything it can—including encouraging sharing and photo uploads—to make sure users consume that capacity.

Consider a project management startup that lets users try its product, but charges for more than three concurrent projects. It offers four tiers: free, 10 projects, 100 projects, and unlimited. It runs ads on several platforms to attract users to its site, and each time a user invites someone else to join a project, that person becomes a user.

The company cares about the following key metrics:

Attention

How effectively the business attracts visitors.

Enrollment

How many visitors become free or trial users, if you're relying on one of these models to market the service.

Stickiness

How much the customers use the product.

Conversion

How many of the users become paying customers, and how many of those switch to a higher-paying tier.

Revenue per customer

How much money a customer brings in within a given time period.

Customer acquisition cost

How much it costs to get a paying user.

Virality

How likely customers are to invite others and spread the word, and how long it takes them to do so.

Upselling

What makes customers increase their spending, and how often that happens.

Uptime and reliability

How many complaints, problem escalations, or outages the company has.

Churn

How many users and customers leave in a given time period.

Lifetime value

How much customers are worth from cradle to grave.

These metrics follow a natural, logical order. Consider the customer's lifecycle: the company acquires a user through viral or paid marketing. Hopefully, that user continues to use the service, and eventually pays for a subscription. The user invites others, and perhaps upgrades to a higher tier. As a customer, she may have issues. In the end, she stops using the service—at which point, we know how much revenue she contributed to the business.

Describing a customer lifecycle in this way is a good method for understanding the key metrics that drive your business. This is where Lean Startup helps. You need to know *which aspects of your business are too risky* and then work to improve the metric that represents that risk.

Unfortunately, that's not always possible. There's no way to measure conversion rates if there are no users to convert. You can't quantify virality if no paid customers are inviting new users. And you probably can't measure stickiness for just a few people if the service requires a critical mass of users to be useful. This means you have to *know where the risk is*, but focus, in the right order, on *just enough optimization to get the business to a place where that risk can be quantified and understood.*

Let's say that the company in our example is concerned about whether the product is good enough to make people use it consistently. This is usually the right place to focus for SaaS companies, because they seldom get a second chance to make a first impression, and need users to keep coming back. In other words, they care about stickiness.

The company will, of course, need some amount of conversion (and therefore some amount of attention), but *only enough to test stickiness.* Those initial users could be acquired by word of mouth, or by direct selling, or by engaging with users on social networks. There's probably no need for a full-blown, automated marketing campaign at this stage.

| # Backupify's Customer Lifecycle Learning

Backupify is a leading backup provider for cloud-based data. The company was founded in 2008 by Robert May and Vik Chadha, and has gone on to raise $19.5M in several rounds of financing.

Backupify was good at focusing on a specific metric at a specific stage, in order to grow the company. "Initially, we focused on site visitors, because we just wanted to get people to our site," said CEO and co-founder Robert May. "Then we focused on trials, because we needed people testing out our product."

Once Backupify had people trialing the product in sufficient numbers, Robert focused on signups (conversions from free trial to paying customer). Now, the primary focus is *monthly recurring revenue* (MRR).

The cloud storage industry has matured a lot in a handful of years, but back in 2008 it was a nascent market. At the time, the company was focused on consumers and realized that, while revenue was going up, the customer acquisition cost (CAC) was too high. "In early 2010 we were paying $243 to acquire a customer, who only paid us $39 per year," explained Robert. "Those are horrible economics. Most consumer apps get around the high acquisition costs with some sort of virality, but backup isn't viral. So we had to pivot [from consumer sales] to go after businesses."

The pivot for Backupify was a success. The company is growing successfully. For now, it remains focused on MRR, but it also tracks how much a customer is worth in the entirety of his relationship with the company—the customer lifetime value (CLV). CLV and CAC are the two essential metrics for a subscription business.

In Backupify's case, the ratio of CLV to CAC is 5–6x, meaning that for every dollar the company invests in finding a customer, it makes back $5 to $6. This is excellent, and it's partly due to its low churn. As it turns out, lock-in is high for cloud storage, which gives the company plenty of time to make back its acquisition costs in the form of revenues. We'll look at the CAC/CLV ratio in more detail later in the book.

"MRR growth will probably be our top metric until we hit $10M in annual recurring revenue," said Robert. "I watch churn, but I'm more focused on customer acquisition payback in months, which is how quickly I make my money back on each customer." Robert's target for that metric is 12 months or less for any given channel. Customer acquisition payback is a great example of a single number that encompasses many things, since it rolls up marketing efficiency, customer revenue, cash flow, and churn rate.

Summary

- Before focusing on sophisticated financial metrics, start with revenue. But don't ignore costs, because profitability is the real key to growth.

- You know it's time to scale when your paid engine is humming along nicely, which happens when the CAC is a small fraction of the CLV—a sure sign you're getting a good return on your investment.

- Most SaaS businesses thrive on monthly recurring revenue—customers continue to pay month after month—which is a great foundation on which to build a business.

Analytics Lessons Learned

There's a natural progression of metrics that matter for a business that change over time as the business evolves. The metrics start by tracking questions like "Does anyone care about this at all?" and then get more sophisticated, asking questions like "Can this business actually scale?" As you start to look at more sophisticated metrics, you may realize your business model is fundamentally flawed and unsustainable. Don't just start from scratch: sometimes what you need is a new market, not a new product, and that market may be closer than you think.

Measuring Engagement

The ultimate metric for engagement is daily use. How many of your customers use your product on a daily basis? If your product isn't a daily use app, establishing a minimum baseline of engagement takes longer, and the time it takes to iterate through a cycle of learning is longer. It's also hard to demonstrate enough value, quickly enough, to keep people from churning. Habits are hard to form—and with any new product, you're creating new habits, which you want to do as quickly and intensely as possible.

Evernote is an example of a daily use application (at least, its creators would like you to use it on a daily basis!). The people who pay for Evernote are most likely those who use it daily. Evernote has reported that only 1% of users convert into paid customers,[*] but for CEO Phil Libin that's OK—after all, the company has over 40 million users, and this year it's focused

---

* http://econsultancy.com/ca/blog/10599-10-tips-for-b2b-freemiums

further on engagement, which is why it's acquiring companies like Skitch and adding image upload features.

After years of operation, the company has also learned that users take months or even years to become paying customers. Investors likely agree with the company's focus on engagement, since they're giving the company deep cash reserves to keep growing. In other words, conversion isn't Evernote's main concern right now, although once it improves engagement that's absolutely what it will concentrate on.[*]

Consider two other applications we use heavily but don't consider daily use applications: Expensify for expense reporting, and Balsamiq for wireframing. Just because *we* don't use them every day doesn't mean that a travelling sales rep, or a UI designer, isn't a daily user.

That's an important lesson around business models and Lean Startup—you bring an early version of your product to the market, test its usage, and look for where it's got the highest engagement among your customers. If there's a subsection of users who are hooked on your product—your early adopters—figure out what's common to them, refocus on their needs, and grow from there. Claim your beachhead. It will allow you to iterate much more quickly on a highly engaged segment of the market.

Some applications—such as a wedding gift registry, a reservation tool for a visit to the dentist, or a tax preparation site—simply aren't meant to be used on a daily basis. But you still need to set a high bar for engagement and measure against it. It's critical that you understand customers' behavior, and draw lines in the sand appropriate to that. Perhaps the goal is weekly or monthly use.

If you're building something genuinely disruptive, you need to consider the technology adoption lifecycle, from early to mainstream. Hybrid cars, Linux servers, home stereos, and microwaves were first adopted by a small segment of their markets, but took years of evangelism and millions of marketing dollars to be considered conventional.

In the first stages of your company, you typically have a small, devoted, unreasonably passionate following. This happens because new products initially appeal only to early adopters comfortable with change, or to that segment of the market so desperate for your solution that it's willing to tolerate something that's still rough around the edges. Those early adopters will be vocal, but beware. Their needs might not reflect those of the bigger, more lucrative mainstream. Google Wave attracted a flurry of early attention, but failed to achieve mainstream interest despite its powerful, flexible feature set.

---

[*] *http://gigaom.com/2012/08/27/evernote-ceo-phil-libin/*

You hope your first users are reflective of the mainstream, so you can reach a bigger market—something Geoffrey Moore famously referred to as "crossing the chasm." This isn't always the case. You also won't have the same volume of metrics on which to base your decisions.

When measuring engagement, don't just look at a coarse metric like visit frequency. Look for usage patterns throughout your application. For example, it's interesting to know that people log in three times per week, but what are they actually doing inside your application? What if they're only spending a few minutes each time? Is that good or bad? Are there specific features they're using versus others? Is there one feature that they always use, and are there others they never touch? Did they return of their own accord, or in response to an email?

Finding these engagement patterns means analyzing data in two ways:

- To find ways you might improve things, segment users who do what you want from those who don't, and identify ways in which they're different. Do the engaged users all live in the same city? Do all users who eventually become loyal contributors learn about you from one social network? Are the users who successfully invite friends all under 30 years old? If you find a concentration of desirable behavior in one segment, you can then target it.

- To decide whether a change worked, test the change on a subset of your users and compare that subset's results to others. If you put in a new reporting feature, reveal it to half of your users, and see if more of them stick around for several months. If you can't test features in this way without fallout—the customers who *didn't* get the new feature might get angry—then at the very least, compare the cohort of users who joined after the feature was added to those who came before.

A data-driven approach to measuring engagement should show you not only *how sticky* your product or service is, but also *who stuck and whether your efforts are paying off.*

Churn

Churn is the percentage of people who abandon your service over time. This can be measured weekly, monthly, quarterly, etc., but you should pick a timespan for all your metrics and stick to it in order to make comparing them easier. In a freemium or free-trial business model, you have both users (not paid) and customers (paid), and you should track churn for both groups separately. While churn might seem like a simple metric, there are a number of complications that can make it misleading, particularly for companies that have a highly variable growth rate.

Unpaid users "churn" by cancelling their accounts or simply not coming back; paid users churn by cancelling their accounts, stopping their payments, or reverting to an unpaid version. We recommend defining an inactive user as someone who hasn't logged in within 90 days (or less). At that point, they've churned out; in an always-connected world, 90 days is an eternity.

Remember, however, that you may still be able to invite them back to the service later if you have significant feature upgrades—as Path did when it redesigned its application—or if you've found a way to reach them with daily content, as Memolane did when it sent users memories from past years.

As Shopify data scientist Steven H. Noble[*] explains in a detailed blog post,[†] the simple formula for churn is:

$$\frac{\text{(Number of churns during period)}}{\text{(\# customers at beginning of period)}}$$

Table 9-1 shows a simple example of a freemium SaaS company's churn calculations.

	Jan	Feb	Mar	Apr	May	Jun
Users						
Starting with	50,000	53,000	56,300	59,930	63,923	68,315
Newly acquired	3,000	3,600	4,320	5,184	6,221	7,465
Total	53,000	56,600	60,920	66,104	72,325	79,790
Active users						
Starting with	14,151	15,000	15,900	16,980	18,276	19,831
Newly active	849	900	1080	1,296	1,555	1,866
Total	15,000	15,900	16,980	18,276	19,831	21,697
Paying users						
Starting with	1,000	1,035	1,035	1049	1,079	1,128
Newly acquired	60	72	86	104	124	149
Lost	(25)	(26)	(27)	(29)	(30)	(33)
Total	1,035	1,081	1,140	1,216	1,310	1,426

Table 9-1. Example of churn calculations

---

* *http://blog.noblemail.ca/*

† *http://www.shopify.com/technology/4018382-defining-churn-rate-no-really-this-actually-requires-an-entire-blog-post*

Table 9-1 shows users, active users, and paying users. Active users are those who have logged in at least once in the month after signing up. New users are growing at 20% a month, 30% use the service at least once (in the month after signing up), and 2% convert into paid customers.

Here's the churn calculation for February:

$$\frac{26 \text{ users lost during the period}}{1035 \text{ paying users at the start of the period}} \times 100$$

If 2.5% of customers churn every month, it means that the average customer stays around for 40 months (100/2.5). This is how you can start to calculate the lifetime value of a customer (40 months × average monthly revenue per user).

Churn Complications

Noble explains that because the number of churns in a particular period is affected by the entire period, but the number of customers at the beginning of a period is a moment-in-time snapshot, calculating churn in this simple manner can give misleading results in startups where growth is varied or unusually fast. In other words, churn isn't normalized for behavior and size—you can get different churn rates for the same kind of user behavior if you're not careful.

To fix this, you need to calculate churn in a less simple, but more accurate, way: average out the number of customers in the period you're analyzing, so you're not just looking at how many you had at the beginning:

$$\frac{(\text{Number of churns during period})}{[(\text{\# customers at beginning of period}) + (\text{\# customers at end of period})]/ \, 2}$$

This spreads out the total number of customers across the period, which is better, but it still presents a problem if things are growing quickly. If you have 100 customers at the start of the month, and 10,000 at the end, this formula assumes you have 5,050 customers in the middle of the month—which you don't, if you're on a hockey stick. Most of your new customers come in the later part of the month, so an average won't work. What's more, most of your churns will, too.

Worse: if you're counting churns as "someone who hasn't come back in 30 days," then you're comparing last month's losses to this month's gains, which is even more dangerous, because you're looking at a lagging indicator (last month's bad news). So by the time you find out something is wrong, it'll be next month.

Ultimately, the math gets really complex. There are two ways to simplify it. The first is to measure churn *by cohort*, so you're comparing new to churned users based on when they first became users. The second way is really, really simple, which is why we like it: measure churn each day. The shorter the time period you measure, the less that changes during that specific period will distort things.

Visualizing the SaaS Business

Figure 9-1 represents a user's flow through a SaaS business, along with the key metrics at each stage.

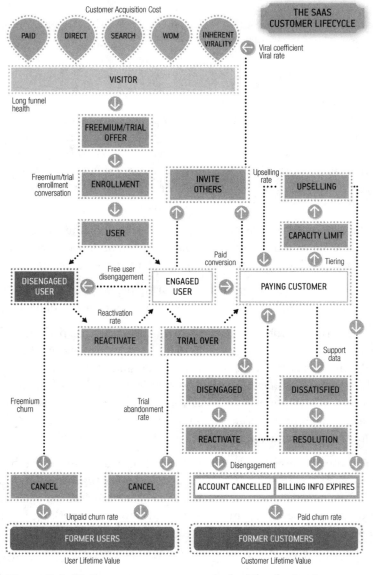

Figure 9-1. Visitors, users, customers: the life of a SaaS company

| # ClearFit Abandons Monthly Subscriptions for 10x Growth

ClearFit is a SaaS provider of recruitment software aimed at helping small businesses find job candidates and predict their success. When they started, founders Ben Baldwin and Jamie Schneiderman offered a $99/month (per job posting) package. "We kept hearing over and over that monthly subscriptions were the key to growing a successful SaaS business," says Ben. "So that's the direction we took, but it didn't work as planned."

Two things confused ClearFit's customers: the price point and the monthly subscription. Ben and Jamie wanted to price ClearFit below what customers paid for job boards (typically more than $300 per job posting), but customers were so used to that price point that they were skeptical of ClearFit's value at $99/month. Ben says, "We don't compete with job boards, we partner with them, but at the time it seemed reasonable to have a lower price point to garner attention." Customers didn't understand why they would pay a subscription fee for something that they would most likely use sporadically. "When a company needs to hire, they want to do it fast and they're willing to invest at that moment in time," says Ben. "Our customers are too small to have dedicated HR staff or recruiters that are constantly looking for talent, and their hiring needs go up and down frequently."

Ben and Jamie decided to abandon their low monthly subscription and switch to a model that their customers understood: a per-job fee. ClearFit launched its new price point at $350 for a single job (for 30 days) and almost immediately saw three times the sales. The increase in volume and the higher price point improved revenue tenfold. "When we increased the price," Ben says, "it was an important signal to our customers. They understood the model and could more easily compare the value against other solutions they use. Even though what we do is different than a job board, we wanted our customers to feel comfortable with purchasing from us, and we wanted to fit into how they budget for recruiting."

In ClearFit's case, innovating on the business model didn't make sense. Ben says, "People don't do subscriptions for haircuts, hamburgers, and hiring. You have to understand your customer, who they are, how and why they buy, and how they value your product or service."

ClearFit's switch to a per-job-posting model may go against the popular grain of subscription-based SaaS businesses, but the company continues to see great success with 30% month-over-month revenue growth.

Summary

- ClearFit initially focused on a subscription model for revenue, but customers misinterpreted its low pricing as a sign of a weak offering.

- The company switched to a paid listing model, and tripled sales while improving revenue tenfold.

- The problem wasn't the business model—it was the pricing and the messages it sent to prospects.

Analytics Lessons Learned

Just because SaaS is a recurring service doesn't mean it needs to be priced that way. If your product is ephemeral—like a transient job posting—it might be better to offer more transactional pricing. Pricing is a tricky beast. You need to test different price points qualitatively (by getting feedback from customers) and quantitatively. Don't assume a low price is the answer; customers might not attribute enough value to your offering. And remember that everything, including price, makes up the "product" you're offering.

Wrinkles: Freemium, Tiers, and Other Pricing Models

In a SaaS model, most of the complexity comes from two things: the promotional approach you choose, and pricing tiers.

As we've seen, some SaaS companies use a freemium model to convince people to use the service, and then make money when those users exceed some kind of cap. A second approach is a free trial, which converts to a paid subscription if the customer doesn't explicitly cancel after a certain time. A third approach is paid-only. There are others. Each has its benefits and drawbacks—paid-only controls cost, is more predictable, and gives you an immediate idea of whether your offering is valuable; freemium allows you to learn how people are using your service and builds goodwill. The difference between these user groups can complicate analysis.

The second wrinkle comes from how you tier pricing. Since different customers have different levels of consumption, the price they pay may change over time. This means you're constantly trying to upsell users to bigger tiers, and predicting growth adds to the dimensions of a model, making it harder to predict and explain your business.

For the most part, we've talked about SaaS as a service provided to customers on a monthly subscription. But there are other revenue models that can work as well. While a subscription model lends itself to more predictive financial planning and less volatile revenue numbers, it doesn't always fit the value proposition, or how customers expect to pay.

Key Takeaways

- While freemium gets a lot of visibility, it's actually a sales tactic, and one you need to use carefully.

- In SaaS, churn is everything. If you can build a group of loyal users faster than they erode, you'll thrive.

- You need to measure user engagement long before the users become customers, and measure customer activity long before they vanish, to stay ahead of the game.

- Many people equate SaaS models with subscription, but you can monetize on-demand software in many other ways, sometimes to great effect.

SaaS businesses share much with mobile applications. Both business models care about customer churn, recurring revenue, and creating enough user engagement to convince users to pay for the product. You can read Chapter 10 to learn more, or you can skip to Chapter 14 to understand how your current stage affects the metrics you should watch.

Model Three: Free Mobile App

A third business model that's increasingly common is the mobile app. If you're selling a mobile application for money, you have a fairly straightforward sales funnel—you promote the application, and people pay you for it. But when you derive your revenue from other sources, such as in-game content, paying for features, or advertising, the model gets more complex. If, after looking at the business model flipbook in Chapter 7, you've decided you're running a mobile app business, then this is what analytics look like for you.

The mobile application has emerged as a startup business model with the rise of iPhone and Android smartphone ecosystems. Apple's application model is tightly regimented, with the company controlling what's allowed and reviewing submissions. Applications for the Android platform may be downloaded from the Android store or "side-loaded" from sources that aren't tightly controlled.

For Lean startups, an app store model[*] presents a challenge. Unlike web applications, where it's easy to do A/B testing and continuous deployment, mobile apps go through the app store gatekeeper—which limits the number of iterations a company can undergo, and hampers experimentation. Modern mobile apps are getting around the gatekeepers to some degree

---

[*] To be clear: Apple has an App Store, and may have claim to the name. But there are plenty of stores from which users can purchase an application for a platform like Android or Kindle. Even the Wii and Salesforce's App Exchange share the dynamics we're talking about here. So when we refer to "an app store," we mean any marketplace for new products created by the maker of a platform. When we're referring to Apple's, we'll capitalize it.

by feeding in online content without requiring an actual app upgrade, but this takes extra work to set up. Some developers advocate trying out the Android platform first because it's easier to push frequent updates to users. Once those developers have validated their MVP on Android, they move to Apple's more constrained deployment environment. Others choose a smaller, secondary market (like the Canadian App Store) and work the bugs out there first.

Mobile app developers make money within their applications in several ways:

Downloadable content (such as new maps or vehicles)

> *Tower Madness*, a popular Tower Defense game for the iPhone, sells additional map sets at a small cost.

Flair and customization of in-character appearance and gaming content (a pet, clothing for a player's avatar)

> Blizzard sells non-combat enhancements like pets or vanity mounts.

Advantages (better weapons, upgrades, etc.)

> *Draw Something* charges for colors that make drawing easier.

Saving time

> A respawn rather than having to run a long distance, a strategy employed by many casual web-based MMOs.

Elimination of countdown timers

> Topping up energy levels that would normally take a day to refresh, which *Please Stay Calm* uses.

Upselling to a paid version

> Some applications constrain features. As of this writing, Evernote's mobile application doesn't allow offline synchronization of files unless a user has upgraded to the paid client, for example.

In-game ads

> Some games include in-game advertising, where the player watches promotional content in return for credits in the in-game currency.

Consider a mobile game that makes money from in-game purchases and advertising. Users find the application in an app store, either by searching or because it's showcased due to popularity or as part of a list. They consider the application—consulting ratings, number of downloads, other titles, and written reviews—and ultimately download the application. Then they launch it and start playing.

The game has an in-game economy (gold coins) that can be used to buy weapons or health more quickly than by simply playing the game. There's also a way to watch ads that pays gold coins. The company spends considerable time striking a balance between making it enjoyable for casual players (who don't want to pay) while still making a purchase attractive (so players pay a small amount). This is where the science of economics meets the psychology of game design.

The company cares about the following key metrics:

Downloads

How many people have downloaded the application, as well as related metrics such as app store placement, and ratings.

Customer acquisition cost (CAC)

How much it costs to get a user and to get a paying customer.

Launch rate

The percentage of people who download the app, actually launch it, and create an account.

Percent of active users/players

The percentage of users who've launched the application and use it on a daily and monthly basis: these are your daily active users (DAU) and monthly active users (MAU).

Percentage of users who pay

How many of your users ever pay for anything.

Time to first purchase

How long it takes after activation for a user to make a purchase.

Monthly average revenue per user (ARPU)

This is taken from both purchases and watched ads. Typically, this also includes application-specific information—such as which screens or items encourage the most purchases. Also look at your ARPPU, which is the average revenue per *paying* user.

Ratings click-through

The percentage of users who put a rating or a review in an app store.

Virality

On average, how many other users a user invites.

Churn

How many customers have uninstalled the application, or haven't launched it in a certain time period.

Customer lifetime value

How much a user is worth from cradle to grave.

We've seen several of these metrics in the previous section on the SaaS business model, but there are some that differ significantly in a mobile app world.

Installation Volume

According to mobile analytics consultancy and developer Distimo, getting featured in an app store has a huge impact on app sales.[*] An app that's already in the top 100 and then gets featured will jump up an average of 42 places on the Android market, 27 places on the iPad App Store, and 15 places on the iPhone App Store.

For mobile developers, the dynamics of an app store matter more than almost anything else when it comes to achieving significant traction. Being showcased on the home page of Apple's App Store routinely yields a hundredfold increase in traffic.[†] Analytics firm Flurry estimates that in 2012, the top 25 applications in the iPhone App Store accounted for roughly 15% of all revenue, and the rest of the top 100 accounted for roughly 17%. Lenny Rachitsky, founder of Localmind, a social mobile location app that was part of Year One Labs, said, "Getting featured is the single biggest thing that ever happened to us. It even matters what slot you're featured in on the App Store, which affects whether you appear above the fold or not."

Alexandre Pelletier-Normand, co-founder of Execution Labs, a game development accelerator, says that getting featured on Google Play is even more beneficial for revenue than being featured in Apple's App Store. "Getting featured on Google Play boosts your ranking, and the rankings in Google Play are quite static compared to the App Store. That means you'll rank higher for longer, which in turn means more revenue."

While this unfair advantage is gradually changing—revenues for less popular applications are growing overall—the facts are simple: if you want to make money, you need to be ranked highly in app stores, and getting featured helps a great deal.

---

[*]   http://www.distimo.com/wp-content/uploads/2012/01/Distimo-Publication-January-2012.pdf

[†]   http://blog.flurry.com/bid/88014/The-Great-Distribution-of-Wealth-Across-iOS-and-Android-Apps

Average Revenue Per User

Mobile app developers are constantly finding ingenious ways to monetize their applications. These developers focus on the average revenue per user (ARPU) on a monthly or lifetime basis. Many game developers instrument their applications heavily themselves, since there isn't a dominant, open way to collect data from applications easily.

If you're making a game, you don't just care about revenue. You're walking a fine line between the compelling content and addictive gameplay that makes things fun and the in-game purchases that bring in money. Avoiding the "money grab" that turns players off is hard: you need to keep users coming back and inviting their friends while still extracting a pound of flesh each month (or at least a few dollars!). As a result, in addition to ARPU, some metrics relate to playability (ensuring the game is neither too hard nor too easy, and that players don't get stuck) and player engagement.

ARPU is simply the revenue you've made, divided by the number of active users or players you have. If you inflate the number of active players to make yourself look good, you'll reduce the ARPU, so this metric forces you to draw a realistic line in the sand about what "engaged" means. Typically, ARPU is calculated on a monthly period.

For mobile games, you can measure customer lifetime value (CLV) by calculating the averages of the money spent by every player post-churn. But because it will (hopefully!) take months or years for a player to leave you, it's easier to estimate the CLV in the way we did for a SaaS company.

Let's return to our example of a free mobile game that makes money from in-game purchases and ads. This month, it's had just over 12,300 downloads, and 96% of those people launch the app and connect to the company's servers. Of these, 30% become "engaged" players that use the application on three separate days.

Each engaged player generates, on average, $3.20 a month in revenue, from a mix of in-game purchases and advertising. This means that the current month's downloads will generate about $11,339 in revenue (though it may take time for the company to receive that revenue because of the app store's payment model).

Of the total players, 15% churn every month, which means the average player lifetime is 6.67 months (1/0.15). This in turn means that the company's monthly revenue is around $75,500. The player lifetime value is the ARPU multiplied by the player lifetime—in this case, $21.33. If the company knows the cost of acquiring an engaged player, it can also calculate the amount each player contributes to the bottom line, the return on investment in advertising efforts, and how long it takes to recover the investment made in acquiring an engaged user. Figure 10-1 shows how all these calculations are performed.

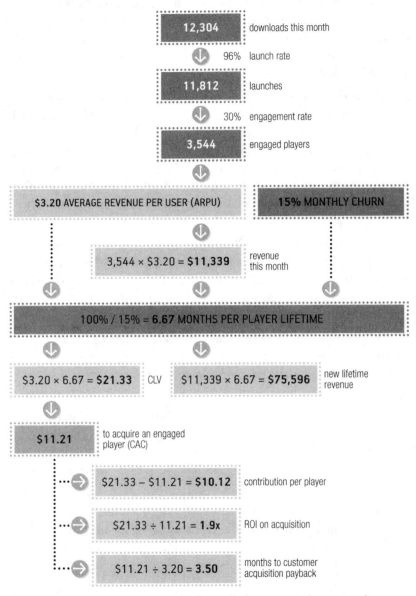

Figure 10-1. How to calculate all the essential metrics for a mobile app

The business model for the company hinges on these numbers. The company needs to increase download volumes, increase the engagement rate, maximize ARPU, minimize churn, and improve virality so customer acquisition costs go down. There's a natural tension between these goals—

for example, making the game more enjoyable so people don't churn versus extracting money so ARPU is high—and this is where the art and finesse of game design comes in.

Percentage of Users Who Pay

There are some players who simply won't spend money in a game. And there are others (often referred to as "whales") who will spend literally *thousands* of dollars to gain the upper hand in a game they love. Knowing the difference between the two—and finding ways to make more users purchase things within the application—is the key to a successfully monetized free mobile application.

The most basic metric here is the percentage of users who pay something. Beyond this basic metric, you want to do segmentation and cohort analysis. If, for example, you know that a particular ad campaign brought in users who were more likely to make in-game purchases, you should be running more campaigns like that. You also need to be sophisticated in terms of what you market to users in-game: whales are more likely to make bigger in-app purchases, whereas users who haven't bought anything yet should be offered something inexpensive to start.

Measuring your ARPU gives you a good idea of how much paying users are spending. Convincing an already-paying user to pay more may not have a significant impact on your ARPU because most users won't pay, but it could absolutely move the needle on revenue in a significant way. Treat your *paying* users as a separate customer base and track their behavior, churn, and revenue separately from your nonpaying ones.

Churn

We've looked at churn in detail in Chapter 9. It's also a critical metric for mobile applications. Keith Katz, co-founder of Execution Labs, a game development accelerator, and former Vice President of Monetization for OpenFeint, recommends looking at churn in specific time periods:

> Track churn at 1 day, 1 week, and 1 month, because users leave at different times for different reasons. After one day it could be you have a lousy tutorial or just aren't hooking users. After a week it could be that your game isn't "deep enough," and after a month it could be poor update planning.

Knowing when users churn gives you an indication of why they're churning and what you can try in order to keep them longer.

Visualizing the Mobile App Business

Figure 10-2 represents a user's flow through a mobile app business, along with the key metrics at each stage.

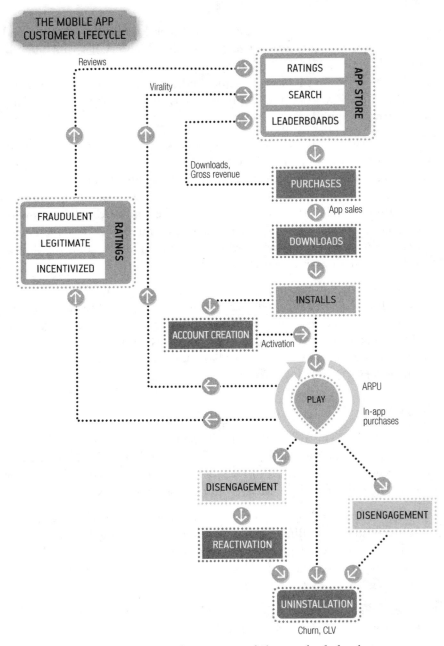

Figure 10-2. Everything in a mobile app feeds back to the app store

German game developer Wooga is a master of metrics. The company is building a formula for successful social games that's completely driven by numbers. The company has over 32 million active monthly users from 231 countries, and over 7 million daily users. In a 2012 *Wired* article, founder Jens Begemann shared his company's approach.[*]

Wooga iterates constantly and releases updates on a weekly basis. It picks a key metric to focus on for an update—retention, for example— and identifies a number of tactics to try to improve it. When the update is released, it measures the changes rigorously and adapts from there. All told, Jens reviews 128 data points on a daily basis. If he sees something that doesn't make sense to him, he sends that to the product teams. It's up to the product people at that point to home in on the number in question and figure out what's going on, and how to make it better.

Wrinkles: In-App Monetization Versus Advertising

One of the factors that can complicate this model is the monetization approach. As we've seen, there are a wide variety of ways in which companies monetize their mobile applications. Some advertising consists of in-app videos; in other cases, it can be a "promoted download" where the user is encouraged to try out another app. When this happens, the user leaves the current application—which can increase churn, reduce engagement, and hamper the experience.

Game developers have to find ways to carefully integrate monetization, particularly when it doesn't fit the theme of the game, and must measure the impact of these revenue sources on their players' subsequent behavior.

Key Takeaways

- Mobile apps make their money in a variety of ways.

- Most of the money comes from a small number of users; these should be segmented and analyzed as a distinct group. The key metric is average revenue per user, but you may also track the average revenue per *paying* user, since these "whales" are so distinct.

Mobile businesses are a lot like SaaS businesses: both try to engage users, extract money from them repeatedly, and reduce churn. You can jump back to Chapter 9 to learn more about SaaS metrics, or you can skip to Chapter 14 to find out how the stage of your business drives the metrics that matter to you.

---

[*] *http://www.wired.co.uk/magazine/archive/2012/01/features/test-test-test?page=all*

CHAPTER 11

Model Four: Media Site

Advertising pays for the Internet. It's so easy to insert advertising into online content that for many companies, ad-based monetization is a fallback revenue source, which subsidizes a cheaply priced game or helps pay for the cost of operating a freemium product. Many websites rely on advertising to pay the bills, but few do it well. Those that do are generally content-focused, trying to attract repeat visitors who will spend a decent amount of time on the site and view many pages.

If your business model most closely resembles a media site, then your primary focus is sharing advertisers' messages with viewers, and getting paid for impressions, click-throughs, or sales. Google's search engine, CNET's home page, and CNN's website are all media sites.

Ad revenue comes in a variety of formats. Some sites make money when they display banners or have sponsorship agreements. Sometimes revenue is tied to the number of clicks on ads or to a kickback from affiliates. Sometimes it's simply display advertising shown each time there's an engagement with a visitor.

Media sites care most of all about click-through or display rates, because those are actual revenue, but they also need to maximize the time visitors spend on the site, the number of pages they see, and the number of unique visitors (versus repeat visitors who keep coming back), because this represents inventory—chances to show ads to visitors—and a growing reach of new people in whom advertisers might be interested.

Imagine a sporting news site that makes money from all four revenue models (sponsorship, display advertising, click-based advertising, and affiliate). The site has 20,000 unique visitors who come to the site an average of 12 times a month, and each time they visit, they spend an average of 17 minutes on the site (see Table 11-1).

Traffic	Example	Notes
Unique visitors per month	20,000	
Sessions per month	12	
Pages per visit	11	
Time on site per visit (m)	17	
Monthly minutes on site	4,080,000	
Monthly page views (inventory)	2,640,000	

Table 11-1. Calculating monthly page inventory

The site has a partnership with a local sports team, and a standing contract to display banners for it on every page in return for $4,000 a month (see Table 11-2).

Sponsor revenue	Example	Notes
Monthly sponsorship rates	$4,000	From your signed contract
Number of sponsored banners	1	From your web layout
Total sponsorship contribution	$4,000	

Table 11-2. Calculating monthly sponsorship revenue

The site also has a display-ad contract that nets it $2 for every thousand times someone sees a banner (see Table 11-3).

Display ad revenue	Example	Notes
Display ad rates (per thousand views)	$2	Whatever you negotiate
Banners per page	1	From your web layout
Total display ad contribution	$5,280	Page views × display rate / 1,000

Table 11-3. Calculating display ad revenue

So far, these are relatively simple revenue models. But the company also has pay-per-click revenue. A portion of its web layout is reserved for ads from a third-party advertising network, which inserts ads relevant to the visitor and the site content (see Table 11-4).

Click-through revenue	Example	Notes
Click-through ads per page	2	From your web layout
Total click-through ads shown	5,280,000	Page views × ads per page
Ad click percentage	0.80%	Depends on ad effectiveness
Total ad clicks	42,240	Ads shown × click-through rate
Average revenue per click	$0.37	From the auction rate for your ads
Total click-through contribution	$15,628.80	Ad clicks × revenue per click

Table 11-4. Calculating click-through revenue

The click-through revenue depends on what percentage of visitors click an ad and the amount paid for the click, which often depends on the value of a particular keyword. As a result, the site may write different kinds of content in order to attract more lucrative ad topics.

Finally, the site sells sports books through an affiliate relationship with an online bookstore. It features a "book of the week" on every page; it doesn't make money when someone clicks the link to that book, but it does make money when someone *buys* the book (see Table 11-5).*

Affiliate revenue	Example	Notes
Affiliate ads per page	1	From your web layout
Affiliate ads shown	2,640,000	Ads per page × page views
Affiliate ad click percentage	1.20%	Depends on ad effectiveness
Total affiliate ad clicks	31,680	Ads shown × affiliate ad clicks
Affilate conversion rate	4.30%	Ability of the affiliate partner to sell stuff
Total affiliate conversions	1,362.24	Ad clicks × conversion rate
Average affiliate sale value	$43.50	Shopping cart size of the affiliate partner
Total affiliate sales	$59,257.44	Revenue the affiliate made
Affiliate percentage	10%	Percentage of affiliate revenue you get
Total affiliate contribution	$5,925.74	Affiliate sales × affiliate percentage

Table 11-5. Calculating affiliate revenue

The affiliate model is complex (and often, site operators won't know what the visitor's purchases were—they'll just get a check). It relies on several funnels: the one that brought the visitor to the site, the one that convinced the visitor to click, and the one that ended in a purchase on a third-party site.

Our sports site is taking advantage of four distinct media monetization models. To do this, it's had to set aside a considerable amount of its screen real estate to accommodate a sponsor, a display banner, two click-through ads, and an affiliate ad for a book. Of course, this undermines the site's quality and leaves less room for valuable content that will keep visitors

---

* Depending on the merchant, the affiliate may make money from the *entire* purchase, not just the item listed on the affiliate site. If you buy a book on Amazon, and also buy a computer, the affiliate that referred you via the book makes a percentage of the computer sale—which gives Amazon a strong advantage when competing for affiliate ad real estate.

coming back. Striking a balance between commercial screen space and valuable content is tricky.

Pricing for sponsorships and display advertising is often negotiated directly, and depends on the reputation of the site, since it's a subtle form of endorsement and the advertiser is hoping for credibility. Ad networks set pricing for affiliate and pay-per-click advertising based on bidding by ad buyers.

Media sites involve a lot of math; sometimes they feel like they're being designed by spreadsheets rather than editors. Many of the vanity metrics we've warned you about earlier are actually relevant to media sites, since those sites make money from popularity.

Ultimately, then, media sites care about:

Audience and churn
> How many people visit the site and how loyal they are.

Ad inventory
> The number of impressions that can be monetized.

Ad rates
> Sometimes measured in *cost per engagement*—essentially how much a site can make from those impressions based on the content it covers and the people who visit.

Click-through rates
> How many of the impressions actually turn into money.

Content/advertising balance
> The balance of ad inventory rates and content that maximizes overall performance.

Audience and Churn

The most obvious metric for a media site is audience size. If we assume that an ad will get industry-standard click-through rates, then the more people who visit your site, the more money you'll make.

Tracking the growth in audience size—usually measured as the number of unique visitors a month—is essential. But measuring unique visitors can lead us astray if we focus on it too much; as we've noted earlier, engagement is much more important than traffic, so knowing how many visitors you're losing, as well as adding, is critical.

You can calculate audience churn on a media site by looking at the change in unique visitors in a specific month and the number of new visitors that month (see Table 11-6).

	Jan	Feb	Mar	Apr	May	June	July
Unique visitors	3,000	4,000	5,000	7,000	6,000	7,000	8,000
Change from last month	N/A	1,000	1,000	2,000	(1,000)	1,000	1,000
New (first-time) visitors	3,000	1,200	1,400	3,000	1,000	1,200	1,100
Churn	N/A	200	400	1,000	2,000	200	100

Table 11-6. Calculating audience churn

In this example, a website launches in January, and gets 3,000 unique visitors that month. Each month, it adds a certain number of unique first-time visitors to the site, but it also loses some visitors. You can calculate the churn by subtracting the number of unique first-time visitors from the change over the previous month—the new visitors are "making up" the last month's loss.

Note that sometimes an effective campaign can mask a churn problem. In this example, even though the site grew by 2,000 unique visitors in April, it managed to lose 1,000 visitors as well.

If you have the ability to test different layouts—one with fewer ads, for example—across visitor segments, you can determine the level of "churn tax" you're paying for having commercial content on the page. Then you can balance this against the revenue you're earning from advertising.

Inventory

Tracking unique visitors is a good start, but you need to measure ad inventory as well. This is the total number of unique page views in a given period of time, since each page view is a chance to show a visitor an ad. You can estimate inventory from visitors and pages per visit, but most analytics packages show the number automatically (see Table 11-7).

	Jan	Feb	Mar	Apr	May	June	July
Unique visitors	3,000	4,000	5,000	7,000	6,000	7,000	8,000
Pages per visit	11	14	16	10	8	11	13
Page inventory	33,000	56,000	80,000	0,000	48,000	77,000	104,000

Table 11-7. Calculating page inventory

The actual inventory depends on page layout and how many advertising elements are on each page.

PATTERN | Performance and the Sessions-to-Clicks Ratio

One other factor to consider is the sessions-to-clicks ratio. Every website loses a certain number of visitors before they ever come to the site. For every 100 web searches that link to you and get clicked, roughly 95 will actually land on your site. Basically, this says that five of those people hit the back button, or decide your site is taking too long to load, or change their mind about visiting.

The ratio of sessions (on your site) to clicks (from search links or referring links) is an indicator of web performance and reliability. Shopzilla's Jody Mulkey and Phillip Dixon did a detailed analysis of the impact of performance improvement on the sessions-to-clicks ratio when the company rebuilt its site to make it load quickly and reliably.[*] Ultimately, the makeover landed the site 3–4% more visitors. But within a short while, the site slowed down again as a result of ongoing changes, and the ratio worsened once more. Keeping a site fast is a constant battle.

---

[*] Phillip Dixon presented the results of Shopzilla's makeover, as well as its initial baseline, at Velocity Santa Clara in 2009. The full video is available at *http://www.youtube.com/watch?v=nKsxy8QJtds*.

Ad Rates

The rate advertising networks will pay you for an ad depends on your content and the going rate for a particular search term or keyword. For a straight-up media site, the ad rate is driven by the topic of your site and the content you publish. For a social network, the demographics of your audience drive ad rates. Visitor demographics will become increasingly important as social platforms like Facebook introduce third-party-placed advertising based on demographic segments—you'll get paid based on *who* your visitors are rather than *what* your site contains.

Content/Advertising Trade-off

The big decision any media site makes is how to pay the bills without selling out. This manifests itself in two ways. First, ad space: too many ads leads to lousy content and reduced visitor loyalty. Second, content: if your content is written to attract lucrative ad keywords, it'll feel forced and seem like a paid promotion.

Layout design and copywriting style are aesthetic issues, but those aesthetic decisions are grist for the analytical mill. If you're serious about content, you need to test different layouts for revenue-versus-churn, and different copy for content-versus-ad-value.

There are commercial tools to help with this. Parse.ly, for example, tries to analyze which content is getting the most traction. You might also segment key metrics like revenue or percentage of visitors who exit on a particular page by author, topic, or layout.

Visualizing the Media Business

Figure 11-1 represents a user's flow through a media business, along with the key metrics at each stage.

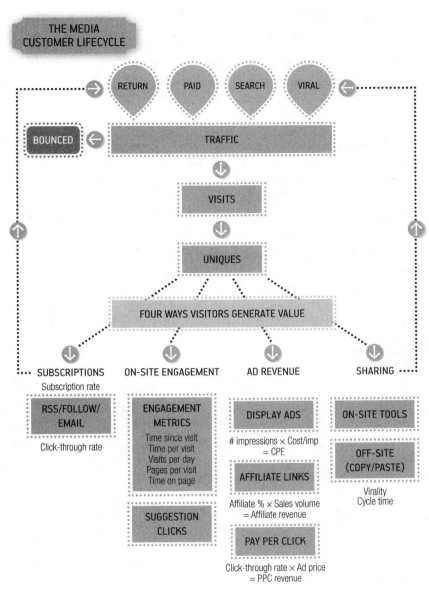

Figure 11-1. Calculating the value of media site customers is complicated

Wrinkles: Hidden Affiliates, Background Noise, Ad Blockers, and Paywalls

The variety of business relationships in online media can make finding the right key performance indicator (KPI) complex. Here are four examples of the kinds of complexity you need to watch out for.

Hidden affiliate models

Pinterest, an online pinboard of images, used to rewrite URLs for pictures of products its users had uploaded using a tool called Skimlinks. But as the site grew, its affiliate revenue quickly outstripped that of other big networks,[*] and it was called out for the practice.[†]

Pinterest was able to monetize traffic quickly with this strategy, and cared not only about how many people contributed content (a user-generated content, or UGC, metric), but also about the likelihood that someone would click on a picture and in turn make a purchase. Affiliate rewriting is a good way to monetize user-generated content without ads—effectively turning everything that's posted into an ad—but complicates business modeling, and can backfire.

Background noise

In one test, blank ads bearing no information had a click-through rate of roughly 0.08%—comparable to that of some paid campaigns.[‡] The ads invited those who'd clicked to explain why they did so; respondents were evenly divided between simple curiosity and accidental clicking. If your ads are getting revenues that are hardly better than the background noise a blank ad would get, you need to find out why.

Ad blockers

Technical users sometimes install ad-blocking software in their browsers that blocks ads from known ad-serving companies. This reduces your inventory, and can mess with your analytics. Reddit actually runs some ads containing funny content, mini-games, or messages thanking visitors for not blocking ads.

---

[*] http://www.digitaltrends.com/social-media/pinterest-drives-more-traffic-to-sites-than-100-million-google-users/

[†] http://llsocial.com/2012/02/pinterest-modifying-user-submitted-pins/

[‡] A June 2012 study by the Advertising Research Foundation conducted across a half-million ad impressions showed these rates; the rate varied by type of site. See http://adage.com/article/digital/incredible-click-rate/236233/.

Unsatisfied with the revenues from online advertising, some media sites run paywalls that charge users to access content. The paywall model runs the spectrum from voluntary donations (usually in the form of a pop up when the visitor first arrives) to fully paid sites where content is accessible only for a recurring fee.

Some media sites adopt a middle ground where visitors can access a quota of articles each month, as shown in Figure 11-2, but must pay to see more than this limit. Such sites are trying to strike a balance between "referred" content (e.g., an article mentioned on Twitter, which might generate ad revenue) and "subscribed" content (where the site is a user's primary daily news source).

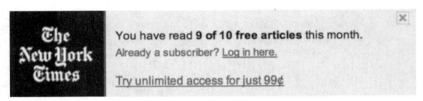

Figure 11-2. The inexorable rise of the paywall

The paywall model complicates analytics because there's a trade-off between ad and subscription revenue, and because there's a new e-commerce funnel to measure: trying to convert casual referred visitors into recurring-revenue subscribers.

Key Takeaways

- For media sites, ad revenue is everything—but advertising may include displays, pay-per-view, pay-per-click, and affiliate models, so tracking revenues is complex.

- Media sites need inventory (in the form of visitor eyeballs) and desirability, which comes from content that attracts a demographic advertisers want.

- It's hard to strike a balance between having good content and enough ads to pay the bills.

Media sites traditionally generate their own content, in the form of blogging, videos, and reported articles. But more and more of today's online content is from users themselves. If you want to learn more about the user-generated content business model and the metrics it tracks, continue to Chapter 12. If, on the other hand, you want to get right to the stages of a startup and how they affect your media business, jump to Chapter 14.

Model Five: User-Generated Content

You might think that Facebook, reddit, and Twitter are media sites, and you'd be right: they make their money from advertising. But their primary goal is rallying an engaged community that creates content. Similarly focused sites like Wikipedia make their money from other sources, such as donations.

We call these businesses *user-generated content* (UGC) sites. They deserve their own business model because their primary concern is the growth of an engaged community that creates content; without user activity, the sites stop functioning entirely. If you've decided that you're in the UGC business, then this chapter explains what metrics you'll need to track.

In this model, you're focused on the creation of good content, which means not only posts and uploads but also votes, comments, spam flagging, and other valuable activity. UGC is about the amount of good content versus bad, and the percentage of users who are lurkers versus creators. This is an *engagement funnel*,[*] similar to the traditional conversion funnels of an e-commerce model—only instead of moving prospects toward buying, you're constantly trying to move your user population to higher and higher levels of engagement, turning lurkers into voters, voters into commenters, and so on.

---

[*] Altimeter Group's Charlene Li refers to this as an *engagement pyramid*.

Wikipedia is an example of a UGC site—good, reliable, well-referenced content helps the site; flame wars or frequent edits between two battling contributors are bad for it. Just as an e-commerce site creates a funnel out of the steps through which a buyer must proceed, a UGC site measures the percentage of users who behave in certain ways. Revenue often comes from advertising or donations, but it's incidental to the core business of engaging users.

Consider a social network focused on link sharing, such as reddit. Anyone can read content and share it using social buttons on the site. Once a user has an account, she can vote content up or down, comment on content, or post content of her own. She can create her own group discussion around a topic. And she can use her account to message other users privately.

The tiers of engagement create a natural funnel, from the completely disengaged, fly-by visitors who come just once, to the hardcore. One of the core functions of the site is to acquire one-time visitors and turn them into users with accounts, and ultimately, into collaborators. Figure 12-1 shows an example engagement funnel, and lists what reddit, Facebook, and YouTube call *tiers*. Note that not every UGC site has all of these tiers.

	EXAMPLES		
	reddit	Facebook	Youtube
DRIVE-BY (ONE-TIME) VISITORS	Visitors	Visitors	Viewers
RETURNING VISITORS	Lurkers	Lurkers	Viewers
ENROLLED USERS	redditors	Users	Google account holders
VOTERS/FLAGGERS	Vote up/down	Like, flag	Thumb up/down
COMMENTERS	Post a reply	Post a comment	Post a comment
CONTENT CREATORS	Original posters (OP)	Poster	Uploader
MODERATORS	Subreddit mods	Group admin	
GROUP CREATORS	Subreddit creators	Event, place, or group creators	Channel owner

Figure 12-1. Every social network in the world just wants you to love it

This pattern of gradually increasing engagement isn't true only of websites—it's an archetype that happens time and again online. Twitter is similar to reddit: people use it to chat, to share links, and to comment on links. Instead of up-voting, there's a retweet button; instead of down-voting, there's blocking. Flickr, Facebook, LinkedIn, and YouTube all have roughly similar engagement tiers.

A UGC company cares about several metrics in addition to those we've seen in the media model in Figure 12-1:

Number of engaged visitors

How often people come back, and how long they stick around.

Content creation

The percentage of visitors who interact with content in some way, from creating it to voting on it.

Engagement funnel changes

How well the site moves people to more engaged levels of content over time.

Value of created content

The business benefit of content, from donations to media clicks.

Content sharing and virality

How content gets shared, and how this drives growth.

Notification effectiveness

The percentage of users who, when told something by push, email, or another means, act on it.

Visitor Engagement

A UGC site is successful when its visitors become regulars. As we've seen with SaaS churn, we look at recency to understand this—that is, when was the last time someone came back to the site? One quick way to measure this is the day-to-week ratio: how many of today's visitors were here earlier in the week? It's an indicator of whether people are returning on a regular basis, even if users don't create an account.

Another metric is the average days since last visit, although you need to exclude users who are beyond some cutoff limit (such as 30 days) from this calculation; otherwise, churned users will skew your numbers. For users who have accounts and take actions, you can measure engagement in other ways: days since last post, number of votes per day, and so on.

Content Creation and Interaction

User participation varies wildly by UGC site. On Facebook, every user logs in to do more than view a profile because it's a "walled garden" for content. Reddit is more open, but still has a high percentage of users who log in, because being logged in is required to up-vote posts.* On the other hand, sites like Wikipedia or YouTube, where the vast majority of users are simply consuming content, must rely on passive signals such as clickstreams or time on page, which serve as a proxy for ratings.

Interaction also varies significantly depending on what you're asking users to do. A few years ago, Rubicon Consulting published a study of online community participation rates. It looked at how often respondents performed certain actions online. As Figure 12-2 shows, there's significant variance in levels of engagement.

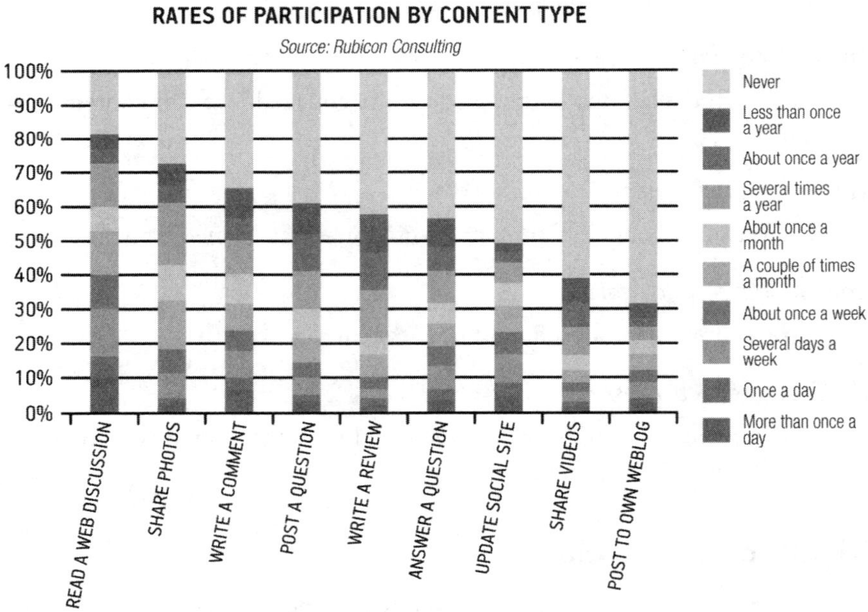

RATES OF PARTICIPATION BY CONTENT TYPE

Source: Rubicon Consulting

Figure 12-2. So much for a community to do, so little time

Early on, UGC sites need to solve a chicken-and-egg problem. They need content to draw in users, and users to create content. Sometimes, this content can be seeded from elsewhere: Wikimedia was originally going to be a site written by experts, but eventually pivoted to a community-edited

---

* It may also be because the login process doesn't demand an email confirmation—meaning users can be anonymous.

model—it overcame the chicken-and-egg issue by having content in place at the start.

The rate of content creation and the rate of enrollment matter a lot at the outset. Later, the question becomes whether good content is rising to the top, and whether people are commenting on it—signs that your user base cares about the discussion and is building a community.

Engagement Funnel Changes

On reddit, there are several tiers of engagement: lurking, voting, commenting, subscribing to a subreddit, submitting links, and creating subreddits. Each tier represents a degree of involvement and content generation by a user, and each type of user represents a different business value to the company. Every UGC site has a similar funnel, though the steps may be different.

The steps in the funnel aren't mutually exclusive—someone can comment without voting, for example—but these steps should be arranged in an order of increasing value to your business model as a user moves down the funnel. In other words, if someone who posts content is "better" for you than someone who simply shares a story, she's in a later tier of the funnel. The key is to move as many users into the more lucrative tiers as possible (making more content and better selection of content that will be popular).

One way to visualize this is by comparing the tiers of engagement over time. This is very similar to the SaaS upselling model: for a given cohort of users, how long does it take them to move to a more valuable stage in the engagement funnel? To see this, lay out the funnel by time period (for example, per month) or by cohort (see Table 12-1).

Totals	Jan	Feb	Mar	Apr
Unique visitors	13,201	21,621	26,557	38,922
Returning visitors	7,453	14,232	16,743	20,035
Active user accounts	5,639	8,473	9,822	11,682
Active voters	4,921	5,521	6,001	7,462
New subscribers/members	4,390	5,017	5,601	6,453
Active commenters	3,177	4,211	4,982	5,801
Active posters	904	1,302	1,750	2,107
Active group creators	32	31	49	54

Table 12-1. Visitor funnel by monthly cohort

If we assume that each tier of the engagement funnel does all the "previous" actions—for example, commenters vote, posters comment, and so on—we can display the change over time as a stacked graph (see Figure 12-3).

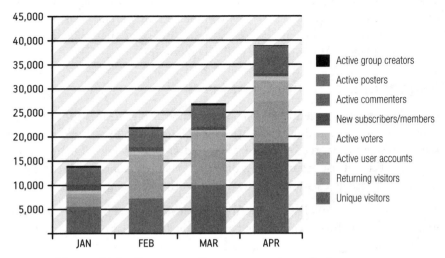

Figure 12-3. Can you split your users into distinct groups based on behavior?

This gives us an idea of growth for each segment, but it doesn't really show us what parts of the engagement process are getting better or worse. For this, we need to first calculate the conversion rates of the engagement funnel for each month (see Table 12-2).

Change from past period	Jan	Feb	Mar	Apr
Unique visitors	N/A	163.8%	122.8%	146.6%
Returning visitors	N/A	191.0%	117.6%	119.7%
Active user accounts	N/A	150.3%	115.9%	118.9%
Active voters	N/A	112.2%	108.7%	124.3%
New subscribers/members	N/A	114.3%	111.6%	115.2%
Active commenters	N/A	132.5%	118.3%	116.4%
Active posters	N/A	144.0%	134.4%	120.4%
Active group creators	N/A	96.9%	158.1%	110.2%

Table 12-2. Conversion rates of the engagement funnel by month

Once we know the conversion rates for each step, we can look at relative changes in rates from month to month (see Table 12-3).

Change in funnel	Jan	Feb	Mar	Apr
Unique visitors	N/A	N/A	N/A	N/A
Returning visitors	N/A	↑ 116.6%	→ 95.8%	↓ 81.6%
Active user accounts	N/A	↓ 78.7%	→ 98.5%	→ 99.4%
Active voters	N/A	↓ 74.7%	↓ 93.8%	↑ 104.5%
New subscribers/ members	N/A	↑ 101.9%	↑ 102.7%	↓ 92.7%
Active commenters	N/A	↑ 118.1%	↑ 108.8%	↓ 93.6%
Active posters	N/A	↑ 108.7%	↑ 113.6%	↑ 103.4%
Active group creators	N/A	↓ 67.3%	↑ 117.6%	↓ 91.5%

Table 12-3. Relative changes in conversion rates by month

With this data, we can see which things got better or worse based on changes we've made, or the different experience a particular cohort had on the site. For example, a smaller percentage of first-time visitors returned to the site in March, but a greater percentage of people commented and created posts that month. This lets us make changes and keep score.

Eventually, you'll hit a "normal" engagement funnel where a stable percentage of people are participating in each stage. This is OK; UGC sites have a power curve of content creation, where a small number of people create the vast majority of content. We'll give you some examples of ideal conversion rates for engagement funnels in Chapter 27.

Value of Created Content

The content your users create has a value. That might be the number of unique visitors who see it (in the case of a site like Wikipedia), the number of page views that represent ad inventory (Facebook), or a more complicated measurement like affiliate revenues generated by clicks on content users post (as in the Pinterest affiliate model).[*]

Regardless of how you value content, you'll want to measure it by cohort or traffic segment. If you're trying to decide where to invest in visitor acquisition, you'll want to know which referring sites bring valuable users. Perhaps you're looking for a particular demographic (as Mike Greenfield

---

[*] Earlier we warned that the number of unique visitors was a vanity metric, but that's when it's applied to site growth. As a measure of the value of an individual piece of content, it's a useful rating.

did when he compared engagement and value across user segments on Circle of Friends and launched Circle of Moms as a result).*

Content Sharing and Virality

A UGC site thrives on its visitors' behavior, and key among those behaviors is sharing. YouTube monetizes user content, relying on popular videos with virality to drive traffic and ad inventory. If your site is an unwalled garden— that is, users can share freely with the rest of the world—then tracking how content is shared is critical. It's less important for walled-garden sites like Facebook, whose goal is to keep users within the application.

While tweeting and liking content is useful, remember that a lot of sharing happens through other systems—RSS feeds and email, in particular. In fact Tynt, which makes tools for publishers to tag sharing when a link is copied and pasted, estimates that as much as 80% of sharing happens through email.†

You want to track how content is shared for several reasons:

- You need to know if you're achieving a level of virality that will sustain your business.

- You want to understand how content is shared and with whom. If every reader sends a URL to someone else, and that person then returns, you need to know that the visit was the result of a share, because the value of the content wasn't just the ad inventory it presented, but also the additional visit it generated.

- It will help you understand whether you should consider a paywall-style monetization strategy.

Notification Effectiveness

We used to design exclusively for the Web. In recent years, designers rallied around portable devices with cries of "design for mobile" or "mobile first." But there's good reason to think that the future of applications isn't mobility—it's notification.

Today's mobile device is a prosthetic brain. We rely on it to remind us of meetings, tell us when others are thinking of us, and find our way home. Smart agent technologies like Siri and Google Now will only reinforce this.

---

* See "Case Study: Circle of Moms Explores Its Way to Success" in Chapter 2.

† *http://www.mediapost.com/publications/article/181944/quick-whats-the-largest-digital-social-media-pla.html*

Already, our mobile devices' notification systems are a battleground, with applications fighting for our attention.

In a UGC model, the ability to keep pulling users back in through notifications is an essential part of sustaining engagement.

Fred Wilson calls mobile notification a game changer:[*]

> Notifications become the primary way I use the phone and the apps. I rarely open Twitter directly. I see that I have "10 new @mentions" and I click on the notification and go to [the] Twitter @mention tab. I see that I have "20 new checkins" and I click on the notification and go to the Foursquare friends tab.

He cites three main reasons why this is such a significant shift:

> First, it allows me to use a lot more engagement apps on my phone. I don't need them all on the main page. As long as I am getting notifications when there are new engagements, I don't really care where they are on the phone.

> Second, I can have as many communications apps as I want. I've currently got SMS, Kik, Skype, Beluga, and GroupMe on my phone. I could have plenty more. I don't need to be loyal to any one communication system, I just need to be loyal to my notification inbox.

> And finally, the notification screen is the new home screen. When I pull out my phone, it is the first thing I do.

You measure notification effectiveness in much the same way as you measure email delivery rates: you're sending out a certain number of messages, and some of those messages produce the outcome you're hoping for. This is true whether those messages are sent by email, SMS, or mobile application.

Visualizing a UCG Business

Figure 12-4 represents a user's flow through a UGC business, along with the key metrics at each stage.

---

[*]   *http://www.avc.com/a_vc/2011/03/mobile-notifications.html*

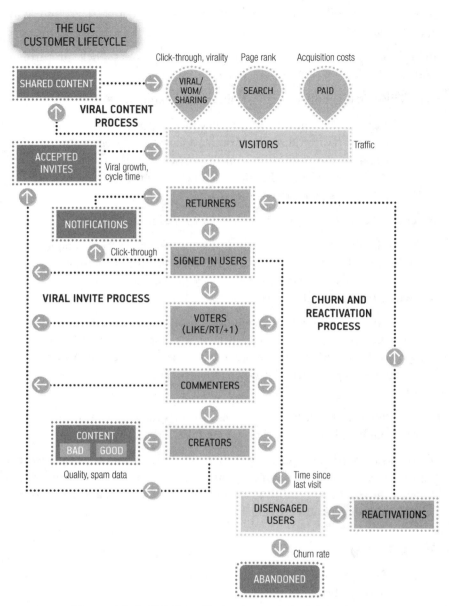

Figure 12-4. UGC is all about turning visitors into creators

Wrinkles: Passive Content Creation

Just as notifications happen in the background but are in many ways the new foreground interface, so too does content creation often happen stealthily. Google has been able to pack its social network, Google+, with information and updates across its user base simply by enabling background features like Latitude and image uploads, and by linking to external sites based on your profile.

As more and more mobile devices become sensors that track our health, our location, our purchases, and our habits, we'll see a split into active content generation (sharing a link, writing a post) and passive content generation (automatically populating a timeline with our actions; helping the system learn from our clickstream). This shift gives a huge advantage to those who make the tools for collecting data—mobile device makers, payment companies, and so on.

Consider three changes on the horizon: ambient check-ins, in which your smart device registers changes in location and shares them; digital wallets designed to store loyalty, ticket, and membership data; and near-field communications technology that make it possible to share information or pay by bumping your device against something. These three technologies alone will provide a treasure trove of passive data that, given the right permissions, can populate someone's timeline in detailed ways that might pass for user-generated content, even when they're happening in the background.

While this doesn't change the UGC world today, it'll gradually cloud the simple sharing measurements we have at the moment and introduce a lot more noise—is a user engaged, or did he simply forget to turn off some kind of passive engagement? Are certain kinds of passive sharing better for the business? If so, what can we do to encourage or reward them?

Key Takeaways

- Visitor engagement is everything in UGC. You track visitors' involvement in an "engagement funnel."

- Many users will lurk, some will contribute lightly, and others will become dedicated content creators. This 80/20 split exists throughout the activities you want your users to accomplish.

- To keep users coming back and engaged, you'll need to notify them of activity through email and other forms of "interruption."

- Fraud prevention is a significant amount of work for a UGC site.

The UGC business might focus on user contribution above all else, but it still pays its bills with advertising most of the time. If you want to learn more about advertising and the media business, head back to Chapter 11. If you want to get straight to the stages of a startup and how they affect metrics, jump to Chapter 14.

CHAPTER 13

Model Six: Two-Sided Marketplaces

Two-sided marketplaces are a variation on e-commerce sites, but they're different enough to warrant a separate discussion. If, after reading Chapter 7, you've concluded that you're running this kind of company, here's what you need to know.

In this model, the company makes money when a buyer and seller come together to complete a transaction. While eBay is undoubtedly the most famous example of a two-sided marketplace, the underlying pattern is fairly common. Consider the following business models, all of which have an aspect of a two-sided market:

- Real estate listing services allow prospective buyers to identify properties by a wide range of criteria, and then extract a fee for setting up the transaction, either as a one-time cost or a percentage.

- Indiegogo lets artists list projects and collect the support of backers. Backers are able to browse projects and find those they want to support. The site takes a percentage of monies raised.

- eBay and Craigslist let sellers list and promote items, and let buyers purchase from them. In the case of Craigslist, a very small number of transactions (rentals in certain cities, for example) cost money, making the rest of the site free.

- App stores let software developers list their wares in exchange for sharing the revenues. The app store not only handles the catalog of apps and the delivery, it also distributes updates, helps with litigation, and manages currency transactions.

- Dating sites allow an inventory of prospective partners to browse one another, and charge a fee for completing an introduction or for revealing additional information in a paid subscription.

- Hotwire and Priceline let hotels list additional inventory, then find buyers willing to buy it at a discount. They hide the identity of the hotel until after the purchase.

All of these examples include a shared inventory model and two stakeholders—buyers and sellers, creators and supporters, prospective partners,* or hotels and travellers. They all make money when the two stakeholders come together, and they often differentiate based on a particular set of search parameters or qualifications (e.g., apartments that have been vetted, seller ratings). And they all need an inventory to get started.

In this section, we're going to define two-sided marketplaces more narrowly, which will exclude some of the aforementioned examples. In our definition:

- The seller is responsible for listing and promoting the product. A real estate service that simply publishes realtor listings wouldn't qualify, but a for-sale-by-owner site would.

- The marketplace owner has a "hands off" approach to the individual transactions. Sites like Hotwire that create the hotel profiles wouldn't be included.

- The buyer and seller have competing interests. In most marketplace models the seller wants to extract as much money as possible, while the buyer wants to spend as little as possible. In a dating site, regardless of gender differences, both parties have a shared interest—a compatible partner—so we'll leave them out of this discussion.

Two-sided marketplaces face a unique problem: they have to attract both buyers and sellers. That looks like twice as much work. As we'll see in some of the case studies ahead, companies like DuProprio/Comfree, Etsy, Uber, and Amazon found ways around this dilemma, but they all boil down to one thing: *focus on whomever has the money*. Usually, that's buyers: if you can find a group that wants to *spend* money, it's easy to find a group that wants to *make* money.

---

* While there's technically only one stakeholder in a dating site—someone who wants to date—many of the sites that focus on heterosexual relationships treat men and women differently (for example, free enrollment for female users). We mention it here because the technique has been used to break the chicken-and-egg problem from which marketplaces suffer, but as online dating becomes more mainstream this is less common.

CASE STUDY | What DuProprio Watches

DuProprio/Comfree is the largest for-sale-by-owner marketplace, and second-most-visited real estate network in Canada. Founded in 1997 by co-president Nicolas Bouchard, it lists 17,000 properties and has roughly 5 million visits a month. The company charges a one-time fee of around $900 for a listing, assistance with pricing, signage, and HDR photography. Additional tools, from legal advice to real estate coaching, are available for an extra fee. The company also has affiliate listing relationships with a prominent newspaper.

Nicolas was Lean before Lean came along. The son of a realtor and an entrepreneur from a young age—already running a hardwood flooring business while in high school—he helped his father build a website in the early days of the Web. Then he had an epiphany. "I started to notice the black-and-orange 'for sale by owner' signs in hardware stores. So I made the connection, and said, 'let's do a real estate website for owners.' I launched it in my parents' basement."

The first version of the website was static, built on Microsoft Frontpage. There was no staff. Nicolas acquired new sellers by scouring the classified ads and driving around looking for "for sale by owner" signs, convincing sellers to list with his site. "Back then, the only KPI was the number of signs we had on people's lawns—because that's how buyers found my website," he recalls. "That, and of course, the number of properties listed on the website."

Gradually, Nicolas found other sources of potential sellers, looking at sites like Craigslist and Kijiji. "It was the beginning of the Internet," he says. "I was still playing with how to pitch the service and how to use the Web to my advantage, and that of my clients."

In early 2000, once the company had found some traction, it switched from a static site to a dynamic one, and manually transferred all the seller listings to the new site. Until that point, it had only rudimentary analytics—little more than a page hit counter. It added Webtrends for analytics. With the dynamic version of the site came a seller login, which allowed sellers to update data on their property by themselves. "At this point, sellers could see more about how they were doing, including how many times their listing appeared in search results, how many times the listing was clicked, and so on," he says.

A couple of years later, the company added client-side logins. This allowed prospective buyers to set their search criteria, and eventually to subscribe to notifications when suitable properties came up for sale. The emphasis was on search.

"With the advent of the dynamic site, we tracked the number of visitors versus the number of seller subscriptions, because that's bread and butter to us," says Nicolas. But the data still wasn't precise: the company was still focusing on visits, not visitors.

One reason for this was that the two-sided marketplace was more complicated than it might seem. Often, someone selling a house was also looking for a new one—which made it hard to segment traffic cleanly between the two groups—so Nicolas settled for a simple rule of thumb. "At some point we had a metric that 1,000 visits on the website equals 1 subscription." Despite the coarseness of this baseline, it was enough to draw a line in the sand. "This was a rudimentary conversion rate," he says. "The objective was to generate more conversions per visit."

As the company became more sophisticated about analysis, it improved its analytics further. "We started to look at the conversion rate of visitors coming to the subscription page, where we display the various packages we offer," he says. "We started to be a bit more disciplined, but this was long before we did any real A/B testing." The company was making modifications to its website to see if they improved conversions or the visits-to-listings ratio, but this was still a month-by-month process.

While the company has detailed analytics from Google today, Nicolas doesn't concern himself with details. "There are always more visitors looking to buy a property," he points out. He also doesn't focus as much on buyer-side account creation. "In Québec alone, we have 3 millions visits a month, and 1.2 million unique visitors a month, but only a small fraction of those—5% or less—create an account."

Nicolas does care a lot about competitors, however. "We want to be as good as possible, and better than real estate agents. We have data from the Canada Mortgage and Housing Corporation and the Canadian Real Estate Board, so we know exactly how many properties were listed and sold. We benchmark ourselves against these numbers all the time, region by region."

Today, the company has three big goals. It wants to convince sellers to list their property on the site, it wants to convince buyers to register for notifications when a property becomes available, and it wants to sell the properties.

DuProprio is a great example of how a company moves through several stages as it grows. The metrics the company tracked changed over time:

- Early on, a static site was fine—the focus was on acquisition (signs on lawns, volume of houses listed).

- Then its focus shifted to the visitor-to-listing ratio, which was a measure of whether the marketplace was healthy.

- As the marketplace emerged, it focused on revenue metrics such as the list-to-sold ratio, and the average package sale price.

- Now it's adding new metrics to optimize the email click-through rate, search results, and use of its recently launched mobile applications. "Currently, because of the way the system is built, it's hard to know where blank searches are occurring on the website, but it's something we're working on."

Ultimately, in this two-sided marketplace, Nicolas has clearly chosen to focus on the source of the money.

"For us, today, one big metric is the number of sales. An even bigger metric than that is the sold-to-list ratio: what's the total number of properties listed versus the total number of properties sold," he says. "If the property doesn't sell, we don't have a business. There will be no word of mouth, no good reviews, no 15,000 testimonials from satisfied sellers, no 'I sold' stickers on lawn signs. Even if tomorrow I'm listing 10,000 more properties, if no properties are selling, I'm dead."

Summary

- Early on, a marketplace can grow its inventory by hand, using decidedly low-tech approaches. Do things that don't scale.

- For some marketplaces, a per-listing or per-transaction fee, rather than a commission, works well.

- If you can build buyer attention, it'll be easy to convince sellers to join you, so go where the money is.

- A static, curated site can be enough to prove the viability of a big-ticket, slow-turnover marketplace.

- Ultimately, volume of sales, and the resulting revenue, is the only metric that matters.

Analytics Lessons Learned

Start with the minimum marketplace that proves you have demand, supply, and a desire for buyers and sellers to transact. Then find ways of making money from that activity. The metrics you track will depend on transaction size, frequency, and other unique characteristics of the business. But the fundamentals are the same: revenue from transactions.

Imagine you're launching a two-sided marketplace for secondhand game consoles. Those with a console to sell can list it, and those looking for a console to buy can browse by a variety of criteria. The transactions are handled through PayPal, and you retain a portion of the proceeds above a minimum amount.

Because you're not a vendor of consoles yourself, you need to find a way to produce *either* an inventory of consoles, *or* a large group of customers. You need to pick which side of the market you're going to "seed."

If you want to seed the seller side, you might crawl Craigslist and approach console owners to see if they have inventory, encouraging them to list items. If you want to seed the buyer side, you might set up a forum for nostalgic game players, bringing them together and inviting them from social sites.

You could create an artificial inventory by selling consoles to start with, and then gradually adding inventory from others. Car-service provider Uber overcame the chicken-and-egg problem in new markets by simply buying up available towncars: when the company launched in Seattle, it paid drivers $30 an hour to drive passengers around, and switched to a commission model only once it had sufficient demand to make it worthwhile for the drivers. *The company created supply.*

On the other hand, if you want to seed the buyer side, you probably need to pick something for which you can command an initial inventory, then purchase some; or you might take orders with a promise of fulfilling them later, knowing you have access to that inventory. Amazon, for example, started selling books, which allowed it to streamline its order, search, and logistics processes. Then it could offer a broader range of its own goods. Eventually, with access to many buyers and their search patterns, Amazon became a marketplace for goods from many other suppliers. Salesforce.com created a CRM product, and then created an app exchange ecosystem where third-party developers could sell software to existing customers. With respect to their marketplace offerings, *both companies first created demand.*

The health of their chicken-and-egg-defeating strategy was a critical metric:

- For Uber, this meant measuring how much drivers would be making on a commission basis, as well as the inventory and the time it took a driver to pick up a customer. When those metrics were sustainable (with a reasonable margin of error), it was time to switch from the "artificial" market of paid drivers to the "sustainable" two-sided marketplace of commissions.

- For Amazon, this meant measuring the number of retained book buyers who were comfortable with the purchase and delivery process, and then trying out new offerings , such as electronics or kitchenware, that those buyers might purchase.

The first step of a two-sided marketplace—and the first thing to measure— is your ability to create an inventory (supply) or an audience (demand). DuProprio looked for "for sale by owner" signs and classified listings to build its initial set of listings, and the seller's lawn sign then drove buyer traffic, so its metrics were listings and lawn signs. The metrics you'll care about first are around the attraction, engagement, and growth of this seed group.

Josh Breinlinger, a venture capitalist at Sigma West who previously ran marketing at labor marketplace oDesk, breaks up the key marketplace metrics into three categories: buyer activity, seller activity, and transactions. "I almost always recommend modeling the buyer side as your primary focus, and then you model supply, more in the sense of total inventory," he says. "It's easy to find people that want to make money; it's much harder to find people that want to spend money."

Josh cautions that just tracking buyer, seller, and inventory numbers isn't enough: you have to be sure those numbers relate to the actual activity that's at the core of your business model. "If you wanted to juice those numbers you could do so quite easily by tweaking algorithms, but you're not necessarily providing a better experience to users," he says. "I believe the better focus is on more explicit marketplace activity like bids, messages, listings, or applications."

Once you've got both sides of the market together, your attention (and analytics) will shift to maximizing the proceeds from the market—the number of listings, the quality of buyers and sellers, the percentage of searches for which you have at least one item in inventory, the marketplace-specific metrics Josh mentions, and ultimately, the sales volume and resulting revenue. You'll also focus on understanding what makes a listing desirable so you can attract more like it. And you'll start tracking fraud and bad offerings that can undermine the quality of the marketplace and send buyers and sellers away.

Our game console company starts by tracking the growth of buyers within the marketplace, and their interest in sellers' listings. To track buyers, we start by tracking visitors who aren't sellers (see Table 13-1). One useful metric is the ratio of buyers to sellers—a higher number should convince more sellers to list their merchandise.

	Jan	Feb	Mar	Apr	May	Jun
Unique visitors	3,921	5,677	6,501	8,729	10,291	9,025
Returning visitors	2,804	4,331	5,103	6,448	7,463	6,271
Registered visitors	571	928	1,203	3,256	4,004	4,863
Visitor/seller ratio	12.10	13.33	11.57	11.91	12.83	10.45

Table 13-1. Site visitors (potential buyers)

But this data looks a lot like vanity metrics. What we *really* care about are engaged buyers who've made a purchase. Drawing a line in the sand, we decide someone is a buyer if she's made at least one purchase, and that a buyer is engaged if she's searched for something in the last 30 days (see Table 13-2).

	Jan	Feb	Mar	Apr	May	Jun
Buyers (1+ purchase)	412	677	835	1,302	1,988	2,763
Engaged buyers (search in last 30 days)	214	482	552	926	1,429	1,826
Engaged buyer/ active seller ratio	1.95	3.09	2.33	4.61	5.67	6.81
Engaged buyer/ active listing ratio	1.37	1.17	0.84	1.05	1.34	1.62

Table 13-2. Number of engaged buyers

Next we look at sellers, their growth in the marketplace, and the listings they create (see Table 13-3).

	Jan	Feb	Mar	Apr	May	Jun
Sellers	324	426	562	733	802	864
Listings	372	765	1,180	1,452	1,571	1,912
Average listings/seller	1.15	1.80	2.10	1.98	1.96	2.21

Table 13-3. Growth of sellers and listings

This is a bit simplistic, however: it breaks our rule that good metrics are ratios or rates, and it doesn't distinguish between active and disengaged sellers. A better set of data might dig a bit deeper. We draw some lines in the sand: sellers are disengaged if they haven't added a listing in the last 30 days, and listings are inactive if they don't show up in buyers' search results at least five times a week (see Table 13-4).

	Jan	Feb	Mar	Apr	May	Jun
Active sellers (new listing in last 30 days)	110	156	237	201	252	268
% active sellers	34.0%	36.6%	42.2%	27.4%	31.4%	31.0%
Active listings (five views in last week)	156	413	660	885	1,068	1,128
% active listings	41.9%	54.0%	55.9%	61.0%	68.0%	59.0%

Table 13-4. Number and percent of active sellers and listings

Now that we have some data on buyers and sellers, we need to map out the conversion funnel leading to a purchase. We look at the number of searches, how many of them produce results, and how many of those results lead to a viewing of a detailed listing of the product. We also track the sale, and whether the buyer and seller were satisfied (see Table 13-5).

	Jan	Feb	Mar	Apr	May	Jun
Total searches	18,271	31,021	35,261	64,021	55,372	62,012
Searches with >1 match	9,135	17,061	23,624	48,015	44,853	59,261
Click-through to listings	1,370	2,921	4,476	10,524	15,520	12,448
Total purchase count	71	146	223	562	931	622
Remaining inventory	301	920	1,877	2,767	3,407	4,697
Satisfied transactions	69.00	140.00	161.00	521.00	921.00	590.00
Percent satisfied transactions	97.18%	95.89%	72.20%	92.70%	98.93%	94.86%
Total revenue	$22,152	$42,196	$70,032	$182,012	$272,311	$228,161
Average transaction size	$312.00	$289.01	$314.04	$323.86	$292.49	$366.82

Table 13-5. Sales, satisfaction, and revenue

Finally, we track the quality of the listings and the buyers' and sellers' reputations (see Table 13-6).

	Jan	Feb	Mar	Apr	May	Jun
Searches per buyer per day	1.48	1.53	1.41	1.64	0.93	0.75
New listings per day	12.00	22.11	30.87	29.67	20.65	43.00
Average search result count	2.1	3.1	3.4	4.2	5.2	9.1
Flagged listings	12	18	24	54	65	71
Percent flagged listings	3.23%	2.35%	2.03%	3.72%	4.14%	3.71%
Sellers rated below 3/5	4.0%	7.1%	10.0%	8.2%	7.0%	9.1%
Buyers rated below 3/5	1.2%	1.4%	1.8%	2.1%	1.9%	1.6%

Table 13-6. Quality of listings

There's a lot of data to track here, because you're monitoring both buyer e-commerce funnels and seller content creation, as well as looking for signs of fraud or declining content quality.

Which metrics you focus on will depend on what you're trying to improve: inventory, conversion rate, search results, content quality, and so on. For example, if you're not getting enough click-through from search results to individual listings, you can show less information in initial search results to see if that encourages more click-through.

So the metrics you'll want to watch include:

Buyer and seller growth

> The rate at which you're adding new buyers and sellers, as measured by return visitors.

Inventory growth

> The rate at which sellers are adding inventory—such as new listings— as well as completeness of those listings.

Search effectiveness

> What buyers are searching for, and whether it matches the inventory you're building.

Conversion funnels

> The conversion rates for items sold, and any segmentation that reveals what helps sell items—such as the professional photographs of a property mentioned in the Airbnb case study in Chapter 1.

Ratings and signs of fraud

> The ratings for buyers and sellers, signs of fraud, and tone of the comments.

Pricing metrics

> If you have a bidding method in place (as eBay does), then you care whether sellers are setting prices too high or leaving money on the table.

All of the metrics that matter to an e-commerce site matter to a two-sided marketplace. But the metrics listed here focus specifically on the creation of a fluid market with buyers and sellers coming together.

Rate at Which You're Adding Buyers and Sellers

This metric is particularly important in the early stages of the business. If you're competing with others, then your line in the sand is an inventory of sellers that's comparable to that of your competitors, so it's worth a buyer's time to search you. If you're in a relatively unique market, then your line in the sand is enough inventory that buyers' searches are returning one or more valid results.

Track the change in these metrics over periods of time to understand if things are getting better or worse. You're already tracking the sellers and listings, but what you really want to know is how fast those numbers are growing.

This makes it easier to pinpoint changes that are worth investigating. You'll want to track how fast you're adding sellers to the marketplace and whether the rate of addition is growing or slowing. If it's growing, then you may want to focus on onboarding new sellers so they become active and list inventory right away; if it's stalling, then you may want to spend more money to find new sellers or focus on increasing the number of listings per seller as well as the conversion rate of those listings.

Long-term, you can always buy supply, but you can't buy demand. In an attention economy, having an engaged, attentive user base is priceless. It's the reason Walmart can coerce favorable terms from suppliers and that Amazon can build a network of merchants even though it's a seller itself. When it comes to sustainable competitive advantage, *demand beats supply*.

Rate of Inventory Growth

In addition to sellers, you need to track listings they create. Focus on the number of listings per seller and whether that's growing, as well as the completeness of those listings (are sellers completing the description of their offering?).

A bigger inventory means more searches are likely to yield results. If you start to saturate your marketplace (i.e., if most of the sellers in your market have already become members), then your growth will come from increasing their listings and the effectiveness of those listings.

Buyer Searches

In many two-sided markets, searches are the primary way in which buyers find sellers. You need to track the number of searches that return no results—this is a lost sales opportunity. For example, you might track the change in daily searches, new listings, and result counts, which will show you whether you're growing the business (see Table 13-7).

	Feb	Mar	Apr	May	Jun
Change in daily searches per buyer	103.3%	92.2%	116.4%	56.6%	80.6%
Change in new listings per day	184.2%	139.6%	96.1%	69.6%	208.3%
Change in average result count per search	147.6%	109.7%	123.5%	123.8%	175.0%

Table 13-7. Buyer searches month over month

In this example, buyers performed fewer daily searches in May and June than beforehand, relatively speaking. The number of listings in May also declined.

You should also look at the search terms themselves. By looking at the most common search terms that yield nothing, you'll find out what your buyers are after. A dominant search term—say, "Nintendo"—might suggest a category you could add to the site to make navigation easier, or a keyword campaign you could undertake to attract more buyers. You'll want to know what the most lucrative search terms are, too, because that tells you what kind of seller you should attract to the site.

The ratio of searches to clicked listings is also an important step in your conversion funnel.

Conversion Rates and Segmentation

The conversion funnel will have several stages, starting with the number of searches done by visitors. You should also measure the number of *satisfied* transactions, because a spike in transactions where one party is unsatisfied suggests that the site is focused on short-term gain (more sales) for long-term pain (a bad reputation, demands for refunds, and so on). See Table 13-8.

	May	Funnel
Total searches	55,372	100.00%
Searches with >1 match	44,853	81.00%
Click-through to listings	15,520	28.03%
Total purchase count	931	1.68%
Satisfied transactions	921	1.66%

Table 13-8. Measuring conversions in a marketplace

Buyer and Seller Ratings

Shared marketplaces are often regulated by the users themselves—users rate one another based on their experience with a transaction. The easiest way to implement this system is to let users flag something that's wrong, or that violates the terms of service. Users can also rank one another, and sellers work hard to earn a good reputation when the ratings system works well.

Percent of Flagged Listings

You'll want to track the percentage of listings that are flagged, and whether this number is increasing or decreasing. A sharp increase in the percentage of listings your users are flagging indicates fraud. See Table 13-9.

	Jan	Feb	Mar	Apr	May	Jun
Percent of listings flagged	3.23%	2.35%	2.03%	3.72%	4.14%	3.71%
Change in percent flagged listings		72.9%	86.4%	182.9%	111.3%	89.7%
Change in sellers rated below 3/5		177.5%	140.8%	82.0%	85.4%	130.0%
Change in buyers rated below 3/5		116.7%	128.6%	116.7%	90.5%	84.2%

Table 13-9. Flagged listings

Similarly, a rise in poor ratings shows a problem with expectations, and may indicate that sellers aren't delivering or buyers aren't paying. In every case, you'll have to start with these metrics, then investigate individually to see if there's a technical problem, a malicious user, or something else behind the change.

Visualizing a Two-Sided Marketplace

Figure 13-1 illustrates a user's flow through a two-sided marketplace, along with the key metrics at each stage.

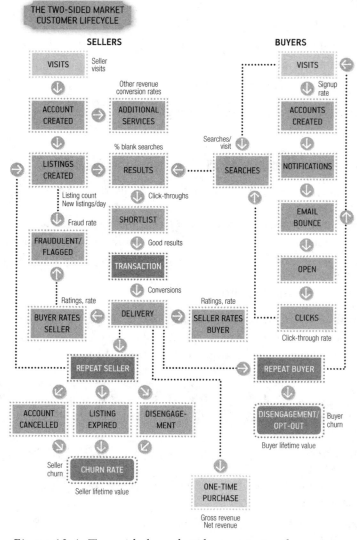

Figure 13-1. Two-sided marketplaces—twice the metrics, twice the fun

Wrinkles: Chicken and Egg, Fraud, Keeping the Transaction, and Auctions

In the early days of the Web, pundits predicted an open, utopian world of frictionless markets that were transparent and efficient. But as Internet giants like Google, Amazon, and Facebook have shown, parts of the Web are dystopian. Two-sided marketplaces are subject to strong network effects—the more inventory they have to offer, the more useful they become. A marketplace with no inventory, on the other hand, is useless.

Successful two-sided marketplaces find a way to artificially populate either the buyer or the seller side early on. As a particular niche matures, this network effect means there will be a few dominant players—as is the case with Airbnb, VRBO, and a few others in the rental property space.

Fraud and trust are the other big issues for such marketplaces. You don't want to assume responsibility for the delivery of goods or services within your marketplace, but you need to ensure that there are reliable reputation systems. Buyer and seller ratings are one approach to this, but there are other ways. Some dating sites offer guarantees (for example, that they will prosecute if a person turns out to be married).

One more major issue is keeping the transaction within the network. In the case of a sailboat or house marketplace, the transaction may be tens or even hundreds of thousands of dollars. That's not really suitable for a PayPal transaction, and it's hard to stop "leakage"—buyers and sellers find one another through your marketplace, and then conclude their business without you getting a transaction fee.

There are a number of ways to overcome this—all of which you should test to see if they work for your product and market. For example, you might:

- Refer users to an outside agent to conclude the transaction (e.g., a realtor) and monetize the referral.

- Charge a fee (instead of a percentage) proportional to the value of the item the seller is listing.

- Monetize something else about the market, such as in-site advertising, shipping services, or favorable placement.

- Make it impossible for the two parties to connect or find each other's identity until after the transaction is confirmed (as discount travel site Hotwire does).

- Offer value-added services (such as purchase insurance or escrow) that encourage participants to keep you in the deal.

Finally, there are auction marketplaces such as eBay where the price of an item isn't fixed. The seller may set the minimum price, as well as a "Buy now" value, but the final price is what the market is willing to pay. If this is your model, you'll need to analyze how many sales failed to receive a bid (indicating overpricing), how many sold for the "Buy now" price (indicating underpricing), and the duration and outcome of auctions. You might use this information to improve the prices your sellers set—and your resulting revenues.

Key Takeaways

- Two-sided markets come in all shapes and sizes.

- Early on, the big challenge is solving the "chicken and egg" problem of finding enough buyers and sellers. It's usually good to focus on the people who have money to spend first.

- Since sellers are inventory, you need to track the growth of that inventory and how well it fits what buyers are looking for.

- While many marketplaces take a percentage of transactions, you may be able to make money in other ways, by helping sellers promote their products or charging a listing fee.

Two-sided marketplaces are a variant of traditional e-commerce sites. We've focused on what makes marketplaces unique in this chapter, but if you want to learn more about e-commerce and the metrics that drive that business model, jump back to Chapter 8. If, on the other hand, you want to learn how the stage of your business drives the metrics you need to watch, continue to Chapter 14.

What Stage Are You At?

You can't just start measuring everything at once. You have to measure your assumptions in the right order. To do that, you need to know what stage you're at.

Our Lean Analytics stages suggest an order to the metrics you should focus on. The stages won't apply perfectly to everyone. We'll probably get yelled at for being so prescriptive—in fact, we already have, as we've tested the material for the book online and in events. That's OK; we have thick skins.

In a startup, your business *model*—and proof that your assumptions are reasonably accurate—is far more important than your business *plan*. Business plans are for bankers; business models are for founders. Deciding what business you're in is usually quite easy. Deciding on the *stage* you're at is complicated. This is where founders tend to lie to themselves. They believe they're further along than they really are.

The reality is that every startup goes through stages, beginning with problem discovery, then building something, then finding out if what was built is good enough, then spreading the word and collecting money. These stages—Empathy, Stickiness, Virality, Revenue, and Scale—closely mirror what other Lean Startup advocates advise.

1. First, you need *empathy*. You need to get inside your target market's head and be sure you're solving a problem people care about in a way someone will pay for. That means getting out of the building, interviewing people, and running surveys.

2. Second, you need *stickiness*, which comes from a good product. You need to find out if you can build a solution to the problem you've discovered. There's no point in promoting something awful if your visitors will bounce right off it in disgust. Companies like Color that attempted to scale prematurely, without having proven stickiness, haven't fared well.

3. Third, you need *virality*. Once you've got a product or service that's sticky, it's time to use word of mouth. That way, you'll test out your acquisition and onboarding processes on new visitors who are motivated to try you, because you have an implied endorsement from an existing user. Virality is also a force multiplier for paid promotion, so you want to get it right before you start spending money on customer acquisition through inorganic methods like advertising.

4. Fourth, you need *revenue*. You'll want to monetize things at this point. That doesn't mean you haven't already been charging—for many businesses, even the first customer has to pay. It just means that earlier on, you're less focused on revenue than on growth. You're giving away free trials, free drinks, or free copies. Now you're focused on maximizing and optimizing revenue.

5. Fifth, you need *scale*. With revenues coming in, it's time to move from growing your business to growing your market. You need to acquire more customers from new verticals and geographies. You can invest in channels and distribution to help grow your user base, since direct interaction with individual customers is less critical—you're past product/market fit and you're analyzing things quantitatively.

So, as we shared in Chapter 5, we suggest these five Lean Analytics stages, and we believe you should go through them in the order shown in Figure 14-1, unless you have a really good reason to do otherwise.

While many of the examples we've looked at are technology companies— and many of those are B2C (business to consumer) companies—these five stages apply equally well to a restaurant as they do to an enterprise software company.

LEAN ANALYTICS STAGE	RATIONALE
EMPATHY	Identifying a real problem and a real solution is the cheapest thing to do (since it costs only a cup of coffee). It also addresses the riskiest question: will anyone care? It comes first.
STICKINESS	Will the dogs eat the dog food? Make your mistakes with a small, friendly audience you can love and nurture before throwing the unwashed masses at it.
VIRALITY	Sharing helps grow, but also verifies that what you've made is good. Word of mouth is endorsement. And virality is a "force multiplier" for paid customer acquisition.
REVENUE	Will people open their pocketbooks? And can you charge them enough to fund your ongoing operations, plus your artificial acquisition of users?
SCALE	You need channels to amortize the cost of sales and distribution. You need an ecosystem to cross the "hole in the middle" from niche player to big company.

Figure 14-1. Why we put the five stages of Lean Analytics in that order

Consider a restaurant:

1. **Empathy:** Before opening, the owner first learns about the diners in the area, their desires, what foods aren't available, and trends in eating.

2. **Stickiness:** Then he develops a menu and tests it out with consumers, making frequent adjustments until tables are full and patrons return regularly. He's giving things away, testing things, and asking diners what they think. Costs are high because of variance and uncertain inventory.

3. **Virality:** He starts loyalty programs to bring frequent diners back, or to encourage people to share with their friends. He engages on Yelp and Foursquare.

4. **Revenue:** With virality kicked off, he works on margins—fewer free meals, tighter controls on costs, and more standardization.

5. **Scale:** Finally, knowing he can run a profitable business, he pours some of the revenues into marketing and promotion. He reaches out to food reviewers, travel magazines, and radio stations. He launches a second restaurant, or a franchise based on the initial one.

Now consider a company selling software to large enterprises:

1. **Empathy:** The founder finds an unmet need because she has a background in a particular industry and has worked with existing solutions that are being disrupted.

2. **Stickiness:** She meets with an initial group of prospects and signs contracts that look more like consulting agreements, which she uses to build an initial product. She's careful not to commit to exclusivity, and tries to steer customers toward standardized solutions, charging heavily for custom features. Her engineers handle customer support directly, rather than having an "insulating layer" of support staff in this early stage, so they have to confront the warts and wrinkles of what they've created.

3. **Virality:** Product in hand, she asks for references from satisfied customers and uses those as testimonials. She starts direct sales and grows the customer base. She launches a user group and starts to automate support. She releases an API, encouraging third-party development and scaling potential market size without direct development.

4. **Revenue:** She focuses on growing the pipeline, sales margins, and revenues while controlling costs. Tasks are automated, outsourced, or offshored. Feature enhancements are scored based on anticipated payoff and development cost. Recurring license and support revenue becomes an increasingly large component of overall revenues.

5. **Scale:** She signs deals with large distributors, and works with global consulting firms to have them deploy and integrate her tool. She attends trade shows to collect leads, carefully measuring cost of acquisition against close rate and lead value.

We'll continue to use these five stages and correlate them to other frameworks as we did in Chapter 5. We'll also outline the individual gates that you need to pass through as you move from one stage to the next.[*]

We care a lot about company stage because the metrics you focus on will be significantly impacted by the stage of your business. Premature focus or optimization of things that don't really matter is a surefire way of killing your startup. So let's dig into the five Lean Analytics stages.

---

[*] It's worth pointing out that Lean founders consider payment, virality, and stickiness three Engines of Growth, and that a company can pivot from one to the next. We prefer to think of them as three things to optimize: a good startup has payment (and investment in customer acquisition), stickiness (and recurring revenue), and virality (and the resulting word of mouth). You can focus on one at a time, but we think you should build all three—and their related metrics—into your startup as you grow.

EXERCISE | Pick the Stage That You're At

What stage do you think you're at? Write it down. After reading the following chapters on the five Lean Analytics stages, see if your answer changes. It will likely require more detail as well—zeroing in on a specific aspect of a stage that you're focused on (for example, problem validation or solution validation in the Empathy stage). You may be overlapping between stages, too, so read them all before deciding.

CHAPTER 15

Stage One: Empathy

At the outset, you're spending your time discovering what's important to people and being empathetic to their problems. You're searching through listening. You're digging for opportunity through caring about others. Right now, your job isn't to prove you're smart, or that you've found a solution.

Your job is to *get inside someone else's head.*

That means discovering and validating a problem and then finding out whether your proposed solution to that problem is likely to work.

Metrics for the Empathy Stage

In the Empathy stage, your focus is on gathering qualitative feedback, primarily through problem and solution interviews. Your goal is to find a problem worth solving and a solution that's sufficiently good to garner early traction. You're collecting this information by *getting out of the building.* If you haven't gotten out of the building enough—and spoken to at least 15 people at each interviewing stage—you should be very concerned about rushing ahead.

Early on, you'll keep copious notes. Later, you might score the interviews to keep track of which needs and solutions were of the greatest interest, because this will tell you what features need to be in your minimum viable product (MVP).

This Is the Best Idea I've Ever Had! (or, How to Discover Problems Worth Solving)

Entrepreneurs are always coming up with ideas. While some people say "ideas are easy," that's not entirely true. Coming up with an idea is hard. Coming up with a good idea is harder. Coming up with an idea that you go out and validate to the point where it makes sense to build something is really, really hard.

Problem (or idea) discovery often starts with listening. After all, people love to complain about their problems. But take their complaining with a grain of salt. You need to listen actively, almost aggressively, for the nugget of truth or the underlying pattern. Big, lucrative startups are often the result of wildly audacious solutions to problems people didn't realize they had.

Discovery is the muse that launches startups.

In some cases, you won't need to discover a problem. It will be the reason you founded a startup in the first place. This is particularly true for enterprise-focused initiatives or startup efforts that happen within a willing host company. As an intrapreneur, you may have noticed a pattern in customer support issues that suggests the need for a new product. If you're selling to enterprises, maybe you were an end user who realized something was missing, or a former employee of a vendor who saw an opportunity.

Your idea is simply a starting point. You should let it marinate awhile before jumping into it. We're huge believers in doing things quickly, but there's a difference between focused speed in a smart direction and being ridiculously hasty. Your first instinct will be to talk to your friends. This isn't a genuine or measurable part of Lean Startup, but it's not a bad first step. Ideally, you've got a group of friends, or trusted advisors, who are in and around the relevant space of interest, from whom you can get a quick reality check.

Your trusted friends and advisors will give you their gut reaction (see—we don't hate guts at all!), and if they're not pandering to you or trying to avoid hurting your feelings, then you'll get at least semi-honest feedback. You may also get some insight that you hadn't thought of: information about competitors, target markets, different takes on the idea, and so on.

This quick "sniff test" is an excellent investment for the first few days after you get an idea, before committing any formal work to it. If the idea passes the sniff test, it's time to apply the Lean Startup process.

Finding a Problem to Fix
(or, How to Validate a Problem)

The goal of the first Lean stage is to decide whether the problem is *painful enough* for *enough people* and to learn *how* they are currently trying to solve it. Let's break down what that means:

The problem is painful enough

> People are full of inertia. You want them to act, and you want them to do so in a way that helps your business. This requires enough discomfort with their situation that they actually do what you want—signing up, paying your price, etc.

Enough people care

> Solving a problem for one person is called consulting. You need an addressable market. Marketers want audiences that are *homogeneous within* (that is, members of the segment have things in common to which you can appeal) and *heterogeneous between* (that is, you can segment and target each market segment in a focused manner with a tailored message).

They're already trying to solve it

> If the problem is real and known, people are dealing with it somehow. Maybe they're doing something manually, because they don't have a better way. The current solution, whatever it is, will be your biggest competitor at first, because it's the path of least resistance for people.

Note that in some cases, your market won't know it has a problem. Before the Walkman, the minivan, or the tablet computer, people didn't know they had a need—indeed, Apple's ill-fated Newton a decade before the iPad showed that the need didn't exist. In this case, rather than just testing for a problem people know they have, you're also interested in *what it takes to make them aware of the problem*. If you're going to have to "plow the snow" in your market, you want to know how much effort it will be so you can factor that into your business models.

You need to validate each of these (and a few more things too) before moving to the next stage. And analytics plays a key role in doing so.

Initially, as we've pointed out, you'll use qualitative metrics to measure whether or not the problem you've identified is worth pursuing. You start this process by conducting problem interviews with prospective customers.

We suggest that you speak with 15 prospective customers to start. After the first handful of interviews, you'll likely see patterns emerging already. Don't stop talking to people. Once you get to 15 interviews, you should have the validation (or invalidation) that you need to help clarify the next steps.

If you can't find 15 people to talk to, well, imagine how hard it's going to be to sell to them. So suck it up and get out of the office. Otherwise, you're wasting time and money building something nobody wants.

While the data you're collecting at this stage is qualitative, it has to be material enough so that you can honestly say, "Yes, this problem is painful enough that I should go ahead and build a solution." One customer doesn't make a market. You can't speak with a few people, get generic positive feedback, and decide it's worth jumping in.

PATTERN | **Signs You've Found a Problem Worth Tackling**

The key to qualitative data is patterns and pattern recognition. Here are a few positive patterns to look out for when interviewing people:

- They want to pay you right away.
- They're actively trying to (or have tried to) solve the problem in question.
- They talk a lot and ask a lot of questions demonstrating a passion for the problem.
- They lean forward and are animated (positive body language).

Here are a few negative patterns to look out for:

- They're distracted.
- They talk a lot, but it's not about the problem or the issues at hand (they're rambling).
- Their shoulders are slumped or they're slouching in their chairs (negative body language).

At the end of the problem interviews, it's time for a gut check. Ask yourself: "am I prepared to spend the next five years of my life doing nothing else but solving the problem in question?"

| PATTERN | # Running Lean and How to Conduct a Good Interview |

Ash Maurya is one of the leaders in the Lean Startup movement. He's experimented and documented Lean Startup practices for several years with his own startups, and he wrote a great book called *Running Lean* (O'Reilly). It's a good complement to this book.

Ash describes a prescriptive, systematic approach for interviewing people during the early stages of the Lean Startup process.

For starters, you need to conduct problem interviews. You decouple the solution (which we know you're excited about!) from the problem, and focus on the problem alone. The goal is to find a problem worth solving. And remember, customers are tired of solutions—they get pitched continually on magical doohickeys that will make their lives easier. But most of the time, the people pitching don't understand the customers' real problems.

Here are some tips from Ash and *Running Lean* for conducting good interviews:

- **Aim for face-to-face interviews.** You not only want to hear what people are saying, you also want to see how they're saying it. People are generally much less distracted when meeting face-to-face, so you'll get a higher quality of response.

- **Pick a neutral location.** If you go to a subject's office, it's going to feel more like a sales pitch. Find a coffee shop or something casual.

- **Avoid recording interviews.** Ash notes that in his experience, subjects get more self-conscious if the interview is being recorded, and the quality of interviews subsequently drops.

- **Make sure you have a script.** While you may adjust the script a bit over time, you're not tweaking it constantly in order to "get the answers you want" or rig anything in your favor. You have to stay honest throughout the process.

The script is probably the hardest thing to do well. Early on, you may not even be sure what questions to ask. In fact, that's why surveys don't work at an early stage—you just don't know what to ask in order to collect meaningful information. But a script will give you enough consistency from interview to interview that you can compare notes.

Most of the problem interview is fairly open-ended. You want to give subjects the opportunity to tell you whatever they want to, and you want them to do so in a comfortable free-form manner.

In *Running Lean*, Ash provides a very good breakdown of interview scripts. We've summarized the problem interview script as follows:

- Briefly **set the stage** for how the interview works. This is the point where you tell the interviewee what you're going to tell (or ask) her. Highlight the goals of the interview to put the interviewee in the right frame of mind.

- **Test the customer segment** by collecting demographics. Ask the subject some basic questions to learn more about her and understand what market segment she represents. These questions depend a great deal on the types of people you speak to. Ultimately, you want to learn about their business or their lifestyle (in the context of the problems you're proposing to solve), and learn more about their role.

- **Set the problem context** by telling a story. Connect with the subject by walking her through how you identified the problems you're hoping to solve, and why you think these problems matter. If you're scratching your own itch, this will be a lot easier. If you don't understand the problems clearly, or you don't have good hypotheses for the problems you're looking to solve, it's going to show at this point.

- **Test the problem** by getting the subject to rank the problems. Restate the problems you've described and ask the subject to rank them in order of importance. Don't dig too deeply, but make sure to ask her if there are other related problems that you didn't touch on.

- **Test the solution.** Explore the subject's worldview. Hand things over to the customer and listen. Go through each problem—in the order the subject ranked them—and ask the subject how she solves it today. There's no more script. Just let the subject talk. This is the point in the interview when you can really do a qualitative assessment of whether or not you've found problems worth solving. It may go well, with subjects begging you to solve the problem, or you might get a resounding "meh," in which case there's a clear disconnect between your business and the real world.

- **Ask for something** now that you're done. You don't want to discuss your solution at length here, because it will feel too much like a sales call, but you should use a high-level pitch to keep the subject excited. Ideally, you want her to agree to do a solution interview with you when you're ready with something to show—these initial subjects can become your first customers—and you want her to refer other people like her so you can do more interviews.

As you can tell, there's a lot that goes into conducting a good interview. You won't be great at it the first time, but that's OK. Hopefully some of what we've covered here and other resources will give you the tools you need. Get a good script in place, practice it, and get out there as quickly as you can. After a handful of interviews, you'll be very comfortable with the process and you'll start seeing trends and collecting information that's incredibly valuable. You'll also be immeasurably better at stating the problem clearly and succinctly, and you'll collect anecdotes that will help with blogger outreach, investor discussions, and marketing collateral.

Qualitative metrics are all about trends. You're trying to tease out the truth by identifying patterns in people's feedback. You have to be an exceptionally good listener, at once empathetic and dispassionate. You have to be a great detective, chasing the "red threads" of the underlying narrative, the commonalities between multiple interviewees that suggest the right direction. Ultimately, those patterns become the things you test quantitatively, at scale. You're looking for hypotheses.

The reality of qualitative metrics is that they turn wild hunches—your gut instinct, that nagging feeling in the back of your mind—into educated guesses you can run with. Unfortunately, because they're subjective and gathered interactively, qualitative metrics are the ones that are easiest to fake.

While *quantitative* metrics can be wrong, they don't lie. You might be collecting the wrong numbers, making statistical errors, or misinterpreting the results, but the raw data itself is right. Qualitative metrics are notoriously easy for you to bias. If you're not ruthlessly honest, you'll hear what you want to hear in interviews. We love to believe what we already believe—and our subjects love to agree with us.

PATTERN | How to Avoid Leading the Witness

We're a weak, shallow species. Human beings tend to tell you what they think you want to hear. We go along with the herd and side with the majority. This has disastrous effects on the results you get from respondents: you don't want to make something nobody wants, but everybody lies about wanting it. What's a founder to do?

You can't change people's fundamental nature. Response bias is a well-understood type of cognitive bias, exploited by political campaigners to get the answer they want by leading the witness (this is known as *push polling*).

You can, however, do four things: don't tip your hand, make the question real, keep digging, and look for other clues.

Don't Tip Your Hand

We're surprisingly good at figuring out what someone else wants from us. The people you interview will do everything they can, at a subconscious level, to guess what you want them to say. They'll pick up on a variety of cues.

- **Biased wording,** such as "do you agree that…" is one such cue. This leads to an effect called *acquiescence* bias, where a respondent will try to agree with the positive statement. You can get around this by asking people the *opposite* of what you're hoping they'll say—if they are willing to disagree with you in order to express their need for a particular solution, that's a stronger signal that you've found a problem worth solving.

- This is one reason why, early in the customer development process, open-ended questions are useful: they color the answers less and give the respondent a chance to ramble.

- **Preconceptions** are another strong influencer. If the subject knows things about you, he'll likely go along with them. For example, he'll answer more positively to questions on the need for environmental protection if he knows you're a vegetarian. The fewer things he knows about you, the less he'll be able to skew things. Anonymity can be a useful asset here; this is a big reason to keep your mouth shut and let him talk, and to work from a standardized script.

- Other social cues come from **appearance.** Everything in your demeanor gives the respondent clues about how to answer you. These days, it's probably hard for you to hide details about yourself, since we live fairly transparently online and you may have met your respondents through social networks. But you'll get better data if you dress blandly and act in a manner that doesn't take strong positions or give off signals.

Make the Questions Real

One way to get the real answer is to make the person uncomfortable.

People only get really interesting when they start to rattle the bars of their cages.

Alain de Botton, author and philosopher

Next time you're interviewing someone, instead of asking "Would you use this product?" (and getting a meaningless, but well-intentioned, "yes"), ask for a $100 pre-order payment. You'll likely get a resounding "no." And that's where the interesting stuff starts.

Asking someone for money will definitely rattle her cage. Will it make both of you uncomfortable? Absolutely. Should you care? Not if you're interested in building something people will actually pay for.

The more concrete you can make the question, the more real the answer. Get subjects to purchase, rather than indicating preference. Ask them to open their wallets. Get the names of five friends they're sure will use the product, and request introductions. Suddenly, they're invested. There's a real cost to acting on your behalf. This discomfort will quickly wash away the need to be liked, and will show you how people really feel.

One other trick to overcome a subject's desire to please an interviewer is to ask her how her friends would act. Asking "Do you smoke pot?" might make someone answer untruthfully to avoid moral criticism, but asking "What percentage of your friends smoke pot?" is likely to get an accurate answer that still reflects the person's perception of the overall population.

Keep Digging

A great trick for customer development interviews is to ask "why?" three times. It might make you sound like a two-year-old, but it works. Ask a question; wait for the person to finish. Pause for three seconds (which signals to her that you're listening, and also makes sure she was really done). Then ask why.

By asking "why?" several times, you force a respondent to explain the reasoning behind a statement. Often, the reasoning will be inconsistent or contradictory. That's good—it means you've identified the gap between *what people say they will do and what they will actually do.*

As an entrepreneur, you care about the latter; it's hard to convince people to act against their inner, moral compasses. "Anyone who values truth," says Jonathan Haidt, author of *The Righteous Mind* (Pantheon), "should stop worshipping reason." The reasoning of your interview subjects is far less interesting than their true beliefs and motivations.

You can also take a cue from interrogators and leave lingering, uncomfortable silences in the interview—your subject is likely to fill that empty air with useful, relevant insights or colorful anecdotes that can reveal a lot about her problems and needs.

Look for Other Clues

Much of what people say isn't verbal. While the amount of nonverbal communication has been widely overstated in popular research, body language often conveys feelings and emotions more than words do. Nervous tics and "tells" can reveal when someone is uncomfortable with a statement, or looking to another person for authority, for example.

When you're interviewing someone, you need to be directly engaged with that person. Have a colleague tag along and take notes with you, and ask him to watch for nonverbal signals as well. This will help you build a bond with the subject and focus on her answers, and still capture important subliminal messages.

And never forget to ask the "Columbo" question. Like Peter Falk's TV detective, save one disarming, unexpected question for the very end, after you've said your goodbyes. This will often catch people off guard, and can be used to confirm or repudiate something significant they've said in the interview.

Convergent and Divergent Problem Interviews

As we wrote this book, we tested out several ideas on entrepreneurs and blog readers. One of the more contentious ideas we discussed was that of scoring problem validation interviews. Several readers felt that this was a good idea, allowing them to understand how well their discovery of needs was proceeding and to rate the demand for a solution. Others protested, sometimes vociferously: scoring was a bad idea, because it interfered with the open, speculative nature of this stage.

We'll share our scoring framework later in the book. First, however, we'd like to propose a compromise: *problem validation can actually happen in two distinct stages.*

While the goal of a problem interview is always the same—decide if you have enough information and confidence to move to the next stage—the tactics to achieve this do vary.

In Ash Maurya's framework from earlier in this chapter, he suggests telling a story first to create context around the problem. Then he suggests introducing more specific problems and asking interviewees to rank them. This is a *convergent* approach: it's directed, focused, and intended to quantify the urgency and prevalence of the problems, so you can compare the many issues you've identified. In a convergent problem interview, you're zeroing in on specifics—and while you want interviewees to speak freely, and the interviews aren't heavily structured—you're not on a fishing expedition with no idea what you're fishing for.

A convergent problem interview gives you a clear course of action at the risk of focusing too narrowly on the problems that you think matter, rather than freeing interviewees to identify other problems that may be more important to them. For example, you might steer subjects back to your line of questioning at the expense of having them reveal an unexpected adjacent market or need.

On the other hand, a *divergent* problem interview is much more speculative, intended to broaden your search for something useful you might go build. In this type of problem interview, you're discussing a big problem space (healthcare, task management, transportation, booking a vacation, etc.) with interviewees, and letting them tell you what problems they have. You're not suggesting problems and asking them to rank them. You probably have a problem or two that you're looking to identify, and you'll measure the success of the interviews, in part, by how often interviewees mention those problems (without you having done so first).

The risk with a divergent problem interview is that you venture too broadly on too many issues and never get interviewees to focus. Divergent problem interviews run the risk of giving you too many problems, or not enough similar problems, and no clarity on what to do next.

It takes practice to strike the right balance when doing interviews. On the one hand, you want to give interviewees the opportunity to tell you what they want, but you have to be ready to focus them when you think you've found something worthwhile. At the same time, you shouldn't hammer away at the problems you're presenting if they're not resonating.

If you're just starting out, and really focused on an exploratory exercise, then try a divergent problem interview. Scoring in this case is less relevant. Collect initial feedback and see how many of the problems people freely described to you match up. If that goes well, you can move to convergent problem interviews with other people and see if the problems resonate at a larger scale.

How Do I Know If the Problem Is Really Painful Enough?

While the data you've collected to this point is qualitative, there are ways of helping you quantify that data to make an informed decision on whether you want to move forward or not. Ultimately, the One Metric That Matters here is *pain*—specifically, your interviewees' pain as it pertains to the problems you've shared with them. So how can you measure pain?

A simple approach is to score your problem interviews. This is not perfectly scientific; your scoring will be somewhat arbitrary, but if you have someone assisting you during the interviews and taking good notes it should be possible to score things consistently and get value out of this exercise.

There are a few criteria you can score against based on the questions you've asked in a convergent problem interview. Each answer has a weight; by adding the results up, you'll have a sense of where you stand.

After completing each interview, ask yourself the following questions.

1. Did the interviewee successfully rank the problems you presented?		
Yes	**Sort of**	**No**
The interviewee ranked the problems with strong interest (irrespective of the ranking).	He couldn't decide which problem was really painful, but he was still really interested in the problems.	He struggled with this, or he spent more time talking about other problems he has.
10 points	5 points	0 points

Even in a convergent problem interview where you've focused on a specific set of problems, the interview is open-ended enough to allow interviewees to discuss other issues. That's completely fine, and is extremely important. There's nothing that says the problems you've presented are the right ones—that's precisely what you're trying to measure and justify. So stay open-minded throughout the process.

For the purposes of scoring the interview and measuring pain, a bad score means the interview is a failure—the interviewee's pain with the problems you're considering isn't substantial enough if she spends all her time talking about other problems she has. A failed interview is OK; it may lead you to something even more interesting and save you a lot of heartache.

2. Is the interviewee actively trying to solve the problems, or has he done so in the past?		
Yes	**Sort of**	**No**
He's trying to solve the problem with Excel and fax machines. You may have struck gold.	He spends a bit of time fixing the problem, but just considers it the price of doing his job. He's not trying to fix it.	He doesn't really spend time tackling the problem, and is OK with the status quo. It's not a big problem.
10 points	5 points	0 points

The more effort the interviewee has put into trying to solve the problems you're discussing, the better.

3. Was the interviewee engaged and focused throughout the interview?		
Yes	**Sort of**	**No**
He was hanging on your every word, finishing your sentences, and ignoring his smartphone.	He was interested, but showed distraction or didn't contribute comments unless you actively solicited him.	He tuned out, looked at his phone, cut the meeting short, or generally seemed entirely detached—like he was doing you a favor by meeting with you.
8 points	4 points	0 points

Ideally, your interviewees were completely engaged in the process: listening, talking (being animated is a good thing), leaning forward, and so on. After enough interviews you'll know the difference between someone who's focused and engaged, and someone who is not.

The point totals for this question are lower than the previous two. For one, engagement in an interview is harder to measure; it's more subjective than the other questions. We also don't want to weigh engagement in the interview as heavily—it's just not as important. Someone may seem somewhat disengaged but has spent the last five years trying to solve the problems you're discussing. That's someone with a lot of pain . . . maybe he's just easily distracted.

4. Did the interviewee agree to a follow-up meeting/interview (where you'll present your solution)?		
Yes, without being asked to	**Yes, when you asked him to**	**No**
He's demanding the solution "yesterday."	He's OK with scheduling another meeting, but suddenly his calendar is booked for the next month or so.	You both realize there's no point showing him anything in terms of a solution.
8 points	4 points	0 points

The goal of the problem interview is to discover a problem painful enough that you know people want it solved. And ideally, the people you're speaking to are begging you for the solution. The next step in the process is the solution interview, so if you get there with people that's a good sign.

5. Did the interviewee offer to refer others to you for interviews?		
Yes, without being asked to	**Yes, when you asked him to**	**No**
He actively suggested people you should talk to without being asked.	He suggested others at the end, in response to your question.	He couldn't recommend people you should speak with.
4 points	2 points	0 points (and ask yourself some hard questions about whether you can reach the market at scale)

At the end of every interview, you should be asking for referrals to other interviewees. There's a good chance the people your subjects recommend are similar in demographics and share the same problems.

Perhaps more importantly at this stage, you want to see if the subjects are willing to help out further by referring people in their network. This is a clear indicator that they don't feel sheepish about introducing you, and that they think you'll make them look smarter. If they found you annoying, they likely won't suggest others you might speak with.

6. Did the interviewee offer to pay you immediately for the solution?		
Yes, without being asked to	**Yes, when you asked him to**	**No**
He offered to pay you for the product without being asked, and named a price.	He offered to pay you for the product.	He didn't offer to buy and use it.
3 points	1 points	0 points (and ask yourself some hard questions about whether you can reach the market at scale).

Although having someone offer you money is more likely during the solution interviews (when you're actually walking through the solution with people), this is still a good "gut check" moment. And certainly it's a bonus if people are reaching for their wallets.

Calculating the Scores

A score of 31 or higher is a good score. Anything under is not. Try scoring all the interviews, and see how many have a good score. This is a decent indication of whether you're onto something or not with the problems you want to solve. Then ask yourself what makes the good-score interviews different from the bad-score ones. Maybe you've identified a market segment, maybe you have better results when you dress well, maybe you shouldn't do interviews in a coffee shop. *Everything is an experiment you can learn from.*

You can also sum up the rankings for the problems that you presented. If you presented three problems, which one had the most first-place rankings? That's where you'll want to dig in further and start proposing solutions (during solution interviews).

The best-case scenario is very high interview scores within a subsection of interviewees where those interviewees all had the same (or very similar) rankings of the problems. That should give you *more confidence* that you've found the right problem and the right market.

| # Cloud9 IDE Interviews Existing Customers

Cloud9 IDE is a cloud-based integrated development environment (IDE) that enables web and mobile developers to work together and collaborate in remote teams anywhere, anytime. The platform is primarily for JavaScript and Node.js applications, but it's expanding to support other languages as well. The company has raised Series A financing from Accel and Atlassian.

Although the Cloud9 IDE team is well past the initial problem interview stage, they regularly speak with customers and engage in systematic customer development. Product Manager Ivar Pruijn says, "We're close to product/market fit, and it helps us a great deal to speak with customers, understanding if we're meeting their needs and how they're using our product."

Ivar took the scoring framework outlined previously and modified some of the questions for the types of interviews he was doing. "Since we're now speaking with customers using our product, we asked slightly different questions, but we scored them just the same," he says. The first two questions that Ivar asked himself after conducting an interview were:

1. Did the interviewee mention problems in his/her workflow that our product solves or will solve soon?

2. Is the interviewee actively trying to solve the problems our product solves/will solve soon, or has he/she done so in the past?

"With these questions, we're trying to determine how well we're solving problems for actual customers. If many of the scores would have been low, we would have known something was wrong," he says.

Happily, most of the interview scores were good, but Ivar was able to dig deeper and learn more. "I was able to identify the customer types to focus on for product improvements. I noticed that two specific customer segments scored the highest on the interviews, especially the first two scoring criteria about meeting their needs and solving their problems."

After scoring the initial interviews, Ivar then verified the results and the scoring in two ways. First, he interviewed some of the company's top active users, gaining an in-depth knowledge of how they work. Second, he analyzed the data warehouse, which has information on how the product is being used. Both of these confirmed his initial findings: two specific segments of customers were getting significantly more value from the product. "Interestingly, both of these customer groups weren't the initial ones we were going after," he says. "So now we know where we can invest more of our time and energy."

In this case, open-ended discussions followed by scoring—even when the company was beyond the initial Empathy stage—revealed a market segment that had better stickiness and was ripe for rapid growth. What's more, Ivar says that scoring the interview questions helped him improve his interviewing over time, focusing on results that could be acted upon.

Summary

- Cloud9 IDE decided to run scored customer interviews even though the company was well past the Empathy stage.

- The interviews showed that customers were happy, but also revealed two specific customer segments that derived higher value from the product.

- Using this insight, the company compared analytics data and verified that these groups were indeed using the product differently, which is now driving the prioritization of features and marketing.

Analytics Lessons Learned

You can talk to customers and score interviews at any stage of your startup. Those interviews don't just give you feedback,they also help you identify segments of the market with unique problems or needs that you might target.

How Are People Solving the Problem Now?

One of the telltale signs that a problem is worth solving is when a lot of people are already trying to solve it or have tried to do so in the past. People will go to amazing lengths to solve really painful problems that matter to them. Typically, they're using another product that wasn't meant to solve their problem, but it's "good enough," or they've built something themselves. Even though you're doing qualitative interviews, you can still crunch some numbers afterward:

- How many people aren't trying to solve the problem at all? If people haven't really made an attempt to solve the problem, you have to be very cautious about moving forward. You'll have to make them aware of the problem in the first place.

- How many volunteer a solution that's "good enough"? You'll spend more time on solutions when you do solution interviews, but startups regularly underestimate the power of "good enough." Mismatched socks are a universal problem nobody's getting rich fixing.

Too often, idealistic startups underestimate a market's inertia. They attack market leaders with features, functionality, and strategies that aren't meaningful enough to customers. Their MVP has too much "minimum" to provoke a change. They assume that what they're doing—whether it's a slicker UI, simpler system, social functionality, or something else—is an obvious win. Then "good enough" bites them in the ass.

The bar for startups to succeed at any real scale is much higher than that of the market leaders. The market leaders are already there, and even if they're losing ground, it's generally at a slow pace. Startups need to scale as quickly as possible. You have to be 10 times better than the market leader before anyone will really notice, which means you have to be 100 times more creative, strategic, sneaky, and aggressive. Market leaders may be losing touch with their customers, but they still know them better than anyone else.

You need to work much harder to win customers from incumbents. Don't just look at the "obvious" flaws of the incumbents (like an outdated design) and assume that's what needs fixing. You'll have to dig far deeper in order to find the real customer pain points and make sure you address them quickly and successfully.

Are There Enough People Who Care About This Problem? (or, Understanding the Market)

If you find a problem that's painful enough for people, the next step is to understand the market size and potential. Remember, one customer isn't a market, and you have to be careful about solving a problem that too few people genuinely care about.

If you're trying to estimate the size of a market, it's a good idea to do both a top-down and a bottom-up analysis, and compare the results. This helps to check your math.

A top-down analysis starts with a big number and breaks it into smaller parts. A bottom-up one does the reverse. Consider, for example, a restaurant in New York City.

- A top-down model would look at the total money people spend dining out in the US, then the percentage of that in New York, then the number of restaurants in the city, and finally calculate the revenues for a single restaurant.

- A bottom-up model would look at the number of tables in a restaurant, the percent that are occupied, and the average price per party. Then it would multiply this by days of the year (adjusting for seasonality).

This is an oversimplification—there are plenty of other factors to consider such as location, type of restaurant, and so on. But the end result should provide two estimates of annual revenue. If they're wildly different, something is wrong with your business model.

As you're conducting problem interviews, remember to ask enough demographic-type questions to understand who the interviewees are. The questions you'll ask will depend a great deal on who you're speaking to and the type of business you're starting. If you're going after a business market, you'll want to know more about a person's position in the company, buying power, budgeting, seasonal influences, and industry. If you're going after a consumer, you're much more interested in lifestyle, interests, social circles, and so on.

What Will It Take to Make Them Aware of the Problem?

If the subjects don't know they have the problem—but you have good evidence that the need really exists—then you need to understand how easily they'll come to realize it, and the vectors of awareness.

Be careful. Most of the time, when people don't have a problem, they'll still agree with you. They don't want to hurt your feelings. To be nice, they'll pretend they have the problem once you alert them to it. If you're convinced that people have the problem—and just need to be made aware of it—you need to find ways to test that assumption.

Some ways to get a more honest answer from people are:

- Get them a prototype early on.
- Use paper prototyping, or a really simple mockup in PowerPoint, Keynote, or Balsamiq, to watch how they interact with your idea without coaching.
- See if they'll pay immediately.
- Watch them explain it to their friends and see if they understand how to spread the message.
- Ask for referrals to others who might care.

A "Day in the Life" of Your Customer

During problem interviews, you want to get a deep understanding of your customer. We mentioned collecting demographics earlier and looking for ways to bucket customers into different groups, but you can take this a step further and gain a lot more insight. You can get inside their heads.

Customers are people. They lead lives. They have kids, they eat too much, they don't sleep well, they phone in sick, they get bored, they watch too much reality TV. If you're building for some kind of idealized, economically rational buyer, you'll fail. But if you know your customers, warts and all, and you build things that naturally fit into their lives, they'll love you.

To do this, you need to infiltrate your customer's daily life. Don't think of "infiltrate" as a bad word. In order for you to succeed, customers need to use your application; if you want them to do so, you need to slot yourself into their lives in an effortless, seamless way. Understanding customers' daily lives means you can map out everything they do, and when they do it. With the right approach, you'll start to understand *why* as well. You'll identify influences (bosses, friends, family members, employees, etc.), limitations, constraints, and opportunities.

One tactic for mapping this out is a "day in the life" storyboard. A storyboard is visual—it's going to involve lots of multicolored sticky notes plastered on the wall—and it allows you to navigate through a customer's life and figure out where your solution will have the most impact. Figure 15-1 shows an example of a storyboard.

Having this map in place makes it much easier to come up with good hypotheses around how, when, and by whom your solution will be used. You can experiment with different tactics for interrupting users and infiltrating their lives. The right level of positive access will allow to use your product successfully..

Mapping a day in the life of your customer will also reveal obvious holes in your understanding of your customer, and those are areas of risk you may want to tackle quickly. With a clearer understanding of when and how your solution will be used, you have a better chance of defining a minimum viable product feature set that hits the mark.

The "day in the life" exercise is a way of describing a very detailed, human use case for your solution that goes beyond simply defining target markets and customer segments. After all, you'll be selling to people. You need to know how to reach them, interrupt them, and make a difference in their lives at the exact moment when they need your solution.

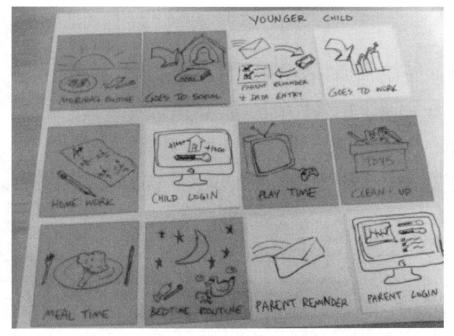

Figure 15-1. How HighScore House mapped the chaos of parenting

User experience designers also rely on mental models of their users to understand how people think about something. A mental model is simply the mental representation of something in the real world—often a simplified version of reality that helps someone work with a thing. Sometimes these are metaphors—the recycle bin on a computer, for example. Other times, they're simple, fundamental patterns that live deep down in our reptile brains—team allegiance, or xenophobia.

Adaptive Path co-founder Indi Young has written extensively about mental models, developing a number of ways to link your customers' lives and patterns with the products, services, and interactions you have with them.* Figure 15-2 shows an example of Indi's work, listing a customer's morning behaviors alongside various product categories.†

---

* *http://rosenfeldmedia.com/books/mental-models/info/description/*

† Mental model diagram from Indi Young's *Mental Models: Aligning Design Strategy with Human Behavior* (Rosenfeld Media). Shared on Flickr (*http://www.flickr.com/photos/ rosenfeldmedia/2125040269/in/set-72157603511616271*) under a Creative Commons Attribution-ShareAlike 2.0 Generic license.

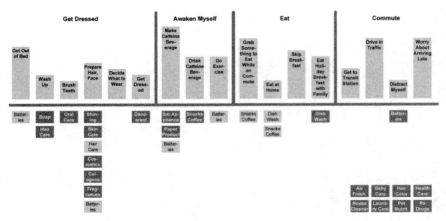

Figure 15-2. Overanalyzing the day's ablutions with a mental model

Outlining your customers' behaviors as they go about a particular task, then aligning your activities and features with those behaviors, is a good way to identify missed opportunities to improve engagement, upsell, endorse, or otherwise influence your buyers. If you're making a personal fitness tool, timing interactions with gym visits, holiday binges, and morning ablutions lets you create a more tailored, engaging experience.

PATTERN | ## Finding People to Talk To

The modern world isn't inclined to physical interaction. We have dozens of ways to engage people at a distance, and when you're trying to find a need, they're mostly bad. Unless you're face-to-face with prospects, you won't see the flinches, the subtle body language, and the little gasps and shrugs that mean the difference between a real problem and a waste of everyone's time.

That doesn't mean technology is bad. We have a set of tools for finding prospects that would have seemed like superpowers to our predecessors. Before you get the hell out of the office, you need to find people to talk with. If you can find these people efficiently, that bodes well: it means that, if they're receptive to your idea, you can find more like them and build your customer base.

Here are some dumb, obvious, why-didn't-I-think-of-that ways to find people to talk to, mail, and learn from.

Twitter's Advanced Search

For startups, Twitter is a goldmine. Its asymmetric nature—I can follow you, but you don't have to follow me back—and relatively unwalled garden means people expect interactions. And we're vain; if you mention someone, he'll probably come find out what you said and who you are. Provided you don't abuse this privilege, it's a great way to find people.

Let's say you're building a product for lawyers and want to talk to people nearby. Put keywords and location information into Twitter's Advanced Search, as shown in Figure 15-3.

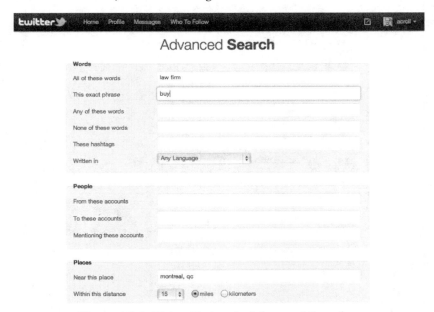

Figure 15-3. Using Twitter's Advanced Search to stalk people

You'll get a list of organizations and people who might qualify similar to the one in Figure 15-4.

Now, if you're careful, you can reach out to them. Don't spam them; get to know them a bit, see where they live and what they say, and when they mention something relevant—or when you feel comfortable doing so—speak up. Just mention them by name, invite them to take a survey, and so on.

There are other interesting tools for digging into Twitter and finding people. Moz has a tool called Followerwonk, and there's also the freely available people search engine, Twellow.

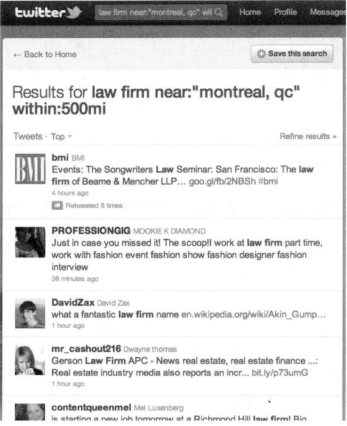

Figure 15-4. Real customers are just a few tweets away

LinkedIn

Another huge boon to startups everywhere is LinkedIn. You can access a tremendous amount of demographic data through searches like the one in Figure 15-5.

You don't need to connect to these people on LinkedIn, because you can just find their names and numbers, look up their firms' phone numbers, and start dialing. But if you do have a friend in common, you'll find that a warm intro works wonders.

LinkedIn also has groups which you can search through and join. Most of these groups are aligned around particular interests, so you can find relevant people and also do some background research.

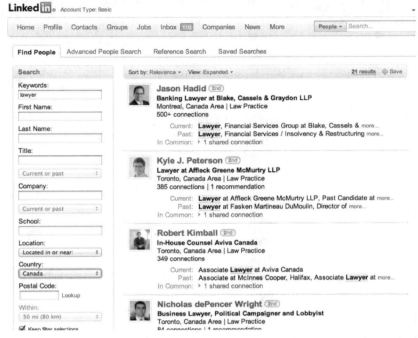

Figure 15-5. All this information is just lying around for you to use

Facebook

Facebook is a bit more risky to mine, since it's a reciprocal relationship (people have to friend you back). But you'll get a sense of the size of a market from your search results alone, as seen in Figure 15-6, and you might find useful groups to join and invite to take a test or meet for a focus-group discussion.

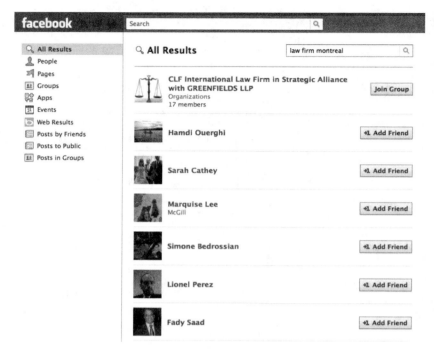

Figure 15-6. Even without details, Facebook shows you who to follow up with

Some of these approaches seem blindingly obvious. But a little preparation before you get out of the office—physically or virtually—can make all the difference, giving you better data sooner and validating or repudiating business assumptions in days instead of weeks.

Getting Answers at Scale

You should continue doing customer interviews (after the first 10–20 or so) and iterate on the questions you ask, dig deeper with people, and learn as much as you can. But you can also expand the scope of your efforts and move into doing some quantitative analysis. It's time to talk to people *at scale*.

This does several things:

- It forces you to formalize your discussions, moving from subjective to objective.

- It tests whether you can command the attention—at scale—that you'll need to thrive.

- It gives you quantitative information you can analyze and segment, which can reveal patterns you won't get from individual groups.

- The respondents may become your beta users and the base of your community.

To talk with people at scale you can employ a number of tactics, including surveys and landing pages. These give you the opportunity to reach a wider audience and build a stronger, data-driven case for the qualitative feedback you received during interviews.

CASE STUDY	## LikeBright "Mechanical Turks" Its Way into TechStars

LikeBright is an early-stage startup in the dating space that joined the TechStars Seattle accelerator program in 2011. But it wasn't an easy road. Founder Nick Soman says that at first Andy Sack, managing director of the Seattle program, rejected LikeBright, saying, "We don't think you understand your customer well enough."

With the application deadline looming, Andy gave Nick a challenge: go speak to 100 single women about their frustrations with dating, and then tell TechStars what he'd learned.

Nick was stuck. How was he going to speak with that many women quickly enough? He didn't think it was possible, at least not easily. And then he decided to run an experiment with Mechanical Turk.[*]

Mechanical Turk is a service provided by Amazon that allows you to pay small amounts of money for people to complete simple tasks. It's often used to get quick feedback on things like logos and color choices, or to perform small tasks such as tagging a picture or flagging spam.

The idea was to use Mechanical Turk to survey 100 single women, putting out a task (or what Mechanical Turk calls a HIT) asking women (who fit a particular profile) to call Nick. In exchange he paid them $2. The interviews typically lasted 10–15 minutes.

"In my research, I found that there's a good cross-section of people on Mechanical Turk," says Nick. "We found lots of highly educated, diverse women that were very willing to speak with us about their dating experiences."

---

[*] *http://customerdevlabs.com/2012/08/21/using-mturk-to-interview-100-customers-in-4-hours/*

Nick set up several Google Voice phone numbers (throwaway numbers that couldn't be tracked or reused) and recruited a few friends to help him out.

He prepared a simple interview script with open-ended questions, since he was digging into the problem validation stage of his startup. Nick says, "I was amazed at the feedback I got. We were able to speak with 100 single women that met our criteria in four hours on one evening."

As a result, Nick gained incredible insight into LikeBright's potential customers and the challenges he would face building the startup. He went back to TechStars and Andy Sack with that know-how and impressed them enough to get accepted. LikeBright's website is now live with a 50% female user base, and recently raised a round of funding. Nick remains a fan of Mechanical Turk. "Since that first foray into interviewing customers, I've probably spoken with over 1,000 people through Mechanical Turk," he says.

Summary

- LikeBright used a technical solution to talk to many end users in a short amount of time.

- After talking to 100 prospects in 24 hours, the founders were accepted to a startup accelerator.

- The combination of Google Voice and Mechanical Turk proved so successful that LikeBright continues to use it regularly.

Analytics Lessons Learned

While there's no substitute for qualitative data, you can use technology to dramatically improve the efficiency of collecting that data. In the Empathy stage, focus on building tools for getting good feedback quickly from many people. Just because customer development isn't code doesn't mean you shouldn't invest heavily in it.

LikeBright chose Mechanical Turk to reach people at scale, but there are plenty of other tools. Surveys can be effective, assuming you've done enough customer development already to know what questions to ask. The challenge with surveys is finding people to answer them. Unlike the one-to-one interviews you've been conducting so far, here you need to automate the task and deal with the inevitable statistical noise.

If you have a social following or access to a mailing list, you can start there, but often, you're trying to find new people to speak with. They're new sources of information, and they're less likely to be biased. That means reaching out to groups with whom you aren't already in touch, ideally through software, so you're not curating each invitation by hand.

Facebook has an advertising platform for reaching very targeted groups of people. You can segment your audience by demographics, interests, and more. Although the click-through rate on Facebook ads is extremely low, you're not necessarily looking for volume at this stage. Finding 20 or 30 people to speak with is a great start, plus you can test messaging this way, through the ads you publish, as well as the subsequent landing pages you have to encourage people to connect with you.

You can advertise on LinkedIn to very targeted audiences. This will cost you some money, but if you've identified a good audience of people through searching LinkedIn contacts and groups, you might consider testing some early messaging through its ad platform.

Google makes it really easy to target campaigns. If you want to promote a survey or signup on the Web, you can do so with remarkable precision. In the first step of setting up an AdWords campaign, you get to specify the location, language, and other information that targets the ad, as shown in Figure 15-7.

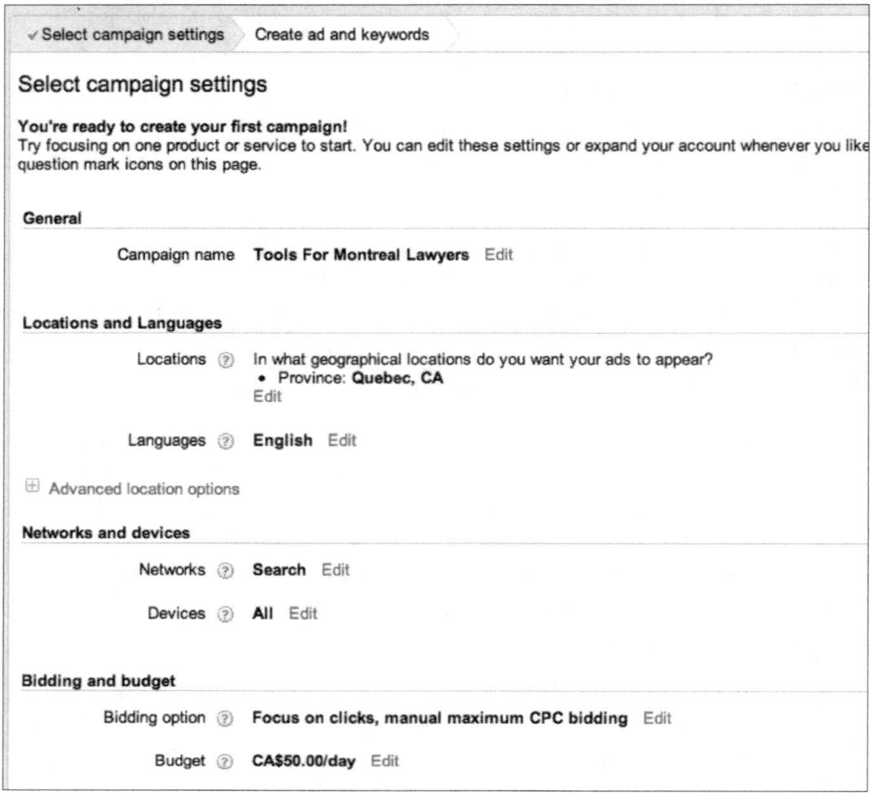

Figure 15-7. Some of the ways you can control who sees your ad

Once you've done that, you can create your message, using a screen like the one in Figure 15-8. This is an excellent way to try out different taglines and approaches: even the ones that don't get clicks show you something, because you know what not to say. Try different appeals to basic emotions: fear, greed, love, wealth, and so on. Learn what gets people clicking and what keeps them around long enough to fill out a survey or submit an email.

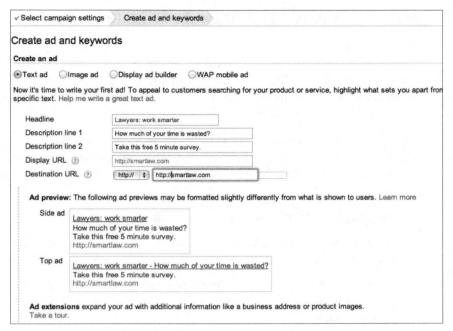

Figure 15-8. Would you click on these ads?

Google also has a survey offering, called Google Consumer Surveys, that's specifically designed to collect consumer information.* Because of the wide reach of Google's publishing and advertising network, the company can generate results that are statistically representative of segments of the population as a whole.

Google's technique uses a "survey wall" approach, but by simplifying the survey process to individual questions requiring only a click or two, the company achieves a 23.1% response rate (compared to less than 1% for "intercept" surveys, 7–14% for phone surveys, and 15% for Internet panels).† However, because of the quick-response format, it's hard to collect multiple responses and correlate them, which limits the kinds of analysis and segmentation you can do.

---

*   *http://www.google.com/insights/consumersurveys/how*

†   *http://www.google.com/insights/consumersurveys/static/consumer_surveys_whitepaper_v2.pdf*

PATTERN | Creating an Answers-at-Scale Campaign

An effective survey involves several critical steps: survey design, testing, distribution, and analysis. But before you do any of these, know why you're asking the questions in the first place. Lean is all about identifying and quantifying the risk. What kind of uncertainty are you trying to quantify by doing a survey?

- If you're asking what existing brands come to mind in a particular industry, will you use this information to market alongside them? Address competitive threats? Choose partners?

- If you're asking how customers try to find a product or service, will this inform your marketing campaigns and choice of media?

- If you're asking how much money people spend on a problem you're planning to address, how will this shape your pricing strategy?

- If you're testing which tagline or unique value proposition resonates best with customers, will you choose the winning one, or just take that as advice?

Don't just ask questions. Know *how the answers to the questions will change your behavior.* In other words, draw a line in the sand before you run the survey. Your earlier problem interviews showed you an opportunity; now, you're checking to see whether that opportunity exists in the market as a whole. For each quantifiable question, decide what would be a "good" score. Write it down somewhere so you'll remember.

Survey Design

Your survey should include three kinds of questions:

- Demographics and psychographics you can use to segment the responses, such as age, gender, or Internet usage.

- Quantifiable questions that you can analyze statistically, such as ratings, agreement or disagreement with a statement, or selecting something from a list.

- Open-ended questions that allow respondents to add qualitative data.

Always ask the segmentation questions up front and the open-ended ones at the end. That way you know if your sample was representative of the market you're targeting, and if people don't finish the last questions, you still have enough quantitative responses to generate results in which you can be confident.

Test the Survey

Before sending it out, try the survey on people who haven't seen it. You'll almost always find they get stuck or don't understand something. You're not ready to send the survey out until at least three people who haven't seen it, and are in your target market, can complete it without questions and then *explain to you what each question meant*. This is no exaggeration: everyone gets surveys wrong.

Send the Survey Out

You want to reach people you don't know. You could tweet out a link to the survey form or landing page, but you'll naturally get respondents who are in your extended social circle. This is a time when it makes sense to pay for access to a new audience.

Design several ads that link to the survey. They can take several forms:

- **Name the audience you're targeting.** ("Are you a single mom? Take this brief survey and help us address a big challenge.")

- **Mention the problem you're dealing with.** ("Can't sleep? We're trying to fix that, and want your input.")

- **Mention the solution or your unique value proposition, without a sales pitch.** ("Our accounting software automatically finds tax breaks. Help us plan the product roadmap.") Be careful not to lead the witness; don't use this if you're still trying to settle on positioning.

Remember, too, that the first question you're asking is "Was my message compelling enough to convince them to take the survey?" You're trying out a number of different value propositions. In some cases, you don't even care about a survey—we know one entrepreneur who tried out various taglines, all of which pointed to a spam site. All he needed to know was which one got the most clicks, and he didn't want to tell anyone who he was yet.

You can also use mailing lists. Some user groups or newsletters may be willing to feature you on their page or in a mail-out if what you're doing is relevant to their audience.

Collect the Information

When you run the survey, measure your cost per completed response. Do a small test of a few dozen responses first. If your numbers are low, check whether people are abandoning on a particular form field—some analytics tools like ClickTale let you do this. Then remove that field and see if completion rates go up. You can also try breaking up the survey into smaller ones, asking fewer questions, or changing your call to action.

While you're collecting information, don't forget to also request permission to contact respondents and collect contact information. If you've found a workable solution to a real problem, some of them may become your beta customers.

Analyze the Data

Finally, crunch the data properly. You're actually looking at three things.

- First, were you able to capture the attention of the market? Did people click on your ads and links? Which ones worked best?

- Second, are you on the right track? What decisions can you now make with the data you've collected?

- Third, will people try out your solution/product? How many of your respondents were willing to be contacted? How many agreed to join a forum or a beta? How many asked for access in their open-ended responses?

Statistics are important here. Don't skimp on the math—make sure you learn everything you can from your efforts.

- Calculate the average, mean, and standard deviation of the quantifiable questions. Which slogan won? Which competitor is most common? Was there a clear winner, or was the difference marginal?

- Analyze each quantifiable question by each segment to see if a particular group of your respondents answered differently. Use pivot tables for this kind of analysis (see the upcoming sidebar "What's a Pivot Table?" for details); you'll quickly see if a particular response correlated to a particular group. This will help you focus your efforts or see where one set of answers is skewing the rest.

What's a Pivot Table?

Most of us have used a spreadsheet. But if you want to take your analytical skills to the next level, you need to move up to pivot tables. This feature lets you quickly analyze many rows of data as if it were a database, without, well, the database.

Imagine that you have 1,000 responses to a survey. Each response is a row in a spreadsheet, containing a number of fields of data. The first column has time and date, the next has email, and the rest have the individual responses that particular respondents gave. Imagine, for example, that your survey asked respondents their gender, the number of hours per week that they play video games, and their age, as shown in the following table.

Gender	Hours Played	Age
M	8	50–60
F	7	50–60
M	12	30–40
F	10	20–30
F	7	40–50
M	14	20–30
F	7	50–60
M	11	30–40
F	8	30–40
M	11	40–50
M	6	60–70
F	5	50–60
F	9	40–50
Average:	**8.85**	

You can simply tally up the columns and see what the average responses were—that people play 8.85 hours a week (as shown in the preceding figure). But that's only a basic analysis, and a misleading one.

More often, you want to compare responses against one another—for example, do men play more video games than women? That's what a pivot table is for. First, you tell the pivot table where to get the source data, then you specify the dimension by which to segment, and then you set what kind of computation you want (such as the average, the maximum value, or the standard deviation) as shown here:

Gender	Total
F	7.57
M	10.33
Grand Total:	8.85

The real power of pivot tables, however, comes when you analyze two segments against each other. For example, if we have categories for gender and age, we can gain even more insight, as shown here:

Age	F	M	Grand Total
20–30	10.00	14.00	12.00
30–40	8.00	11.50	10.33
40–50	8.00	11.00	9.00
50–60	6.33	8.00	6.75
60–70		6.00	6.00
Grand Total:	7.57	10.33	8.85

This analysis shows that game-playing behavior is more influenced by age than by gender, which suggests a particular target demographic. Pivot tables are a powerful tool that every analyst should be comfortable with, yet they're often overlooked.

Build It Before You Build It
(or, How to Validate the Solution)

With a validated problem in hand, it's time to validate the solution.

Once again, this starts with interviewing customers (what Lean Startup describes as *solution interviews*) to get the qualitative feedback and confidence necessary to build a minimum viable product. You can also continue and expand on quantitative testing through surveys and landing pages. This provides you with a great opportunity to start testing your messaging (unique value proposition from Lean Canvas) and the initial feature set.

There are other practical ways of testing your solution prior to actually building it. By this point, you should have identified the riskiest aspects of the solution and what you need people to do with the solution (if it existed) in order to be successful. Now look for a way of testing your hypotheses through a proxy. Map the behavior you want people to do onto a similar platform or product, and experiment. Hack an adjacent system.

CASE STUDY | Localmind Hacks Twitter

Localmind is a real-time question-and-answer platform tied to locations. Whenever you have a question that's relevant to a location—whether that's a specific place or an area—you can use Localmind to get an answer. You send the question out through the mobile application, and people answer.

Before writing a line of code, Localmind was concerned that people would never answer questions. The company felt this was a huge risk; if questions went unanswered, users would have a terrible experience and stop using Localmind. But how could it prove (or disprove) that people would answer questions from strangers without building the app?

The team looked to Twitter and ran an experiment. Tracking geolocated tweets (primarily in Times Square, because there were lots of them there over several days), they sent @ messages to people who had just tweeted. The messages would be questions about the area: how busy is it, is the subway running on time, is something open, etc. These were the types of questions they believed people would ask through Localmind.

The response rate to their tweeted questions was very high. This gave the team the confidence to assume that people would answer questions about where they were, even if they didn't know who was asking. Even though Twitter wasn't the "perfect system" for this kind of test because there were lots of variables (e.g., the team didn't know if people would get a push notification on a tweet to them or notice the tweet), it was a good enough proxy to de-risk the solution, and convince the team that it was worth building Localmind.

Summary

- Localmind identified a big risk in its plan—whether people would answer questions from strangers—and decided to quantify it.

- Rather than writing code, the team used tweets with location information.

- The results were quick and easy, and sufficient for the team to move forward with an MVP.

Analytics Lessons Learned

Your job isn't to build a product; it's to de-risk a business model. Sometimes the only way to do this is to build something, but always be on the lookout for measurable ways to quantify risk without a lot of effort.

Before You Launch the MVP

As you're building your bare-minimum product—just enough functionality to test the risks you've identified in the Empathy stage—you'll continue to gather feedback (in the form of surveys) and acquire early adopters (through a beta enrollment site, social media, and other forms of teasing). In this way, by the time you launch the MVP you'll have a critical mass of testers and early adopters eager to give you feedback. You're farming test subjects. Your OMTM at this point is enrollments, social reach, and other indicators that you'll be able to drive actual users to your MVP so you can learn and iterate quickly. This is the reverse *Field of Dreams* moment: *if they come, you will build it.*

It's hard to decide how good your minimum product should be. On the one hand, time is precious, and you need to cut things ruthlessly. On the other hand, you want users to have an "aha!" moment, that sense of having discovered something important and memorable worth solving. You need to keep the magic.

> *Clarke's Third Law: Any sufficiently advanced technology is indistinguishable from magic.*
>
> Arthur C. Clarke, *Profiles of the Future*, 1961

Gehm's Corrollary: Any technology distinguishable from magic is insufficiently advanced.

Barry Gehm, *ANALOG*, 1991

Deciding What Goes into the MVP

Take all of your solution interviews, quantitative analysis, and "hacks," and decide what feature set to launch for your MVP.

The MVP has to generate the value you've promised to users and customers. If it's too shallow, people will be disinterested and disappointed. If it's too bloated, people will be confused and frustrated. In both cases, you'll fail.

It's important to contrast an MVP with a smoke-test approach where you build a teaser site—for example, a simple page generated in LaunchRock with links to social networks. With a smoke-test page, you're testing the risk that the message isn't compelling enough to get signups. With the MVP, you're testing the risk that the product won't solve a need that people want solved in a way that will make them permanently change their behavior. The former tests the problem messaging; the latter, the solution effectiveness.

Circle back with interviewees as you're designing the MVP. Show them wireframes, prototypes, and mockups. Make sure you get the strong, positive reaction you're looking for before building anything. Cut everything out that doesn't draw an extremely straight line, from your validated problem, to the unique value proposition, to the MVP, to the metrics you'll use to validate success.

It's important to note that the MVP is a process, not a product. This is something we learned at Year One Labs working with multiple startups all at a similar stage. The knee-jerk reaction once you've decided on the feature set is to build it and gun for traction as quickly as possible, turning on all the marketing tactics possible. As much as we all understand that seeing our name in lights on a popular tech blog doesn't really make a huge difference, it's still great when it's there. But sticking with Lean Startup's core tenet—*build→measure→learn*—it's important to realize that an MVP will go through numerous iterations before you're ready to go to the next step.

Measuring the MVP

The real analytical work starts the minute you develop and launch an MVP, because every interaction between a customer and the MVP results in data you can analyze.

For starters, you need to pick the OMTM. If you don't know what it should be, and you haven't defined "success" for that metric, you shouldn't be building anything. Everything you build into the initial MVP should relate to and impact the OMTM. And the line in the sand has to be clearly drawn.

At this stage, metrics around user acquisition are irrelevant. You don't need hundreds of thousands of users to prove if something is working or not. You don't even need thousands. Even with the most complicated of businesses, you can narrow things down significantly:

- If you're building a marketplace for used goods, you might focus on one tiny geographic area, such as house listings in Miami.

- The same holds true for any location-based application where density is important—a garage sale finder that's limited to one or two neighborhoods.

- You might pick one product type for your marketplace test—say, X-Men comics from the 80s—validate the business there, and then expand.

- Maybe you want to test the core game mechanics of your game. Release a mini-game as a solo application and see what engagement is like.

- Perhaps you're building a tool for parents to connect. See if it works in a single school.

The key is to identify the riskiest parts of your business and de-risk them through a constant cycle of testing and learning. Metrics is how you measure and learn whether the risk has been overcome.

Entrepreneur, author, and investor Tim Ferriss, in an interview with Kevin Rose, said that if you focus on making 10,000 people really happy, you could reach millions later.* For the first launch of your MVP, you can think even smaller, but Ferriss's point is absolutely correct: total focus is necessary in order to make genuine progress.

The most important metrics will be around engagement. *Are people using the product? How are they using the product? Are they using all of the product or only pieces of it? Is their usage and behavior as expected or different?*

---

*   *http://youtu.be/ccFYnEGWoOc*

No feature should be built without a corresponding metric on usage and engagement. These sub-metrics all bubble up to the OMTM; they're pieces of data that, aggregated, tell a more complete story. If you can't instrument a feature or component of your product, be very careful about adding it in—you're introducing variables that will become harder and harder to control.

Even as you focus on a single metric, you need to be sure you're actually adding value. Let's say you launch a new SaaS product, and you assume that if someone doesn't use it in 30 days, he's churned. That means it'll be 30 days before you know your churn rate. That's much too long. Customers always churn, but if you're not writing them off quickly, you may think you have more engagement than you really do. Even if initial engagement is strong, you need to measure whether you're delivering value. You might, for example, look at the time between visits. Is it the same? Or does it gradually drop off? You might find a useful leading indicator along the way.

Don't Ignore Qualitative Analytics

You should be speaking with users and customers throughout the MVP process. Now that they have a product in their hands, you can learn a great deal from them. They'll be less inclined to lie or sugarcoat things—after all, you made a promise of some kind and now they have a high expectation that you'll deliver. Early adopters are forgiving, and they're OK with (and in fact, crave) roughly hewn products, but at the same time their feedback will become more honest and transparent as their time with the MVP increases.

Be Prepared to Kill Features

It's incredibly hard to do, but it can make a huge difference. If a feature isn't being used, or it's not creating value through its use, get rid of it and see what happens. Once you've removed a feature, continue to measure engagement and usage with existing users. *Did it make a difference?*

If nobody minds, you've cleaned things up. If the existing users protest, you may need to revisit your decision. And if a new cohort of users—who'd never seen the feature before it was removed—start asking for it, they may represent a new segment with different needs than your existing user base.

The narrowing of your focus and value proposition through the elimination of features should have an impact on how customers respond.

| # Static Pixels Eliminates a Step in Its Order Process

Static Pixels is an early-stage startup founded by Massimo Farina. The company allows you to order prints of your Instagram photos on recycled cardboard. When the company first launched, it had a feature called InstaOrder, which allowed you to order photos directly from Instagram. Massimo believed that InstaOrder would make it easier for customers to use his service and increase the volume of orders. "We built the feature based on pre-launch feedback, and the assumption that users would like it," Massimo said.

The company spent two weeks building the feature—a costly amount of development time for a small team—but after releasing the feature found it wasn't used much. Massimo said, "Turns out, the feature was confusing people and making the checkout process more complicated."

As Figure 15-9 shows, the first-time ordering process with InstaOrder had an extra step, and that step required going to PayPal to pre-authorize payments. The hypothesis was that the feature would be worth the first-time ordering pain, after which ordering would be much easier directly through Instagram. "Convenience was the hypothesis," noted Massimo.

But Massimo and his team were wrong. Not only were orders low, but page views started to drop on the landing page that promoted the feature, and bounce rate was high as well. It just wasn't resonating.

Two weeks after the feature was removed, the number of transactions doubled, and it continues to increase. The bounce rate on the new landing page improved while sign-in goal completions increased.

So what did the Static Pixels team learn? "For starters, I think people didn't transact through Instagram because it's a very new and foreign process," Massimo said. "Ordering products via a native social platform interface hasn't really been done before. Also, I believe that when people are posting photos to Instagram, they aren't necessarily thinking about ordering prints of that photo."

The company lost some development time, but through a focus on analytics—particularly on its key metric of prints ordered—it identified roadblocks in its process, made tough decisions on removing a feature (which it originally thought was one of its unique value propositions), and then tracked the results.

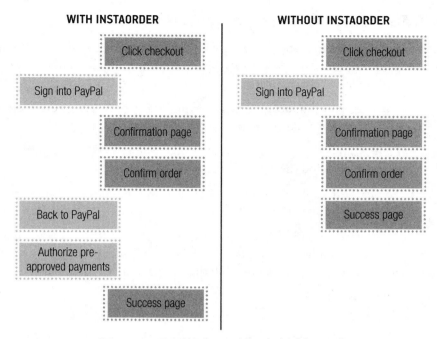

Figure 15-9. Which model worked better?

Summary

- The way Static Pixels asked users to buy had too much friction.

- A lighter-weight approach, with fewer steps, was both easier to implement and increased conversion rates.

Analytics Lessons Learned

Building a more advanced purchasing system that sacrificed first-purchase simplicity for long-term ease of repeat purchases seemed like a good idea, but it was premature. This early in the company's life, the question was "Will people buy prints?" and not "Will we have loyal buyers?" The feature the team had built was de-risking the wrong question. Always know what risk you're eliminating, and then design the minimum functionality to measure whether you've overcome it.

A Summary of the Empathy Stage

- Your goal is to identify a need you can solve in a way people will pay money for at scale. Analytics is how you measure your way from your initial idea to the realization of that goal.

- Early on, you conduct qualitative, exploratory, open-ended discussions to discover the unknown opportunities.

- Later, your discussions become more quantitative and more convergent, as you try to find the right solution for a problem.

- You can use tools to get answers at scale and build up an audience as you figure out what product to build.

Once you have a good idea of a problem you're going to solve, and you're confident that you have real interest from a sizeable market you know how to reach, it's time to build something that keeps users coming back.

It's time to get sticky.

EXERCISE | Should You Move to the Next Stage?

Answer the following questions.

Have I conducted enough quality customer interviews to feel confident that I've found a problem worth solving?	
Yes	**No**
List the reasons why you think the problem is painful enough to solve.	Conduct more interviews. Use Mechanical Turk or other resources to reach more people quickly.

Do I understand my customer well enough?	
Yes	**No**
List the reasons why you think this is the case. What have you done to understand your customer?	Try developing a "day in the life" storyboard to identify gaps in your understanding of the customer.

Do I believe my solution will meet the needs of customers?	
Yes	**No**
List the reasons why you think this is the case. What have you done to validate the solution?	Show your solution (in whatever form it's in) to more customers, collect more feedback, and dig deeper.

CHAPTER 16

Stage Two: Stickiness

Having climbed inside your market's head, it's time to build something. The big question now is whether or not what you've built is sticky, so that when you throw users at it, they'll engage. You want to be, as Rowan Atkinson's *Blackadder* put it, "in the stickiest situation since Sticky the stick insect got stuck on a sticky bun." That's how you make the business sustainable.

MVP Stickiness

The focus now is squarely on retention and engagement. You can look at daily, weekly, and/or monthly active users; how long it takes someone to become inactive; how many inactive users can be reactivated when sent an email; and which features engaged users spend time with, and which they ignore. Segment these metrics by cohort to see if your changes convince additional users to behave differently. Did users who signed up in February stick around longer than those who joined in January?

You don't just want signs of engagement. You want *proof* that your product is becoming an integral part of your users' lives, and that it'll be hard for them to switch. You're not looking for, nor should you expect, rapid growth. You're throwing things at the wall to test stickiness, not measuring how fast you can throw. And by "things," we mean users. After all, if you can't convince a hundred users to stick around today, you're unlikely to convince a million to do so later.[*]

Your top priority is to build a core set of features that gets used regularly and successfully, even by a small group of initial users. Without that, you don't have a solid enough foundation for growth. Your initial target market can be very small, hyper-focused on the smallest subset of users that you think will generate meaningful results.

Ultimately, you need to prove two things before you can move on to the Virality stage:

- Are people using the product as you expected? If they aren't, maybe you should switch to that new use case or market, as PayPal did when it changed from PalmPilot to web-based payment or when Autodesk stopped making desktop automation and instead focused on design tools.

- Are people getting enough value out of it? They may like it, but if they won't pay, click ads, or invite their friends, you may not have a business.

Don't drive new traffic until you know you can turn that extra attention into engagement. When you know users keep coming back, it's time to grow your user base.

Iterating the MVP

As we've said, the MVP is a process, not a product. You don't pass Go just because you put something into people's hands. Expect to go through many iterations of your MVP before it's time to shift your focus to customer acquisition.

Iterating on your MVP is difficult, tedious work. It's methodical. Sometimes it doesn't feel like innovation. Iterations are evolutionary; pivots are revolutionary. This is one of the reasons founders get frustrated and decide

---

[*] One exception to this rule is a business that requires a critical mass of activity to be useful. If your service is engaging only when it has, say, 1,000 property listings, or 10,000 prospective mates, or cars less than three minutes away, then you'll need to artificially seed it somehow before you can focus on testing stickiness. This is a common problem for two-sided marketplaces.

instead to pivot repeatedly in the hopes that something will accidentally engage their users. Resist that temptation.

As you iterate, your goal is to improve on the core metrics that you're tracking. If a new feature doesn't significantly improve the One Metric That Matters, remove it. Don't get caught tinkering and polishing. You're not fine-tuning at this point; you're searching for the right product and market.

CASE STUDY | **qidiq Changes How It Adds Users**

Qidiq is a tool—for doing really simple surveys of small groups via email or a mobile application—that was launched through startup accelerator Year One Labs. In early versions of the product, a survey creator invited respondents to join a group. Once those respondents had signed up and created an account, they could answer surveys delivered by email or pushed to an iPhone client.

Only a small percentage of people who were invited actually created an account and responded. So the founders devised a test: why not act as if the recipient already had an account, send her a survey question she can respond to with a single click or tap, and see what the response rate is like? The act of responding could be treated as tacit acceptance of enrollment; later, if the recipient wanted to log into her account, she could do so through a password recovery.

The qidiq team quickly changed their application, as illustrated in Figure 16-1, and sent out more surveys to personal groups they'd created. These initial surveys were sent via email alone. The results were striking: response rates went from 10–25% with the enroll-first model to 70–90% with the vote-first model. This made the team rethink their plans to develop a mobile application, since mobile applications couldn't compete with the cross-platform ubiquity and immediacy of email. Maybe email was good enough, and they shouldn't build their mobile app any more, or port it to Android.

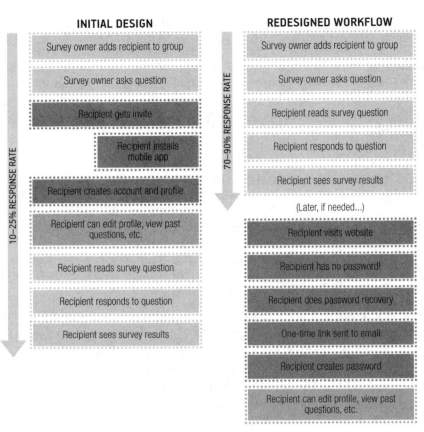

INITIAL DESIGN

- Survey owner adds recipient to group
- Survey owner asks question
- Recipient gets invite
- Recipient installs mobile app
- Recipient creates account and profile
- Recipient can edit profile, view past questions, etc.
- Recipient reads survey question
- Recipient responds to question
- Recipient sees survey results

10–25% RESPONSE RATE

REDESIGNED WORKFLOW

- Survey owner adds recipient to group
- Survey owner asks question
- Recipient reads survey question
- Recipient responds to question
- Recipient sees survey results

(Later, if needed...)

- Recipient visits website
- Recipient has no password!
- Recipient does password recovery
- One-time link sent to email
- Recipient creates password
- Recipient can edit profile, view past questions, etc.

70–90% RESPONSE RATE

Figure 16-1. Don't let details like account creation
get in the way of your core functionality

"By focusing on the key metric of response rate, we were able to avoid the temptation of wasting our energy on the sexier mobile app," says co-founder Jonathan Abrams. "Because it was the response rate that mattered, it became clear early on that email, while less sexy, was the better strategy for our startup."

The metric qidiq was tracking, which was the basis of its whole product, was the number of people who would respond to a question. That was the right metric, and when the team found a product change that moved it dramatically in the right direction, it made them rethink the design of their entire service.

Summary

- The MVP should include the simplest, least-friction path between your user and the "aha!" moment you're trying to deliver.

- Everything is on the table. While you shouldn't reinvent well-understood concepts like an enrollment process with which people are familiar, you should also feel free to ignore them for the sake of a test.

- Focusing on a single metric—in this case, survey response rate—let the team tweak every other part of the business, from sign-up to platform.

Analytics Lessons Learned

When you've got an MVP, you don't have a product. You have a tool for figuring out what product to build. By asking an unorthodox question—in this case, "What if users were already registered?"—the qidiq team not only quadrupled response rates, but also avoided a costly, distracting development rathole.

Premature Virality

Many startups—particularly in the consumer space—focus on virality first. They implement features and tactics to try to increase user acquisition as much as possible, before really understanding what those users will do. This is common for two reasons:

- First, the bar for success in a consumer application is always going up. A few years ago, hundreds of thousands of users was considered big. Today, 1 million users is the benchmark, but it's quickly going to 10 million. That's a lot of users. Certain categories of product, such as social networks and e-commerce, are ossifying, with a few gigantic players competing and leaving little room for upstarts.

- Second, many consumer applications rely on network effects. The more users, the more value created for everyone. Nobody wants to use the telephone when they're the only one with a telephone. Location-based applications typically require lots of scale, as do most marketplaces and user-generated content businesses, so that there are enough transactions and discussions to make things interesting. Without a critical mass of users, Facebook is an empty shell. Reaching this critical mass quickly is the first step in delivering the anticipated value of the product.

As a result, founders of consumer startups and multiplayer games often argue that they need to focus on virality and user acquisition because it will solve all their other problems. But having lots of users isn't traction unless those users are engaged and sticking around.

The results of premature scaling can be disastrous if startups invest all of their time and money into user acquisition, only to watch those users churn too quickly. By the time they go back and try to recover those users, they're gone. You never get a second chance to have a first enrollment.

The Goal Is Retention

The more engaged that people are with your product (and potentially other users of your product), the more likely they'll stay. By ignoring growth from virality (for now), you can simplify how you decide what to build next into your MVP. Ask yourself, "Do we believe that the feature we want to build (or the feature we want to change) will improve stickiness?" Put the feature aside if the answer is "no." But if the answer is "yes," figure out how to test that belief and start building the feature.

PATTERN | ## Seven Questions to Ask Yourself Before Building a Feature

You probably have a long list of feature ideas you believe will improve retention. You need to further prioritize. Here are seven questions you can ask yourself (and your team) before building a new feature.

1. Why Will It Make Things Better?

You can't build a feature without having a reason for building it. In the Stickiness stage, your focus is retention. Look at your potential feature list and ask yourself, "Why do I think this will improve retention?"

You'll be tempted to copy what others are doing—say, using gamification to drive engagement (and in turn retention)—just because it looks like it's working for the competition. Don't. Qidiq ignored common wisdom around the sign-up process and the creation of a mobile app and quadrupled engagement. It's OK to copy existing patterns, but know why you're doing so.

Asking "Why will it make it better?" forces you to write out (on paper!) a hypothesis. This naturally leads to a good experiment that will test that hypothesis. Feature experiments, if they're tied to a specific metric (such as retention) are usually easy: you believe feature X will improve retention by Y percent. The second part of that statement is as important as the first part; you need to draw that line in the sand.

2. Can You Measure the Effect of the Feature?

Feature experiments require that you measure the impact of the feature. That impact has to be quantifiable. Too often, features get added to a product without any quantifiable validation—which is a direct path toward scope creep and feature bloat.

If you're unable to quantify the impact of a new feature, you can't assess its value, and you won't really know what to do with the feature over time. If this is the case, leave it as is, iterate on it, or kill it.

3. How Long Will the Feature Take to Build?

Time is a precious resource you never get back. You have to compare the relative development time of each feature on your list. If something is going to take months to build, you need good confidence that it will have a significant impact. Can you break it into smaller parts, or test the inherent risk with a curated MVP or a prototype instead?

4. Will the Feature Overcomplicate Things?

Complexity kills products. It's most obvious in the user experience of many web applications: they become so convoluted and confusing that users leave for a simpler alternative.

"And" is the enemy of success. When discussing a feature with your team, pay attention to how it's being described. "The feature will allow you to do this, *and* it'd be great if it did this other thing, *and* this other thing, *and* this other thing too." Warning bells should be going off at this point. If you're trying to justify a feature by saying it satisfies several needs a little bit, know that it's almost always better to satisfy *one* need in an absolutely epic, remarkable way.

One mobile analytics expert for an adult-content site told us his rule for new features is simple: "If you can't do it in three taps with one hand, it's broken." Knowing your user's behavior and expectations is everything. Having feature complexity get in the way of the real testing you need to do around your market, customer acquisition, and retention is extremely painful.

5. How Much Risk Is There in This New Feature?

Building new features always comes with some amount of risk. There's technical risk related to how a feature may impact the code base. There's user risk in terms of how people might respond to the feature. There's also risk in terms of how a new feature drives future development, potentially setting you on a path you don't want to pursue.

Each feature you add creates an emotional commitment for your development team, and sometimes for your customers. Analytics helps break that bond so that you can measure things honestly and make the best decisions possible, with the most information available.

6. How Innovative Is the New Feature?

Not everything you do will be innovative. Most features aren't innovative, they're small tweaks to a product in the hope that the whole is more valuable than the individual parts.

But consider innovation when prioritizing feature development; generally, the easiest things to do rarely have a big impact. You're still in the Stickiness stage, trying to find the right product. Changing a submit button from red to blue may result in a good jump in signup conversions (a classic A/B test), but it's probably not going to turn your business from a failure into a giant success; it's also easy for others to copy.

It's better to make big bets, swing for the fences, try more radical experiments, and build more disruptive things, particularly since you have fewer user expectations to contend with than you will later on.

7. What Do Users *Say* They Want?

Your users are important. Their feedback is important. But relying on what they say is risky. Be careful about over-prioritizing based on user input alone. Users lie, and they don't like hurting your feelings.

Prioritizing feature development during an MVP isn't an exact science. User actions speak louder than words. Aim for a genuinely testable hypothesis for every feature you build, and you'll have a much better chance of quickly validating success or failure. Simply tracking how popular various features are within the application will reveal what's working and what's not. Looking at what feature a user was using before he hit "undo" or the back button will pinpoint possible problem areas.

Building features is easy if you plan them beforehand and truly understand why you're doing something. It's important to tie your high-level vision and long-term goals down to the feature level. Without that alignment, you run the risk of building features that can't be properly tested and don't drive the business forward.

| # How Rally Builds New Features with a Lean Approach

Rally Software makes Agile application lifecycle management software. The company was founded in 2002 and has pioneered a number of Agile best practices. We spoke with Chief Technologist Zach Nies about how the company continues to successfully build its products.

Establishing a Company Vision

Everything at Rally starts with a three- to five-year company vision that is refreshed every 18 months. The entire company aligns around the vision, which is the first waypoint in turning a big, distant goal into something more attainable. This longer-term vision becomes a key input into annual planning each year. Zach says, "When we were younger and smaller we didn't bother looking three years into the future, but it's an important part of the process for a company of our size."

Annual planning is initially done by a small group of executives. Zach calls this the first iteration. The output of the initial planning is a draft corporate strategy, which provides a clear, concise picture of Rally's performance gaps and targets, reflections, and rationale for the year. The executive team also identifies three or four high-level places where they believe the company needs to focus action to accomplish the annual vision. "This work creates a draft of ideas to bring back to Rally for reflection," Zach says. "They provide a summary of what the executive group saw as critically valuable to address in our upcoming year."

The second iteration of annual planning takes the form of departmental annual retrospectives. Rally uses an approach called ORID (Objective, Reflective, Interpretive, Decisional) from *The Art of Focused Conversation* by R. Brian Stanfield (New Society Publishers).[*] Zach says:

> This process invites insights from all employees, and provides a valuable narrative about the past, present, and future. From each ORID within each department, we learn about completed work, the current work in progress, planned work, specific annual metrics, the implications for the coming year, and the overall mood for the year. Kids are learning machines, but adults

---

* *http://www.amazon.com/Art-Focused-Conversation-Access-Workplace/dp/0865714169*

need structured reflection to learn; this process provides that structure.

Both the executive planning and the ORIDs feed into the next step of the annual planning process: gathering 60 people from the company in a highly-facilitated meeting to clearly articulate the vision for the year and align around how to accomplish it.

Developing a Product Plan

The product team is actively involved in defining the company's annual strategy. A big part of this is aligning the directions of the company and product. The product team focuses on answering the question "Why?" above everything else. "The articulation of why we're doing something, and always questioning our focus, rallies everyone around one compelling vision, company, and product, and creates a vital emotional connection with our customers," Zach says. "Only once we understand 'why' can we really look at 'what' and 'how'."

Now Rally is ready to dig into product. While this process may seem like a lot, it's very iterative and Lean. The company goes through a *build→measure→learn* cycle at several levels before getting to the point where it's actually developing features.

Deciding What to Build

Feature development begins in earnest with deciding what to build and how to build it. Rally has an open, but process-oriented, way of making feature decisions. Each quarter, employees submit short proposals for changes to the company's product direction. These proposals come from anyone in the organization, but are typically highly influenced by interactions with customers.

Zach says:

> We include almost everyone who does product-management-type work in the decision-making process, including product marketing, product owners, engineering managers, sales leadership, and executives. It may seem like this is quite a bit of process, but the benefits of everyone's input and alignment far outweigh the 10 or so hours a quarter we spend running the process. We find strong alignment enables great execution.

Rally doesn't release software, but instead "turns features on for users and customers." Most features have a toggle that allows Rally to turn them on or off for specific customers. This allows the company to roll out code to progressively larger groups of users, generating feedback from early adopters while mitigating the risk of exposing problems to a lot of customers.

Measuring Progress

Underneath Rally's feature development process, the company is focused on measurement. "We have an internal data warehouse in which we record everything from server/database kernel-level performance measurements to high-level user gestures derived from HTTP interactions between the browser and our servers," says Zach. The goal is to make sure the team can measure feature usage and performance. "When we develop a feature our product team can form theories about how much usage warrants further development of that feature," Zach says. "As we are toggling on the feature we can compare our theories to actual data. Because the data includes both usage and performance information, we can quickly understand, in real time, the impact a feature is having on the performance and stability of our production environment."

Learning Through Experiments

Even with such a deep level of planning and an all-inclusive approach to product development, Zach still says that the company is careful not to "blindly build features based on internal or customer requests." Instead, it runs experiments to learn more.

According to Zach, every experiment starts with a series of questions:

- What do we want to learn and why?

- What's the underlying problem we are trying to solve, and who is feeling the pain? This helps everyone involved have empathy for what we are doing.

- What's our hypothesis? This is written in the form: "[Specific repeatable action] will create [expected result]." We make sure the hypothesis is written in such a way that the experiment is capable of invalidating it.

- How will we run the experiment, and what will we build to support it?

- Is the experiment safe to run?

- How will we conclude the experiment, and what steps will be taken to mitigate issues that result from the experiment's conclusion?

- What measures will we use to invalidate our hypothesis with data? We also include what measures will indicate the experiment isn't safe to continue.

In a three-month period, over 20 experiments were run to learn exactly what would satisfy users in a critical part of the user interface. Rather than guessing, this was a disciplined process of discovery. This area of the user interface was a focus because refining it was a major part of the product vision for the year , and directly supported one of Rally's corporate goals for the year.

Summary

- Data-driven product direction starts at the top, and it's an iterative, methodical process.

- Everything is an experiment, even when you have an established product and a loyal set of customers.

- It takes extra engineering effort to be able to turn on and off individual features, and to measure the resulting change in user behavior, but that investment pays off in reduced cycle time and better learning.

Analytics Lessons Learned

Rally has taken measurement to the next level. In a way, Rally is two companies—one making lifecycle management software, and one running a gigantic, continuous experiment on its users to better understand how they interact with the product itself. This requires a lot of discipline and focus, as well as considerable engineering effort to make every feature testable and measurable, but it's paid off in less waste, a better product, and a consistent alignment with what customers want.

How to Handle User Feedback

Customers have something in common with entrepreneurs—they're liars too. They don't lie intentionally, but often they forget how your product really works or what they were doing in the product.

Many of the reviews for personal banking app Mint give the product one star, saying, "Warning! This product will try to collect your banking information and connect to your bank account!" as shown in Figure 16-2. *But that's what Mint is for.*

*Figure 16-2. Warning—banking app may want your
banking details*

If you're the product manager, you might be tempted to ignore this feedback, but what it's really telling you is that your marketing and product descriptions aren't working, bringing down your product ratings and reducing your addressable market.

Customers may give you feedback you don't like. Just remember that they don't have the same mental model you do, they aren't in your target market. They often lack training to use your product properly.

We've already seen some of the cognitive biases demonstrated by interview subjects. Existing users suffer from similar biases. They have different expectations and context from you. You need to view their feedback with that in mind.

For one thing, user feedback suffers from horrible sampling bias. Few people provide feedback when they have a predictable, tepid experience. They reach out when they're ecstatic or furious. If they're feeling aggrieved, you'll hear from them.

What's more, they don't know their value to you. They may feel entitled to a free product because that's how you've positioned your SaaS offering, or to free breadsticks because that's how you've priced your buffet. You know their value to your business—they don't. To each unhappy user he or she is, they're the most important person in the world. And he or she has been wronged or celebrated.

Finally, customers aren't aware of the constraints and nuances of their problems. It's easy to complain about US television programming not being available overseas; it's unlikely that those complaining are aware of the intricacies of foreign currency exchange, censorship, and copyright licensing. They want their problem solved, but they have little insight into how to solve it the *right* way.

Laura Klein is a user experience (UX) professional and consultant, as well as the author of *UX for Lean Startups* (forthcoming from O'Reilly), part of the Lean Series along with this book. She writes a great blog called Users Know. You should read her post, "Why Your Customer Feedback is Useless," in its entirety.*

To improve how you interpret feedback, Laura has three suggestions:

- Plan tests ahead of time, and know what you want to learn before you get started. "A big reason that feedback is hard to interpret is because there's just too much of it, and it's not well organized or about a particular topic," says Laura. "If you know exactly what you're gathering feedback on, and you're disciplined about the methods you use to gather it, it becomes very simple to interpret the responses."

- Don't talk to just anybody. "You should group feedback from similar personas," says Laura. "For example, if I ask a Formula 1 driver and my mom about how they feel about their cars, I'm going to get inconsistent responses." Balancing feedback like that is very difficult because it's from such different types of people. "Figure out who your customers are and focus your research on a particular type of person."

- Review results quickly as you collect data. "Don't leave it all until the end," Laura notes. "If you talk to five people for an hour each over the course of a few days, it can be really hard to remember what the first person said." Laura recommends having someone else in each session, so that you can debrief with that person after and pull out the top takeaways from the session.

The reality is, users will always complain. That's just the way it goes. Even if people are using your product, you have good engagement metrics, and your product is sticky, they're still going to complain. Listen to their complaints, and try to get to the root of the issue as quickly as possible without overreacting.

---

* *http://usersknow.blogspot.ca/2010/03/why-your-customer-feedback-is-useless.html*

The Minimum Viable Vision

The *minimum viable vision* is a term coined by entrepreneur and Year One Labs partner Raymond Luk. He says, "If you're trying to build a great company and get others involved, it's not enough to find an MVP—you need an MVV, too."

A minimum viable vision (MVV) is one that captivates. It scales. It has potential. It's audacious and compelling. As a founder, you have to hold that huge, hairy, world-changing vision in one hand, and the practical, pragmatic, seat-of-the-pants reality in the other. The MVV you need in order to get funding demands a convincing explanation of how you can become a dominant, disruptive player in your market.

Here are some signs that suggest you've got the makings of an MVV:

- *You're building a platform.* If you're creating an environment in which other things can be created, this is a good sign. Google Maps was just one of the many mapping tools available, alongside MapQuest and others, but Google made it easy to embed and annotate those maps, leading to thousands of mashups and clever uses. It quickly became the de facto platform for entry-level geographic information systems (GIS), and all those annotations made its maps even more useful.

- *You have recurring ways to make money.* It's one thing to take money from someone once, but if you can convince that person to pay every month as well, you're onto something. Just look at Blizzard's revenues from *World of Warcraft*: purchase of the paid desktop client is a fraction of the money the company makes compared to revenue from $14.95 per month subscriber fees.

- *You've got naturally tiered pricing.* If you can find ways for customers to self-upsell, as companies like 37Signals, Wufoo, and FreshBooks have done, then you can hook your users on basic features and tempt them with an upgrade path that adds functionality as they need it. This means you'll not only add revenue from new users, but from existing ones, too.

- *You're tied to a disruptive change.* If you're part of a growing trend—people sharing information, mobile devices, cloud computing—then you've got a better chance of growth. A rising tide floats all boats, and a rising tech sector floats all valuations and exits.

- *Adopters automatically become advocates.* Just look at the classic example of online marketing—Hotmail. A simple message appended to every email invited the recipient to switch to Hotmail. The result was an exponential growth rate and a huge exit for the founders.* An expense management system like Expensify makes it as easy as possible to add others to the approval workflow, because this is a vector for inherent virality.

- *You can create a bidding war.* If you've got a solution that several industry giants will want, you're in a great place. While big companies can build anything given enough time, they'll buy you if you're stealing their sales or if your product helps them sell dramatically more easily. Beverage giants like Pepsico, Cadbury-Schweppes, and Coca-Cola regularly buy out promising incumbents, like Odwalla, Tropicana, Minute Maid, RC Cola, and others, knowing they can make back their investment easily through their existing supply chains.

- *You're riding an environmental change.* We don't mean the Green movement here. In strategic marketing, environmental forces include everything you're subject to in your business ecosystem, such as government-mandated privacy laws or anti-pollution regulations. If you're building something that everyone will be forced to adopt (such as a product that complies with soon-to-be-signed health or payment privacy legislation), you've got a promising exit and a chance to take over the sector.

- *You've got a sustainable unfair advantage.* There's nothing investors like more than unfairness. If you can maintain an unfair advantage— lower costs, better market attention, partners, proprietary formulae, and so on—then you can scale your business to a degree where it's interesting to investors. But be careful: outside of government-mandated monopolies, few advantages are truly sustainable in the long term.

- *Your marginal costs trend to zero.* If as you add users your incremental costs go down—so that the nth customer costs almost nothing to add—that's a great place to be. You're enjoying healthy economies of scale. For example, an antivirus company has fixed costs of software development and research that must be amortized across all customers, but the addition of one more client adds only a vanishingly small cost to this total. Businesses that can grow revenues while incremental costs stay still or decline have the potential to grow massively overnight.

- *There are inherent network effects in the model.* The phone system is the classic example of a business with a network effect: the more people who use it, the more useful it becomes. Network-effect businesses are wonderful, but they often have a two-edged sword: it's great when you

---

* *http://www.menlovc.com/portfolio/hotmail*

PART TWO: FINDING THE RIGHT METRIC FOR RIGHT NOW

have 10 million users, but you may be deluding yourself about how easily users will adopt the product or service, and it's hard to test the basic value with a small market at first. You need a plan for getting to the point where the network effects kick in and become obvious.

- *You have several ways to monetize.* It's unlikely that any one payment model will work, but if you can find several ways to make money from a business—one obvious one, and several incidental ones—then you can diversify your revenue streams and iterate more easily, improving your chances of success. Quick note: AdWords and selling your analytical data probably aren't enough.

- *You make money when your customers make money.* Humans are, at their most basic, motivated by two things: fear and greed. While that might seem a bit cynical, it's how we evolved. In business, fear means things like costs and risks, and if you reduce risks or cut costs, that's nice—but it's not compelling. Customers will often rationalize away the risk and pocket the savings. But if you make money from greed (or, as it's known in the business world, revenues) then the customer will likely split the winnings with you. Products that boost revenues are easier for people to believe in—just look at lotteries and get-rich-quick schemes versus savings plans and life insurance. Eventbrite and Kickstarter know this.

- *An ecosystem will form around you.* This is similar to the platform model. Salesforce and Photoshop are good examples of this: Salesforce's App Exchange has thousands of third-party applications that make the CRM (customer relationship management) provider more useful and customizable, and Photoshop's plug-in model added features to the application far more quickly than if Adobe had coded them all itself.

In the end, you have to be audacious. You need to understand how your company can become a Big Idea, something that's truly new, and either widely appealing to a broad market or a must-have for a well-heeled niche.

The Problem-Solution Canvas

At Year One Labs, we developed a tool called the *Problem-Solution Canvas* to help our startups maintain discipline and focus on a weekly basis. It's inspired by Ash Maurya's Lean Canvas, but focused on the day-to-day operations of a startup. We used it to home in on the key one to three problems the startups were facing. It allowed us all to agree on those problems and prioritize them.

It was fairly common for founders to incorrectly prioritize the key issues at hand. It's not surprising; startup founders are juggling a ton at once, wearing hats stacked to the sky like crazed circus performers, and as we well know, they're a bunch of liars (but we love 'em just the same!). As mentors and advisors, we knew that a big part of our job—where we could provide significant value because of our detachment—was to guide entrepreneurs back to what was most important.

The Problem-Solution Canvas is a two-page document. Like a Lean Canvas it's divided into a few boxes. On a weekly basis we'd ask founders to prepare a Problem-Solution Canvas and present it. The canvas became the focal point for our status meetings, and it was extremely helpful for keeping those meetings productive.

Figure 16-3 shows the first page of the template.

THE GOAL IS TO LEARN

CURRENT STATUS	LAST WEEK'S LESSON LEARNED (AND ACCOMPLISHMENTS)
- List key metrics you're tracking, where they're at, and compare with last few weeks - How are things trending?	- What did you learn last week? - What was accomplished? - On track: YES / NO
TOP PROBLEMS	
- List and describe the top problems - Prioritize them	

Figure 16-3. If you filled in this page every week, what would you learn?

The first thing you'll notice is the title: *The Goal Is to Learn*. This is important, because it reminded the entrepreneurs about what they were setting out to do. It wasn't about building "stuff." It wasn't about adding features. It wasn't about getting PR, or anything else. Learning was the measure of success.

Next, founders would fill in a brief update on their current status, focusing on the key metrics (qualitative and/or quantitative) that they were tracking. Notice how small this box is compared to the others.

The Lessons Learned box is a quick bulleted summary of key learning. The title says "and Accomplishments" because we wanted to give entrepreneurs a place to brag—at least a little bit. Not surprisingly, they'd include some vanity metrics in here and we wouldn't spend a lot of time on them. The "On track: Yes/No" benchmark is designed as a test of intellectual honesty. Can entrepreneurs really come clean on what's going on, good and bad? If so, we could be much more valuable.

Finally, we asked entrepreneurs to list the top problems they were facing at that moment. At most they would include three problems prioritized in order of importance. This section of the Problem-Solution Canvas often elicited the most debate, but it was always healthy and critical for resetting everyone's goals and expectations.

With the problems now well understood, along with the startup's current status, we'd move to the second page of the canvas, shown in Figure 16-4.

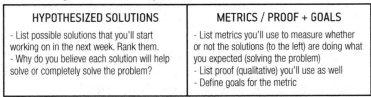

Problem #1: [put name of it here]

HYPOTHESIZED SOLUTIONS	METRICS / PROOF + GOALS
- List possible solutions that you'll start working on in the next week. Rank them. - Why do you believe each solution will help solve or completely solve the problem?	- List metrics you'll use to measure whether or not the solutions (to the left) are doing what you expected (solving the problem) - List proof (qualitative) you'll use as well - Define goals for the metric

Problem #2: [put name of it here]

HYPOTHESIZED SOLUTIONS	METRICS / PROOF + GOALS
- List possible solutions that you'll start working on in the next week. Rank them. - Why do you believe each solution will help solve or completely solve the problem?	- List metrics you'll use to measure whether or not the solutions (to the left) are doing what you expected (solving the problem) - List proof (qualitative) you'll use as well - Define goals for the metric

Figure 16-4. We've all got problems—but can you pick just three?

In this section, the founders re-list the problems and include hypothesized solutions. These solutions are hypothesized because we don't know if they'll work. These are experiments that the founders will run in the next week. We always asked them to define the metrics they'd use to measure success (or failure) and draw a line in the sand. If engagement was the most important problem, they had to include possible solutions they'd experiment with to increase engagement, define the metric (e.g., % daily active users), and set a target. *What's the problem, how do you propose to fix it, and how will you know if you succeeded?* That's the core of the Problem-Solution Canvas.

For us (as mentors and advisors), it was an extremely valuable exercise. The Problem-Solution Canvas is also useful for internal decision making. It sits a level below the Lean Canvas, focusing on very specific details in a very specific time period (one to two weeks).

| # VNN Uses the Problem-Solution Canvas to Solve Business Problems

Varsity News Network (VNN) is an early-stage startup based in Michigan. Ben met one of the founders there, Ryan Vaughn, when speaking at a conference in 2012. The company's platform makes it easy for athletic directors to manage social communication, creating hyper-local media coverage about athletics at their high schools. The goal is to leverage that awareness creation into ongoing financial and emotional support for high school sports.

Ryan was introduced to the Problem-Solution Canvas and started using it immediately with his board of directors. "We had just raised financing and had to solve a number of key business problems very quickly," said Ryan. "We used the Problem-Solution Canvas to get all our board members on the same page, focused on what we had to do in order to move forward."

VNN followed a Lean process, particularly in the beginning of the company in order to determine its value proposition and how that tied into producing content about high school sports. The company remains Lean today, testing and iterating each new feature or initiative it launches, measuring effectiveness and value creation.

Still, Ryan was concerned that his board wouldn't embrace the Problem-Solution Canvas. He said, "The Lean Startup process has not been widely adopted in the Midwest yet, but our board had been exposed to the methodology, which helped speed up our initial progress with the canvas."

VNN used the canvas for a few months, during a critical time of problem solving. The result was that everyone involved stayed focused on the major tasks at hand. Through the Problem-Solution Canvas, VNN validated a number of its core assumptions and designed a scalable growth model involving direct sales. This allowed it to prove enough of its business to start generating revenue and plan for a second round of financing.

Figures 16-5 and 16-6 show an example of one of its canvases.

MAY PROBLEM/SOLUTION DASHBOARD

METRICS	LAST MONTH'S LESSON LEARNED (AND ACCOMPLISHMENTS)

- Schools sold: 1
  - Last month: 3
  - Total: 34
- Ad sales/school: $4,750
- Ad sales/rep/mo: $6,150
- Traffic/school: 1931.9 visits
  - +200 visits over last 3 months
  (new theme)
	- What did you learn last month?
	  - One sales rep can sell $10k+ in one month
	  - A market exists for individual sport websites
	  - Schedules > photos > articles
	- What was accomplished?
	  - Photogs sponsored for right to submit pics
	  - Secured second test market in Indianapolis
	- On track: YES

TOP PROBLEMS

- 1. We still don't know what one full-time rep can sell
  - We believe $10k in ads and 2 schools, based on limited data
  - 1 part-time rep sold 5+ schools in multiple months
  - 1 part-time rep sold $10,000 in ads two months in a row
- 2. We don't know the market for sport-specific sites
  - Coaches will pay $20–30/month. How should we sell/support these?
- 3. We don't yet show enough value to advertisers
  - We will need a 50%+ renewal rate year-over-year, current rate = 50%

Figure 16-5. VNN spends some time on introspection

Problem #1: We still don't know what 1 full-time rep can sell in a month

HYPOTHESIZED SOLUTIONS	METRICS / PROOF + GOALS

- 1. Hire full-time rep in Ann Arbor to sell both schools and ads in East Michigan
  - Shows what average rep can do
- 2. Contract with two guys out of Indianapolis to start new market
  - Shows what elite-rep can do
	- Metrics: School and ad sales/rep
	- Ann Arbor: Will have sold $8,500 and 3 schools by end-July
	- Indianapolis: Will have sold $7,500 and 4 schools by end-July

Problem #2: We don't know the market for sport-specific websites

HYPOTHESIZED SOLUTIONS	METRICS / PROOF + GOALS

- 1. Interview coaches in/out of Michigan
  - Big questions are if there is demand, pricing, and features
- 2. If market, build and sell MVP to coaches
  - This is the ultimate test of market
  - Question is *how* best to sell it
	- Metrics: Interview responses and sales
	- 1. Interviews with coaches
	  - Stated interest and payment amount
	Pre-purchase orders

Figure 16-6. Knowing how much you can sell, and the size of the market, matters a lot

Summary

- Having raised funding, VNN used the Problem-Solution Canvas to communicate with its board of directors in an effective manner.

- The canvas helped the company iterate to revenue and position itself for additional financing.

Analytics Lessons Learned

Never underestimate the power of getting everyone on the same page—literally. A single sheet of consistent information that forces all stakeholders to be succinct and to agree really helps clarify and define a problem, particularly in a fast-changing environment.

A Summary of the Stickiness Stage

- Your goal is to prove that you've solved a problem in a way that keeps people coming back.

- The key at this stage is engagement, which is measured by the time spent interacting with you, the rate at which people return, and so on. You might track revenue or virality, but they aren't your focus yet.

- Even though you're building the minimal product, your vision should still be big enough to inspire customers, employees, and investors—and there has to be a credible way to get from the current proof to the future vision.

- Don't step on the gas until you've proven that people will do what you want reliably. Otherwise, you're spending money and time attracting users who will leave immediately.

- Rely on cohort analysis to measure the impact of your continuous improvements as you optimize the stickiness of your product.

When your engagement numbers are healthy and churn is relatively low, it's time to focus on growing your user base. Don't run out and buy ads immediately, though. First, you need to leverage the best, most convincing campaign platform you have—your current users. It's time to go viral.

EXERCISE #1 | Should You Move to the Next Stage?

1. Are people using the product as expected?

   - If they are, move to the next step.

   - If they aren't, are they still getting enough value out of it, but using it differently? Or is the value not there?

2. Define an active user. What percentage of your users/customers is active? Write this down. Could this be higher? What can you do to improve engagement?

3. Evaluate your feature roadmap against our seven questions to ask before building more features. Does this change the priorities of feature development?

4. Evaluate the complaints you're getting from users. How does this impact feature development going forward?

EXERCISE #2 | Have You Identified Your Biggest Problems?

Create a Problem-Solution Canvas. This should take no more than 15–20 minutes. Share your canvas with others (investors, advisors, employees) and ask yourself if it really addresses the key concerns you're facing today.

CHAPTER 17

Stage Three: Virality

In 1997, venture capital firm Draper Fisher Jurvetson first used the term *viral marketing* to describe network-assisted word of mouth.[*] The firm had seen the power of virality firsthand with Hotmail, which included a vector for infection in every email—the now-famous link at the bottom of a message that invited recipients to get their own Hotmail account.

Decades earlier, Frank Bass, one of the founders of marketing science, described how messages propagated out in a marketplace.[†] His 1969 paper, "A New Product Growth Model for Consumer Durables," explained how messages trickle out into a market through word of mouth. At first, the spread starts slowly, but as more and more people start talking about it, spread accelerates. However, as the market becomes saturated with people who've heard the message, spread slows down again. This model is represented by a characteristic *S*-shape known as the Bass diffusion curve, shown in Figure 17-1.

---

* *http://www.dfj.com/news/article_25.shtml*
† *http://en.wikipedia.org/wiki/Bass_diffusion_model*

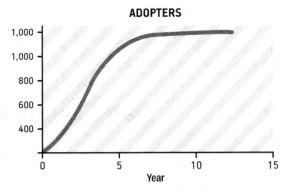

Figure 17-1. Three certainties: death, taxes, and market saturation

When researchers compared the spread of Hotmail to the predictions from Bass's model, they found an almost perfect fit.

In the Virality stage, it's time to focus on user acquisition and growth, but keep an eye on your stickiness too.

- There's a risk that you build virality and word of mouth at the expense of engagement. Perhaps you're bringing in new users who are different from your earlier adopters, and as a result they don't engage with the product. Or maybe your unique value proposition is getting lost in your marketing efforts, and your new users have different expectations from earlier ones.

- Be careful that you haven't moved on from stickiness too soon. If you're investing in adding users, but your churn is high, you may not be getting a good enough return on investment. Premature growth burns money and time, and will quickly kill your startup.

The Three Ways Things Spread

Virality is simply users sharing your product or service with others. There are three kinds of virality:

- **Inherent** virality is built into the product, and happens as a function of use.

- **Artificial** virality is forced, and often built into a reward system.

- **Word-of-mouth** virality is the conversations generated by satisfied users, independent of your product or service.

All three matter, but should be treated as distinct forms of growth and analyzed in terms of the kind of traffic they bring in. For example, you may find that artificial virality brings in plenty of drive-by traffic, but inherent virality brings in engaged customers who actually turn into revenue.

Inherent Virality

Many products have inherent virality. When you use TripIt, you share your travel plans with colleagues, which they can view better when signed in; when you use Expensify, you forward expense reports to others for approval; when you use FreshBooks, your customers view their electronic invoices on the site.

This is the best kind of virality. It feels genuine, and the recipient is motivated to start using the product or service. It's like an epidemic. It's not voluntary. It's not something that you opt into doing or experiencing, it just happens.

Artificial Virality

While inherent virality is best, artificial virality can be bought. Parts of Dropbox are inherently viral—users share files with colleagues and friends—but the company isn't afraid to compensate its users. It offers additional storage for tweeting or liking the product, and rewards users for helping it to acquire new customers. The rapid growth of the service happened because of existing users trying to convince friends to sign up so they can grow their free online storage capacity.

Artificial virality comes from incentivizing existing users to tell their friends. Done right, it can work well—as Dropbox has shown—but it can also be awkward and feel forced if done poorly. You're essentially building self-funded marketing activities into the product itself, sometimes at the expense of legitimate functionality.

Word-of-Mouth Virality

Finally, there's natural word of mouth. Harder to track, it's also extremely effective, because it amounts to an endorsement by a trusted advisor. You can see some of this activity by simply monitoring blogs and social platforms for mentions of your startup—and when you see one it's a good idea to engage with the endorser, find out what made him share your product or service, and try to turn that into a repeatable, sustainable part of the viral growth strategy.

You may even want to use tools like Klout or PeerReach to try to score the impact that those who are discussing you can have on awareness of your product or service, since their rankings act as a proxy for a person's ability to spread a message.

Metrics for the Viral Phase

Measuring your viral growth turns out to be really important if you don't want to pay for customers. The number you're after is your viral coefficient, which venture capitalist David Skok sums up nicely as "the number of new customers that each existing customer is able to successfully convert."[*]

To calculate your viral coefficient:

1. First calculate the invitation rate, which is the number of invites sent divided by the number of users you have.

2. Then calculate the acceptance rate, which is the number of signups or enrollments divided by the number of invites.

3. Then multiply the two together.

Table 17-1 shows sample math for a company with 2,000 customers who send 5,000 invitations, 500 of which are accepted.

Existing customers	2,000		
Total invitations sent	5,000	Invitation rate	2.5
Number that get clicked	500	Acceptance rate	10%
		Viral coefficient	25%

Table 17-1. Sample math for a viral coefficient calculation

This might seem overly simple, because in theory, that quarter of a customer will, in turn, invite another 25% of a customer (6.25% of a customer), and so on. In reality, as David points out, it's unlikely that users will continue to invite their friends as time goes by—instead, they'll invite those friends who they think are relevant and then stop inviting, and many of those they invite will have the same groups of friends. The invitation roster will get saturated.

There's another factor to consider here: cycle time. If it takes only a day for someone to use the site and invite others, you'll see fast growth. On the other hand, if it takes someone months before she invites others, you'll see much slower growth.

Cycle time makes a huge difference—so much so, David feels it's more important than viral coefficient. Using sample data from a worksheet he

---

[*] David Skok's explanation of viral coefficient calculation includes two spreadsheets you can play with at *http://www.forentrepreneurs.com/lessons-learnt-viral-marketing/*.

created, David underscores this in one of his examples: "After 20 days with a cycle time of two days, you will have 20,470 users, but if you halved that cycle time to one day, you would have over 20 million users!"

Bass's equations took many of these factors into consideration when he was trying to explain how messages propagate out into a marketplace and how customers gradually adopt innovation.

Ultimately, what we're after is a viral coefficient above 1, because this means the product is self-sustaining. With a viral coefficient above 1, every single user is inviting at least another user, and that new user invites another user in turn. That way, after you have some initial users your product grows by itself. In the preceding example, we could do several things to push the viral coefficient toward 1:

- Focus on increasing the acceptance rate.

- Try to extend the lifetime of the customer so he has more time to invite people.

- Try to shorten the cycle time for invitations to get growth faster.

- Work on convincing customers to invite more people.

Beyond the Viral Coefficient

Treat the three kinds of viral growth differently. Each of them will have different conversion rates, and users who come from each kind of growth will have different engagement levels. That'll tell you where to focus your efforts.

The metrics that matter in the virality phase are about outreach and new user adoption. While the most fundamental of these is the viral coefficient, you can also measure the volume of invites sent by a user, or the time it takes her to invite someone.

For companies selling to an enterprise market, where click-to-invite virality isn't the norm, there are other metrics that might work better. One is the *net promoter score*, which simply asks how likely a user is to tell his friends about your product and compares the number of strong advocates to those who are unwilling to recommend it.* It's a good proxy for virality, because

---

* The NPS, first championed by Enterprise Rent-A-Car and written about by Frederick F. Reichfeld, considered only strongly enthusiastic respondents because those are the "customers who not only return to rent again but also recommend Enterprise to their friends"; see *http://hbr.org/2003/12/the-one-number-you-need-to-grow/ar/1*.

it suggests customers who will act as references, refer you business, or be quoted in marketing collateral.

Virality doesn't play a key role in every business. Some products are just not naturally viral, and hardly any are wildly so. Much has been made of getting a viral coefficient above 1—in other words, getting every user to invite at least one other user. This means, in theory, you can grow forever.

Unfortunately, a sustained viral coefficient above 1 is a Holy Grail for startups.

That doesn't mean you should ignore virality; rather, it means you need to treat it as a force multiplier that will make your paid marketing initiatives more successful. That's why the Virality stage comes before the Revenue and Scale stages: you want to get the biggest bang for your marketing buck, and to do so, you need to optimize your viral engines first.

| CASE STUDY | **Timehop Experiments with Content Sharing to Achieve Virality** |

Jonathan Wegener and Benny Wong started Timehop in February 2011 as a hackathon project. The original product—built in a single day and called 4SquareAnd7YearsAgo—aggregated your Foursquare check-ins and sent them to you in a daily email from one year ago. It was a fun way of looking back at where you had been each day last year. The project got a lot of attention, and after a few months of watching organic growth, the founders decided to focus on it full-time. They rebranded as Timehop and raised $1.1 million in financing from venture and angel investors.

The founders spent most of their time at the beginning focusing on engagement. Luckily for them, people were hooked on the product, and it showed in the core metrics. "We consistently saw 40–50% open rates on our emails, and still do," says Jonathan. "So we knew we had a sticky, engaging product that people cared about."

Proving that Timehop was an engaging product was essential, but so was proving that engagement led to retention. "People have been on Timehop for close to two years without ever getting bored and leaving," says Jonathan. "Originally we tracked open rates, unsubscribes, and content density [how many users get emails each day because they did something a year ago] religiously, but all of that's in very good shape." It was time to change their One Metric That Matters.

That engagement and retention gave the founders the confidence they needed to tackle the next big challenge: growth. "We saw through pixel tracking in emails that 50% of emails were being opened on iOS devices," says Jonathan. "That led us to focus on a mobile app, which is also a better tool for encouraging growth through sharing."

While people do share Timehop emails, email itself is not truly social. People *received* emails, but they didn't share them. Since Timehop wants to build what Jonathan describes as a "social network for your past," the move to mobile helps to encourage social behaviors. In fact, mobile users share 20 times more than email-only users. But it still wasn't enough.

"All of our focus right now is on sharing," says Jonathan. "The metric we're watching is percent of daily active users that share something. We don't focus on the viral coefficient right now—we know it's below 1— and we want to track numbers that are closer to what people are doing in our app." The company is now experimenting and testing rapidly to see if it can significantly improve this number. It builds fast and focuses on learning and tracking results. And it has a line in the sand: "We'd like to have at least 20–30% of our daily active users share something on a daily basis," Jonathan says.

Timehop cares only about growth through virality (and using sharing of content as the primary mechanism for encouraging that virality). "All that matters now is virality," says Jonathan. "Everything else—be it press, publicity stunts, or something else—is like pushing a rock up a mountain: it will never scale. But being viral will."

Summary

- Timehop's founders turned a one-day hackathon project into a real company when they saw consistent, organic growth and significant engagement.

- After seeing that 50% of users opened up daily Timehop emails on an iOS device, the founders built a mobile application. They also changed their OMTM from engagement and retention to virality.

- The founders are focused almost exclusively on content sharing, and increasing the percentage of daily active users who share content, in an effort to create sustainable growth in their user base.

Analytics Lessons Learned

Understanding how people use your product can provide key insight into what direction to go and how to move from one stage to the next—for example, from stickiness to virality. Focusing on a metric like viral coefficient may be too high level; instead, look for the actions within your product that drive virality and make sure you're measuring those properly and have lines in the sand that you're targeting.

Instrumenting the Viral Pattern

Hiten Shah's ProductPlanner site was a tremendously valuable source of acquisition patterns.[*] From enrollment processes to viral email loops to friend invitations, the site catalogued dozens of customer acquisition workflows and would suggest metrics for each stage of the process. For example, Figure 17-2 shows the email invite loop for Tagged.

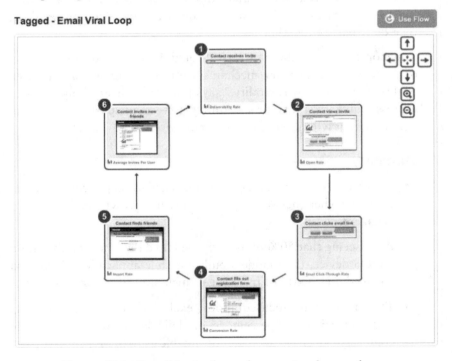

Figure 17-2. Email invite loops have a simple set of steps and metrics to track

---

* *ProductPlanner was recently taken down. It used to live at* http://productplanner.com.

While ProductPlanner is no longer available—its founders are focusing on KISSmetrics instead—you can design patterns of your own using this model, then quickly see what metrics you should be tracking within a process. Then you can instrument the viral loop you've built, see where it's collapsing, and tweak it, edging your way toward that elusive coefficient of 1.

Growth Hacking

Most startups won't survive on gradual growth alone. It's just too slow. If you want to grow, you need an unfair advantage. You need to tweak the future. You need a hack.

Growth hacking is an increasingly popular term for data-driven guerilla marketing. It relies on a deep understanding of how parts of the business are related, and how tweaks to one aspect of a customer's experience impact others. It involves:

- Finding a metric you can measure early in a user's lifecycle (e.g., number of friends a user invites) through experimentation , or, if you have the data, an analysis of what good users have in common

- Understanding how that metric is correlated to a critical business goal (e.g., long-term engagement)

- Building predictions of that goal (e.g., how many engaged users you'll have in 90 days) based on where the early metric is today

- Modifying the user experience today in order to improve the business goal tomorrow (e.g., suggesting people a user might know), assuming today's metric is *causing* a change in tomorrow's goal

The key to the growth hacking process is the early metric, (which is also known as a *leading indicator*—something you know today that predicts tomorrow). While this seems relatively straightforward, finding a good leading indicator, and experimenting to determine how it affects the future of the company, is hard work. It's also how many of today's break-out entrepreneurs drove their growth.

Attacking the Leading Indicator

Academia.edu founder Richard Price shared stories* from a recent Growth Hacking conference† at which several veterans of successful startups shared their leading indicators.

- Former Facebook growth-team leader Chamath Palihapitiya said a user would become "engaged" later if he reached seven friends within 10 days of creating an account. Josh Elman, who worked at Twitter, said the company had a similar metric: when a new user follows a minimum number of people—and some of those follow back—the user is likely to become engaged. In fact, Twitter has two kinds of users: "active" ones who've visited at least once in the last month, and "core" ones who've visited seven times in the last month.

- Onetime Zynga GM Nabeel Hyatt, who ran a 40-million-player game, said the company looked at first-day retention: if someone came back the day after she signed up for a game, she was likely to become an engaged user (and even one who paid for in-game purchases). Hyatt also underscored the importance of identifying One Metric That Matters, then optimizing it before moving on to the next one.

- Dropbox's ChenLi Wang said the chances that someone becomes an engaged user increase significantly when he puts at least one file in one folder on one of his devices.

- LinkedIn's Elliot Schmukler said the company tracks how many connections a user establishes in a certain number of days in order to estimate longer-term engagement.

User growth isn't everything, however. You may be trying to hack other critical goals like revenue. Josh Elman told us that early on Twitter focused its energy on increasing feed views because it knew its revenue would be tied to advertising—and that advertising could happen only when a user looked at her Twitter feed. Number of feed views was a leading indicator of revenue potential even before the company hit the Revenue stage.

What Makes a Good Leading Indicator?

Good leading indicators have a few common characteristics:

---

* *http://www.richardprice.io/post/34652740246/growth-hacking-leading-indicators-of-engaged-users*

† *http://growthhackersconference.com/*

- Leading indicators tend to relate to social engagement (links to friends), content creation (posts, shares, likes), or return frequency (days since last visit, time on site, pages per visit).

- The leading indicator should be clearly tied to a part of the business model (such as users, daily traffic, viral spread, or revenue). After all, it's the business model that you're trying to improve. You're not just trying to increase number of friends per user—you're trying to increase the number of loyal users.

- The indicator should come early in the *user's* lifecycle or conversion funnel. This is a simple numbers game: if you look at something that happens on a user's first day, you'll have data points for every user, butif you wait for users to visit several times, you'll have fewer data points (since many of those users will have churned out already), which means the indicator will be less accurate.

- It should also be an early extrapolation so you get a prediction sooner. Recall from Chapter 8 that Kevin Hillstrom says the best way to understand whether an e-commerce company is a "loyalty" or an "acquisition"-focused organization is to look at how many second purchases happen in the first 90 days. Rather than wait a year to understand what mode you're in, look at the first three months and extrapolate.

You find leading indicators by segmentation and cohort analysis. Looking at one group of users who stuck around and another group who didn't, you might see something they all have in common.

Correlation Predicts Tomorrow

If you've found a leading indicator that's correlated with something, you can predict the future. That's good. In the case of Solare, the Italian restaurant we described in Chapter 6, the number of reservations at 5 p.m. is a leading indicator of the total number of customers who dine on any given night—letting the team make last-minute staffing adjustments or buy additional food.

UGC site reddit has been fairly public about its traffic and user engagement—after all, it derives revenue from advertising, and wants to convince advertisers it's a good bet.[*] About half of all *visits* to the site are logged-in users, but these users generate a disproportionate amount of site traffic. Reddit's engagement is good. "Almost everyone who makes an

---

* *http://www.reddit.com/about*

account comes back a month later," says Jeremy Edberg. "It's a couple of months before people stop coming back."

Is there a leading indicator in reddit's site traffic? Table 17-2 compares logged-in users (those with accounts) to anonymous visitors by the number of pages they view in a visit.

	Logged-in users			All users		
Days since last visit	Visits	Page views	Pages per visit	Visits	Page views	Pages per visit
0	127,797,781	1.925B	15.06	242,650,914	3.478B	14.33
1	5,816,594	87,339,766	15.02	13,021,131	187,992,129	14.44
2	1,997,585	27,970,618	14.00	4,958,931	69,268,831	13.97
3	955,029	13,257,404	13.88	2,620,037	34,047,741	13.00
4	625,976	8,905,483	14.23	1,675,476	20,644,331	12.32
5	355,643	4,256,639	11.97	1,206,731	14,162,572	11.74

Table 17-2. Reddit's page views for logged-in versus non-logged-in users

This data suggests that loyal, enrolled users—those who return each day to the site and have an account—view a higher number of pages per visit. Is that high number of page views by a first-time visitor a leading indicator of enrollment?

Causality Hacks the Future

Correlation is nice. But if you've found a leading indicator that *causes* a change later on, that's a superpower, because it means you can change the future. If a high number of page views on a first visit to reddit *causes* enrollment, what could reddit do to increase the number of page views, and therefore increase enrollment? This is how growth hackers think.

Recall from Chapter 2 what Circle of Friends founder Mike Greenfield did when he compared engaged to not-engaged users—and found out that many of the engaged users were moms. Whether or not someone was a mother was, for Mike, a market-focused leading indicator of that person's future engagement. He could decide how many servers to buy in six months' time based on how many moms signed up today. But what really mattered was this: he could target moms in his marketing, and change the engagement of his users dramatically.

Mike's hack was market-related, but growth hacks come in all shapes and sizes. Maybe it's a change in pricing, or a time-limited offer, or a form of personalization. The point is to experiment in a disciplined manner.

Product-focused growth hacks—what Chamath Palihapitiya calls "aha moments"—need to happen early in the user's lifecycle in order to have an impact on the greatest number of possible users. That's why social sites suggest friends for you almost immediately.

You can use promotions and experiments to try to identify a leading indicator, too. Music retailer Beatport ran a Cyber Monday promotion to maximize total purchases. A week before the holiday, it sent all its customers a 10% discount code. Those customers who purchased something with the code were then sent a second, personalized code for 20% off. If they used that code, they were sent a final, one-time-only, time-limited code for Cyber Monday that gave them 50% off their purchase. This approach increased purchase frequency, and encouraged customers to max out their shopping cart each time.

While we don't have data on the effectiveness of the campaign itself, it's clear that the company now has a wealth of information on who will respond best to a promotion and how discounts relate to purchase volume—and it's made its loyal customers feel loved as well.

Growth hacking combines many of the disciplines we've looked at in the book: finding a business model, identifying the most important metric for your current stage, and constantly learning and optimizing that metric to create a better future for your organization.

A Summary of the Virality Stage

- Virality refers to the spread of a message from existing, "infected" users to new users.

- If every user successfully invites more than one other user, your growth is almost assured. While this is seldom the case, any word of mouth adds to customer growth and reduces your overall customer acquisition costs.

- Inherent virality happens naturally as users interact with your product. Artificial virality is incentivized and less genuine. And word of mouth, while hard to create and track, drives a lot of early adoption. You need to segment users who come from all three kinds of virality.

- In addition to viral coefficient, you care about viral cycle time. The sooner each user invites another one, the faster you'll grow.

- As you grow in the Virality and Revenue stages, you're trying to find leading indicators of future growth: metrics that can be measured early in a user's lifecycle that predict—or, better yet, control—what the future will be.

When you're growing organically from referrals and invitations, you'll get the most out of every dollar you spend acquiring customers. It's time to focus on maximizing revenue, and pouring some of that money back into additional acquisition. It's time for the Revenue stage.

EXERCISE | Should You Move On to the Revenue Stage?

Ask yourself these questions:

- Are you using any of the three types of virality (inherent, artificial, word of mouth) for your startup? Describe how. If virality is a weak aspect of your startup, write down three to five ideas for how you could build more virality into your product.

- What's your viral coefficient? Even if it's below 1 (which it likely is), do you feel like the virality that exists is good enough to help sustain growth and lower customer acquisition costs?

- What's your viral cycle time? How could you speed it up?

What are the segments or cohorts of users who do what your business model wants them to do? What do they have in common? What can you change about your product, market, pricing, or another aspect of your business to address this as early as possible in their customer lifecycle?

CHAPTER 18

Stage Four: Revenue

At some point, you have to make money. As you move beyond stickiness and virality, your metrics change. You'll track new data and find a new OMTM as you funnel some of the money you collect back into acquiring new users. Customer lifetime value and customer acquisition cost drive your growth, and you'll run experiments to try to capture more loyal users for less, tweaking how you charge, when you charge, and what you charge for. Welcome to the Revenue stage of Lean Analytics.

The goal in the Revenue stage is to turn your focus from *proving your idea is right* to *proving you can make money* in a scalable, consistent, self-sustaining way. Think of this as the piñata phase, where you beat on your business model in different ways until candy pours out.

Some startup advocates recommend charging for the product at the outset. This depends on several factors, from churn to cost of acquisition to the kind of application you're building. But there's a difference between *charging up front* and *focusing on revenue and margins*. In the earlier stages, it's OK to run the business at a loss, or to give away accounts, or to issue refunds, or to let highly paid developers field support calls. Now, that has to change. Now, you're not just building a product—you're building a business.

Metrics for the Revenue Stage

Measuring revenue is easy enough, but remember that while raw revenue might be going "up and to the right," revenue per customer is a better indicator of actual health. It's a ratio, after all, and there's a lot more you can learn from it. For example, if revenue is going up but revenue per customer is going down, it tells you that you're going to need a lot more customers to continue growing at the same pace. Is that doable? Does that make sense? The ratio helps you focus on making real decisions for your startup.

As a result, you'll be looking at click-through rates and ad revenue, or conversion rate and shopping cart size, or subscriptions and customer lifetime value—or whatever brings in money. You'll be comparing this to the cost of acquiring new users faster than they churn—because the net addition of visitors, users, and customers you can monetize is your growth rate.

You'll also work hard at getting pricing right, balancing the highest price with the most paying customers. And you'll be experimenting with bundles, subscription tiers, discounts, and other mechanisms to determine the best price.

The Penny Machine

An entrepreneur walks into a maple-paneled boardroom just off the 280, glances around the table at the well-groomed investors gathered there, and reaches into a large leather bag. She pulls out a strange machine, roughly two feet high by one foot wide, sets it carefully on the table, and plugs it in.

The room is expectantly quiet.

"Does anyone have a penny on them?" she asks. The general partner raises an eyebrow as one of the junior staff members hands over a faded copper piece.

"Now watch."

The entrepreneur inserts the coin into the top of the machine and pulls a small lever. There is a low-pitched whirring, followed by a pause, and then a shiny new nickel tumbles into the small shelf at the bottom of the machine.

The only sound in the room is the ventilation system, cooling the warm Palo Alto air.

"That's a neat trick," says the silver-haired general partner, straightening up in his seat and grinding his brown Mephistos into the hypoallergenic rug beneath him. "Do it again."

The staffer hands her another coin. She slides the second penny into the top of the machine, and again pulls the lever. Out slides another nickel.

"You've got a bag of nickels in there," accuses a slightly disheveled technical analyst, somewhat defensively. "Open it up."

Wordlessly, the entrepreneur releases a small clasp on the side of the machine and swings it open. Within are a series of tubes and wires, but nowhere is big enough to conceal nickels. The analyst looks mildly offended, but the general partner is on the edge of his seat as she closes the machine back up.

"How many pennies can I put in there per hour?" he asks.

"It takes five seconds to cool down, so you can insert 720 pennies an hour. That's $36 in nickels for a profit of $28.80 an hour, with a margin of 80%."

The general partner leans back in his Aeron chair and gazes out across the highway, into the Woodside hills. He pauses for a minute. "Can I put nickels into it?" he inquires.

"I've tried it with dimes. It works. Produces neatly folded dollar bills. I haven't tried anything more than that yet, but I'm hoping it will handle fives," replies the entrepreneur.

"How many can you make and run at once?" asks the partner, oblivious to the rest of the room.

"I think we can have 500 machines running around the clock. They cost $30,000 apiece and take two months to make."

"One more question," says the partner, "and I think we have a deal. Why can't someone else build one?"

"I have intellectual property protection on the core mechanism, and I've signed an exclusive agreement with the US Mint to be the only producer of legal currency."

Of course, this isn't a real venture capital pitch. But it's as close to perfect as one can get. We can learn a lot from the penny machine, and it's a great metaphor to get startup CEOs thinking like investors.

The penny machine has an obvious money-making ability: you put in money, and more comes out. People understand what a penny is. While no business is as clear-cut as the penny machine, every CEO needs to make his business model as straightforward as possible, particularly to outsiders, so it's painfully obvious why the venture will yield revenues.

The entrepreneur had reasonable answers to key questions: how big can the business grow, how good can the margins get, and what kinds of barriers to entry does it have?

The presenter engaged the audience, and let them help her tell the story. They were smart people who asked the questions she wanted, and she showed them that she'd anticipated their questions by providing slightly more detail than they asked for without going into too much depth.

There was no need for a detailed technical explanation at this stage. Later, the investors would certainly go over the technology carefully to ensure that it wasn't illegal, immoral, or outright trickery. But this meeting wasn't about that. Opening the machine up served as a simple proof that everyone in the room understood well enough.

The entrepreneur didn't set a valuation. She gave the investors all the details they needed to form one of their own, based on revenue potential, margin, costs, and so on. They could also calculate the working capital needed to fund the creation of the machines, based on cost and time, as well as return on investment.

Startup CEOs seeking venture capital would do well to remember the penny machine. It's a good way to ensure you're thinking like a venture capitalist. Every time your pitch strays from the simplicity of this meeting, it's a warning sign that you need to go back and tighten it up.

Penny Machines and Magic Numbers

This isn't just an entertaining metaphor for entrepreneurs preparing to pitch. Think of your company as a machine that predictably generates more money than you put into it. Measuring the ratio of inputs to outputs tells you whether you have a good machine or a broken one.

In 2008, Ominture's Josh James suggested one way to understand how a SaaS company is doing, and to decide whether it's time to step on the gas or to reconsider the business model.[*] It's pretty simple, really: look at the return on investment of your marketing dollar. In a SaaS company, you spend money on sales and marketing in the hopes that you'll sign up new customers. If all goes well, the following quarter your revenues will have increased.

To measure the health of the machine, divide how much you changed the annual recurring revenue in the past quarter by what it cost you to do so. You need three numbers to do this calculation:

- Your quarterly recurring revenue for quarter x ($QRR[x]$)
- Your quarterly recurring revenue for the quarter before x ($QRR[x-1]$)
- Your sales and marketing expense for the quarter before x ($QExpSM[x-1]$)

If you don't have quarterly sales and marketing spending, you can take the annual spending and divide it by four. This also helps smooth out spikes

---

[*]   *http://larsleckie.blogspot.ca/2008/03/magic-number-for-saas-companies.html*

in marketing spend or seasonal shifts, since not all the sales you get this quarter are a result of last quarter's sales efforts—some may have benefitted from previous quarters.

The formula looks like this:

$$\frac{(QRR[x]-QRR[x-1])}{QExpSM[x-1]}$$

If the result is below 0.75, you have a problem. When you pump money into the machine, less money comes out. That's a bad thing for this stage of your business, because it means there's a fundamental flaw in your business model. If the result is better than 1, you're doing well—you can fund your growth with the proceeds, funneling revenue increases back into the machine to increase sales and marketing spend.

Finding Your Revenue Groove

At this stage in your startup, you've got a product that users like and tell other users about. You're trying to figure out the best way to monetize the product. Recall Sergio Zyman's definition of marketing (*more stuff to more people for more money more often more efficiently*) using. In the Revenue stage, you need to figure out which "more" increases your revenues per engaged customer the most:

- If you're dependent on physical, per-transaction costs (like direct sales, shipping products to a buyer, or signing up merchants), then *more efficiently* will figure prominently on either the supply or demand side of your business model.

- If you've found a high viral coefficient, then *more people* makes sense, because you've got a strong force multiplier added to every dollar you pour into customer acquisition.

- If you've got a loyal, returning set of customers who buy from you every time, then *more often* makes sense, and you're going to emphasize getting them to come back more frequently.

- If you've got a one-time, big-ticket transaction, then *more money* will help a lot, because you've got only one chance to extract revenue from the customer and need to leave as little money as possible on the table.

- If you're a subscription model, and you're fighting churn, then upselling customers to higher-capacity packages with broader features is your best way of growing existing revenues, so you'll spend a lot of time on *more stuff*.

Where Does the Money Come From?

For many services that charge a recurring fee, you need to decide if you're charging everyone, or just premium users. A freemium model may work, but it's not always a good thing—particularly if free users cost you money, and if you can't naturally distinguish the paid version of your service with tiers that a regular user will naturally encounter, such as number of projects or gigabytes of storage.

One variant on freemium is pay-for-privacy, where the content your users create is available to everyone unless they explicitly pay to keep it to themselves. SlideShare uses a variant of this. While the site does make money from advertising, it also charges users for a premium model where the content they upload isn't available to everyone. Now that they're part of LinkedIn, they're also subsidized by that company's business model.

If your users all pay, then you need to decide if you'll have trial periods, discounts, or other incentives. Ultimately, the best revenue strategy is to make a great product: the best startups have what Steve Jobs referred to as the "insanely great," with customers eager to give them money for what they see as true value.

If none of your users pay, then you're relying on advertising, or other behind-the-scenes subsidies, to pay the bills.

Many startups blend several of the six business models we've seen to form their own unique revenue model. They then find ways to pour that revenue into their own mix of virality and customer acquisition, investing some amount of their income into growth.

Customer Lifetime Value > Customer Acquisition Cost

When it comes to turning revenues into additional customers, the most basic rule is simple: spend less money acquiring customers than you get from them.

That's hugely oversimplified, because you really want to spend only a fraction of your revenue on acquisition if you're going to keep the lights on, hire in anticipation of growth, spend money on research, and generate a return on investment.

The CLV-CAC math also needs to reflect the fact that there's a delay between paying to acquire customers and those customers paying you back. Any investment or loans you take aren't just paying for you to get to breakeven, they're also paying for the anticipated revenue from customers.

Balancing acquisition, revenue, and cash flow is at the core of running many business models, particularly those that rely on subscription revenue and paying to gain customers. As you play with the numbers to strike that balance, there are really four variables you work on:

- The money in the bank at the outset (i.e., your investment)
- The amount of money spent on customer acquisition each month
- The revenue you bring in from users
- The rate of churn from users

Get the math right. Take too much, and you dilute your ownership; take too little, and you run out of cash simply because your users pay you over time but you have to acquire them up front.

CASE STUDY | Parse.ly and the Pivot to Revenue

Parse.ly makes an analytics tool that helps the Web's big publishers understand what content is driving traffic. It was first launched in 2009 out of Philadelphia's Dreamit Ventures as a reader tool for consumers to find stories they'd like. A year later, the company changed its approach: since it knew what a reader might like to read next, it could help publishers suggest content that would keep readers on the site for longer. And in 2011, it changed again, this time offering reporting tools to publishers who wanted to know what was working. The current product, Parse.ly Dash, is an analytics tool for publishers.[*]

While Dash is a successful product today, the company had to abandon its earlier work in its search for a sustainable business model. "It was very hard for us to shift away from our consumer newsreader product. That's because all the metrics were actually quite positive," says Mike Sukmanowsky, Parse.ly's Product Lead.

"We had thousands of users and the product was growing rapidly. We were written up in top technology press like TechCrunch, ReadWriteWeb, and ZDNet. The product worked and we had a million ideas for how to improve it even further. However, it was lacking one critical metric for any growing business—revenue. We ran tests and surveys, and learned that though our users loved Parse.ly Reader, they didn't love it so much that they'd be willing to pay for it."

The founders had plenty of code, but no revenue, and costs were growing. Mike attributes part of this to the focus that startup accelerators have

---

[*] The Parse.ly team has written a detailed explanation of these changes at *http://blog.parse.ly/post/16388310218/hello-publishers-meet-dash*.

on rapid prototyping, often at the expense of customer development. "One of the challenges of an accelerator is that they are so product-focused (ship it quick) and pressure-oriented (two months to demo) that a lot of our customer development had to happen parallel to product development. And, in fact, some of the biggest questions were answered after shipping our first version."*

Once the company had decided to change business models, it stopped development on the reader entirely. While the new offering was built from scratch, it leveraged much of the technology and many of the architectural lessons learned from the first product. Now a direct sales team sells its current offering, using a trial period for evaluation, and then charging a monthly fee.

As you might expect from an analytics firm, the Parse.ly team collects and analyzes a lot of data. In addition to using Dash themselves, they rely on Woopra for engagement and to arm their sales team, Graphite for tracking time-series data, and Pingdom for uptime and availability.

As the company iterated through various business models, the metrics it tracked changed accordingly.

"For Parse.ly Reader, our core metrics were new signups and user engagement. We would pay close attention to how many signups per day we were getting based on our press write-ups and how many logins per day we were getting from user accounts," says Mike. "In the Parse.ly Publisher Platform, we focused entirely on number of recommendation impressions served, and click-through rate of our recommendations. We still pay close attention to these metrics for users of our API."

For the current reporting product, the company tracks a broader set of metrics, including:

- New signups per day for trial accounts
- Conversion rate on the signup flow and account activation process
- Number of active users (seats) per account and account invitation activity
- User engagement (based on Woopra data)
- API calls in Graphite

---

* Mike is quick to point out that this is changing, with an increased emphasis on revenue generation. See *http://go.bloomberg.com/tech-deals/2012-08-22-y-combinators-young-startups-tout-revenue-over-users/*

- Website activity in Google Analytics
- Tracked page views and unique visitors across all the sites running within the network of monitored sites

Since its software is installed on a number of sites, it also tracks data for those sites, including the average number of posts published, average page views, and top referrers. And it tracks fundamental business metrics—head count, customer count, server count, revenue, costs, and profit.

In the end, *Parse.ly* had to make some painful decisions despite the apparent success of a consumer business. It didn't test the monetization of its initial product, even though that was one of the riskiest aspects. But when, before its second pivot, it spent time talking to its enterprise customers about the dashboard, the answer was clear: "We'd show them proof of concepts of the analytics tool we could deliver to them, and they began to clamor for the insights we were proposing," recalls Mike. "They cared more about the prospect of this tool than the recommendations we were providing."

Summary

- Even if you have healthy growth in an important dimension (like user count or engagement), it's not worth much if you can't convert it to money and pay the bills.
- Pivoting the business changed the OMTM immediately.
- Every company lives in an ecosystem—in this case, of readers, publishers, and advertisers. It's often easier to pivot to a new market than to create an entirely new product, and, once you've done so, for the market to help you realize what product you should have made in the first place.

Analytics Lessons Learned

Recognize that being able to make money is an inherent assumption of most business models, but that to de-risk the model you need to test it early. Be prepared to radically change, or even shut down, parts of your company in your quest for revenue.

Market/Product Fit

Most people's first instinct when things aren't going incredibly well is to build more features. Hopefully we've demonstrated that this isn't the right approach, because the likelihood that any one feature is going to suddenly solve your customers' problems is very small.

Instead, try pivoting into a new market. The assumption here is that the product isn't the problem, it's the target customer. In a perfect world, you've validated the market before building anything, but mistakes happen, and in some cases you're not starting at step one of the customer development process and don't want to throw away everything you've built. It may be easier to change markets than products.

Many startup founders discover Lean Startup at a specific point in their growth: they've built a product and it has a bit of traction, but not enough to be exciting. They're facing a difficult decision. Should they continue on the current path or change something? They're looking for answers. They're searching for ways to build more traction and they're not ready to give up. This is common for bigger companies and intrapreneurs as well: they have something in the market, but it's not at the scale they want and they're looking for ways to increase growth rate or market share.

Instead of building new features or rebuilding from scratch, try pointing your product at a new market. We think of this as *market/product fit* instead of *product/market fit*, because you're trying to find a market that fits your existing product. This also applies to changing your business model, which is a completely reasonable approach to finding scale. Again, it's market/product fit because you're changing a market variable (the business model) and keeping the product static (or relatively so).

Here are some suggestions for taking an existing product and finding a new market.

Review Your Old Assumptions

Look back at the old assumptions you had about the markets you were going after with the product. If you didn't have any assumptions around why a particular market would work, now is the time to do a postmortem on that and use the benefit of hindsight. Why didn't it work? What's holding back traction in the market? Are the pain points you're solving genuinely painful enough to the markets you were going after?

Now look at markets related to those you tackled previously. What do you know about these markets? What makes these markets similar or different from the ones you went after?

Going out and doing problem interviews in new markets will help you figure out if your product is going to solve painful enough problems. You should be able to compare what you hear from new markets with the hindsight analysis you have of your existing customer base.

Begin a Process of Elimination

You'll be able to drop some markets and/or business models pretty quickly. For example, a freemium model requires a huge base of prospective customers. Lincoln Murphy does a great job of laying out the math on addressable market size in a presentation entitled *The Reality of Freemium in SaaS.*[*] One of his big conclusions: without a huge potential market and a number of other factors, freemium just doesn't work.

Understanding the mechanics of various markets and business models helps you triangulate the combinations that work best.

Deep Dive

When you've identified potential new markets and a prospective business model, it's time to do a deep dive and get into the full swing of customer development. Speak with 10–15 prospects in each market to validate your assumptions around their problems. This may feel like a slow process—after all, you have a product ready to sell—but the effort will be worthwhile, because you'll avoid going into markets that aren't a good fit.

In parallel, you can also take a broader approach and look to reach customers at scale, using landing pages and advertising to gauge interest. But don't skip steps and ignore the problem interviews completely.

Find Similarities

When looking at a market at this stage, you need to narrow it down and go niche. Using "size of company" as your metric for market definition isn't good enough. We see this all the time, but SMBs (small and medium businesses) are not a market; the category's just too broad.

Look for important similarities between companies inside of a broadly defined market. Industry is a good place to start. But also consider geography, how they purchase products, what they've recently purchased, budgets, industry growth, seasonality, legislative constraints, and decision makers. All of these factors help define a true market you can go after quickly.

---

*   http://www.slideshare.net/sixteenventures/the-reality-of-freemium-in-saas

Pitch the product you have, but don't feel obligated to pitch it exactly as it works today. Simultaneous with your efforts to find the right market and business model, you need to envision how the product will change and be repackaged. This isn't a complete rebuild that will take huge amounts of effort, but there's no reason you can't pitch a modified version of your existing product based on what you've learned about your new target market.

Essentially, your existing product is the MVP, and hopefully it suffices as the MVP and doesn't require major change. A few nips and tucks are all that's needed—and suddenly customers are thrilled with the speed with which you've delivered the product.

Finding a new market for an existing product is difficult. And the reality is that there may not be a market for the product you have, and you'll be moving into a much more substantial pivot or a complete redo. But before you get to that stage, stop, pull back, and look for a customer base that will pay you for what you already have. To succeed at this, you need to remain committed to the Lean Startup process and customer development, but you can start part-way through the process instead of going completely back to square one.

The Breakeven Lines in the Sand

Revenue is not the only financial metric that matters. You want to be *breakeven*—meaning your revenues exceed your costs on a regular basis. Driving toward profitability may not be the right thing to do—you may be focused on another metric, such as user acquisition. But it's irresponsible not to think about breakeven, because if there's no way you can ever get there, you're just burning money and time.

This means looking at business metrics such as operating costs, marginal costs, and so on. You may discover that it's a good idea to fire a segment of your customers because of the drain they represent on the business—this is particularly true in B2B startups. With that in mind, here are some possible "gates" you may want to use to decide if you're ready to move to the Scale stage.

Breakeven on Variable Costs

As a startup, you're probably spending more on growth than you're making on revenue, particularly if you've taken funding and aren't bootstrapping the business from your own resources. Your investors don't want to own part of a breakeven company—they want shares that pay back multiples on a lucrative acquisition or IPO.

If the money you make from a customer exceeds the cost of acquiring that customer and delivering the service, you're doing well. You may be pouring money into new features, recruiting, and so on—but each customer isn't costing you anything.

Time to Customer Breakeven

A key measurement of successful revenue growth is whether the customer lifetime value exceeds the customer acquisition cost. But this is useful for strategic budgeting, too. Imagine a company where customers spend $27 during their 11 months of activity, and it costs $14 to acquire them, as shown in Table 18-1.

$27	Customer lifetime value
11	Months from activation to departure
$2.45	Average revenue per customer per month
$14	Cost to acquire a customer
5.7	Months to customer breakeven

Table 18-1. Working out how long a customer takes to pay you back

If you're relying on this revenue to grow, you'll need some money. This is a good time to fire up a spreadsheet and start playing with numbers: you now know you need 5.7 months' burn to keep the company running.

EBITDA Breakeven

EBITDA—earnings before income tax, depreciation, and amortization—is an accounting term that fell out of favor when the dot-com bubble burst. Many companies used this model because it let them ignore their large capital investments and crushing debt. But in today's startup world, where up-front capital expenses have been replaced by pay-as-you-go costs like cloud computing, EBITDA is an acceptable way to consider how well you're doing.

Hibernation Breakeven

A particularly conservative breakeven metric is hibernation. If you reduced the company to its minimum—keeping the lights on, servicing existing customers, but doing little else—could you survive? This is often referred to as "ramen profitability." There's no new marketing spend. Your only growth would come from word of mouth or virality, and customers wouldn't get new features. But it's a breakeven point at which you're "master of your own destiny" because you can survive indefinitely. For some startups, particularly self-funded ones, this may be a good model to use because it gives you a much stronger negotiating position if you're seeking financing.

Revenue Stage Summary

- The core equation for the Revenue stage is the money a customer brings in minus the cost of acquiring that customer. This is the return on acquisition investment that drives your growth.

- You're moving from proving you have the right product to proving you have a real business. As a result, your metrics shift from usage patterns to business ratios.

- Think of a business as a machine that converts money into greater sums of money. The ratio of money in to money out, as well as the maximum amount of money you can put in, dictates the value of the business.

- You're trying to figure out where to focus: more revenue per customer, more customers, more efficiencies, greater frequency, and so on.

- If things aren't working, it may be easier to pivot your initial product to a new market rather than starting from scratch.

- While your goal is to grow, you should also keep an eye on breakeven, because once you can pay your own bills you can survive indefinitely.

Once revenues and margins are within the targets you've set out in your business model, it's time to grow as an organization. Much of what you've done by hand must now be done by other people: your employees, sales channels, and third parties. It's time for the Scale stage.

CHAPTER 19

Stage Five: Scale

You have a product that's sticky. You've got virality that's multiplying the effectiveness of your marketing efforts. And you have revenues coming in to fuel those user and customer acquisition efforts.

The final stage for startups is Scale, which represents not only a wider audience, but also entry into new markets, a modicum of predictability and sustainability, and deals with new partners. Your startup is becoming part of a broader ecosystem, in which you're a known and active participant. If the Revenue stage was about proving a business, the Scale stage is about proving a market.

The Hole in the Middle

Harvard professor Michael Porter describes a variety of generic strategies by which companies compete.[*] Firms can focus on a niche market (a segmentation strategy), they can focus on being efficient (a cost strategy), or they can try to be unique (a differentiation strategy). A local, gluten-free coffee shop focuses on a specific customer niche, Costco focuses on efficiency and low costs, and Apple focuses on branded design and uniqueness.[†] Some companies have different focuses for supply and demand—Amazon, for

---

[*]   http://en.wikipedia.org/wiki/Porter_generic_strategies

[†]   The best companies focus on both efficiency and differentiation, which is why Coca-Cola and Red Bull pay handsomely for brand advertising, why Costco has its own Kirkland line, and why Apple designs new manufacturing systems. But most companies emphasize one over the other.

example, is ruthlessly efficient on backend infrastructure from suppliers, and brand-heavy on differentiating for demand.

Porter observed that firms with a large market share (Apple, Costco, Amazon) were often profitable, but so were those with a small market share (the coffee shop). The problem was companies that were neither small nor large. He termed this the "hole in the middle" problem—the challenge facing firms that are too big to adopt a niche strategy efficiently, but too small to compete on cost or scale. They need to differentiate themselves to survive the midsize gap, and then achieve scale and efficiency.

This is why the Scale stage is so critical. It's the last test before you've identified and quantified all of the risks in your startup. It's where you find out what you'll be when you grow up.

Metrics for the Scale Stage

This stage is where you look beyond your own company. If you focus too early on competitors, you can be blinded by what they're doing, rather than learning what your customers actually need. But by now, you have enough of a groove to look outside. You'll find that it's a crowded world, where you're competing with everyone for attention.

We've known that getting enough of the right kind of attention was going to be a problem for three decades. In 1981, cognitive scientist and economist Herbert Simon observed that we live in an information age, and that information consumes attention—in other words, attention is a precious commodity, and its value grows as we're flooded with more and more information. In this stage, you're checking whether analysts, competitors, and distributors care about you as much as your core group of initial customers does. Getting attention at scale means your product or service can stand on its own, without your constant love and feeding.

In the Scale stage, you want to compare higher-order metrics like Backupify's OMTM—customer acquisition payback—across channels, regions, and marketing campaigns. For example: is a customer you acquire through channels less valuable than one you acquire yourself? Does it take longer to pay back direct sales or telemarketing? Are international revenues hampered by taxes? These are signs that you won't be able to scale independent of your own organizational growth.

Is My Business Model Right?

In the Scale stage, many of the metrics you've used to optimize a particular part of the business now become inputs into your accounting system. Data like sales, margins, and customer support costs now help you project cash flow and understand how much investment you'll need.

Lean tends not to touch on these things, but they're important for bigger, more established organizations that have found their product/market fit, and for intrapreneurs trying to convince more risk-averse stakeholders within their organization. Even though you may not be "Lean" in the strict sense of the word, you may still have to pivot in order to operate at scale.

Consider, for example, a product sold through direct sales. If you try to introduce the product to channels, those channels may not be equipped to sell and support the product. Your own support costs go up; returns or abandonment from channel-sold customers climbs. What should you do?

One approach is to change the market the channel serves. You could handle high-touch customers with consulting needs through direct sales, but offer a simplified version that's less customizable to the channel. Or you could try changing the markets at which your channel is aimed—focusing on government sales, or buyers in higher education, who are better able to serve themselves.

These might not seem like Lean pivots, but they're done with the same kind of discipline and experimentation that informed your earlier product and pricing decisions.

If you're in a good business, you'll soon have an ecosystem of competitors, channel partners, third-party developers, and more. To thrive, you need to claim your place in this market and establish the kinds of barriers to entry that maintain margins in the face of competition. At this point, you've moved beyond the Lean Startup model, but that doesn't mean you've stopped obsessing over iterative learning.

Scaling is good if it brings in incremental revenue, but you have to watch for a decrease in engagement, a gradual saturation of the initial market, or a rising cost of customer acquisition. Changes in churn, segmented by channels, show whether you're growing your most important asset—your customers—or hemorrhaging attention as you scale.

CASE STUDY | Buffer Goes from Stickiness to Scale (Through Revenue)

Buffer is a startup that was founded in 2010 by Tom Moor, Leo Widrich, and Joel Gascoigne. Joel kick-started Buffer because of a pain he was experiencing: the difficulty of posting great content he was finding regularly to Twitter. Solutions already existed for scheduling tweets, but nothing as simple and easy to use as what Joel was looking for, so he joined forces with Tom and Leo, and they built Buffer.

Unlike most companies in the social software space, they decided to charge customers right off the bat. Joel had two assumptions: that the problem was painful enough for people, and that they would pay. Taking a very Lean approach, the trio built and launched the app and had their first paying customers in seven weeks.*

For Buffer, their One Metric That Matters was revenue. As Joel says, "We were constrained by our situation: track record and location [being based in New Zealand] made it a challenge to seriously consider raising funding, and I had no funds to dip into and was working full-time for other clients. This meant the most important metric was revenue, since I needed to grow the revenue in my spare time to a position where I could quit my existing work."

Joel and his team decided to go with a freemium approach (which they still have today), so along with the all-important metric of revenue, they were looking at other metrics around signups, activation, and conversion. "Early on, the most important metrics were activation, retention, and revenue," says Joel. "I think good metrics here are the signs of a solid product. Revenue mattered the most because I was literally calculating how many users we'd need based on our conversion in order for me to quit my work. As soon as we hit that amount, we grew faster, and shortly after hitting 'ramen profitability' we jumped on a plane to San Francisco, went through the AngelPad incubator, and raised our seed round."

Joel shared some numbers with us:

- 20% of visitors create an account (acquisition).

- 64% of people who sign up become "active" (which the founders define as posting one status update using Buffer).

- 60% of people who sign up come back in the first month (engagement/stickiness).

- 20% of people who sign up come back (are still active) after six months (engagement/stickiness).

Their conversion is between 1.5% and 2.5% from free to paid. Joel uses cohort analysis to measure these results, and says that Buffer sees a similar result to what Evernote has, where over time more users

---

* *http://blog.bufferapp.com/idea-to-paying-customers-in-7-weeks-how-we-did-it*

convert into paying customers. "For example, for the cohort of users who signed up in February 2012, 1.3% upgraded in their first month using the product," says Joel. "After six months, 1.9% of the same cohort is paying customers."

Once these numbers became clear and consistent, and revenue got to the point where Buffer was profitable, Joel felt it was time to make the switch and focus on acquisition. This was a big shift from proving the product and its stickiness at a small scale to trying to grow at a much faster pace. "For starters, we realized that personally, it would be most satisfying if we could make Buffer a very widespread service with millions of users," says Joel. "Then we checked our churn, because we know that it's vital before focusing on acquisition." Joel's target was below 5%, and in fact Buffer's churn hovers around 2%, so, the team doesn't invest a lot of time trying to improve it, which gives them the comfort to focus on acquisition.

Buffer is also profitable, which gives them the flexibility to push acquisition, try new channels, and not burn cash or be forced to raise more capital. Before finally deciding to focus on acquisition, they did look at other metrics. Joel says, "We could probably double our conversion to paying customers if we worked hard on it, but that requires focus just like anything else. And that can come later, because what we want the most is to have a huge user base."

The company is now in growth mode, trying new channels and focusing on user acquisition—but it still keeps an eye on conversion and revenue. Joel points out, "We measure the funnel of our new channels to ensure that they still convert to paying customers."

Summary

- Buffer used revenue early on as a measure of stickiness; the founders' goal wasn't to generate tons of revenue and scale, but to generate enough to prove they had a legitimate, scalable business.

- Buffer runs ongoing cohort analysis to assess changes it's making in its product as well as in its marketing initiatives.

- When it proved its product was sticky, it moved its focus to acquisition and how to acquire more users at a low cost.

Analytics Lessons Learned

Reality counts. Your choice of when to focus on revenue may be dictated by realities of your industry or your economic climate. If you prove that early users will pay for the initial offering in sufficient numbers, you not only have clear proof that you've found a good market, but you also have much more freedom to grow and evolve on your own terms. Combine revenue and engagement, and you know if your product has enough long-term value to be scalable. When you get to that point, you can start to scale acquisition.

By now, you're a bigger organization. You're worrying about more people, doing more things, in more ways. It's easy to get distracted. So we'd like to propose a simple way of focusing on metrics that gives you the ability to change while avoiding the back-and-forth whipsawing that can come from management-by-opinion. We call it the *Three-Threes Model*. It's really the organizational implementation of the Problem-Solution Canvas we saw in Chapter 16.

PATTERN | The Three-Threes Model

At this stage, you probably have three tiers of management. There's the board and founders, focused on strategic issues and major shifts, meeting monthly or quarterly. There's the executive team, focused on tactics and oversight, meeting weekly. And there's the rank-and-file, focused on execution, and meeting daily.

Don't get us wrong: for many startups, the same people may be at all three of these meetings. It's just that you'll have very different mindsets as a board than you will as the person who's writing code, stuffing boxes, or negotiating a sale.

We've also found that it's hard to keep more than three things in your mind at once. But if you can limit what you're working on to just three big things, then everyone in the company knows what they're doing and why they're doing it.

Three Big Assumptions

In your current business model, you have some fundamental assumptions, such as "people will answer questions," or "organizers are frustrated with how to run conferences," or "we'll make money from parents." Some of these may be platform assumptions too: "Amazon Web Services are reliable enough for our users."

Each assumption has a metric associated with it, and a line in the sand. This is your big bet. These are the cells in your spreadsheet that you obsess over as a board. They're what you look at to see if you can make payroll, or how much investment you're going to need, or whether the marketing campaigns are bringing in more than they're costing, or whether your business model is hopelessly, fatally, doomed.

Assumptions like these shouldn't change more than once a month (unless you're in an accelerator program or have an artificial time constraint). They certainly shouldn't change that often when you're at the Scale stage; that kind of thrashing dulls momentum, like pumping the tiller on a sailboat. Changing fundamental assumptions around your business model may require board approval, and will likely alienate your customers and bewilder your employees unless properly communicated. The board and your advisors should be involved in the assumptions at the Scale stage.

These three assumptions should leap off the page of your Lean Canvas if you're doing it right. Of course, if you change business models entirely, you'll have another big three assumptions because you now have another canvas.

Each month, the three assumptions should be communicated to the entire organization. The executive team is responsible for validating or repudiating them at the next meeting.

Three Actions to Take

At the executive level, you need to define the tactics that will make the big assumptions happen. The whole company should know them, and it's the executive team's job to break each of them down into three actions that can happen this week.

For each board-level assumption, what three tactical actions are you taking to get those metrics to move in the right direction? These may be product enhancements or marketing strategies that you think will make the product better. They're your feature roadmap and your marketing campaign for the week. They'll change regularly. You need to survey, test, and prototype quickly to approve or kill things. It's like a scrum in Agile.

While there's a lot of latitude for executives to try to move the needle, they have to report back to the founders and board at the end of the month. This keeps them from straying too far from the prescribed business model—striking a balance between innovation and predictability that's needed for later-stage companies.

Three Experiments to Run

On a daily basis, the company is performing individual tasks to try to complete the tactical actions. Anyone in the company can run a test—from speaking with customers to tweaking features to running a survey to conducting a pricing experiment—provided it's documented beforehand and the results contribute to the week's actions. The test is the only indicator of what you're doing right or wrong. It's done daily, and it's like a sprint in Agile.

For each of those actions, what three tasks are you performing? What three experiments are you running? How will you choose the winner? This is execution, discussed with the action owner every day. Again, this means a wide range of flexibility at the ground level, while introducing a degree of structure.

Finding Discipline as You Scale

Discipline is key to success in a larger, later-stage startup, particularly in the furious heat of execution. You can't thrash wildly in search of inspiration—you have investors, employees, and expectations. But at the same time, you need the latitude that made you agile and adaptive in the first place.

Know, clearly, what assumptions underpin your fundamental business model. Then, with the approval of stakeholders, change one of them. Hand that change to the executive team: which features do you think will improve that basic assumption? Plan out your daily activities to test those features: have conversations with customers, run surveys, create a segment that tests the new code, try mockups. This combination of agility and methodical precision is what distinguishes great startups from stalled ones.

It's almost a cliché at some tech events to ask, "What's your latest pivot?" This is horrible. Plenty of disenchanted founders say, "I'm pivoting" when they should be saying, "I'm a confused idiot with ADHD!" *Avoid the "lazy pivot."* Without a plan, it's just flapping in the wind. Discipline makes everyone accountable to one another.

A Summary of the Scale Stage

- When you're scaling, you know your product and your market. Your metrics are now focused on the health of your ecosystem, and your ability to enter new markets.

- You'll look at compensation, API traffic, channel relationships, and competitors at this stage—whereas before, these were distractions.

- You need to understand if you're focused on efficiency or differentiation. Trying to do both as a way of scaling is difficult. If you're efficiency-focused, you're trying to reduce costs; if you're differentiation-focused, you're increasing margins.

- As you grow, you'll need to have more than one metric at a time. Set up a hierarchy of metrics that keeps the strategy, the tactics, and the implementation aligned with a consistent set of goals. We call this the *three threes*.

You never really leave the Scale stage, although as your organization becomes more and more like a "big company" you may find yourself having a hard time innovating. Congratulations—you're now an intrapreneur, fighting the status quo and trying to change things from within. As we'll see in Chapter 30, innovating from within has some unique challenges. But first, let's combine your business model and stage to find the metrics that matter to you right now.

CHAPTER 20

Model + Stage Drives the Metric You Track

The core idea behind Lean Analytics is this: by knowing the kind of business you are, and the stage you're at, you can track and optimize the One Metric That Matters to your startup right now. By repeating this process, you'll overcome many of the risks inherent in early-stage companies or projects, avoid premature growth, and build atop a solid foundation of true needs, well-defined solutions, and satisfied customers.

Figure 20-1 shows these Lean Analytics stages, along with the "gates" you need to clear to move to the next phase and some of the metrics that will indicate when you're ready to move forward.

Now that you know your business model and your current stage, you're in a good position to pick a few metrics that will help you make it to the next stage of growth. Table 20-1 gives you some examples of what things matter to a particular model as it grows.

Once you've identified the metrics you should worry about, your next question is clear: *what should I be trying for, and what's normal?*

We decided to find out.

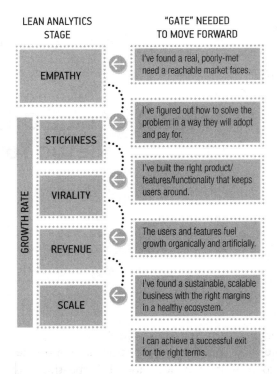

Figure 20-1. Where are you today? What will it take to move forward?

Business model						
Company stage	E-commerce	Two-sided marketplace	Software as a Service	Free mobile app	Media	User-generated content
The really big question	**Will they buy enough for enough money from you?**		**Will it solve a pain they'll pay for?**		**Will they engage with content in a repeatable manner?**	
Empathy stage: Problem validation: getting inside your market's head to discover real needs you can solve. *These tend to be qualitative discussions and open questions.*	How do buyers become aware of the need? How do they try to find a solution? What pain do they encounter as a result? What are their demographics and tech profiles?	Do buyers need a place to sell? Do sellers need a place to buy? How do they transact today? How do they find items? What prevents them from buying through those channels?	Do prospects have a known need they are pained to solve today? Can they do it with software? How do they learn about such solutions? What's the buying process?	What's your target market? What similar games and models have worked? Are there examples of similar pricing and gameplay habits?	Can you get enough attention around a subject? How do people consume information?	Does a community exist? What makes it special and unique? How do others join it? How fast is it growing?
Empathy stage: Solution validation. *This happens in both qualitative and quantitative approaches, and in some cases curated MVPs or regional tests.*	What competes with the product you're proposing? What's the price elasticity of the product or service?	Will buyers share sales revenue, or go outside the market? What added-value features entitle you to a portion of the proceeds? Will you be able to generate listings? Will they come to the marketplace?	Will the features you're offering fit their processes and solve a pain well enough for them to part with money and tell their friends?	Does the basic game structure function? Do users like a basic MVP of core gameplay, as shown by user testing?	Why will they consume your content? What tools, apps, and platforms deliver content to them today?	Will the community come to you? Where does it convene today? How does it like to interact? What are its privacy needs, and its tolerance for sharing and advertising?

Business model						
Company stage	E-commerce	Two-sided marketplace	Software as a Service	Free mobile app	Media	User-generated content
Will it grow?	Will they find you and tell others?		Will they sign up, stick around, and tell others?		Can you grow traffic to a level that can be profitably monetized?	
Stickiness stage: Achieving a minimum viable product that engages customers in a meaningful, valuable way.	Conversion, shopping cart size. For acquisition: cost of finding new buyers. For loyalty: percent of buyers who return in 90 days.	Rate of inventory creation, search type and frequency, price elasticity, listing quality, fraud rates.	Engagement, churn, visitor/user/customer funnel, capacity tiers, feature utilization (or neglect).	Onboarding; adoption; ease of play; time to "hooks"; day-, week-, and month-long churn; launches; abandonment; time played; regional testing.	Traffic, visits, returns; segmenting business metrics by topic, category, author; RSS, email, Twitter followers and click-throughs.	Content creation, engagement funnel, spam rates, content and word-of-mouth sharing, primary acquisition channels.
Virality stage: Growing adoption through inherent, artificial, and word-of-mouth virality; optimizing viral coefficient and cycle time.	Acquisition-mode: customer acquisition costs, volume of sharing. Loyalty model: ability to reactivate, volume of buyers who return.	Acquisition of sellers, acquisition of buyers, inherent and word-of-mouth sharing. Account creation and configuration.	Inherent virality, customer acquisition cost.	App store ratings, sharing, invites, rankings.	Content, virality, search engine marketing and optimization; promoting long time on page.	Content invites, user invites, in-site messaging, off-site sharing.

Business model						
Company stage	**E-commerce**	**Two-sided marketplace**	**Software as a Service**	**Free mobile app**	**Media**	**User-generated content**
Primary source of money	Transactions		Active users		Ad revenue	
Revenue stage: Convincing users to pay with optimal pricing, then pouring some of that money back into customer acquisition.	Transaction value, revenue per customer, ratio of acquisition cost to lifetime value, direct sales metrics.	Transactions, commissions, per-listing pricing, value-added services such as promotion, photography.	Upselling, customer acquisition cost, customer lifetime value, upselling path and roadmap.	Download volumes, average revenue per player, average revenue per *paying* player, acquisition costs.	Cost per engagement, affiliate revenues, click-through percentages, number of impressions.	Ads (same as media), donations, user data licensing.
Scale stage: Growing the organization through customer acquisition, channel relationships, finding efficiencies, and participating in a market ecosystem.	Affiliates, channels, white-label, product ratings, reviews, support costs, returns, RMAs and refunds, channel conflict.	Other verticals, related products; bundling third-party offers (e.g., car rental in a vacation rental site, shipping in a craft marketplace, etc.)	Application programming interface (API) traffic, Magic Number, app ecosystem, channels, resellers, support costs, compliance, on-premise/private versions.	Spinoffs, publisher and distribution deals, international versions.	Syndication, licenses, media and event partnerships.	Analytics, user data, private and third-party ad models, APIs.

Table 20-1. What metrics matters depending on your business model and stage

PART THREE:

LINES IN THE SAND

You know your model, your stage, and even what metric matters most to you right now. But what's normal? Unless you have a line in the sand, you don't know if you're crushing it or being crushed. We've collected data from startups, analysts, and vendors to try to paint a picture of what's typical. Your mileage will vary—but at least you'll know what mileage looks like.

Success is not final, failure is not fatal: it is the courage to continue that counts.

Sir Winston Churchill

CHAPTER 21

Am I Good Enough?

One of the biggest questions we wanted to tackle with *Lean Analytics* is "what's normal?" It's something we get asked all the time: "How do I know what's a normal or ideal value for the metrics I'm tracking? How do I know if it's going well or not? Should I keep optimizing this metric, or move on to something else?"

At the outset, many people cautioned us against trying to find a typical value for a particular metric. After all, startups are, by definition, trying to break the rules, which means the rules are being rewritten all the time. But we think it's important to try to define "normal" for two big reasons.

First, you need to know if you're in the ballpark. If your current behavior is outrageously far from that of everyone else, you should be aware of it. If, on the other hand, you're already as good as you're going to get—move on. You've already optimized a key metric, and you'll get diminishing returns trying to improve it further.

Second, you need to know what sport you're playing. Online metrics are in flux, which makes it hard to find a realistic baseline. Only a few years ago, for example, typical e-commerce conversion rates were in the 1–3% range. The best-in-class online retailers got a 7–15% conversion rate, because they had offline mindshare or had worked hard to become the "default" tool for purchase. These numbers have changed in recent years, though, because people now consider the Web the "default" storefront for many purchases. Today, pizza delivery companies have *extremely* high conversion rates because, well, that's how you buy pizza.

In other words: there is a normal or ideal for most metrics, and that normal will change significantly as a particular business model goes from being novel to being mainstream.

| CASE STUDY | # WP Engine Discovers the 2% Cancellation Rate |

WP Engine is a fast-growing hosting company specializing exclusively in hosting WordPress sites.* Successful entrepreneur and popular blogger Jason Cohen founded the company in July 2010. In November 2011, WP Engine raised $1.2M in financing to accelerate growth and handle the ongoing challenges of scaling the business.

WP Engine is a service company. Its customers rely on WP Engine to provide fast, quality hosting with constant uptime. WP Engine is doing a great job, but customers still cancel. All companies have cancellations (or churn), and it's one of the most critical metrics to track and understand—not only is it essential for calculating metrics like customer lifetime value, but it's also an early warning signal that something is going wrong or that a competing solution has emerged.

Having a cancellation number isn't enough; you need to understand *why* people are abandoning your product or service. Jason did just that by calling customers who cancelled. "Not everyone wanted to speak with me; some people never responded to my calls," he recalls. "But enough people were willing to talk, even after they had left WP Engine, that I learned a lot about why they were leaving." According to Jason, most people leave WP Engine because of factors outside of the company's control (such as the project ending where hosting was needed), but Jason wanted to dig further.

Having a metric and an understanding of the reasons people were leaving wasn't enough. Jason went out and found a benchmark for cancellation rate. This is one of the most challenging things for a startup to do: find a relevant number (or line in the sand) against which to compare yourself. Jason researched the hosting space using his investors and advisors. One of WP Engine's investors is Automattic, the company behind WordPress, which also has a sizeable hosting business.

---

* For full disclosure, it also hosts the companion website to this book.

Jason found that for established hosting companies, there's a "best case scenario" benchmark for cancellation rate per month, which is 2%. That means every month—for even the best and biggest hosting companies around—you can expect 2% of your customers to leave.

On the surface, that looks like a huge number. "When I first saw our churn, which was around 2%, I was very concerned," Jason says. "But when I found out that 2% is pretty much the lowest churn you'll get in the hosting business, it changed my perspective a great deal." Had Jason not known that this is simply a fact of life in the hosting industry, WP Engine might have invested time and money trying to move a metric that wouldn't budge—money that would have been far better spent elsewhere.

Instead, with a benchmark in hand, Jason was able to focus on other issues and key performance indicators (KPIs), all the while keeping his eye on any fluctuation in cancellation rate. He doesn't rule out the possibility of trying to break through the 2% cancellation rate at some point (after all, there can be significant value in reducing that churn), but he's able to prioritize according to what's going on in his business today, and where the biggest trouble spots lie, all while keeping an eye on the future success of the company.

Summary

- WP Engine built a healthy WordPress hosting business, but losing 24% of customers every year concerned its founders.

- By asking around, the founder discovered that a 2% per month churn rate was normal—even good—for that industry.

- Knowing a good line in the sand allowed him to focus on other, more important business objectives instead of trying to over-optimize churn.

Analytics Lessons Learned

It's easy to get stuck on one specific metric that looks bad and invest considerable time and money trying to improve it. Until you know where you stand against competitors and industry averages, you're blind. Having benchmarks helps you decide whether to keep working on a specific metric or move on to the next challenge.

Average Isn't Good Enough

The Startup Genome project has collected key metrics from thousands of startups through its Startup Compass site.[*] Co-founder Bjoern Lasse Herrmann shared some of the metrics he's gathered about an "average" startup. They serve as a sobering reminder that being average simply isn't good enough. There's a line in the sand, a point where you know you're ready to move to the next KPI—and most companies aren't anywhere near it.

Consider this: if you get your churn rate below 5%—ideally as low as 2%—each month, you have a reasonably sticky product. Bjoern's average is between 12% (for indirectly monetized sites) and 19% (for those that monetize directly from users)—nowhere near good enough to move to the next stage.

Furthermore, consumer applications have a nearly 1:1 CAC to CLV ratio. That means they're spending all the money they make acquiring new users. As we've seen, you're doing well when you spend less than a third of your customer revenue acquiring new customers. For bigger-ticket applications (with a CLV of over $50K) things are less bleak, with most companies spending between 0.2% and 2% of CLV on acquisition.

Startup Compass has some great comparative insight, and we encourage you to use it to measure yourself against other companies. But realize that there's a reason most startups fail: *average is nowhere near good enough.*

What Is Good Enough?

There are a few metrics—like growth rate, visitor engagement, pricing targets, customer acquisition, virality, mailing list effectiveness, uptime, and time on site—that apply to most (if not all) business models. We'll look at these next. Then, in the following chapters, we'll dig into metrics specific to the six business models we've covered earlier. Remember, though, that while you might turn immediately to the chapter for your business model, there's always some overlap and relevant metrics in other business models that should be helpful to you. So we encourage you to look at what's normal for other business models, too.

---

[*] *http://www.startupcompass.co*

Growth Rate

Investor Paul Graham makes a good case* that above all else, a startup is a company designed to grow fast. In fact, it's this growth that distinguishes a startup from other new ventures like a cobbler or a restaurant. Startups, Paul says, go through three distinct growth phases: slow, where the organization is searching for a product and market to tackle; fast, where it has figured out how to make and sell it at scale; and slow again, as it becomes a big company and encounters internal constraints or market saturation, and tries to overcome Porter's "hole in the middle."

At Paul's startup accelerator, Y Combinator, teams track growth rate weekly because of the short timeframe. "A good growth rate during YC is 5–7% a week," he says. "If you can hit 10% a week you're doing exceptionally well. If you can only manage 1%, it's a sign you haven't yet figured out what you're doing." If the company is at the Revenue stage, then growth is measured in revenue; if it's not charging money yet, growth is measured in active users.

Is Growth at All Costs a Good Thing?

There's no question that growth is important. But focusing on growth too soon is bad. We've seen how inherent virality—that's built into your product's use—is better than artificial virality you've added as an afterthought. A flood of new visitors might grow your user base, but might also be detrimental to your business. Similarly, while some kinds of growth are good, other kinds aren't sustainable. Premature scaling, such as firing up the paid engine before you're sticky, can exacerbate issues with product quality, cash flow, and user satisfaction. It kills you just as you're getting started.

Sean Ellis notes that growth hackers are constantly testing and tweaking new ways of achieving growth, but that "during this process it is easy to lose sight of the big picture. When this happens, growth eventually falls off a cliff." †

He goes on to say, "Sustainable growth programs are built on a core understanding of the value of your solution in the minds of your most passionate customers." As we saw in Chapter 5, Sean's Startup Growth Pyramid illustrates that scaling your business comes only after you've found

---

* *http://paulgraham.com/growth.html*

† *http://startup-marketing.com/authentic-growth-hacks/*

product/market fit and your unfair advantage. In other words: stickiness comes before virality, and virality comes before scale.

Most Y Combinator startups (and most startups, for that matter) focus on growth before they hit product/market fit. In some cases this is a necessity, particularly if the value of the startup depends on a network effect—after all, Skype's no good if nobody else is using it. But while rapid growth can accelerate the discovery of product/market fit, it can just as easily destroy the startup if the timing isn't right.

Paul's growth strategy is also a very B2C-biased way to look at the world. B2B organizations have a different flow, from a few early customers for whom they look like consultants, to later-stage customers who tolerate a more generic, standardized product or service. Growing a B2B organization prematurely can alienate your core of loyal customers who are helping to build your business, stalling revenue and eliminating the referrals, case studies, and testimonials needed to grow your sales.

This is a universal problem, best described by the *technology lifecycle adoption* model, first proposed by George Beal, Everett Rogers, and Joe Bohlen,* and expanded by Geoffrey Moore:† it takes a lot of work to move from early adopters to laggards as the product becomes more mainstream and the barriers to adoption fall.

Bottom Line

As you're validating your problem and solution, ask yourself whether there are enough people who really care enough to sustain a 5% growth rate—but don't strive for that rate of growth at the expense of really understanding your customers and building a meaningful solution. When you're a pre-revenue startup at or near product/market fit, your line in the sand should be 5% growth for active users each week, and once you're generating revenues, they should grow at 5% a week.

Number of Engaged Visitors

Fred Wilson says that across Union Square Ventures' portfolio companies, there's a consistent ratio for engagement and concurrent users.‡ He says that for a web service or mobile application:

---

* *http://en.wikipedia.org/wiki/Technology_adoption_lifecycle*

† *http://www.chasminstitute.com/METHODOLOGY/TechnologyAdoptionLifeCycle/tabid/89/Default.aspx*

‡ *http://www.avc.com/a_vc/2011/07/301010.html/*

- 30% of registered users will use a web-based service at least once a month. For mobile applications, 30% of the people who download the app use it each month.

- 10% of registered users will use the service or mobile app every day.

- The maximum number of concurrent users will be 10% of the number of daily users.

While it's a huge generalization, Fred says this 30/10/10 ratio is consistent across a wide variety of applications, from social to music to games. Getting to this stage of regular use and engagement is a sign that you're ready to start growing, and to move into the Virality, Revenue, and Scale stages of your business.

Bottom Line

Aim for 30% of your registered users to visit once a month, and 10% of them to come daily. Figure out your reliable leading indicators of growth, and measure them against your business model predictions.

Pricing Metrics

It's hard to know what to charge. Every startup makes money from different things, so there's no easy way to compare pricing across companies. But you can learn some lessons from different pricing approaches.

A fundamental element of any pricing strategy is elasticity: when you charge more, you sell less; when you charge less, you sell more. Back in 1890, Alfred Marshall defined the *price elasticity of demand* as follows:

> The elasticity (or responsiveness) of demand in a market is great or small according as the amount demanded increases much or little for a given fall in price, and diminishes much or little for a given rise in price.*

Unlike Marshall, you have the world's greatest pricing laboratory at your disposal: the Internet. You can test out discount codes, promotions, and even varied pricing on your customers and see what happens.

Let's say you've run a series of tests on the price of your product. You know that when you change the price, you sell a certain number of items (see Table 21-1).

---

* *http://en.wikipedia.org/wiki/Price_elasticity_of_demand*

Price	$5	$6	$7	$8	$9	$10	$11	$12	$13	$14	$15
Buyers per month	100	90	80	75	70	65	60	55	50	45	40
Revenue	$500	$540	$560	$600	$630	$650	$660	$660	$650	$630	$600

Table 21-1. How changing price affects sales

When we chart the resulting revenues, we get a characteristic curve (Figure 21-1). The best pricing is somewhere between $11 and $12, since this maximizes revenues.

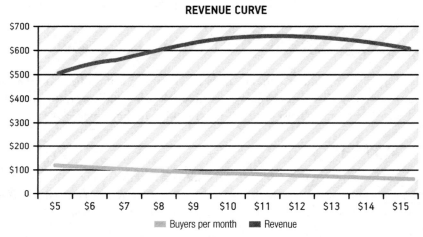

Figure 21-1. Aim for the top of the curve

If all we're hoping for is revenue optimization, this is the optimal price point. But revenue isn't everything:

- Price yourself too high, and you may lose the war. Apple's FireWire was a better communications technology, but Apple wanted to charge to license its patents, so USB won.* Sometimes charging too much can stall a market.

- If you experiment with your users and word gets out, it can backfire, as it did for Orbitz when the company recommended more expensive products to visitors using Macs.

- If you charge too little, you'll arouse suspicion from buyers, who may wonder if you're up to no good or you're a scam. You may end up devaluing your offering in customers' eyes.

---

* *http://www.guardian.co.uk/technology/2012/oct/22/smartphone-patent-wars-explained*

- If you charge too much, you may slow down the much-needed viral growth or take too long to achieve network effects that improve your product's functionality.

- Some things—like healthcare—you can sell at nearly any price; others, like bottled water, sell more when a price boost increases perceived quality, as Pellegrino and Perrier will happily tell you.

- If you make your pricing tiers simple, you'll see better conversions. Patrick Campbell, co-founder and CEO of pricing service Price Intelligently, says that based on his data, companies with easy-to-understand tiers and a clear path up differentiated pricing plans convert customers at a much higher rate than companies with complicated tiers, features that aren't always applicable, and hard-to-follow pricing paths.

- Products that "fly under the radar" and don't need a boss's approval convert at a much higher rate, because expensing something is easier.

Neil Davidson, joint CEO at Red Gate Software Ltd and author of *Don't Just Roll the Dice* (Red Gate Books), says, "One of the biggest misconceptions around pricing is that what you charge for your product or service is directly related to how much it costs you to build or run it. That's not the case. Price is related to what your customers are prepared to pay."

CASE STUDY | ## Socialight Discovers the Underlying Metrics of Pricing

Socialight was founded in 2005 by Dan Melinger and Michael Sharon, and sold to Group Commerce in 2011. The idea came from work Dan was doing in 2004 with a team at NYU focused on how digital media was changing how people communicated.

This was in the early days of social networking: Friendster was the dominant social platform. Socialight's first incarnation was as a destination social network for Java-enabled mobile phones, which were considered the pinnacle of mobile app technology at the time. People could place "sticky notes" around the world, and then collaborate, organize, and share them with friends or the community as a whole.

Back then, Dan wasn't focused on pricing, but shortly after launching Socialight, the founders realized that power users were looking for different feature sets based on how they were using the product. "The mobile software market was starting to mature, along with location-based services and devices like iPhones," said Dan. "We also started getting approached by companies that wanted to pay for us to build and host mobile and social apps for them."

This started the company's pivot from B2C to B2B. It built an API to let others build their own applications, and then built a more advanced mobile app-maker product. This achieved good traction, with over 1,000 communities built atop it.

As Socialight moved into the B2B space, it launched a three-tiered freemium business model. The two paying tiers were called Premium and Pro, and cost $250 and $1,000–$5,500 per month, respectively. The main difference between the Premium and Pro offerings was the amount of involvement Socialight had with those customers—at $1,000–$5,500 per month, Socialight was very involved with lots of hours invested per month to work with customers.

Four months into its freemium launch, the company realized there was a problem. While the Pro customers were great for top-line revenue, they were costing Socialight a *lot* of money. "We realized that the margins we were getting from Pro customers were nowhere near as good as those from Premium, even though the revenue from Pro customers was great. Moreover, Pro customers took a lot longer to close, which is not something we understood well enough early on," says Dan.

This is where a greater understanding and sophistication around price-related metrics becomes so important. Tracking revenue by pricing tier, which Socialight did from the outset, is a good place to start. But the other fundamental business metrics are perhaps even more important. For example, Socialight could have focused on customer acquisition cost versus customer lifetime value to identify its revenue and cost problems. Or it could have focused on margins earlier in the process, which would have helped identify its revenue issues. Eventually, the company increased the Pro tier to $5,500/month exclusively, a reflection of the increased support required by customers.

Socialight never got around to experimenting with different pricing strategies (it was acquired, after all!), but Dan would have liked to. "I think we could have reduced the Pro feature set a small amount and reduced its pricing significantly," he says.

This underscores the tricky balance in a freemium or tiered pricing model: how do you make sure that the features/services being offered fit into the right packages at the right price? Instead of looking at pricing, Dan was able to experiment with other metrics. He looked for ways to encourage customers using the free service to convert to the Premium tier (and focused a lot less on the Pro tier). The focus on conversion (from free to paid) helped Socialight grow its business and get the bulk of its paid users into the profitable tier.

Summary

- Socialight switched from a consumer to business market, which required a change in pricing.

- The founders analyzed not only revenue, but also the cost of service delivery, and realized that high-revenue customers weren't as profitable.

- They intentionally priced one of their tiers unreasonably high to discourage customers from buying it while still being able to claim it publicly.

Analytics Lessons Learned

Consider the impact that pricing has on customer behavior, both in terms of attracting and discouraging them. Price is an important tool for getting your customers to do what you want, and it should always be compared not only to cost of sales, but also to cost of goods sold and marginal cost.

Research on price elasticity suggests that it applies most in young, growing markets. Think about getting a walk-in haircut, for example. You may not check how much the haircut is; you know it'll be within a certain price range. If the stylist presented you with a bill for $500, you'd be outraged. There's a well-defined expectation of pricing. While startups often live in young, growing markets where prices are less established, bigger, more stable markets are often subject to commodity pricing, regulation, bulk discounts, long-term contracts, and other externalities that complicate the simplicity of the elasticity just described.

Your business model will affect the role pricing plays for you. If you're a media site, someone is already optimizing revenue for you in the form of ad auctions. If you're a two-sided marketplace, you may need to help your sellers price their offerings correctly in order to maximize your own profits. And if you're a UGC site, you may not care about pricing—or may want to apply similar approaches to determine the most effective rewards or incentives for your users.

In a study of 133 companies, Patrick Campbell found that most respondents compared themselves to the competition when setting pricing, as shown in Figure 21-2. Some simply guessed, or based their price on the cost plus a profit margin. Only 21% of respondents said they used customer development.

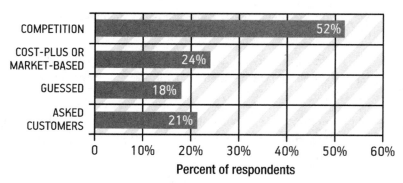

Figure 21-2. *Very few companies take pricing seriously enough*

While it might seem like getting pricing right is a team effort, the reality across these respondents was that the founder ultimately decided final pricing, as shown in Figure 21-3.

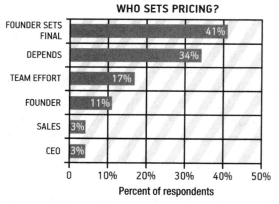

Figure 21-3. *Ultimately, pricing comes from opinions at the top*

Despite the number of testing tools available to organizations that want to get serious about pricing, few companies did much more than check out the competition. As Figure 21-4 shows, only 18% did any kind of customer price sensitivity testing.

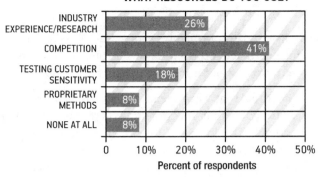

WHAT RESOURCES DO YOU USE?

INDUSTRY EXPERIENCE/RESEARCH	26%
COMPETITION	41%
TESTING CUSTOMER SENSITIVITY	18%
PROPRIETARY METHODS	8%
NONE AT ALL	8%

Percent of respondents
(0, 10%, 20%, 30%, 40%, 50%)

Figure 21-4. Most of us just follow our competitors blindly

Ultimately, what Patrick's research shows is that despite the considerable rewards for getting pricing right, most startups aren't looking at real data—they're shooting from the hip.

Bottom Line

There's no clear rule on what to charge. But whatever your choice of pricing models, testing is key. Understanding the right tiers of pricing and the price elasticity of your market is vital if you're going to balance revenues with adoption. Once you find your revenue "sweet spot," aim about 10% lower to encourage growth of your user base.

Cost of Customer Acquisition

While it's impossible to say what it'll cost to get a new customer, we can define it as a percentage of your customers' lifetime value. This is the total revenue a customer brings to you in the life of her relationship with you. This varies by business model, so we'll tackle it in subsequent, model-specific chapters, but a good rule of thumb is that your acquisition cost should be less than a third of the total value a customer brings you over her lifetime. This isn't a hard-and-fast rule, but it's widely cited. Here's some of the reasoning behind it.

- The CLV you've calculated is probably wrong. There's uncertainty in any business model. You're guessing how much you'll make from a customer in her lifetime. If you're off, you may have spent too much to acquire her, and it'll take a long time to find out whether you've underestimated churn or overestimated customer spend. "In my experience, churn has the biggest impact on CLV, and unfortunately, churn is a lagging indicator," says Zach Nies. He suggests offering only month-to-month subscription plans initially in order to get a better picture of true churn early on.

- The acquisition cost is probably wrong, too. You're paying the costs of acquiring customers up front. New customers incur up-front cost—onboarding, adding more infrastructure, etc.

- Between the time that you spend money to acquire someone and the time you recoup that investment, you're basically "lending" the customer money. The longer it takes you to recoup the money, the more you'll need. And because money comes from either a bank loan or an equity investor, you'll either wind up paying interest, or diluting yourself by taking on investors. This is a complex balance to strike. Bad cash-flow management kills startups.

- Limiting yourself to a customer acquisition cost (CAC) of only a third of your CLV will force you to verify your acquisition costs sooner, which will make you more honest—so you'll recognize a mistake before it's too late. If your product or service costs a lot to deliver and operate, you may not have the operating margins to support even a third, and you may have to lower your CAC to an even smaller percentage of CLV to make your financial model work.

What *really* drives your acquisition costs is your underlying business model. While there may not be an industry standard for acquisition, you should have some target margins that you need to achieve, and the percentage of your revenue that you spend on acquisition drives those margins. So when you're deciding what to spend on customer acquisition, start with your business model.

Bottom Line

Unless you have a good reason to do otherwise, don't spend more than a third of the money you expect to gain from a customer (and the customers she invites downstream) on acquiring that customer.

Virality

Recall that virality is actually two metrics: how many new users each existing user successfully invites (your viral coefficient) and the time it takes her to do so (your viral cycle time). There's no "normal" for virality. Both metrics depend on the nature of your product, as well as market saturation.

A sustained viral coefficient of greater than 1 is an extremely strong indicator of growth, and suggests that you should be focusing on stickiness so you can retain those new users as you add them. But even a lower viral coefficient is useful, because it effectively reduces your customer acquisition cost. Imagine that it costs you $1,000 to acquire 100 new users. Your CAC is therefore $10. But if you have a viral coefficient of 0.4, then those 100 users will invite 40 more, who will in turn invite an additional 16, and so on. In the end, those 100 users are really 165 users. So your CAC is actually $6.06. Put another way, virality is a force multiplier for your attention-generating efforts. Done right, it's one of your unfair advantages.

It's also critical to distinguish between *artificial* virality and *inherent* virality. If your service is inherently viral—meaning that use of the product naturally involves inviting outsiders, as it does with products like Skype or Uberconf—the newly invited users have a legitimate reason to use the product. A Skype user you invite will join in order to get on a call with you. Users who join in this way will be more engaged than those invited in other, less intrinsic ways (for example, through a word-of-mouth mention).

On the other hand, if your virality is forced—for example, if you let people into a beta once they invite five friends, or reward people with extra features for tweeting something—you won't see as much stickiness from the invited users. Dropbox found a clever way around this, by *looking* inherent and giving away something of value (cloud storage) when it was in fact largely artificial. People invited others because they wanted more space for themselves, not because they needed to share content. Only later did the company add more advanced sharing features that made the virality more inherent.

Don't overlook sharing by email, which, as mentioned in Chapter 12, can represent nearly 80% of all online sharing, particularly for media sites and older customers.

Bottom Line

There's no "typical" virality for startups. If virality is below 1, it's helping lower your customer acquisition cost. If it's above 1, you'll grow. And if you're over 0.75, things are pretty good. Try to build inherent virality into the product, and track it against your business model. Treat artificial virality the same way you would customer acquisition, and segment it by the value of the new users it brings in.

Mailing List Effectiveness

Mailing list provider MailChimp shares a considerable amount of data on how well mailing lists work.[*] Mailing list open rates vary widely by

---

[*] *http://mailchimp.com/resources/research/*

industry.* A 2010 study showed that construction, home and garden, and photo emails achieve nearly 30% open rate, but emails related to medicine, politics, and music get as little as 14%. And these are legitimate messages for which recipients have ostensibly signed up—not spam.

There's plenty you can do to improve your email open rate. Targeting your mailings by tailoring messages to different segments of your subscriber base improves clicks and opens by nearly 15%. Email open rates change significantly based on the time of day—3 p.m., as it turns out, is when people are most likely to open something. Few people open emails on the weekend. More links in an email means more clicks. And newer subscribers are more likely to click on a message.

Jason Billingsley recommends testing an individualized send schedule equal to the signup time of the unique user. So, if a user signs up at 9 a.m., schedule to send her updates at 9 a.m. "Most email tools aren't set up for such a tactic, but it's a highly valuable test that could yield significant results," he says.

But by far the biggest factor in mailing list effectiveness is simple: write a decent subject line. A good one gets an open rate of 60–87%, and a bad one suffers a paltry 1–14%.† It turns out that simple, self-explanatory messages that include something about the recipient get opened. Sometimes it's just one word: Experian reported that the word "exclusive" in email promotional campaigns increased unique open rates by 14%.‡

François Lane, CEO of mailing platform CakeMail, has a few additional cautions that underscore how email delivery metrics are interrelated:

- The more frequently you email users, the lower your bounce and human-flagged spam rates (because those addresses quickly get removed from the list), but frequent emailing also tends to reduce engagement metrics like open rate and click-through rate, because recipients get email fatigue.

- A higher rate of machine-flagged spam leads to a lower rate of human-flagged spam, because humans don't complain about mail they don't receive.

- Open rate is a fundamentally flawed metric, because it relies on the mail client to load a hidden pixel—which most modern mail applications

---

* *http://mailchimp.com/resources/research/email-marketing-benchmarks-by-industry/*

† *http://mailchimp.com/resources/research/email-marketing-subject-line-comparison/*

‡ *The 2012 Digital Marketer: Benchmark and Trend Report,* Experian Marketing Services (*http://go.experian.com/forms/experian-digital-marketer-2012*).

don't do by default. This is one of the main reasons newsletter designers focus on imageless layout. Open rates are mainly useful for testing subject lines or different contact lists for a single campaign, but they provide only a sample, and at best a skewed one.

Bottom Line

Open and click-through rates will vary significantly, but a well-run campaign should hit a 20–30% open rate and over 5% click-through.

Uptime and Reliability

The Web isn't perfect. A 2012 study of static websites running on 10 different cloud providers showed that nearly 3% of tests to those clouds resulted in an error.* So even if your site is working all the time, the Internet and the underlying infrastructure will cause problems.

Achieving an uptime of better than 99.95% is costly, too, allowing you to be down only 4.4 hours a year. If your users are loyal and engaged, then they'll tolerate a small amount of downtime—particularly if you're transparent about it on social networks and keep them informed.

Bottom Line

For a paid service that users rely on (such as an email application or a hosted project management application), you should have at least 99.5% uptime, and keep users updated about outages. Other kinds of applications can survive a lower level of service.

Site Engagement

Everyone cares about site engagement (unless you're exclusively mobile, but even then you likely have a web presence driving mobile downloads). In some cases (such as a transaction-focused e-commerce site), you want site visitors to come onto your site and engage quickly, whereas in other cases (such as a media site that monetizes via ads), you want visitors spending as much time as possible.

Analytics firm Chartbeat measures page engagement across a multitude of sites. It defines an "engaged" user as someone who has a page open and has scrolled, typed, or interacted with the page in the last few seconds. "We generally see a separation between how much engagement sites get

---

* From a study of cloud providers conducted by Bitcurrent/CloudOps Research from December 15, 2011, to January 15, 2012, in conjunction with Webmetrics.

on landing pages—which typically get high traffic and low engagement—and other pages," says Joshua Schwartz, a data scientist with the company. "Across my sample of sites, average engaged time on landing pages was 61 seconds and on non-landing pages it was 76 seconds. Of course, this varies widely between pages and between sites, but it's a reasonable benchmark."

Bottom Line

An average engaged time on a page of one minute is normal, but there's wide variance between sites and between pages on a site.

Web Performance

Study after study has proven that fast sites do better across nearly every metric that matters, from time on site to conversion to shopping cart size.[*] Yet many web startups treat page-load time as an afterthought. Chartbeat measures this data across several hundred of its customers who let the company analyze their statistics in an anonymized, aggregate way.[†] Looking at the smaller, lower-traffic sites in its data set, the company found that these took 7–12 seconds to load. It also found that pages with very slow load times have very few concurrent users, as shown in Figure 21-5.

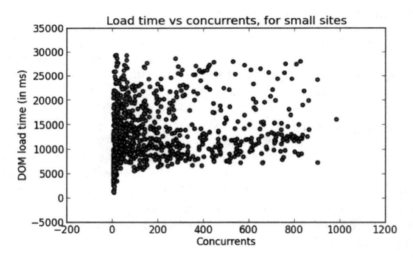

Figure 21-5. After about 10 seconds of load time, people don't stick around

---

[*] http://www.watchingwebsites.com/archives/proof-that-speeding-up-websites-improves-online-business/

[†] Chartbeat did not include data from customers who opted out of this aggregate analysis; it also excluded some periods of unusually high traffic, which was related to the US election period.

"There seems to be a hard threshold at about 15–18 seconds, where after that users simply won't wait, and traffic falls off dramatically," says Joshua. "It's also notable that the largest sites in our sample set, those with thousands of concurrents, had some of the fastest page load times—often under five seconds."

Bottom Line

Site speed is something you can control, and it can give you a real advantage. Get your pages to load for a first-time visitor in less than 5 seconds; after 10, and you'll start to suffer.

EXERCISE | Make Your Own Lines in the Sand

In this chapter and the next six chapters, we share lines in the sand, or baselines, for which you can aim. You should already have a list of key metrics that you're tracking (or would like to track). Now compare those metrics with the lines in the sand provided in the following chapters. How do you compare? Which metric is worst off? Is that metric your One Metric That Matters?

CHAPTER 22

E-commerce: Lines in the Sand

Before we get into specific e-commerce metrics, we want to reinforce an important dimension of storefront segmentation.

There's a tendency to think of all mobile use as the same. That's wrong. "One of my pet peeves these days is how 'mobile' traffic is defined," says investor and entrepreneur Derek Szeto. "It's often defined as tablet plus smartphone, and especially from a commerce perspective, they're *very* different things. If I were managing a marketplace or storefront, I'd segment my analysis into three groups: desktop, tablet, and smartphone."

Part of the difference comes from the fact that users engage with the online world in three postures: creation (often on a computer with a keyboard), interaction (usually with a smartphone), and consumption (with a tablet). Mixing tablets and mobile phones into a single category is a dangerous mistake. And people buy more media on a tablet than they do on a PC because that's where they consume content.

In other words: *your mileage will vary.* It'll depend on whether you're an acquisition- or a loyalty-focused e-commerce site; on whether your buyers are buying from a tablet, a phone, or a desktop; and on a variety of other important dimensions. The only way you can deal with this is to measure, learn, and segment properly.

Conversion Rate

In March 2010, Nielsen Online reported the best conversion rates for online retailers, as shown in Table 22-1.[*]

Company	Conversion rate
Schwan's	40.6%
Woman Within	25.3%
Blair.com	20.4%
1800petmeds.com	17.8%
vitacost.com	16.4%
QVC	16.0%
ProFlowers	15.8%
Office Depot	15.4%

Table 22-1. Top e-commerce conversion rates

Other big e-commerce sites such as Amazon, Tickets.com, and eBay saw lower conversion rates (9.6%, 11.2%, and 11.5%, respectively).[†]

These companies fall into three big categories: catalog sites (which have a considerable number of offline, printed catalogs driving traffic), retail giants like eBay and Amazon, and gift sites tightly linked to intention, such as an online flower shop (people don't browse flowers casually; they go to a flower site with one thing in mind).

Many of Nielsen's highly-ranked companies fall into the loyalty category of online retailers, where you'd expect conversion to be high. Schwan's is an online grocery store; it's not the type of site that many people will browse and comparison shop with. Others, like Amazon and eBay, have incredibly strong brands that exist in the customer's consciousness on and off the Web. "In my experience, most e-commerce startups selling either their own product or retailing others' products can expect conversion rates of 1–3% maximum," says Bill D'Alessandro. "Startups shouldn't plug 8–10% conversion into their models when deciding on the viability of their business—that's never going to happen. The three things that propel you from 2% to 10% are seriously loyal users, lots of SKUs, and repeat customers. And even then it's a big accomplishment."

---

[*] http://www.marketingcharts.com/direct/top-10-online-retailers-by-conversion-rate-march-2010-12774/

[†] http://www.conversionblogger.com/is-amazons-96-conversion-rate-low-heres-why-i-think-so/

More typical conversion rates still vary significantly by industry. A 2007 Invesp post cited FireClick survey data that shows just how different the rates can be (see Table 22-2).[*]

Type of site	Conversion rate
Catalog	5.8%
Software	3.9%
Fashion and apparel	2.3%
Specialty	1.7%
Electronics	0.50%
Outdoor and sports	0.40%

Table 22-2. Conversion rates by vertical

Outside of these categories, there seems to be a widely held notion that a conversion rate of 2–3% is typical for normal websites. Bestselling author, speaker, and digital marketing expert Bryan Eisenberg has an explanation for where this number may have come from: in 2008, Shop.org claimed that its affiliated members had an average within this range, and the FireClick index said the global conversion rate was 2.4%.[†] Bryan argues that leading sites do better because they focus on visitor intent—when you're going to buy flowers, you've already made up your mind; you're just deciding which ones. A more recent 2012 study estimated the average conversion rate across the whole Web at 2.13%.[‡]

Bottom Line

If you're an online retailer, you'll get initial conversion rates of around 2%, which will vary by vertical, but if you can achieve 10%, you're doing incredibly well. If your visitors arrive with a strong intent to buy, you'll do better—but, of course, you'll have to invest elsewhere to get them into that mindset.

Kevin Hillstrom at Mine That Data cautions that averages are dangerous here. Many electronics retailers, which have a lot of "drive-by" visitors doing research, have conversion rates as low as 0.5%. On the other hand, there's a correlation between average order size and conversion rate.

---

[*] http://www.invesp.com/blog/sales-marketing/compare-your-site-conversion-rate-to-ecommerce-site-averages.html

[†] http://www.clickz.com/clickz/column/1718099/the-average-conversion-rate-is-it-myth

[‡] http://www.ritholtz.com/blog/2012/05/shopping-cart-abandonment/

Shopping Cart Abandonment

A 2012 study estimated that just over 65% of buyers abandon their shopping cart.[*] Of those who abandon, 44% do so because of high shipping costs, 41% decide they aren't ready to purchase, and 25% find the price is too high. A February 2012 study estimated abandonment at an even higher 77%.[†] Improving on abandonment beyond 65% seems to be a challenge, but that doesn't stop companies from trying:

- *Fab.com*, a curated catalog site, puts its shopping cart on a timer as a pressure tactic to convince buyers to complete their transaction: buy soon, or someone else may steal your purchase from you. The site's brand of exclusivity and its limited, register-first approach to offers are actually reinforced by the expiry timer.

- If you start to buy Facebook ads, then abandon the process, the company sends you a credit toward your first ads to get you restarted.

Price does seem to be a factor. Listrak might estimate a 77% abandonment rate, but that rate dropped to 67.66% on December 14, 2011—a day that many online retailers declared "free shipping day."[‡]

KP Elements, which sells skin care products to combat keratosis pilaris (a common cosmetic skin condition), ran a pricing test where it compared a $30 price point plus $5 shipping on the buy page, versus a $35 price point for the same product, with free shipping. Conversion went from 5% to 10% with that simple change. The prices were identical—$35—but the free shipping offer was twice as compelling to customers.

In 2012, the Baymard Institute looked at 15 different studies of abandonment and concluded that an abandonment rate of roughly 66% is average, as shown in Figure 22-1.[§]

---

[*] http://www.ritholtz.com/blog/2012/05/shopping-cart-abandonment/

[†] http://www.bizreport.com/2012/02/listrak-77-of-shopping-carts-abandoned-in-last-six-months.html#

[‡] http://www.internetretailer.com/2012/02/02/e-retailers-now-can-track-shopping-cart-abandonment-daily

[§] http://baymard.com/lists/cart-abandonment-rate

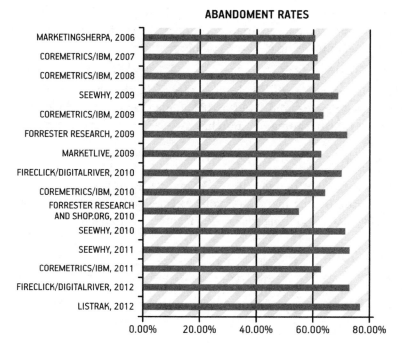

ABANDOMENT RATES

Figure 22-1. Meta-studies are so meta

Price isn't the only cause for abandonment. Jason Billingsley says that most abandonment studies ignore key variables, such as expected delivery date. "As more time-sensitive purchases move online, this becomes critical data," he says. "Retailers must expose estimated arrive dates and not just shipping and fulfillment dates."

Bottom Line

Sixty-five percent of people who start down your purchase funnel will abandon their purchase before paying for it.

Search Effectiveness

Search is now the default way for consumers to research and find products, from their initial investigation of vendors to their navigation within a site. While this is true in e-commerce, it's also relevant for media, user-generated content (UGC), and two-sided marketplaces.

In e-commerce specifically, 79% of online shoppers spend at least 50% of their shopping time researching products. Forty-four percent of online shoppers begin by using a search engine.[*]

Mobile search traffic is particularly focused on purchasing. Fifty-four percent of iOS web traffic is devoted to search, compared to 36% for the Internet as a whole—and 9 out of 10 mobile searches lead to action, with over half of them leading to a purchase.

Bottom Line

Don't just think "mobile first." Think "search first," and invest in instrumenting search metrics on your website and within your product to see what users are looking for and what they're not able to find.

---

[*]   See *http://blog.hubspot.com/Portals/249/docs/ebooks/120-marketing-stats-charts-and-graphs. pdf* for this and many other statistics on search usage. Chikita provided the iOS search number, and Search Engine Land provided the mobile purchase number.

CHAPTER 23

SaaS: Lines in the Sand

Paid Enrollment

Churn, engagement, and upselling metrics are similar across many SaaS companies. But there's one factor that produces a huge difference across many metrics: asking for payment up front during a trial.

Totango, a provider of SaaS customer intelligence and engagement software, has data across more than 100 SaaS companies, measuring trial, conversion, and churn rates. It has found that asking for a credit card during signup means 0.5% to 2% of visitors sign up for a trial, while *not* asking for a credit card means 5% to 10% of visitors will enroll.

Enrollment isn't the only goal, of course. You want users who enroll in a trial to become paying customers. Roughly 15% of trial users who did *not* provide a credit card will sign up for a paid subscription. On the other hand, 40–50% of trial users who *did* provide one will convert to a paid subscription.

Asking for a credit card up front can also mean more churn after the first payment period if users' expectations aren't clearly set. Up to 40% of paid users may cancel their subscriptions—they forgot that they agreed to billing after the trial expired, and when they see a charge on their credit card, they cancel. Once this initial hurdle is over, however, most users stick around each month. A 2009 Pacific Crest study found that best-in-class SaaS companies manage to get their annual churn rates below 15%.[*]

Table 23-1 shows a quick summary of the differences in metrics with and without an upfront credit card.

	Credit card	No credit card
Try it	2%	10%
Become subscribers	50%	15%
Churn on first pay period	Up to 40%	Up to 20%
End to end	0.6%	1.2%

Table 23-1. Impact of requiring a credit card to try a SaaS product

Credit cards aren't the only indicator of conversion rates. Some people who try a SaaS product are just curious; others are seriously evaluating the tool. They show different behaviors, and can be treated as separate segments based on their activities and how much time they invest in exploring the product.

Let's look at two basic funnels to see how both models work, focusing on Totango's analysis of these "serious evaluators," and using the higher values from Table 23-1; see Table 23-2.

5,000 serious evaluators visit the site	
Credit cart up front	**No credit card up front**
100 try it (2%)	500 try it (10%)
50 become subscribers (50%)	75 become subscribers (15%)
20 churn fast (40%)	15 churn fast (20%)
30 customers remain (0.6%)	60 customers remain (1.2%)

Table 23-2. Two engagement and churn funnels

In this simple example, we see that asking for a credit card up front results in a total of 30 paying customers (from 5,000 visitors), whereas not doing so yields double the paying customers (60 in all). A paywall turns away evaluators who aren't serious—but it also turns away people who are on the fence. Totango's data shows that for most SaaS providers, 20% of

---

[*]   http://www.pacificcrest-news.com/saas/Pacific%20Crest%202011%20SaaS%20Workshop.pdf

visitors are serious evaluators, 20% are casual evaluators, and 60% are simply curious.

The best approach is to tailor marketing to users based on their activity. You need to convince serious evaluators that you're the right choice, and convince the casual evaluators that they should become more serious. Identify serious prospects by usage analytics and focus sales resources on those users. Combining usage analytics (finding out who's serious) with an open door (no paywall) yields the best results.

Let's add a third funnel to the previous two—one where the SaaS provider is actively identifying and courting serious evaluators with tailored marketing. In this case, while everyone can try the tool, fewer subscribe, but those who do are more likely to remain (see Table 23-3).

Credit cart up front	No credit card up front	No credit card, focus on serious users
100 try it (2%)	500 try it (10%)	500 try it (10%)
50 become subscribers (50%)	75 become subscribers (15%)	125 become subscribers (25%)
20 churn fast (40%)	15 churn fast (20%)	25 churn fast (20%)
30 customers remain (0.6%)	60 customers remain (1.2%)	100 customers remain (2%)

Table 23-3. Totango's data on a third funnel for serious evaluators

According to Totango's research, the best approach is to not put up a credit card paywall to try the service, but to segment users into three groups—then market to the active ones, nurture the casual ones, and don't waste time on those who are just curious bystanders (or at best, get them to tell friends who might be real prospects about you).

Bottom Line

If you ask for a credit card up front, expect just 2% of visitors to try your service, and 50% of them to use it. If you don't ask for a credit card, expect 10% to try, and up to 25% to buy—but if they're surprised by a payment, you'll lose them quickly. In our preceding example, not having a credit card up front gives you a 40% increase in conversions, provided you can tailor your selling efforts to each segment of your evaluators based on their activity.

Freemium Versus Paid

One of the biggest pricing debates in startups, particularly those based on software, is that of freemium versus paid models.

Proponents of a free model point out that adoption and attention are the most precious of currencies. Twitter waited until it had millions of active users before introducing advertising, and despite the outcry over promoted tweets, growth has continued. Chris Anderson, former editor-in-chief of *Wired* and author of *The Long Tail* (Hyperion), observes that King Gillette pioneered the idea of giving something away (handles) to make money on something else (razor blades).* But in many ways, online users have strong expectations that the Internet should be free, which means it's hard to charge even for valuable things.

Detractors of freemium models observe that for every success like Dropbox or LinkedIn, there's a deadpool of others who went out of business giving things away. In one example cited by the *Wall Street Journal*, billing-management software firm Chargify was on the brink of failure in 2010—but then it switched to a paid model, and in July 2012, became profitable with 900 paying customers.†

Neil Davidson is concerned with the popularity of freemium, particularly among startups. "I think that for most people the freemium model is unsustainable," he says. "It's very hard to create something good enough that people will want to use, but with enough of a feature gap to the paid version so that people will upgrade." Neil believes that too many startups charge too little, and undervalue themselves. "If you're creating something that your customers value, then you shouldn't shy away from asking them to pay for it. If you don't, you haven't got a business."

Even when freemium works, users sometimes take a long time to start paying. Evernote's Phil Libin talks about a "smile graph," shown in Figure 23-1, that illustrates how customers who once abandoned the product eventually return.‡

---

* *http://www.wired.com/techbiz/it/magazine/16-03/ff_free*

† Sarah E. Needleman and Angus Loten, "When Freemium Fails," *Wall Street Journal*, August 22, 2012; *http://online.wsj.com/article/SB10000872396390443713704577603782317318996.html*.

‡ *http://www.inc.com/magazine/201112/evernote-2011-company-of-the-year.html*

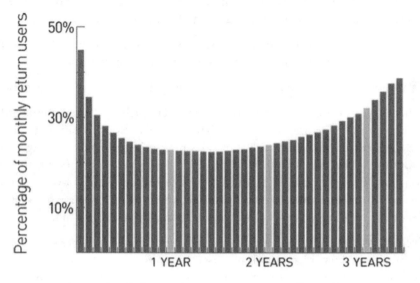

Figure 23-1. *Evernote calls this a smile graph, and not just because of the shape*

Phil estimates that while less than 1% of users upgrade to a paid model after their first month, the number grows to 12% after two years. In fact, having been around long enough to collect a backlog of users who will eventually upgrade, the company experiences what David Skok calls *negative* churn— which happens when product expansions, upselling, and cross-sells to your current customer base exceed the revenue that you are losing because of churn.[*] But many analysts consider Evernote an anomaly: unless you're really good at the freemium approach, your free users can bankrupt you.

Jules Maltz and Daniel Barney of IVP, a late-stage venture capital and growth equity firm, suggest that freemium models work for products that have:[†]

- A low cost of delivering service to an additional user (i.e., low marginal cost).

- Cheap, or even free, marketing that happens as people use the product.

- A relatively simple tool that doesn't require long evaluations or training.

---

[*]   *http://www.forentrepreneurs.com/why-churn-is-critical-in-saas/*

[†]   *http://www.ivp.com/assets/pdf/ivp_freemium_paper.pdf*

- An offering that "feels right" if it's free. Some products (like homeowner's insurance) might make prospects wary if they're offered for free.

- An increase in value the longer someone uses the product. Flickr gets more valuable the more images you store in it, for example.

- A good viral coefficient, so your free users become marketers for you.

What if you *are* charging? Christopher O'Donnell of Price Intelligently points out that startups are trying to balance revenue optimization (making the most money possible) with unit sales maximization (encouraging wide adoption as the business grows) and value perception (not pricing so low you make buyers suspicious).[*] Sellers also have to understand how to bundle several features or services into a package, and how to sell these bundles as tiers in order to reach several markets with different price points.

Even if you're charging every customer, you can still experiment with pricing in the form of promotions, discounts, and time-limited offers. Each of these is a hypothesis suitable for testing across cohorts (if you use time-limited offers) or A/B comparisons (if you offer different pricing to different visitors).

Alex Mehr, the founder of online dating site Zoosk, understands the "optimal revenue" curve. But he argues that startups should err on the side of charging a bit too little.[†] "I prefer to make 10% less money but have 20% more customers. You want to stay a little bit to the left side of the peak. It is around 90% of the revenue maximization point." Alex overlooks the issues of elasticity, value perception, and strategic discounting in his model, however.

Upselling and Growing Revenue

Best-in-class SaaS providers are able to grow revenues per *customer* by 20% from year to year. This comes through additional users added to the subscription, as the application spreads through the organization, as well as a series of tiered offerings and an easy upselling path. Done correctly, the increased revenues from upselling should nearly offset the 2% monthly losses from churn. But these are the best of the best, and they offer a clear path for extracting more money from customers as each customer's use grows.

---

[*] Christopher O'Donnell, *Developing Your Pricing Strategy; price.intelligent.ly/downloads/Developing_Your_Pricing_Strategy.pdf*.

[†] Tarang Shah and Sheetal Shah, *Venture Capitalists at Work: How VCs Identify and Build Billion-Dollar Successes* (Apress), as quoted by Sean Ellis at *http://www.startup-marketing.com/great-guidance-on-pricing-from-zoosk-ceo/*.

Patrick Campbell analyzed aggregate, anonymous data to measure how many of a company's subscribers moved up a tier. He found that across his sample, 0.6% of free users moved up to a paying tier in a given month, and that 2.3% of a company's subscribers moved from a lower-priced tier to a higher-priced one in a given month.

Bottom Line

Try to get to 20% increase in *customer* revenue—which may include additional seat licenses—each year. And try to get 2% of your paying subscribers to increase what they pay each month.

Churn

(Churn is also important in mobile gaming, two-sided marketplaces, and UGC sites)

The best SaaS sites or applications usually have churn ranging from 1.5% to 3% a month. For other sites, it'll vary depending on how you define "disengaged." Mark MacLeod, Partner at Real Ventures, says that you need to get below a 5% monthly churn rate before you know you've got a business that's ready to scale. Remember, though, if you're surprising your subscribers in a bad way (e.g., billing them for something they didn't know they'd ordered), then churn will spike during your first billing period, sometimes to 50%, so you should factor this into your calculations.

David Skok agrees with the 5% churn threshold, but only for early-stage companies, and says that you have to see a clear path to getting churn below 2% if you want to scale significantly:

> In the early days of a SaaS business, churn really doesn't matter
> that much. Let's say you lose 3% of your customers every month.
> When you only have a hundred customers, losing three of them is
> not that terrible. You can easily go and find another three to replace
> them. However, as your business grows in size, the problem becomes
> different. Imagine that you have become really big, and now have a
> million customers. Three percent churn means that you are losing
> 30,000 customers every month. That turns out to be a much harder
> number to replace.

CASE STUDY | OfficeDrop's Key Metric: Paid Churn

OfficeDrop helps small businesses manage paper and digital files in the cloud. Its service provides searchable cloud storage coupled with downloadable apps that allow businesses to sync, scan, search, and share files anywhere at any time. Currently, over 180,000 users store data in the service, and its subscribers access and upload millions of files each month.

The company offers its solution as a freemium model with one free plan and three paid plans. We spoke with Healy Jones, Vice President of Marketing, to learn more about the company's key metrics and lessons learned.

"Our most important number is paid churn," says Healy. OfficeDrop defines paid churn as the number of paying users who downgrade to free or cancel divided by the total number of paying users available to churn at the beginning of the month.

For OfficeDrop, paid churn is a key indicator of the business's overall health. "For example, we can tell how our marketing messaging is doing based on paid user churn—if a lot of new customers churn out, then we know our messaging doesn't match what the customers are actually finding when they start using the product," explains Healy. "We can also tell if our feature development is progressing in the direction that older users want: if they stick around for a long time then we are doing a good job, but if they churn out fast then we are not developing the product in the direction that they want. We can also tell if any bugs are causing people to be upset—if a lot of users cancel on a particular day, then we have to look and see if there was a technical problem that ticked people off."

The company aims for a monthly churn rate below 4%. "Three percent is good," Healy says. "Anything over 5% and we really don't have a business that will generate gross margin positive growth." Most recently, Healy says the company has been hitting a churn rate of 2% and hopes to maintain that.

As is often the case, churn is the inverse of engagement, and this is the second key metric for OfficeDrop. It defines an active user as someone who used the product in the previous month. When OfficeDrop launched, the founders assumed that people would not want to install programs on their computers or devices, that they would want a rich browser experience instead. "We did everything by our gut, and almost everything was wrong," says Healy. "We hypothesized that the browser experience—which is the easiest to get started with and has the lowest barriers to entry for new customers—would be more likely to create engagement, but we didn't start seeing real engagement, and in turn real customer growth and lower churn, until we built downloadable applications."

Figure 23-2 shows a classic hockey stick around June 2011. This measures the increased customer base (which is a result of increased engagement and reduced churn).

OFFICEDROP CLOUD FILING CUSTOMER BASE

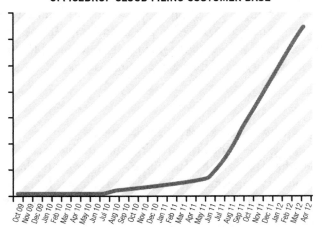

Figure 23-2. Can you tell where OfficeDrop added a mobile client app?

"In mid-2011, we went mobile and first started offering OfficeDrop as a mobile app, and that had a huge impact," says Healy. "A little harder to see—but equally important—was when we released our Mac desktop scanner application in January 2011. That was our first major downloadable app, and it got great press and drove even better engagement."

After seeing that initial uptick in engagement, OfficeDrop made the commitment to develop mobile offerings. The company launched an Android app in May 2011, followed by an iPhone app in June 2011. "Going against our assumptions, we built a desktop application that proved successful. I think of that like a pivot for us, and it gave us the confidence to change our product offering. The results are clear: improved engagement and lower churn," says Healy.

Summary

- OfficeDrop watches paid churn—paying customers who switch to a free model or leave—as its One Metric That Matters.

- The initial product was heavily browser-focused, and assumed users wouldn't want desktop or mobile clients, based on the founders' gut instincts.

- The introduction of a scanner application, followed by mobile client software, dramatically increased the growth of the company.

Analytics Lessons Learned

Always question your assumptions, even when you're seeing traction. Customers want to use certain applications in certain ways—mapping on their mobile phone, for example. Doing a day-in-the-life analysis, or testing a major pivot with the introduction of a simple application, can often prove or invalidate a big assumption quickly, and change your fortunes forever.

Certain products or services are very sticky, in part because of the lock-in users experience. Photo upload sites and online backup services, for example, are hard to leave, because there's a lot of data in place, so churn for those product categories may be lower. On the other hand, in an industry with relatively low switching costs, churn will be substantially higher.

Social sites may have some tricks at their disposal, too. If users try to leave Facebook, they're reminded that some of their close friends will miss them—and they'll lose pictures of those friends. This is an example of how an emotional tweak was later supported by the data: once implemented, this last-ditch guilt trip reduced deactivations by 7%, which at the time meant millions of users stayed on Facebook.*

If you're going to offer users an incentive to stick around—such as a free month or an upgrade to a new phone—you'll have to weigh the cost of doing so against the cost of acquiring another customer. Of course, if word gets out that you're incentivizing disgruntled users to stick around, then many customers may threaten to leave just to receive the discount, and getting the word out is what the Internet is for.

Bottom Line

Try to get down to 5% churn a month before looking at other things to optimize. If churn is higher than that, chances are you're not sticky enough. If you can get churn to around 2%, you're doing exceptionally well.

---

* *http://blog.kissmetrics.com/analytics-that-matter-to-facebook/*

CHAPTER 24

Free Mobile App: Lines in the Sand

Mobile Downloads

The mobile application business suffers from a "long tail" of popularity: a few apps do very well, but most of them flounder. According to Ken Seto, founder and CEO of mobile game company Massive Damage, "Some indie game developers get as few as a couple of downloads a day. This number is entirely dependent on your marketing, virality, and ranking in the app store."

All businesses have competitors. But for mobile apps, the app store ecosystem puts that competition front and center. You can't ignore your standings, and you can't relax. "The tricky part," he says, "is that it's hard to stick at a certain ranking because everyone around you is trying to surpass you. So if your game doesn't have natural hype—or isn't promoted by Apple or paid marketing—you will slip in rankings. There's no 'typical' here."

Bottom Line

Expect yourself to be at the mercy of promotions, marketing, and the whims of the app store environment. The app store battle can be demoralizing, but smart mobile developers use the abundance of information about competitors to see what's working, emulate their successes, and avoid their mistakes.

Mobile Download Size

As mobile applications get more complex, their file sizes increase. This poses a risk for developers, though; consumers on slower connections may abandon a download if it takes too long. Alexandre Pelletier-Normand, co-founder of Execution Labs, a game development accelerator, says, "If you want your app to be easily downloadable by anyone anywhere, it has to be under 50 megabytes, 'on the portal'."

An app that's bigger than 50 MB for iOS devices will require a Wi-Fi connection. If a user doesn't have a Wi-Fi connection, she won't be able to download your app, and it's unlikely she'll bother trying again.

You can download apps that are larger than 50 MB on Android devices, but the process is greatly impacted by a warning from Google Play, which interrupts users and results in significant drop-off in the download process.

Alexandre makes a point of using the phrase "on the portal" to refer to the initial download from Apple's App Store or Android app stores. He says, "Some developers will work around the limitation by having a small app on the Google or Apple portals, and this app will then download additional content 'transparently' from the developer's servers while you play."

Bottom Line

Keep your initial downloads small, and aim for less than 50 MB to minimize download churn.

Mobile Customer Acquisition Cost

Some application developers use third-party marketing services to pay for installations. This is an ethical gray area for mobile developers: you're using mercenaries to artificially inflate your download numbers and juice your ratings, in the hopes that the resulting improvement in rankings will convince real users to download the app. There are legitimate marketing services out there for mobile application and game developers, but be careful who you work with. While few of the people we've talked with will go on record about pricing, such services cost from $0.10 to $0.70 per install at the low end.

Because few of these installations become engaged players, it's critical that you segment out mercenary installers to avoid polluting your other metrics. The metric you really care about is how many *legitimate* users your mercenaries bring in, and how many of those become engaged, paying users.

A more legitimate form of acquisition is banners or ads within other applications. Typically, these cost $1.50 to $4.00 per installation; these installations are more likely to become legitimate users because they found out about the application and chose to install it themselves. "The trick is to get your average cost per installation (across both mercenary and legitimate installations) to somewhere between $0.50 and $0.75," says Ken Seto. "These numbers are all based on free games [with in-game monetization], however. I don't think it's cash-efficient to do paid installs for paid games."

Keith Katz also warns against spending up to your CLV, which he sees a lot of app developers doing:

> Too many mobile game developers seem to think the math works when you spend dollar for dollar against your customer lifetime value. But they tend to forget that you pay tax on your revenue to the government and then there's the "platform tax" incurred by Apple's App Store or Google Play, which is 30%. If you're spending $1 to generate $1 in revenue, you're really spending closer to $1 to generate $0.60.

Bottom Line

Pay around $0.50 for a paid (mercenary) install, and around $2.50 for a legitimate, organic one, but make sure that your overall acquisition cost is less than $0.75 per user (and, of course, less than the lifetime value of a user). These costs are increasing, in part because large studios and publishers are getting more heavily into mobile and driving costs higher, and in part because of the crackdown on some marketing service tactics for delivering paid installs.

CASE STUDY | ## Sincerely Learns the Challenges of Mobile Customer Acquisition

Sincerely Inc. is the maker of the Sincerely gifting network and a number of mobile applications including Postagram, Ink Cards, and Sesame Gifts. The company's first application, Postagram, lets people create and send a custom postcard from anywhere in the world. Ink Cards, its second app, allows you to send personalized greeting cards. And Sesame Gifts allows you to send themed gift sets in a beautiful box. The company has evolved from the simplest shippable item—a postcard—to $30–$50 gifts with Sesame.

When the company first started in 2010, co-founders Matt Brezina and Bryan Kennedy assumed that mobile ads would be like Google AdWords in 2000—early movers (to using mobile advertising) would have a huge advantage in a giant, not-yet-efficient user acquisition channel. "We figured by selling the simplest gift on the planet, a 99-cent postcard, we could easily buy users, get credit cards, and begin to make our gifting network profitable," says Matt. "This strategy was gut instinct and some small experiments we ran on an off-branded app (i.e., one that wasn't obviously affiliated with the Sincerely brand)."

It turns out Sincerely was able to buy users through mobile advertising for Postagram, but not cheaply enough. "Our metric for success was buying a Postagram user cheaply enough that they'd become profitable in under one year," says Matt. "And if not, could we cross-promote them to another, more expensive gifting app to get them profitable within one year, and eventually three months."

Matt and Bryan found that not only were mobile adds too expensive, but also that they were hard to track and the conversion rate from initial acquisition to mobile installation and launch was abysmal. So they launched Ink Cards six months after Postagram and set a price point starting at $1.99 per card. "Through cross-promotion, we increased the lifetime value of an initial Postagram user by around 30%," says Matt. "But the payback time *still* wasn't what we wanted it to be."

Now Sincerely has launched Sesame, which offers gifts at a higher price point. "We now hope to get into the zone of sustainably growing the business through ads," says Matt. But as a result of the cost and challenges with mobile advertising, Sincerely spends a significant amount of time focused on virality. "Through necessity—because the mobile ad equation just doesn't work well enough—we've learned a lot about driving growth by enabling our users to share their great experience with new friends," Matt says. "We do this by giving users free cards for people they've never sent any to." This focus on viral growth reduces the reliance on advertising alone for user acquisition in a mobile industry where acquisition tools aren't yet mature or efficient.

Summary

- Sincerely launched Postagram to allow users to send 99-cent custom postcards, and assumed that mobile advertising would be inexpensive and efficient enough for the company to grow successfully.

- The company was able to acquire users, but it was too expensive (because mobile advertising was hard to measure, and drop-off rates were high) and not rewarding enough (because the lifetime value of the customer was too low).

- The company launched Ink Cards, personalized greeting cards with a higher price point. This improved lifetime value by around 30%, but the payback time was still too slow, and it wasn't enough for mobile advertising to be profitable.

- Now Sincerely has launched Sesame Gifts, curated gifts you can send to people for $30–$50. The founders hope that this new price point will allow them to grow profitably through mobile advertising, while they also focus more on growing virally to reduce their dependency on advertising channels.

Analytics Lessons Learned

Mobile advertising is more complicated and more expensive than you may initially realize, and you need to track the customer acquisition cost carefully. You also need to track how quickly users pay back the cost of acquiring them, as well as their lifetime value. Test different channels and track user behavior, and use virality as a means of lowering your acquisition costs.

Application Launch Rate

Simply downloading an application isn't enough. Users have to launch it, and some wait a long time to do so. In addition to the size constraints outlined previously, multiple tablets and phones connected to a single account may download the application at different times, skewing your launch analytics. In other words: it's complicated.

For free applications, many downloaders are just browsing applications casually and haven't committed to a particular game or application and the related in-game purchases, so a higher percentage of downloads are never launched. For example, Massive Damage sees roughly 83% of downloads for its flagship game, *Please Stay Calm*, lead to an application launch.

Bottom Line

Expect a significant number of downloads to never launch your application, particularly if it's a free app.

Percent Active Mobile Users/Players

When it comes to inactivity, the first day is always the worst. There's a gradual decline in active users over time, but the first day decline can be as high as 80%. Following that, there's a gradual drop-off each day: for a cohort of users, as few as 5% of them may be around after a month.

An October 2012 study by mobile analytics firm Flurry showed that across more than 200,000 applications, only 54% of users were still around at the end of the first month, only 43% were around at the end of the second, and only 35% were using the application by the end of the third.[*] On average, users interacted with the application 3.7 times a day, though these metrics varied highly with the kind of application being used.

It's important to note that overall engagement has increased in the numbers shared by Flurry (from 25% to 35% in the third month), but that frequency of use has dropped (from 6.7 uses a week to 3.7 a week). Flurry also notes that device affects engagement: smartphone users interact with an app 12.9 times a week, on average, but do so for only 4.1 minutes; tablet users interact with an app 9.5 times a week, but do so for 8.2 minutes.[†]

Bottom Line

Assume that a big chunk of the people who try your app once will never do so again—but after that initial cliff drop, you'll see a more gradual decline in engaged users. While the shape of this curve will vary by app, industry, and demographic, the curve always exists, so once you have a few data points you may be able to predict churn and disengagement ahead of time.

Percentage of Mobile Users Who Pay

If your application is paid-only, then this will naturally be "all of them," but if you're running a freemium model where users pay for enhanced functionality, then a good rule of thumb is that 2% of your users will actually sign up for the full offering.

For a free-to-play mobile game with in-app purchases, Ken Seto says that across the industry roughly 1.5% of players will buy something within the game during their use of it.

In-game purchases follow a typical power law, with a few "whales" spending significantly more on in-game activity and the majority spending little or nothing. A key factor in mobile application success is being able to strike a balance between gameplay quality (which increases good ratings and the number of players) and in-app purchases (which drives revenue). In a multiplayer game, maintaining game balance between paid and free players is a constant challenge.

---

[*] *http://blog.flurry.com/bid/90743/App-Engagement-The-Matrix-Reloaded*

[†] *http://blog.flurry.com/bid/90987/The-Truth-About-Cats-and-Dogs-Smartphone-vs-Tablet-Usage-Differences*

Bottom Line

For a freemium model, aim for a conversion from free to paid of 2%. For a mobile application or game with in-app purchases, assume that roughly 1.5% of users will buy something.

Average Revenue Per Daily Active User

The average revenue per daily active user (ARPDAU) is a very granular way of measuring traction and revenue. Most mobile game developers focus on daily active users, and in turn on the revenue those users create.

SuperData Research has published ARPDAU benchmarks for different gaming genres:[*]

- $0.01–$0.05 USD for puzzle, caretaking, and simulation games
- $0.03–$0.07 USD for hidden object, tournament, and adventure games
- $0.05–$0.10 USD for RPGs, gambling, and poker games

GAMESbrief.com collected additional information from three game companies, DeNA, A Thinking Ape, and WGT:

> DeNA[†] and A Thinking Ape[‡] have both claimed that for most mobile games, expected ARPDAU is less than $0.10. However, YuChiang Cheng [CEO] of WGT said at Login Conference 2012 that an ARPDAU of less than $0.05 is a sign of poor performance, and that a good benchmark for ARPDAU is $0.12–015. Cheng also said that ARPDAUs on tablets are 15–25% higher than on smartphones.

Bottom Line

A good metric here is highly dependent on the type of game, but aim for an ARPDAU above $0.05 as a minimum.

Monthly Average Revenue Per Mobile User

There's no good way to generalize this, as it depends entirely on your business model. You should analyze competitors to see what prices and tiers they're charging, but don't be afraid to shake things up with new pricing in the early stages of your launch, provided you can measure the

---

[*] *http://www.gamesbrief.com/2012/09/arpdau/*

[†] *http://techcrunch.com/2012/06/13/the-1-grossing-game-on-android-and-ios-denas-rage-of-bahamut-has-almost-even-revenues-from-both/*

[‡] *http://www.insidemobileapps.com/2011/11/16/a-thinking-ape-interview-kenshi-arasaki/*

effect. Several industry insiders have told us that for mobile games, a decent average is $3 per month per daily active player—or $0.10 per day.

Bottom Line

Like customer acquisition costs, customer revenue comes from your business model and the margin targets you've set. Every vertical has its own value. But in the mobile app world, if you know your ARPDAU, the number of days a user sticks around, and your cost per install, you can do the math fairly quickly and decide if you have a viable business model.

Average Revenue Per Paying User

Figuring out a good benchmark for average revenue per paying user (ARPPU) is hard. It's highly dependent on the type of app (and we're focused primarily on games here) as well as the operating system.

Nicholas Lovell of GAMESBrief.com splits paying users into three categories: minnows, dolphins, and whales:

> Real whales can spend an enormous amount of money. Social Gold reckons the highest group of spenders has a lifetime value of over $1,000, with some spending over $20,000 on a single game.[*] Flurry, meanwhile, says that on iOS and Android in the US, the average transaction value for an in-app purchase is $14, and 51% of revenue is generated from in-app purchase transactions of over $20.[†]

Nicholas recommends looking at ARPPU for whales, dolphins, and minnows separately:

- Whales: 10% of payers, ARPPU of $20
- Dolphins: 40% of payers, ARPPU of $5
- Minnows: 50% of payers, ARPPU of $1

"These [averages] are dependent on your game," says Nicholas. "Not just which platform or genre, but how you design. For your whales to reach an ARPPU of $20, some of them must be spending over $100. Is this possible? Your dolphins need to have a good reason to keep spending a little bit of money each month. Have you created one? Your minnows need to be converted from freeloaders to buyers. What will make them jump?"

---

[*] *http://www.gamesbrief.com/2010/06/whats-the-lifetime-value-of-a-social-game-player/*

[†] *http://blog.flurry.com/bid/67748/Consumers-Spend-Average-of-14-per-Transaction-in-iOS-and-Android-Freemium-Games*

Bottom Line

Recognize that in a free-to-play multiplayer game, most users are just "fodder" for paying users. Early on in the user's lifecycle, identify a leading indicator in her behavior—like time played per day, number of battles, or areas explored—that suggests whether she's a non-payer, minnow, dolphin, or whale. Then provide different kinds of in-game monetization for these four segments—adapting your marketing, pricing, and promotions according to that behavior—selling bling to minnows, content to dolphins, and upgrades to whales (for example).

Mobile App Ratings Click-Through

Good ratings and reviews have a significant impact on downloads, but encouraging users to rate an app can be tough. After a few uses of the application, most developers pop up a message asking for a review; some developers even vary the message to try to encourage ratings. For example, one mobile developer asks questions like "Do you like this application?" or "Would you like to see more features and free content?" in the pop up; clicking "yes" takes the user to the ratings page.

Alexandre Pelletier-Normand warns that any message that offers something in exchange for a rating and isn't neutral could get you blocked from an app store. But he also says, "You must proactively offer users the ability to rate your app at a strategic moment—ideally early in the game, since you want many ratings quickly—after a memorable gameplay sequence. Ratings are the most important factor considered in the ranking of the app."

Review rates vary by app price and type. In one Quora response, a developer said expensive paid apps had a 1.6% review rate; cheap paid apps had a 0.5% review rate; and free trial apps had only a 0.07% review rate.* As that poster observed, sites like *xyologic.com* have detailed data on download and ratings counts, so you can compare yourself to your particular segment. For free games, Massive Damage sees a 0.73% ratio of downloads to ratings.

Bottom Line

Expect less than 1.5% review rate for paid apps, and significantly less than 1% for free apps.

---

* *http://www.quora.com/iOS-App-Store/What-percentage-of-users-rate-apps-on-iTunes*

Mobile Customer Lifetime Value

There's no good way to generalize the lifetime value of a customer, because it's a function of spending, churn, engagement, and application design. But it's a fundamental part of any business model, and it anchors other factors such as customer acquisition cost and cash flow.

GigaOm's Ryan Kim observed[*] that according to recent data,[†] freemium apps (in which users pay for something within the application) have eclipsed premium apps (where the developer offers a second, paid version) in terms of revenue, as shown in Figure 24-1.

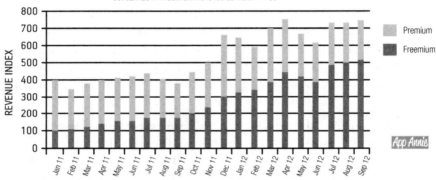

Figure 24-1. Premium is so 2010

Customer loyalty is also linked to lifetime value, and loyalty depends heavily on the kind of application. Flurry has done extensive research, as seen in Figure 24-2, across mobile applications that use its analytical tools.

---

[*] *http://gigaom.com/mobile/freemium-app-revenue-growth-leaves-premium-in-the-dust/*

[†] *http://www.appannie.com/blog/freemium-apps-ios-google-play-japan-china-leaders/*

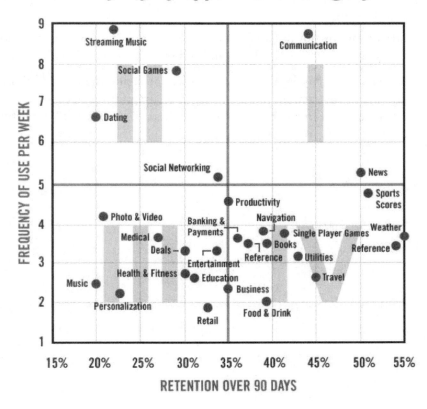

Figure 24-2. Maybe it's not just you: engagement varies by app category

As TechCrunch's Sarah Perez points out, splitting application types into two dimensions—how frequently an application is used, and what kind of user retention the application sees in a 90-day period—suggests different loyalty patterns.* These can in turn inform pricing strategies to maximize user revenue:

- Frequently used apps that retain loyal customers may be a better vehicle for advertising, recurring fees, or well-designed in-app content.

- Frequently used apps that lose users after a while may satisfy a need (such as buying a house, or completing the game) and then go away. A

* http://techcrunch.com/2012/10/22/flurry-examines-app-loyalty-news-communication-apps-top-charts-personalization-apps-see-high-churn/

per-transaction fee on completion, as well as the right to reach out to the user when the need occurs again, will matter more than long-term engagement.

- Infrequent, low-loyalty applications need to "grab money" early on, so they may be better as a sold application or using a one-time fee.

- Infrequent, highly loyal applications need to make the most of those infrequent interactions by upselling, encouraging the user to invite others, and making sure they stay in the user's "utility belt" of useful tools.

CHAPTER 25

Media Site: Lines in the Sand

Click-Through Rates

(Click-through rates also apply to UGC sites)

A well-placed, relevant ad will get clicked more, but no matter what, ads are a numbers game: even the best ads seldom get as much as 5% click-through rates.

A May 2012 study by CPC Strategy listed the top 10 comparative shopping sites, along with their click-through rates where applicable (Bing and TheFind don't charge for clicks).* See Table 25-1.

Comparison shopping engine	Conversion rate	Cost-per-click rate
Google	2.78%	Too early to know**
Nextag	2.06%	$0.43
Pronto	1.97%	$0.45
PriceGrabber	1.75%	$0.27
Shopping.com	1.71%	$0.34
Amazon Product Ads	1.60%	$0.35

---

* *http://www.internetretailer.com/2012/05/03/why-google-converts-best-among-comparison-shopping-sites*

** *http://mashable.com/2012/09/11/google-shopping-to-switch-to-paid-model-in-october/*

Comparison shopping engine	Conversion rate	Cost-per-click rate
Become	1.57%	$0.45
Shopzilla	1.43%	$0.35
Bing	1.35%	N/A
TheFind	0.71%	N/A

Table 25-1. Top 10 comparative shopping sites

Global search marketing agency Covario reported in 2010 that the average click-through rate for paid search, worldwide, was 2% (see Table 25-2).

Bing	2.8%
Google	2.5%
Yahoo!	1.4%
Yandex	1.3%

Table 25-2. Average click-through rate for paid search

Affiliate marketer Titus Hoskins says that 5–10% of the visitors he sends to Amazon ultimately buy something, and that this is significantly higher than revenues from competing affiliate platforms.* Amazon and other general-purpose retailers also reward affiliate partners more handsomely than some more narrowly focused companies, because an affiliate referrer gets a percentage of the entire shopping cart. So if an author sends a visitor to Amazon to buy a book, and that buyer also purchases groceries, the author gets a percentage of the buyer's grocery purchase as well. This encourages affiliate advertisers to give Amazon's ads more prominence, since they're more lucrative.

Derek Szeto feels that because Amazon's conversion rates are high, affiliates are more likely to drive traffic to towards it sites. Amazon balances the richness of its affiliate program with a relatively short cookie lifetime—so an affiliate makes money from an Amazon buyer only if that person buys something within 24 hours of clicking the affiliate link.

Recall that blank ads showed a click-through rate of 0.08% in the Advertising Research Foundation's tests, so if you're seeing a click-through rate below that, you're definitely doing something wrong.

---

* *http://www.sitepronews.com/2011/12/30/what-amazon-shows-us-about-achieving-higher-conversion-rates/*

Bottom Line

Your ads will get 0.5 to 2% click-through rate for most kinds of on-page advertising. Below 0.08%, you're doing something horribly wrong.

Sessions-to-Clicks Ratio

(Sessions-to-clicks ratio also applies to UGC, e-commerce, and two-sided marketplaces)

Expect 4–6% of the clicks that come from search engines or ads to never show up on your site. You can improve this by tweaking the performance and uptime of your website, but doing so requires constant vigilance and tuning that may come at the expense of adding new features or running experiments. Until you've found product/market fit, you probably shouldn't spend a lot of time trying to improve this metric.

Bottom Line

You'll lose around 5% of clicks before the visitor ever gets to your site. Deal with it. If you're sticky enough, the visitor will try again.

Referrers

Media sites rely on referrers from other sites to drive traffic. But not all referrers are created equal. Chartbeat ran some analysis for us comparing a group of sites broadly categorized as tech- and politics-based, versus social referrers including Facebook and Twitter.* An average pickup from any of the sites analyzed resulted in a peak of 70 concurrent users, and in a two-week period users from the referrer spent a total of 9,510 minutes engaged.

Traffic from social referrers was much less engaged. Facebook referrals resulted in an average peak of 51 concurrent users, and 2,670 minutes of engaged time. Twitter referrals resulted in an average peak of 28 concurrent users, and 917 total minutes of engaged time. Chartbeat's Joshua Schwartz says, "the lower total engaged time numbers for social sites, versus those for standard referrers, speaks to the fleeting nature of social pickups; while a referrer pickup may result in a sustained flow of traffic across days, social spikes are more likely to be short-lived."

---

* These sites included TechCrunch.com, Wired.com, HotAir.com, Drudge.com, RealClearPolitics .com, TheDailyBeast.com, HuffingtonPost.com, Engadget.com, TheNextWeb.com, AllThingsD .com, PandoDaily.com, Verge.com, VentureBeat.com, Gawker.com, Jezebel.com, Mashable.com, Cracked.com, and Buzzfeed.com.

Bottom Line

Learn where your most beneficial traffic comes from, and what topics it's after, and spend time cultivating a following around those sources and topics. When you run experiments, segment them by platform: Facebook fans want a different kind of content from Twitter followers.

Engaged Time

Measuring visits or page views tells you how much traffic you had—but it doesn't tell you how much time your visitors spent actually looking at your content (also known as *time on page*). Browsers can capture this data, using a script on the page to report back as long as the visitor is engaged.

We asked Chartbeat to segment its measurement of this "engaged time" metric by the type of site. Sure enough, there's a significant difference between media, e-commerce, and SaaS sites that reflects each site's different usage patterns. Chartbeat's research, aggregated from customers who've agreed to have their data analyzed anonymously, is shown in Figure 25-1.

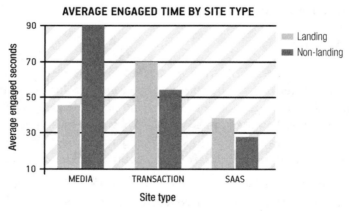

Figure 25-1. You're supposed to stick around for media; SaaS wants you to move on fast

Chartbeat found that the average engaged time on a media site's landing page is only 47 seconds, but the engaged time on a non-landing page is 90 seconds. These numbers are considerably different from the averages previously discussed (61 seconds for landing pages and 76 seconds for non-landing pages). In particular, SaaS sites have a low time on page, which is as it should be if the purpose of the site is to make users complete a task and be productive.

Joshua says, "The more analysis we do, the more we're seeing that engaged time is especially crucial for media sites. While getting lots of eyeballs is important, if the traffic immediately bounces, it doesn't do much good. So engaged time as a metric is essentially measuring the quality of a media site's content."

Bottom Line

Media sites should aim for 90 seconds or more of engaged time on their content pages. Don't expect (or aim for) a high engaged time on landing pages, though; you want people to find the content they want quickly and dig in further.

| PATTERN | **What Onsite Engagement Can Tell You About Goals and Behaviors** |

On average, people spend about a minute on a page when they're engaged with it. This varies widely by type of site, but also by pages within a site. So how can you use this information?

- **Look at the outliers.** "If a page has a large number of visitors and a low engaged time, think about why people are leaving quickly. Did they come expecting something else? Is the layout working? Or is it simply a page that isn't designed to keep users for long?" asks Joshua.

- **Show off your good stuff.** If a page has a high engaged time but few visitors, consider promoting it to a wider audience.

- **Ensure that the purpose of the page matches the engagement.** "If you're an e-commerce site, you might want your landing page to have little engagement time," says Joshua. "But if you're producing editorial content, you should aim for high engaged time on article pages."

Sharing with Others

(Sharing with others also applies to UGC sites)

Sharing is the word-of-mouth form of virality. A March 2012 Adage article by Buzzfeed's Jon Steinberg and StumbleUpon's Jack Krawczyk looked at how much popular stories had been shared.[*] As with many other metrics, there was a strong power law. The vast majority of stories were shared with

---

[*] Buzzfeed president Jon Steinberg and StumbleUpon's Jack Krawczyk looked at sharing behavior across social platforms; see *http://adage.com/article/digitalnext/content-shared-close-friends-influencers/233147/.*

a small group, and only a tiny fraction was shared widely. On Facebook, the top 50 shared stories in the last five years had received hundreds of thousands—even millions—of views.

But despite these outliers, the median ratio of views to shares is just nine. That means that, typically, for every time a story is shared only nine people visited it. In other words, most sharing is intimate, among close-knit groups of peers. On Twitter, the median was 5 to 1; on reddit, which promotes popular links on its home page, it was 36 to 1.

StumbleUpon looked at 5.5 million sharing actions in a 45-day period. It concluded that users shared "intimately" (to another StumbleUpon user, or via email) twice as often as they broadcasted a message to a wider audience using the site.

Bottom Line

With a few notable exceptions, Steinberg and Krawczyk conclude that sharing happens from a groundswell of small interactions among colleagues and friends, rather than through massive actions between one person and an army of minions.

CASE STUDY | JFL Gags Cracks Up YouTube

Since 1983, comedians from around the world have been descending on Montreal every summer for the Just For Laughs festival. Today, it's the world's largest international comedy festival.

In 2000, Just For Laughs Gags, a silent "hidden camera prank" show, began airing on television. You've probably seen these brief sketches; their short format and lack of spoken words makes them great for airplanes and other public places, as well as for global markets.

We talked with Carlos Pacheco, Digital Director at Just For Laughs, about his job monetizing Gags TV, the show's YouTube channel.

The Decline of Existing Channels

"Until recently, the Gags TV series was primarily funded (and profitable) in the old-fashioned TV way," Carlos explains. "With every new season, the TV and digital rights would be sold to local and international TV networks, which has kept the series going since its start 12 years ago." But recently, producers saw a decline in licensing prices—basically, TV networks were no longer willing to pay the prices they had in the past.

The show has had a YouTube channel since 2007, but it didn't have much content and wasn't being regularly maintained. The original plan was to create a dedicated website, relying heavily on Adobe Flash, that featured Just For Laughs content including stand-up and Gags. "Once that fell through, the team at Gags decided to concentrate on YouTube," says Carlos. "Even though the channel had been a YouTube partner since 2009, it was only in early 2011 that the producers started to notice some revenue coming from the few videos that were there." With the hypothesis that more videos would lead to more revenue, the team uploaded over 2,000 prank clips to the site.

Since its creation, Gags was formatted for television, which meant a half-hour show (with commercial breaks) featuring 12 to 14 pranks. On YouTube, the half-hour constraints were gone. In many ways, the short format of a single prank was more suited to the Web than television. "The mass upload wasn't done very strategically," says Carlos, "but out of the 2,000 videos, a few got noticed and went viral, helping the channel grow, and ad revenue became significant in early 2012."

Getting the Ad Balance Right

On YouTube, content owners can run ads in several ways. They can create overlays atop the video with clickable links, and they can screen ads before, during, or after the content. The content provider can also decide whether ads can be skipped or not. The right ad strategy is critical; more impressions and more ads means more revenue (measured in *cost per engagement*, or CPE—the revenue earned from an ad impression), but those ads can turn viewers away.

Initially the only metrics the team looked at were daily views and revenue. Now they're getting much more sophisticated, looking at metrics such as time watched per video, traffic sources, playback locations, demographics, annotations, and audience retention. A key goal is to analyze where people drop off from watching, which helps guide Carlos on the right formats for videos.

"For example, a few months ago we started producing web exclusive 'best of Gags' videos," says Carlos. "The first videos featured a 10- to 15-second intro animation, but looking at the audience retention we saw a 30% drop-off within the first 15 seconds. After that, we modified the initial uploads and all future uploads to remove the intros, which gave our audience the content they really wanted as soon as they pressed play."

Early on, Gags used only overlay ads on its content. Later, the team added a kind of skippable YouTube ad called TrueView pre-roll advertising, which increased overall CPE but didn't slow down growth. "We didn't want to start with anything other than TrueView, since our content is short. We knew our fans weren't interested in sitting through a minute-long pre-roll ad just to watch a one- to two-minute prank video," says Carlos. The team has also experimented with YouTube TV channels like Revision3, with good results.

In early 2012, YouTube announced that longer-form content would be prioritized in recommendations it made to viewers. Since the Gags team had seen other content producers uploading full TV episodes onto the site, they thought this would be a good way to experiment with uncut episodes that had forced pre-roll, mid-roll, and post-roll ads.

The results showed that even though the long form worked, shorter clips were still better:

- In the first 24 hours after a long-form video was uploaded, the number of views was nearly the same as those of a two-minute video clip, averaging 30,000–40,000 views.

- Ad revenue per long-form video was five times higher than that from a two-minute clip. That might seem like a good thing, but a long-form video has around 12 individual clips, so it's actually less lucrative.

- Long-form video episodes have a longer tail of viewing—they keep a higher average number of daily views for a longer period than the short clips.

- Audience retention is very different. Because the long-form episodes have introductions and are longer, there's a 40% audience drop-off halfway into an episode, versus a 15% drop-off halfway into a single short video.

Merchandising on the Channel

Until now, there has been no attempt to sell products via the channel. The Gags team gets requests to buy video, and even the music that accompanies each video. "This is a huge wasted opportunity for us, considering we generate over 4 million impressions a day," says Carlos. "We have 4 to 5 million people walking into our store every day, but there's nothing to buy. I've made it my personal mission to change this using YouTube-approved retailers (which allow us to link out from annotations) for our merchandise, as well as by partnering with digital distributors."

To Take Down or Not?

Gags owns all the rights to the content it uploads. With its viral, broadly appealing content, copying and repurposing material happens a lot, but the team doesn't do any Digital Millennium Copyright Act (DMCA) takedowns. Part of this is simply getting the word out to new markets. "Most of the time, fan-made compilations and uploads to a personal YouTube account go viral in the uploader's specific market," says Carlos. "This has helped us expand our brand and audience to markets we never even thought of."

But there's another, more lucrative, reason for not having these videos taken down. "Every time a fan 'repurposes' our content on his or her personal YouTube channel, we see it in our content management system, and we're given a choice: either take it down, release our claim, or reinstate our claim and monetize the uploaded content," says Pacheco. "In almost every case, we reinstate the content and monetize these user-generated videos."

Since deciding to focus on YouTube, the channel has grown dramatically, "In the last year, on average, there are 100,000 user-generated Gags videos that generate 40–50% of our total monthly views," says Carlos. "I've seen two-hour mash-up videos of our content that have generated millions of views, which is something we would never have thought of doing."

Although fan-made videos bring in less revenue per engagement than Gags' original content, the sheer volume of views represents a significant amount of total ad revenue. Carlos says, "I also pay attention to how fans are compiling these videos to see if we can learn from and mimic their success, since we often see UGC videos generate more views than ours."

A Fundamentally New Opportunity

Carlos points out that Gags' growth on YouTube has happened completely independently from any marketing web support from the Just For Laughs festival or social media channels. Before February 2012, Gags had no official Facebook page, Twitter account, or web presence. "Of course, a key success factor that helped Gags grow is the fact that it's been on the air for over 10 years in over 100 countries. But until recently, our online presence was almost nonexistent," says Carlos.

Originally producers thought that uploading their full catalog to the Web would cannibalize TV sales. That didn't happen. Television sales actually *improved* as a result of Gags being discovered by new, untapped markets, and other online content providers are regularly reaching out to Gags with new monetization opportunities.

"The success of the YouTube channel over the last 12 months has turned things around for Gags," says Carlos. "Producers are no longer at the mercy of television or cable networks. On top of that, with funding opportunities like YouTube original channels, there's space for creators like us to build brand new online properties, which is something we're seriously looking at."

The nature of the Gags content, being mostly silent, helps it transcend borders, cultures, and languages. Carlos feels this has helped the brand expand dramatically: "Although our main channel will hit a billion views within the next few months, behind the scenes our total channel and UGC views are already past 2.1 billion."

Summary

- Just For Laughs Gags produces short, popular comedy reels well suited for the Web.

- Gags' YouTube channel brings in revenue from both its own content and content created by end users.

- Short-form video, without long pre-roll introductions, has proven more lucrative than longer content.

Analytics Lessons Learned

Sometimes it's better to build atop someone else's platform than to build something from scratch, and sometimes user-generated content can be a lucrative revenue model for media sites, particularly when you learn from what users are doing and emulate it yourself. The key is to measure engagement and optimize your content for the medium.

CHAPTER 26

User-Generated Content: Lines in the Sand

Content Upload Success

(Content upload success also applies to two-sided marketplaces)

If there's an action on your site that you want users to take because it's key to success, it has a funnel you can track and optimize. On Facebook, for example, sharing photos is one of the most common things users do. In 2010, Facebook's Adam Mosseri revealed some data on how Facebook's photo upload funnel worked:[*]

- 57% of users successfully find and select their photo files.
- 52% of users find the upload button.
- 42% successfully upload a picture.

Success can be a complicated thing to define. For example, 85% of users chose only one picture for an album, which wasn't good for the way Facebook organized pictures. So the developers added another step that allowed users to select more than one picture more easily. After the change, the number of single-picture albums dropped to 40%.

---

[*]   *http://blog.kissmetrics.com/analytics-that-matter-to-facebook/*

Bottom Line

There's no clear number, but if a content generation function (such as uploading photos) is core to the use of your application, optimize it until all your users can do it, and track error conditions carefully to find out what's causing the problem.

Time on Site Per Day

(Time on site per day also applies to media sites)

There's a surprisingly consistent rule of thumb for social networks and UGC websites. Across many companies we polled, the average time on site per day seemed to be 17 minutes. This number was mentioned several times by companies participating in the TechStars accelerator program at a recent demo day; it's also what reddit sees for an average user. One study showed that Pinterest users spend 14 minutes on the site each day, Tumblr users spend 21 minutes a day, and Facebook users spend an hour a day on the site.[*]

Bottom Line

You'll have a very good indicator of stickiness when site visitors are spending 17 minutes a day on your site.

CASE STUDY | ## Reddit Part 1—From Links to a Community

From humble beginnings as a startup in the first cohort of Paul Graham's Y Combinator accelerator, reddit has grown to be one of the highest-traffic destinations on the Web.

Reddit began as a simple link-sharing site, but over the years it's changed significantly. "A lot of features were just us sitting down and thinking, 'what would be cool to have?'" says Jeremy Edberg, who was reddit's first employee and ran infrastructure operations. "When the site first launched, it was just for sharing and voting on links. The idea to add comments was pretty much because [reddit co-founder] Steve Huffman decided he wanted to comment on some links."

Even after commenting was enabled, there was no way to start a discussion within reddit itself. So users found ways to do this themselves. The comment threads became discussions in their own right. Seeing

---

* *http://tellemgrodypr.com/2012/04/04/how-popular-is-pinterest/*

this, the team added a feature, called *self-posts*, that let someone start a conversation without linking elsewhere on the Web. "When we first did [self-posts], it was pretty much just a response to things users were already doing using hacks, so we decided to make it easier," says Jeremy. This is a great example of what Marc Andreesen says: "In a great market—a market with lots of real potential customers—the market *pulls* product out of the startup."* Self-posts have since become a cornerstone of the site, creating a community of users who interact with one another. "Today, more submissions are self-posts than not."

Reddit has an engaged, passionate community, and it's perfectly designed to collect feedback. "The entire site is set up for giving feedback, which makes it very easy for the users to give direct feedback and for the company to know which feedback is important," says Jeremy. But he cautions that it's not enough to listen to users—you have to watch what they do. "Direct feedback, even on reddit, is usually not an accurate depiction of how users actually feel. The phrase 'actions speak louder than words' applies just as much to business as anything else. Your users' *actions* should drive your business."

Summary

- Reddit pivoted from simple link sharing to commenting to a platform for moderated, on-site discussions by watching how users were using what it had built.

- Despite copious feedback from vocal users, the real test was what users were actually doing.

Analytics Lessons Learned

While it's important not to overbuild beyond your initial feature set or core function—in reddit's case, link sharing—a thriving community will pull features out of you if you know how to listen. Reddit included only basic functionality, but made it easy for users to extend the site, then learned from what was working best and incorporated it into the platform.

---

* *http://www.stanford.edu/class/ee204/ProductMarketFit.html*

Engagement Funnel Changes

Leading web usability consultant Jakob Nielsen once observed that in an online population, 90% of people lurk, 9% contribute intermittently, and 1% are heavy contributors.[*] His numbers suggest that there are power laws at work in engagement funnels. These patterns predate the Web—they occurred in online forums like CompuServe, AOL, and Usenet. Table 26-1 shows some of his estimates.

Platform	Lurkers	Occasional	Frequent
Usenet	?	580,000	19,000
Blogs	95%	5%	0.1%
Wikipedia	99.8%	0.2%	0.003%
Amazon reviews	99%	1%	Tiny
Facebook donation app	99.3%	0.7%	?

Table 26-1. Jakob Nielsen's engagement estimates

Nielsen has a number of approaches for moving lurkers toward participation, including making it easier to participate and making participation an automatic side-effect of usage. For example, if you have a link-sharing site, you might time how long it takes a user to return from viewing a link and use that as a measurement of the link's quality—the user wouldn't have to rate the link. Any attempt to optimize contribution and engagement would then become a hypothesis for testing.

Nielsen's ratio is changing as web use becomes part of our daily lives. A 2012 BBC study of online engagement showed that 77% of the UK's online population is participating online, partly due to the ubiquity of the Internet as a social platform and how easy it is to participate lazily, by uploading a picture or updating a status.[†]

The Altimeter Group's Charlene Li has done a lot of research into engagement. Her engagement pyramid details several kinds of user engagement. In her book *Open Leadership* (Jossey-Bass), she cites the 2010 Global Web Index Source, which surveyed web users from various countries about the kinds of activities in which they engaged online.[‡] Roughly 80% of respondents

---

[*] See *http://www.useit.com/alertbox/participation_inequality.html*, which has a number of excellent tips for improving participation inequality.

[†] *http://www.bbc.co.uk/blogs/bbcinternet/2012/05/bbc_online_briefing_spring_201_1.html*

[‡] Global Web Index Wave 2 (January 2010), *trendstream.net*.

consumed content passively, 62% shared content, 43% commented, and 36% produced content. (See Table 26-2.)

	China	France	Japan	UK	USA
Watchers: Watch video, listen to a podcast, read a blog, visit a consumer review site or forum.	86.0%	75.4%	70.4%	78.9%	78.1%
Sharers: Share videos or photos, update social network or blog.	74.2%	48.9%	29.2%	61.8%	63.0%
Commenters: Comment on a news story, blog, or retail site.	62.1%	35.6%	21.7%	31.9%	34.4%
Producers: Write a blog or news story, upload a video.	59.1%	20.2%	28.0%	21.1%	26.1%

Table 26-2. Engagement by country

The difference between countries is notable—more than half of Chinese web users produced their own content, but only 20% of French and English respondents did. Clearly, "normal" engagement is dependent on user culture.

Participation, then, is tied to cultural expectations and the purpose of the platform. Facebook has a high engagement rate from its users because their interactions are highly personal, and users upload to Flickr because, well, that's where their pictures live. But highly directed participation (like writing a Wikipedia entry, or posting a product review) that isn't the central reason for the platform to exist remains elusive for many startups.

The BBC's model breaks users down into four groups:

- 23% of Internet users are passive, choosing only to consume

- 16% of users will react to something (voting, commenting, or flagging it)

- 44% will initiate something (posting content, starting a thread, etc.)

- 17% of users are contributing intensely, doing something even when it's difficult or not core to the platform, such as reviewing a book on an e-commerce site

A thread on reddit that discussed user engagement on the site had some interesting numbers.* One user posted that he'd submitted a picture that received 75,000 views in 24 hours on Imgur. The topic itself had 1,347 up-votes, 640 down-votes, and 108 comments. That suggests a 2.5% "easy" engagement and a 0.14% "difficult" engagement.

Jeremy Edberg says that in 2009 reddit's user contribution followed the 80/20 rule seen on many UGC sites; that is, 20% of users were logged in and voting, and 20% of *those* were commenting. While the site's behavior has shifted significantly as it has become more social and community-oriented, the percentage of visitors who comment is still small.

Even lurking, disengaged visitors may be doing something. A 2011 study from MIT's Sloane School of Management suggests that many of them share passively, via channels you don't see, such as email or conversations elsewhere.† Yammer says that over 60% of its users subscribe to a regular digest of activity, which means the company has permission to reach them.‡

Bottom Line

By our estimates, expect 25% of your visitors to lurk, 60–70% of your visitors to do things that are easy and central to the purpose of your product or service, and 5–15% of your users to engage and create content for you. Among those engaged users, expect 80% of your content to come from a small, hyperactive group of users, and expect 2.5% of users to interact casually with content and less than 1% to put some effort into interaction.

CASE STUDY | **Reddit Part 2—There's Gold in Those Users**

Once reddit had pivoted from link sharing to a community, it had engaged users, but it still wasn't making money, sometimes struggling to pay for enough infrastructure to handle its growing traffic load. While advertising was a possible source of revenue, it came at the expense of user satisfaction. Enough of reddit's users employed ad-blocking software on their browsers that reddit even ran the occasional ad thanking people for not using it.

---

* *http://www.reddit.com/r/AskReddit/comments/bg7b8/what_percentage_of_redditors_are_lurkers/*

† *http://papers.ssrn.com/sol3/papers.cfm?abstract_id=1041261*

‡ *http://blog.yammer.com/blog/2011/07/your-community-hidden-treasure-lurking.html*

Then the company found an alternate source of revenue: donations. "Users would constantly joke that such-and-such a feature is only available via reddit gold," says Jeremy Edberg. "At some point, our parent company came to us and asked us to think of ways to increase our revenue (which, to their credit, was something that took three years for them to ask). We thought, 'Hey, let's make this reddit gold thing real.'"

The team added the ability to buy "gold," which didn't really have any effect beyond bragging rights. "When it launched, the only benefit you got was access to a secret forum and an (electronic) trophy. We didn't even have a price—we asked people to pay what they thought it was worth. One person paid $1,000 for a month of reddit gold, some paid a penny," says Jeremy. "But the average was right around $4, which is how we set the price."

Over time, reddit gold users got early access to new features. As dedicated users, they were more likely to provide useful feedback—and the limited number of people using the new feature shielded servers from heavy load.

Eventually, reddit added the ability to gift gold to others, and reward good posts with a donation of gold. While the company hasn't disclosed the revenue it makes from gold, it's a significant part of its income, and it's taken steps to build it into the site. "We also realized people were buying gold for others as a way of 'tipping' for great content, so we made that easier to do," says Jeremy.

Summary

- Despite healthy user growth, reddit wasn't paying its bills and was constantly skimping on new infrastructure.

- Building on considerable goodwill and user feedback, the team tried a donation model that fit the tone and culture of the community.

- They analyzed the results of a "pay what you will" campaign to set pricing.

- Once they saw some success, they found ways to make donation easier and expand how it was used.

Analytics Lessons Learned

Remember the business model flipbook: just because you're a UGC business doesn't mean your revenue must come from ads. Wikipedia and reddit both generate revenue from their community, and it helps them stay true to their culture and retain their users.

Spam and Bad Content

UGC sites thrive because they have good content. For many of the UGC companies we spoke with—such as Community Connect and reddit—fraudulent content is a very real problem that requires constant analysis and a significant engineering investment. In addition to algorithms and machine heuristics, companies like Google and Facebook pay people full-time to screen content for criminal or objectionable material, which can be a grueling job.* Jeremy Edberg estimates that 50% of reddit's development time focused on stopping spam and vote cheating—although for the first 18 months of the site's life, user voting was enough to block all spam, and there was no spam protection in place.

Spammers often create one-time accounts, which are easy to spot. Hijacked accounts are harder to pinpoint, but most UGC sites allow users to flag spammy content, which makes it easier to review. But despite the promise of a self-policing community, users aren't a good way to find bad content. Many of the posts flagged on reddit were actually spammers flagging everyone *else* in the hopes of boosting their own content. At reddit, "we had to build a system to analyze the quality of the reports per user (how many reports ultimately turned into verified spam)," says Jeremy.

At reddit, automated filters, along with moderators, catch most of the spam—which, in 2011, represented about half of all submitted content. "That 50% comes from far less than 50% of the users," says Jeremy. "Pretty much the way all the anti-cheating was developed was by finding a case of a cheater who was successful, analyzing why they were successful, finding other examples in the corpus, and then developing a model to find that type of cheating."

Ultimately, spam suggested the site's advertising revenue model, too. "We figured spammers were trying to get their links seen though cheating; why not just let them pay and then make it obvious they paid?" recalls Jeremy. "If you look at the sponsored link today, you'll see that the styling and execution is almost identical to how Google highlighted sponsored links around 2008."

Bottom Line

Expect to spend a significant amount of time and money fighting spam as you become more popular. Start measuring what's good and bad, and which users are good at flagging bad content, early on—the key to effective

---

* *http://www.buzzfeed.com/reyhan/tech-confessional-the-googler-who-looks-at-the-wo*

algorithms is a body of data to train them. Content quality is a leading indicator of user satisfaction, so watch for a decline in quality and deal with it before it alienates your community.

CHAPTER 27

Two-Sided Marketplaces: Lines in the Sand

Two-sided marketplaces are really a blend of two other models: e-commerce (because they're built around transactions between buyers and sellers) and user-generated content (because they rely on sellers to create and manage listings whose quality affects the revenue and health of the marketplace). This means there's a combination of analytics you need to care about.

There is another reason analytics matter to marketplaces. Sellers seldom have the sophistication to analyze pricing, the effectiveness of their pictures, or what copy sells best. As the marketplace owner, you can help them with this analysis. In fact, you can do it better than they can, because you have access to the aggregate data from all sellers on the site.

An individual merchant might not know what price to charge. Even if he could do the analysis, he wouldn't have enough data points. But since you have access to *all* transactions, you may be able to help him optimize pricing (and improve your revenues along the way). Airbnb did this kind of experimental optimization on behalf of its vendors when it tested the impact of paid photography services on rental rates—then rolled the service out to property owners.

We've looked at both the e-commerce and UGC models in other chapters, but here we'll briefly consider some of the unique challenges faced by two-sided marketplaces.

Transaction Size

Some marketplaces are for infrequent, big-ticket items (like houses), while others are for frequent, smaller items (like those listed on eBay). This means that the number of listings per seller, and the transaction price, vary widely, and a useful baseline is impossible.

There are often correlations between purchase size and conversion rate, however. The bigger a purchase, the more consideration and comparison go into it. Smaller purchases carry less risk, and may be more impulsive or whimsical than big ones.

Bottom Line

We can't tell you what your typical transaction size will be, but we can tell you that you should measure it, along with conversion rates, to understand your buyers' behavior—then pass this information along to sellers.

CASE STUDY | What Etsy Watches

Etsy is an online store for creative types to share and sell their work. Founded in 2005 by a painter, a photographer, and a carpenter who had nowhere to sell their work online, the company now sells over half a billion dollars a year through its shared marketplace.

The company looks at a lot of metrics. It tracks revenue metrics such as shopping carts (individual sales), number of items sold, gross monthly sales, and total fees collected from those sales. It also looks at the growth of buyers and sellers by counting the number of new accounts, new sellers, and total confirmed accounts. Over time, the company has started tracking year-on-year increase in these core metrics.

Beyond these fundamentals, Etsy tracks the growth of individual product categories, time to first sale by a user, average order value, percentage of visits that convert to a sale, percentage of return buyers, and distinct sellers within a product category. It also breaks down time-to-first-sale and average order value by product category.

Recently, the company has started looking more closely at values like the total gross margin sold and percent of converting visits by mobile versus desktop, as well as the number of active sellers in a region. It's also calculating smoothed historical averages that act as a baseline against which to identify any anomalies in the data.

Etsy VP of Engineering Kellan Elliott-McCrae says that for any given product, Etsy calculates a number of metrics, particularly within site search. The company runs its search system like any other ad network, and "constantly measures demand (searches) and supply (items) for all the keywords passing through the system, making them available for purchase and pricing them when there is both demand and supply."

When Etsy adopted a continuous deployment approach to engineering, its initial business dashboards included registrations per second, logins per second (against login errors), checkouts per second (against checkout errors), new and renewed listings, and "screwed users" (distinct users seeing an error message). "Importantly, these are all rate-based metrics designed to quickly highlight that we might have broken something," says Kellan. "Later we added metrics like average and 95th percentile page-load times, and monitored for performance regressions."

Most recently, Etsy has been trying to make it clear how various features contribute to a sale. "For example, we can attribute the percentage of sales that come directly from search, but we've found that visitors who first browse, and *then* search, have a higher conversion rate," says Kellan. "Of course, on the flip side, conversion rate is a very difficult metric to get statistical significance on, as purchases happen rarely enough that when analyzing them against the site-wide clickstream, you get anomalous results."

Kellan points out that Etsy's help pages have the best conversion rate for purchases anywhere on the site (because people go there when they're trying to accomplish something), but jokes that the company hasn't followed through on the logical product decision of making help pages the core site experience. "To get meaningful data, you really have to scope your experiments."

Even with the site's huge sales volume, the company hasn't gone after rapid growth. "We play with a very narrow margin and so we've historically been very cautious about stepping on the gas rather than closely monitoring health metrics and growing sustainably," he explains.

Because anticipating demand helps drive sales, the company sends out a monthly newsletter to sellers, which discusses analytical data, market research, and historical trends. The company also has a market research tool for sellers. "If a seller were to search for 'desk'," explains Kellan, "they could check out the market research tool to see that 'desk calendars' generally sell in the $20–$24 range, a downloadable desk calendar PDF sells in the $4 range, desk lamps sell in roughly the $50 range, and only a handful of actual desks are sold each day."

Etsy is a shared marketplace, but it overcame the chicken-and-egg issues that two-sided markets face through serendipity. "Initially our buyers and sellers were the same people. We made this explicit in the beginning by encouraging the sale of both crafts and craft supplies," says Kellan. "Etsy was deeply embedded in a community of makers who supported each other, and initially we were helping them find one another."

Summary

- Etsy is metrics-driven, but those metrics have become increasingly business-focused as it's moved past product/market fit.

- The company sidestepped the chicken-and-egg problem most marketplaces face because initially, its buyers were also sellers.

- Analytics are also shared with vendors, in order to help them sell more successfully—which in turn helps Etsy.

Analytics Lessons Learned

The buyer/seller model in a shared marketplace is a lot like inventory in an advertising network. Knowing what buyers want, and how well you're meeting that demand, is an early indicator of what your revenues will be like. And because you want to help your sellers, you should selectively share analytical data with them that will make them better at selling.

Top 10 Lists

Top 10 lists are a good way to start understanding how your marketplace is working. Run some queries of KPIs like revenue and number of transactions according to product segments:

- Who are your top 10 buyers?

- Who are your top 10 sellers?

- What products or categories generate the majority of your revenues?

- What price ranges, times of day, and days of week experience peak sales?

It might seem simple, but making lists of the top 10 segments or categories, and looking at what's changing, will give you qualitative insights into the health of your marketplace that you can later turn into quantitative tests, and then innovations.

Bottom Line

Unlike a traditional e-commerce company, you don't have a lot of control over inventory and listings. But what you *do* have is insight into what is selling well, so you can go and get more like it. If you find that a particular product category, geographic region, house size, or color is selling well, you can encourage those sellers—and find more like them.

CHAPTER 28

What to Do When You Don't Have a Baseline

We've tried to describe some useful baselines. But if you've read through the past seven chapters, you'll know that these numbers are rudimentary at best: you want churn below 2.5%; you want users to spend 17 minutes on your site if you're in media or UGC; fewer than 2.5% of people will interact with content; 65% of your users will stop using your mobile app within 90 days. *For many metrics, there's simply no "normal."*

The reality is you'll quickly adjust the line in the sand to your particular market or product. That's fine. Just remember that you shouldn't move the line to your ability; rather, you need to move your ability to the line.

Nearly any optimization effort has diminishing returns. Making a website load in 1 second instead of 10 is fairly easy; making it load in 100 milliseconds instead of 1 second is much harder. Ten milliseconds is nearly impossible. Eventually, it's not worth the effort, and that's true of many attempts to improve something.

That shouldn't be discouraging. It's actually useful, because it means that as you approach a local maximum, you can plot your results over time and see an asymptote. In other words, the rate at which your efforts are producing diminishing results can suggest a baseline, and tell you it's time to move to a different metric that matters.

Consider the 30-day optimization effort for a site that's trying to convince visitors to enroll, shown in Figure 28-1. At first, out of over 1,200 visitors, only 4 sign up—an abysmal 0.3% conversion rate. But each day, the company tweaks and tests enrollment even as site traffic grows modestly. By the end of the month, the site is converting 8.2% of its 1,462 visitors.

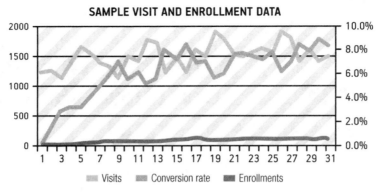

Figure 28-1. Can you see the gradual improvement in this chart?

The question is: should this company keep working on enrollment, or has it hit diminishing returns? By applying a trend line to the conversion rate, we can quickly see the diminishing returns (Figure 28-2).

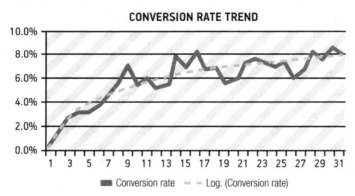

Figure 28-2: Maybe 9% is as good as this will get without a radical change

Ultimately, the best the company will be able to do with *all else being equal* is achieve a conversion rate of around 9%. So on the one hand, that's a good baseline, and gives a sense of the universe it's in. On the other hand, all else is seldom equal. A new strategy for user acquisition could change things significantly.

This recalls our earlier discussion of local maxima. Iterating and improving the current situation will deliver diminishing returns, but that may be good enough to satisfy part of your business model and move forward. In this example, if the company's business model assumes that 7% of visitors will subscribe, then it's time to move on to something else, such as increasing the number of visitors.

If you don't have a good sense of what's normal for the world, use this kind of approach. At least you'll know what's normal—and achievable—for your current business.

At this point, you've got an idea of your business model, the stage you're at, and some of the baselines against which you should be comparing yourself. Now let's move beyond startups into other areas where Lean Analytics still plays an important role: selling to the enterprise and intrapreneurs.

PART FOUR:

PUTTING LEAN ANALYTICS TO WORK

You now know a lot about data. It's time to roll up your sleeves and get to work. In this part of the book, we'll look at how Lean Analytics is different for enterprise-focused startups, as well as for intrapreneurs trying to change things from within. We'll also talk about how to change your organization's culture so the entire team makes smarter, faster, more iterative decisions.

> *He who rejects change is the architect of decay. The only human*
> *institution which rejects progress is the cemetery.*
>
> Harold Wilson

CHAPTER 29

Selling into Enterprise Markets

Think Lean Analytics only applies to consumer-focused businesses? Think again.

Sure, it's easier to experiment on consumers—there are so many of them out there, and they make decisions irrationally, so you can toy with their emotions. There's no doubt that cloud computing and social media have made it easy to launch something and spread the word without significant upfront investment, and consumer startups are media icons, even fodder for Hollywood.* Even business-to-business startups, such as SaaS providers, often target small and medium companies.

But a data-informed approach to business is good for any kind of organization. Plenty of great founders went after big business problems, and got rich doing so. As TechCrunch reporter Alex Williams put it, "While the enterprise can be as boring as hell, the whole goddamn thing is paved with gold."† Enterprise-focused startups do have to deal with some unique challenges along the way, which changes the metrics they watch and how they collect them, but it's worth it.

---

* In February 2012, The Next Web's Allen Gannett listed the rise of the cloud, the consumerization of technology, and the broad adoption of SaaS delivery models as three catalysts for the rapid expansion of acquisitions in enterprise software.

† Williams's reaction after attending a demo day by Acceleprise, an accelerator focused on startups that target enterprise customers; see *http://techcrunch.com/2012/11/09/notes-from-a-startup-night-the-enterprise-can-be-as-boring-as-hell-but-the-whole-goddamn-thing-is-paved-with-gold/*.

Why Are Enterprise Customers Different?

Let's start with the good news: it's easier to find enterprises to talk to. They're in the phone book. They might have time for coffee. They have budgets. And for many of the people in these organizations, it's part of their *job* to evaluate new solutions, meet with vendors, and share their needs to see if someone can solve them more explicitly. Armed with a decent caffeine allowance, you can talk to actual prospects fairly quickly.

That said, there are plenty of important ways that enterprise sales are different and more difficult than selling to a large, unwashed audience. Venture capitalist Ben Horowitz was one of the first to burst this bubble:

> Every day I hear from entrepreneurs, angel investors, and venture capitalists about an exciting new movement called "the consumerization of the enterprise." They tell me how the old, expensive, Rolex-wearing sales forces are a thing of the past and, in the future, companies will "consume" enterprise products proactively like consumers pick up Twitter.

> But when I talk to the most successful new enterprise companies like WorkDay, Apptio, Jive, Zuora, and Cloudera, they all employ serious and large enterprise sales efforts that usually include expensive people, some of whom indeed wear Rolex watches.[*]

Big Ticket, High Touch

The one thing that makes enterprise-focused startups different is this: B2C customer development is polling, B2B customer development is a census.

In most cases, enterprise sales involve bigger-ticket items, sold to fewer customers. That means more money from fewer sources. If you're selling a big-ticket item, this changes the game dramatically. For starters, you can afford to talk to every customer. The high sale price offsets the cost of a direct sales approach, particularly in the early stages of the sale.

The small number of initial users makes an even bigger difference. You aren't talking to a sample of 30 people as a proxy for the market at large. Instead, you're talking to 30 companies who may well become your first 30 customers.

Much of analytics is about trying to understand large amounts of information so you can get a better grasp of underlying patterns and act on

---

[*] *http://bhorowitz.com/2010/11/15/meet-the-new-enterprise-customer-he%E2%80%99s-a-lot-like-the-old-enterprise-customer/*

them. But in the early stages of a B2B startup, there aren't patterns—there are just customers.

- You can pick up the phone and call them right away.

- They'll call you and tell you what they want.

- You can get in a room with them.

- You can't test something on a statistically significant sample of the population and write it off if the test fails—you'll lose customers.

Formality

Enterprise buyers tend to be more regulated. They can't make decisions on gut or emotion—or rather, they can, but it has to be justified with a business case. Big companies are often public companies with checks and balances. The person who pays for the product (finance) isn't the person who uses it (the line of business). Understanding this dichotomy is critical for product development and sales. Initially, you may target early adopters, where the buyer is much closer to the user (they may be the same person at this point), but as you move past early adopters, the buyer and user diverge.

Companies have formal structure for good reasons. It helps prevent corruption, and makes auditing possible. But that structure gets in the way of understanding things. Your contact at a company may be a proponent, but someone else in the organization may be a detractor, or have a concern of which you're not aware. This is one of the reasons direct sales is common in early stages: it lets you navigate the bureaucracy and understand the part of the sales process that's hidden to outsiders.

Legacy Products

Consumers can ditch their old product on a whim. Small businesses can migrate fairly easily, as the recent exodus to cloud-based software demonstrates. Large companies, on the other hand, have a significant capital investment in the past which must be properly depreciated. They also have a significant political investment in past decisions, and often this is the strongest opposition to change.

Most organizations of any real size have developed their own software and processes, and they expect you to adapt to them. They won't change how they work: change is hard, and retraining is a cost. This can increase your deployment costs, because you have to integrate with what's already in place. It also means your products must be more configurable and adaptable, which translates into more complexity and less ease of use.

Incumbents

Those legacy issues are part of another problem—incumbents. If you're trying to disrupt or replace something, you'll have to convince the organization that you're better, despite the efforts of an existing solution. Organizations are averse to change, and love the status quo. If you're trying to sell to them, and your product is still in the early stages of the technology adoption cycle, you're penalized simply for being new. *Consumers love novelty; businesses just call it risk.*

This also means incumbent vendors can stall your sale significantly if they get wind of what you're planning to do just by claiming that they're going to do it too. They can step on your oxygen hose by promising something—then rescind the promise once you're dead.

Of course, big, slow incumbents have plenty of weaknesses. New entrants can disrupt their market simply by being easier to adopt, because they require no training. A decade ago, the only people who knew what a "feed" was were stock traders connecting to Bloomberg terminals; today, everyone who's used Facebook or Twitter is familiar with feeds. They don't need to be trained.

Simplicity isn't just an attribute of enterprise disruption—it's the price of entry. DJ Patil, data scientist in residence at Greylock and former head of product at LinkedIn, calls this the Zero Overhead Principle:

> A central theme to this new wave of innovation is the application
> of core product tenets from the consumer space to the enterprise.
> In particular, a universal lesson that I keep sharing with all
> entrepreneurs building for the enterprise is the Zero Overhead
> Principle: no feature may add training costs to the user.*

Slower Cycle Time

Lean Startup models work because they empower you to learn quickly and iteratively. It's hard to achieve speed when your customer moves sluggishly and carefully, so the slower cycle time of your target market makes it tough to iterate quickly. This is a key reason why many of the early Lean Startup success stories have come from consumer-focused businesses.

The rise of the SaaS market changes this, because it's relatively easy to alter functionality without the market's permission. But if you're selling traditional enterprise software, or delivery trucks, or shredders, you're not going to learn and iterate as quickly as you would from consumers. Of

---

* *http://techcrunch.com/2012/10/05/building-for-the-enterprise-the-zero-overhead-principle-2/*

course, your competitors aren't either. You don't need to be fast—just faster than everyone else.

Rationality (and Lack of Imagination)

Not all companies fit the stereotype of the big, slow, late-adopter customer, but risk aversion is real. Because enterprise buyers can't take the risks consumers can, they limit their own thinking. They demand proof that something will work before they try it out, which means great ideas can often become mired in business cases, return-on-investment analyses, and total-cost-of-ownership spreadsheets.

This rationality is warranted. In 2005, IEEE (Institute of Electrical and Electronics Engineers) committee chair Robert N. Charette estimated that of the $1 trillion spent on software each year, 5–15% would be abandoned before or shortly after delivery, and much of the rest would be late or suffer huge budget overruns.[*] A similar study by PM Solutions estimates that 37% of IT projects are at risk.[†]

Because companies are full of people—for many of whom their job is just a job—their priority is to minimize the chance of them making a mistake even if the organization as a whole might suffer in the long term. It's hard to inspire an organization if its employees are busy wondering whether the changes you promise will cost them their jobs.

This is an unnecessarily bleak view of the world.

For all these reasons, most B2B-focused startups consist of two people: a domain expert and a disruption expert.

- The domain expert knows the industry and the problem domain. He has a Rolodex and can act as a proxy for customers in the early stages of product definition. Often this person is from the line of business, and has a marketing, sales, or business development role.

- The disruption expert knows the technology that will produce a change on which the startup can capitalize. She can see beyond the current model and understand what an industry will look like after the shift, and brings the novel approach to the existing market. This is usually the technologist.

---

[*] http://spectrum.ieee.org/computing/software/why-software-fails/0

[†] http://www.zdnet.com/blog/projectfailures/cio-analysis-why-37-percent-of-projects-fail/12565

The Enterprise Startup Lifecycle

Startups begin in many ways. Over the years, however, we've seen a recurring pattern in how B2B startups grow. It usually happens in one of three ways:

The enterprise pivot

> In this pattern, the company creates a popular consumer product, then pivots to tackle the enterprise. This is what Dropbox did, and to some extent it's the way BlackBerry circumvented enterprise IT by targeting mercenary salespeople. It's not trivial, though: enterprises have very different expectations and concerns from consumers.

Copy and rebuild

> Another approach is to take a consumer idea and make it enterprise-ready. Yammer did this when it rebuilt Facebook's status update model and copied Facebook's feed interface.

Disrupt an existing problem

> There are plenty of disruptions that happen to an industry, from the advent of mobile data, to the Internet of Things,* to the adoption of the fax machine, to location-aware applications. Any of them can offer a big enough advantage to make it worth discarding the old way of doing things. Taleo did this to the traditional business of human resources management.

Inspiration

Many of the enterprise startups we've talked to began with a basic idea, often hatched within the ecosystem they wanted to disrupt. That's because domain knowledge is essential. Important elements of how a business works—particularly back-office operations—are hidden from the outside world. It's only by being an insider that the bottlenecks become painfully obvious.

Take the founders of Taleo. They left enterprise requirements planning (ERP) heavyweight BAAN to bring talent management tools to the enterprise. They had seen that the big challenges of ERP were integration and deployment, and they'd realized that the Web was how many organizations connect with candidates. They also saw that talent management, both before and after hires were made, was increasingly data-driven.

---

* *http://en.wikipedia.org/wiki/Internet_of_Things*

Many of their realizations came from seeing technology trends. But the founders' fundamental knowledge of the HR industry came from their time at BAAN. Clearly, it worked out well: in February 2012, Oracle acquired Taleo for $1.9 billion.

That doesn't mean the founding team *must* include an insider—but it helps. Remember, though, insiders still need to "get out of the building" and validate their assumptions; not doing so because of existing domain expertise can be disastrous.

Let's look at how the five stages of the Lean Analytics framework apply to a B2B-focused company. Figure 29-1 shows what a B2B company needs to do at each stage, as well as what risks it should fear.

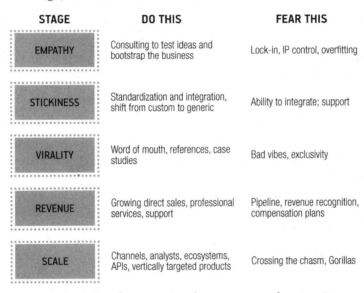

STAGE	DO THIS	FEAR THIS
EMPATHY	Consulting to test ideas and bootstrap the business	Lock-in, IP control, overfitting
STICKINESS	Standardization and integration, shift from custom to generic	Ability to integrate; support
VIRALITY	Word of mouth, references, case studies	Bad vibes, exclusivity
REVENUE	Growing direct sales, professional services, support	Pipeline, revenue recognition, compensation plans
SCALE	Channels, analysts, ecosystems, APIs, vertically targeted products	Crossing the chasm, Gorillas

Figure 29-1. The Lean Analytics stages when you're selling to enterprises

Empathy: Consulting and Segmentation

Many bootstrapped startups begin their lives as consulting organizations. Consulting is a good way to discover customer needs, and it helps pay the bills. It also gives you a way to test out your early ideas, because while every customer has needs, the only needs you can build a business on are those that are consistent across a reasonably large, addressable market.

Having said that, consulting companies struggle a great deal to transition from service providers to product companies because they need to, at some point, abandon service revenues and focus on the product. That transition can be extremely painful—from a cash flow perspective—and most service providers don't make the jump.

It's also necessary to "burn the boats" of the services business to ensure that you commit to the product. After all, you're going to neglect some of your most-loved customers in order to deliver a product the general market wants instead, and it'll be tempting to do custom work to keep them happy. You can't run a product and a services business concurrently. Even IBM had to split itself in two; what makes you think you can do it as a fledgling startup?

CASE STUDY | How Coradiant Found a Market

Coradiant, a maker of web performance equipment, started in 1997 as Networkshop, and was acquired by BMC Software in April 2011.[*] Initially it was an IT infrastructure consulting firm that wrote studies on performance, availability, and web technologies like SSL.[†] Soon, however, enterprises and startups approached the company seeking help with their deployments. These customers needed several pieces of costly network infrastructure—a pair of load balancers, firewalls, crypto accelerators, switches, routers, and related monitoring tools that, together, cost up to $500,000 and handled 100 megabits per second (Mbps) of traffic. But these companies needed only a fraction of that capacity.

Networkshop built a virtualized front-end infrastructure that customers could buy one Mbps at a time. It deployed this in a single data center in one city, and offered fractional capacity to customers in that data center. The economics were good: once the infrastructure had exceeded 35% utilization by customers, every additional dollar went straight to the bottom line.

Armed with this example, Networkshop changed its name to Coradiant and closed Series A funding, using the proceeds to deploy similar "pods" of infrastructure in data centers throughout North America. Wrapping this in support services, the company joined firms like LoudCloud and SiteSmith in the growing managed service provider (MSP) business.

Within a few years, however, the data center owners with whom Coradiant had colocated realized that they needed to make more

---

[*] Full disclosure: Coradiant was co-founded by Alistair Croll and Eric Packman in 1997 as Networkshop; the name was changed to Coradiant in mid-2000.

[†] *http://www.infosecnews.org/hypermail/9905/1667.html*

money from their facilities. To increase their revenue per square foot, they started offering competing services. The Coradiant founders had a decision to make: either compete head-to-head with the very same data centers in which their customers were hosted—a bad idea—or pivot to a new model that didn't need the data center owners' permission.

Coradiant had built a monitoring service (called OutSight) to help manage customers' infrastructure and measure performance. In the summer of 2003, the company scaled back dramatically, laying off most operational staff and hiring developers and architects who focused on building an appliance version of this technology. The new product, dubbed TrueSight, launched in 2004, and this time, Coradiant didn't need the data center owners' permission to be deployed.

Some of Coradiant's MSP customers became TrueSight users, quickly building a stable of reference-worthy household names. The initial version of TrueSight contained only basic features—most reporting, for example, was done by exporting information into Excel. But Coradiant had an extremely hands-on pre- and post-sales engineering team that worked closely with early customers. Once the company saw what kinds of reports customers made, and how they used the appliance, it incorporated those into later versions.

Coradiant didn't use channel sales until the product was relatively mature. The direct contact helped provide frequent feedback from the field. The company also held user conferences twice a year to hear how people were using the product, which led it into new directions such as real-time visualization and data export for vulnerability detection.

Ultimately, the consulting heritage gave Coradiant insight into the needs of a target market. The initial product offering was based on the sharing of IT infrastructure, amortizing the cost of networking components across many customers. That service, in turn, helped the firm learn what features customers needed from a monitoring product, and ultimately led it to build the product for which it was acquired.

Summary

- Coradiant started selling managed services, but a major market shift changed the dynamics of the market significantly.

- The company found that its unique value was a subset of the managed services offered that looked at users' experience on a website.

- Customers wanted this functionality as an appliance rather than a service.

Analytics Lessons Learned

Sometimes, environmental changes such as legislation or competition mean that validated business assumptions are no longer true. When that happens, look at what your core value proposition is and see if you can sell it to a different market or in a different way that overcomes those changes—in this case, keeping only a subset of a service and delivering it as an appliance.

Launching a startup as a consultancy has its risks. It's easy to get trapped in consulting. As the business grows, you'll want to keep customers happy, and won't have the cycles to dedicate to building the product or service you want. Many startups have lost sight of their initial plan and are now consulting firms—some of them happily. But they don't meet Paul Graham's test for scalable, repeatable, rapid growth. They're not startups.

What's more, in order to make the shift from consultancy to startup, you first need to test whether your existing customers' demands are applicable to a broader audience. Doing so may violate privacy agreements you have with your customers, so you need to finesse customer development. Your existing clients may feel that a standardized product you plan to offer will be less tailored to their needs; you need to convince them that a standard product is in fact better for them, because the cost of building future versions will be shared among many buyers.

Once you've found the problem you're going to fix, and have verified that the solution will work with your prospects and clients, you need to segment them. Not all clients are identical, so it's smart to pick a geographic region, a particular vertical, or customers who belong to just one of your sales teams. That way, you can give those early adopters better attention and limit the impact of failure.

Imagine, for example, that you're building a hiring management tool. The way that a legal firm finds and retains candidates is very different from the way a fast-food restaurant does it. Trying to build a single tool for them— particularly at the outset—is a bad idea. Everything from the number of interviews, to the qualifications needed, to the number of years someone stays with the company will be different. Differences mean customization and parameters, which increase complexity, and violates DJ Patil's Zero Overhead Principle.

Stickiness: Standardization and Integration

Once you know the need and have identified your initial segments, you have to standardize the product. With some products, it's possible to sell before building. Instead of an MVP, you may have a prototype, or a set of specifications for which the prospect will commit to paying on delivery. This pipeline of conditional purchases reduces the cost of fundraising, because it increases the chances of success.

In the B2C world, startups worry less about "Can I build it?" and more about "Will anyone care?" In the enterprise market, the risk is more, "Will it integrate?" Integration with existing tools, processes, and environments is the most likely source of problems, and you'll wind up customizing for clients—which undermines the standardization you fought so hard to achieve earlier.

Managing this tension between customization and standardization is one of the biggest challenges of an early-stage enterprise startup. If you can't get the client's users to try the product, you're doomed. And while your technology might work, if it doesn't properly integrate with legacy systems, it'll be seen as your fault, not theirs.

Virality: Word of Mouth, Referrals, and References

Assuming you've successfully sold the standardized product to an initial market segment, you'll need to grow. Because enterprises don't trust newcomers, you'll rely heavily on referrals and word-of-mouth marketing. You'll make case studies from early successes, and ask satisfied users to handle phone calls from new prospects.

Referrals and references are critical to this stage of growth. A couple of household names as customers are priceless. Enterprise-focused vendors will often provide discounts in exchange for case studies.

Revenue: Direct Sales and Support

With the pipeline growing and revenue coming in, you'll worry about cash flow and commission structures for your direct sales team. To know if you have a sustainable business, you'll also look at support costs, churn, trouble tickets, and other indicators of ongoing business costs to learn just how much a particular customer contributes to the bottom line. If the operating margin is bad, it will have a significant drag on profitability.

Feedback from the sales team and the support group is critical at this point, because it indicates whether your initial success is genuine, or simply a case of prospects buying into the story you're telling (which won't be sustainable in the longer term). Zach Nies, Chief Technologist at Rally Software says, "This is absolutely critical for startups, because they have a huge advantage here. In most incumbents, the product development team is so far removed from the field and customers that they have no sense of trends in the market.

Often startups will know a lot more about an incumbent's customers than the incumbent does."

Scale: Channel Sales, Efficiencies, and Ecosystems

In the final stages of an enterprise-focused startup, you'll emphasize scaling. You may have channel sales through value-added resellers and distributors. You'll also have an ecosystem of analysts, developers, APIs (application programming interfaces) and platforms, partners, and competitors that will define and refine the market. These are all good indicators that companies will keep using you, because they're investing in processes, vendor relationships, and technology that will make it harder for them to leave you. Scaling an enterprise software company takes years to accomplish. Zach estimates that it can be as long as 5 to 10 years before a company selling into the enterprise has established and validated channels, and mastered its sales processes.

So What Metrics Matter?

Just as there are plenty of parallels between the way B2C and B2B startups grow, so many of the metrics we've seen for consumer-focused companies apply equally well to enterprise-focused ones. But there are a few metrics that you'll want to consider that apply more to enterprise startups.

Ease of Customer Engagement and Feedback

As you're talking to customers, how easy is it to get meetings with them? If you plan to use a direct sales organization later on, this is an early indicator of what it'll be like to sell the product.

Pipeline for Initial Releases, Betas, and Proof-of-Concept Trials

As you start to sign up prospects, you'll track the usual sales metrics. Unlike B2C platforms where you're looking at subscription and engagement, if you're selling a big-ticket, long-term item, you're looking at contracts. While you may not have recognizable revenue, you'll have lead volume and bookings to analyze, and these should give you an understanding of the cost of sales once the product has launched.

It's important—right from the very beginning—that you articulate the stages of your sales funnel and the conversion rates at each point along the way. The sales cycle needs to be well documented, measured, and understood after the first few sales, to see if you can build a repeatable approach. At that point, you can bring in additional salespeople to increase volume.

Stickiness and Usability

As we've seen, the usability of a disruptive solution is "table stakes" for a new entrant in today's market. Companies expect ease of use, because they didn't have to get trained on Google or Facebook, and thus shouldn't have to get training from you, either. DJ Patil suggests using data to find where the friction is hiding in your usage and adoption. "If you can't measure it, you can't fix it," he says. "Instrument the product to monitor user flows and be able to test new ideas in how to iteratively improve your product."

Integration Costs

In the heat of the moment, it's hard to take notes, but integration plays such a big role in enterprise sales that you have to be disciplined about measuring it. What's the true cost of pre- and post-sales support? How much customization is required? How much training, explaining, and troubleshooting are you doing in order to successfully deliver a product to a customer?

You need to capture this data early on, because later it's an indicator of whether you've built a startup or just created a highly standardized consulting practice. If you prematurely accelerate the latter, thinking it's the former, supporting an expanded market and a sales channel will crush you. This data can also be used against incumbents in a total-cost-of-ownership analysis.

User Engagement

No matter what you're building, the most important metric is whether people are using it. In an enterprise, however, the buyer is less likely to be the user. That means your contact may be an IT project manager, someone in purchasing, or an executive, but your actual users may be rank-and-file employees with whom you have no contact.

You may also have to refrain from talking to users: it's easy to pop up a survey on a consumer website, but employers may frown upon you using up their employees' precious time to answer your questions.

Simply measuring metrics like "time since last use" will be misleading, too, because users are *paid* to use your tool. They may log in every day because it's their job to do so; that doesn't mean they enjoy it. The real questions are whether they *like* logging in, and whether it makes them more productive. Users have a task they want to accomplish, and your product will thrive if it is the perfect tool for that task. Some marketers advocate analyzing customer needs by the job the customer is trying to get done (known as the "jobs-be-done" approach) rather than by segments.*

Get baselines from your clients that apply to their real-world businesses before you deploy. How many orders do they enter a day? How long does it take an employee to get payroll information? How many truck deliveries a day can their warehouse handle? What is the usual call hold time? Once you've deployed, use this information to measure progress, helping your advocates to prove the ROI—and turning it into case studies you can share with other customers.

Disentanglement

As you transition from a high-touch consulting business to a standardized one with less customer interaction, you need to focus on disentanglement. Your goal is to not have "anchor" customers that represent a disproportionate amount of your revenue or your support calls, because you need to scale.

Put your high-touch customers that you acquired early on into a segment and compare them to the rest of your customers. How do they differ? Do they consume a fair proportion of your support resources? Do their feature requests match those of all your customers and prospects? Don't ignore the companies that made you who you are—but do realize they're not in a monogamous relationship with you anymore.

Zach Nies suggests going even further, segmenting customers into three groups. "'A customers' are your really big customers who negotiated a big discount and expect the world from you. 'B customers' are customers who are fairly low maintenance, didn't get a big discount, see themselves as partners with you, and provide useful insights. 'C customers' cause trouble, are a pain to deal with, and demand things from you that you feel will damage your business," he explains. "Don't spend too much time on the A's—they sound good but aren't the best for your business. Bring as many Bs on as customers as possible. And try to get your 'C customers' to be customers of your competitors."

---

*   *http://hbswk.hbs.edu/item/6496.html*

Support Costs

Zach's advice is based on some fundamental truths. In many B2B-focused companies, the top 20% of customers generate 150–300% of profits, while the middle 70% of customers break even, and the lowest 10% of customers reduce 50–200% of profits.[*]

You'll track support metrics like top-requested features, number of outstanding trouble tickets, post-sales support, call center hold time, and so on. This will indicate where you're losing money, and whether the product is standardized and stable enough to move into growth and scaling.

Segment this data, too. Figure out who's costing the most money. Then consider firing them.[†] Once, it was hard to break out individual customer costs, but electronic systems make it possible to assign activities—such as support calls, emails, additional storage, or a truck roll—to individual customers.

You don't actually have to fire customers, of course. You can simply change their pricing enough to make them profitable or encourage them to leave. This is part of getting your pricing right before you grow the business to a point where unprofitable clients can do real damage at scale.

User Groups and Feedback

If your business involves big-ticket sales, you may have few enough customers that you can get many of them in the same room. Informal interaction with existing customers can be a boon to enterprise-focused startups, and resembles the problem and solution validation stages of the Lean Startup process—only rather than validating a solution, you're validating a roadmap. Even with a large number of customers, Zach says, "Identify the real advocates and bring them in for a big hug." He also suggests helping advocates network among themselves, which Rally does on its website.[‡]

Successful user-group meetings require considerable preparation. Users will be eager to please—or quick to complain—so results will be polarized. They'll also agree to every feature you suggest. Force them to choose; they

---

[*] Robert S. Kaplan and V.G. Naranyanan "Measuring and Managing Customer Profitability," *Journal of Cost Management* (2001), 15, 5–15, cited in Shin, Sudhir, and Yoon, "When to 'Fire' Customers."

[†] Jiwoong Shin, K. Sudhir, and Dae-Hee Yoon, "When to 'Fire' Customers: Customer Cost-Based Pricing," *Management Science*, December 2012 (*http://faculty.som.yale.edu/ksudhir/papers/Customer%20Cost%20Based%20Pricing.pdf*).

[‡] *http://www.rallydev.com/community*

can't have everything, and you need to present them with hard alternatives (also known as *discrete choices*).

A lot of work has gone into understanding how people make choices. "A 'discrete' choice," says Berkeley professor Dan McFadden, "is a 'yes/no' decision, or a selection of one alternative from a set of possibilities." His application of discrete choice modeling to estimate the adoption of San Francisco's Bay Area Rapid Transit system—which was under construction at the time of his research—earned him the 2000 Nobel Prize in Economics.[*] One important conclusion from this work is that people find it easier to discard something they don't want than to choose something they do (which feels like commitment), so a series of questions in which they are asked to discard one of two options works well.

The math of choice modeling is complex. There are entire conferences devoted to the subject, and it's widely used in new product development for everything from laundry detergent to cars. But some of the methodologies are instructive. For example, you can get better answers by repeatedly asking your customers to compare two possible feature enhancements and choosing the one they can do without, rather than by simply asking them to rate the possible features on a scale of 1 to 10. You'll do even better if you mix up several attributes in each comparison, regardless of whether a particular combination of attributes makes sense.

Imagine you're trying to find a new diet food to introduce. You know the attributes that might affect buyers include taste, calories, gluten content, and sustainable ingredients. Simply asking prospects whether taste is more important to them than caloric content is informative. But asking them to make a choice between two discrete offerings—even if those offerings are theoretically impossible—is even better. Would you prefer:

- A delicious, gluten-free, high-calorie candy made with artificial ingredients;

- Or a bland, high-gluten, low-calorie candy of organic origin?

Asking customers to trade off variations of combinations, over and over, dramatically improves prediction accuracy. In fact, this is equivalent to the multivariate testing we've discussed before, applied to surveys and interviews.

As you're designing user events, know what you're hoping to learn and invest in the conversations and experimental design needed to get real answers that you can turn into the right product roadmap.

---

[*] *http://elsa.berkeley.edu/~mcfadden/charterday01/charterday_final.pdf*

Pitch Success

You've measured your effectiveness at setting up meetings in the early phases of your startup. It matters later on, when you're about to bring on channels. Your channel partners aren't as clever as you, and you'll need to arm them with collateral and messaging that they can use to close deals without your assistance. If they try to push your product or service and encounter resistance, they'll sell something else. With channels, you seldom get a second chance to make a first impression.

Create marketing tools for your channel and then test them yourselves. Make cold calls with their scripts. Pitch them to new customers. Send out email form letters and test response rates.

This does two things: first, it shows you which script, pitch, or form letter to use (because, after all, everything's an experiment, right?, and second, it gives you a baseline against which to compare channel effectiveness. If a channel partner isn't meeting your baseline, something else is wrong, and you can work to fix it before that partner sours on your product.

If you make channel collateral, tag each piece of collateral with something that identifies the channel. You might use shortened URLs that include a code identifying the partner in PDFs you create, which would let you see which partners' efforts are driving traffic to your site.

Barriers to Exit

As you bring customers on at scale, you want to make them stick around. A vibrant developer ecosystem and a healthy API allow customers to integrate themselves with you, making *you* the incumbent vendor and helping you to counter threats from competitors and new entrants.

Simon Wardley, who studies organizational warfare and evolution for the Leading Edge Forum, points out that companies must prioritize the long list of features customers need. Build too many, and they won't all be profitable; build too few, and you leave the door open to competitors. APIs, he says, offer a solution.[*]

> All innovations... are a gamble and whilst we can reduce costs we can never eliminate it. The future value of something is inversely proportional to the certainty we have over it; we cannot avoid this information barrier any more than we can reliably predict the future. However, there is a means to maximize our advantage.

---

[*] *http://blog.gardeviance.org/2011/03/ecosystem-wars.html*

By making these utility services accessible through APIs, we not only benefit ourselves but we can open up these components to a wider ecosystem. If we can encourage innovation in that wider ecosystem then we do not incur the cost of gambling [and] failure for those new activities. Unfortunately, we do not enjoy the rewards of their success either.

Fortunately, the ecosystem provides an early warning mechanism of success (i.e., adoption)...by creating a large enough ecosystem, we can not only encourage a rapid rate of innovation but also leverage that ecosystem to identify success and then either copy (a weak ecosystem approach) or acquire (a strong ecosystem approach) that activity. This is how we maximize our advantage.

If you have an API, track its usage by clients. Those clients who have a lot of API activity are investing more in extending their relationship with you; those who are inactive could switch vendors more easily. If you have a developer program, examine searches and feature requests to discover what tools your customers want, then find developers to build features you aren't going to create yourself.

The Bottom Line: Startups Are Startups

While enterprise-focused startups must contend with some significant differences, the fundamental Lean Startup model remains: determine the riskiest part of the business, and find a way of quantifying and mitigating that risk quickly by creating something, measuring the result, and learning from it.

CHAPTER 30

Lean from Within: Intrapreneurs

As World War II exploded across Europe, the United States realized it needed a way to counteract German advances in aviation—specifically, jet aircraft. The US military asked Lockheed Martin (then the Lockheed Aircraft Corporation) to build a jet fighter. Desperate times called for desperate measures: in a month, the engineering team had a proposal. Less than six months later, working in a closely guarded circus tent, they built the first plane.*

This group became known as the Skunk Works, a title that's synonymous with an independent, autonomous group charged with innovation inside a bigger, slower-moving organization. Such groups are often immune to the restrictions and budget oversight that guides the rest of the company, and have the specific goal of working "out of the box" to mitigate the inertia of large businesses. Companies like Google and Apple adopt this same approach, creating their own advanced research groups such as the Google X Lab.†

Making things change quickly is hard, and if you're going to do it, you need authority commensurate with responsibility. If you're trying to disrupt from within, you have a lot of work to do. Many of the lessons learned

---

* *http://en.wikipedia.org/wiki/Skunkworks_project*

† *http://www.nytimes.com/2011/11/14/technology/at-google-x-a-top-secret-lab-dreaming-up-the-future.html?_r=2*

from the startup world apply, but they need to be tweaked to survive in a corporate setting.

Span of Control and the Railroads

If you work in a company of any significant size, you owe your organizational chart to an enterprising general superintendent of the railroad era named Daniel C. McCallum.* In the 1850s, railroads were a booming business. Unfortunately for investors, they didn't scale well. Small railroads turned a profit; big ones didn't.

McCallum noticed this, and divided his railroad into smaller sections, each run by subordinates who reported back a standard set of information he defined. McCallum's line—as well as other lines that copied this approach—thrived. McCallum's model, inspired by his time as a soldier and the regimented hierarchies he had learned in the military, was then applied to other industries.

McCallum was the first management scientist, introducing controls, structure, and regulations in order to reduce risk and increase predictability at scale. Unfortunately, intrapreneurs aren't trying to solve for safety and predictability. Their job is to *take* risks, and to uncover the non-obvious and the unpredictable. If you're trying to provoke change and disrupt the status quo, then the organizations McCallum introduced are your kryptonite. You need to shield yourself, just as the engineers within the Skunk Works did decades ago. But you also need to coexist with the organization, because unlike an independent startup, the fruits of your labors must integrate with your host company.

- What you make may **cannibalize the existing business,** or threaten employees' jobs. People will behave irrationally. Marc Andreesen famously said, "software eats everything," and one of its favorite foods is jobs.† When a software company introduces a SaaS version of its application, salespeople who make a living selling enterprise licenses get angry.

- **Inertia is real.** If you're asking people to change how they work, you'll need to give them reason to do so. Consider an Apple store: there's no central cash register, and you're emailed a receipt. It takes a fraction of the time to purchase something, and makes better use of floor space—

---

* *http://en.wikipedia.org/wiki/Daniel_McCallum*

† *http://beforeitsnews.com/banksters/2012/08/the-stanford-lectures-so-is-software-really-eating-the-world-2431478.html*

but convincing an existing retailer to change to this model will require retraining and modifying store layout.

- If you do your job well, you'll **disrupt the ecosystem**. A traditional music label has relationships with distributors and stores. That made it hard for it to move into online music distribution, leaving the opportunity open for online retailers as soon as disruptive technologies like MP3s and fast broadband emerged.

- Your innovation will **live or die in the hands of others**. While it's easy to be myopic about your work—and disdainful of what the rest of the company is doing—you're all in the same boat. "When problems crop up it is easy to see things from your own point of view," says Richard Templar, tongue firmly in cheek, in *The Rules of Work* (Pearson Education), "[but] once you make the leap to corporate speak it gets easier to stop doing this and start seeing problems from the company's point of view."*

In their book *Confronting Reality* (Crown Business), Larry Bossidy and Ram Charan list the six habits of highly unrealistic leaders: filtered information, selective hearing, wishful thinking, fear, emotional over-investment, and unrealistic expectations from capital markets.†

Intrapreneurs need the opposite attributes to thrive—and many of those attributes are driven by data and iteration. You need access to the real information, and you need to go where the data takes you, avoiding confirmation bias. You need to set aside your own assumptions and preconceived notions, and you need to combine high standards with low expectations.

PATTERN | Skunk Works for Intrapreneurs

The Skunk Works needed results and permission to move quickly. It set down 14 guidelines (known as *Kelly's 14 Rules & Practices*, named after engineering team lead Clarence "Kelly" Johnson) that can be adapted to anyone who's trying to change a company from within.‡ With apologies to Johnson, we'd like to share our 14 rules for Lean Intrapreneurs.

---

* Richard Templar, *The Rules of Work* (Upper Saddle River, New Jersey: Pearson Education, 2003), 142.

† Larry Bossidy and Ram Charan, *Confronting Reality* (New York: Crown Business, 2004), 22–24.

‡ *http://www.lockheedmartin.com/us/aeronautics/skunkworks/14rules.html*

1. If you're setting out to break rules, you need the responsibility for making changes happen—and the authority that can come only from high-level buy-in. Get an executive sponsor, and make sure everyone else knows that you've got one.

2. Insist on access both to resources within the host company and to real customers. You'll probably need the permission of the support and sales teams to do this. They won't like the changes and uncertainties you may introduce by talking to customers—but insist on it anyway.

3. Build a small, agile team of high performers who aren't risk-averse, and who lean toward action. If you can't put together such a team it's a sign you don't *really* have the executive buy-in you thought you did.

4. Use tools that can handle rapid change. Rent instead of buying. Favor on-demand technologies like cloud computing, and opex over capex.*

5. Don't get bogged down in meetings, keep the reporting you do simple and consistent, but be disciplined about recording progress in a way that can be analyzed later on.

6. Keep the data current, and don't try to hide things from the organization. Consider the total cost of the innovation you're working on, not just the short-term costs.

7. Don't be afraid to choose new suppliers if they're better, but also leverage the scale and existing contracts of the host organization when it makes sense.

8. Streamline the testing process, and make sure the components of your new product are themselves reliable. Don't reinvent the wheel. Build on building blocks that already exist, particularly in early versions.

9. Eat your own dog food, and get face-time with end users, rather than delegating testing and market research to others.

10. Agree on goals and success criteria before starting the project. This is essential for buy-in from executives, but also reduces confusion and avoids both feature creep and shifting goals.

---

* *http://www.diffen.com/difference/Capex_vs_Opex*

11. Make sure you have access to funds and working capital without a lot of paperwork and the need to "resell" people midway through the project.

12. Get day-to-day interaction with customers, or at the very least, a close proxy to the customer such as someone in support or post-sales, to avoid miscommunication and confusion.

13. Limit access to the team by outsiders as much as possible. Don't poison the team with naysayers, and don't leak half-finished ideas to the company before they're properly tested.

14. Reward performance based on results, and get ready to break the normal compensation models. After all, you're trying to keep entrepreneurs within a company, and if they're talented, they could leave to do their own thing.

Changing—or Innovating to Resist Change?

It takes a dire threat or a top-down leader to force a company to change. If you have both, even a huge company can move quickly. In the late 90s, as the web browser grew in importance, analysts were predicting the downfall of Microsoft, but they underestimated Bill Gates's ability to turn his company quickly. Within a few months, the company had created Internet Explorer and insinuated it throughout its Windows operating system: you'd type a URL, and it would convert it to a hyperlink. You'd save something, and it would have an HTML version. Even the much-maligned paperclip knew about the Web.

While Microsoft did have to contend with antitrust accusations, its quick response staved off irrelevance and kneecapped ascendant Netscape. Jim Clark, Netscape's CEO, called Gates's response ruthless, but noted that his ruthlessness came from the company's dominance in the desktop space. "In order to be ruthless you have to have some kind of power, and in most cases I've been going up against Microsoft, so I never had that power."[*]

Since that time, the company has had to do the same with its Office suite. In 2005, Gates and Ray Ozzie announced the shift from a licensed software package to a hosted, SaaS-based offering.[†] This time, the threat was from Google's nascent office offering, which would be subsidized by Google's money-making ad machine. While Google's product was just a gleam in its

---

[*] http://www.cnn.com/books/news/9906/18/netscape/

[†] http://ross.typepad.com/blog/2005/10/turn_on_a_dime.html

founders' eyes, services like Write.ly made it plain that desktop productivity suites were under siege.*

Critics of Microsoft's reactions complain that the company isn't changing; rather, it's managing to stay the same and exert its dominance, avoiding or delaying market change. "I realized that Microsoft had not turned at all," said Dave Winer in 1999. "What's actually been happening is that Microsoft is exerting tremendous energy to stay right where it is."†

As an intrapreneur, you might find that this "innovate to stay still" notion does not sit well with you. You're a disruptor, right? However, when you're working for an incumbent with large market share, sometimes innovation is about maintaining a company's dominance and suppressing change to continue making money in the traditional ways. If you don't like that, you should probably leave the company and start something of your own.

Stars, Dogs, Cows, and Question Marks

Why might you not want to disrupt things? To understand this, you need to look at how large organizations plan their product and market strategy.

The Boston Consulting Group (BCG) box, shown in Figure 30-1, is a simple way to think about a company's product portfolio. It classifies products or subsidiaries according to two dimensions: how quickly the market is growing, and how big a market share the company has in that market.

Products with high market share but slow growth are "cash cows." They generate revenue, but they aren't worthy of heavy investment. By contrast, products with high growth but small market share are "question marks," candidates for investment and development. Those with both growth and market share are the rising "stars." Those with neither—called "dogs"—are to be sold off or shut down.

The BCG box offers a thumbnail of a company's product portfolio. It's also a good way to think about innovation. If you're trying to change a company, you're either trying to create a new product (hopefully in a growing market) or you're trying to innovate to revitalize an existing product with the addition of new features, markets, or services.

---

* *http://anders.com/cms/108*

† *http://scripting.com/1999/06/19.html*

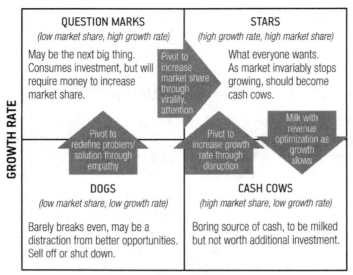

Figure 30-1. The BCG box: ever wonder where "cash cows" came from?

Seen from a Lean Startup perspective, the BCG box shows us what stage we're working on and what metrics should apply. If you're creating new products or companies (question marks), then you need to focus on empathy. If you're trying to rescue a dog, you still need empathy, and you have access to existing customers. You're either going to change the product (to enter an area of increased growth) or the market (to gain market share).

If you have a question mark (high growth but nascent market share), you'll be focusing on growing market share through organic (virality) or inorganic (customer acquisition) means.

If you have a star, and the market's growth is stalling, you need to optimize revenues and reduce costs so your marginal cost of product delivery is healthy. That way you can survive the coming commoditization and price wars. On the other hand, if there's a disruption in the industry that might expand the market—such as the rise of mobile technology, or the emergence of international demand—you'll be focusing on increasing growth rate to return a cash cow to star status.

Companies tend to try to improve what they have, which is one of the reasons that incumbents get disrupted. In his book *Imagine* (Canongate

Books), author Jonah Lehrer talks about the creation of the Swiffer mop.[*] It's a perfect example of how companies look for a local maximum rather than trying to solve a problem.

CASE STUDY | Swiffer Gives Up on Chemistry

Proctor & Gamble (P&G) makes lots of cleaning products. It's constantly trying to improve and revitalize its cash-cow products, but despite the hard work of many highly paid experts, it was stalled in its efforts to invent a better cleaning fluid.

The company's executives knew it was time to disrupt the industry, and they couldn't do it from within. So they brought in Continuum, an outside agency, to help out.[†] Rather than mixing up another batch of chemicals, Continuum's team decided to watch people as they mopped. They focused on recording, testing, and rapid iteration during their investigation phase.[‡]

At one point, they watched a test subject clean up spilled coffee grounds. Rather than breaking out a mop, the subject swept up the dry grounds with a broom, and then wiped the remaining fine dust with a damp cloth.

No mop.

That was an eye-opener for the design team, and they looked at the problem from a different angle. They discovered that the mop—not the liquids—was the key. They looked at the makeup of floor dirt (which is part dust, and thus better picked up without water)[§] and innovated on the cleaning tool itself, giving P&G a $500-million-dollar innovation—the Swiffer, a more user-friendly style of mop—in an otherwise stagnant cleaning industry.

The ability to step outside the frame of reference within which the existing organization works and see the actual need rather than the current solution, is a fundamental ability of any intrapreneur.

---

[*] http://www.npr.org/2012/03/21/148607182/fostering-creativity-and-imagination-in-the-workplace

[†] http://www.kinesisinc.com/business/how-spilt-coffee-created-a-billion-dollar-mop/

[‡] http://www.dcontinuum.com/seoul/portfolio/11/89/

[§] http://www.fastcodesign.com/1671033/why-focus-groups-kill-innovation-from-the-designer-behind-swiffer

Summary

- By using basic customer development approaches, P&G was able to create an entirely new product category.

- Pretending you're a startup, and focusing on disruption in the Empathy stage, is a good way to rediscover what's possible and take off enterprise blinders.

- Resist the temptation to use surveys and quantitative research; the insights from one-on-one observation can unlock an entire market segment.

Analytics Lessons Learned

For intrapreneurs, sometimes starting back at the beginning, with a reconsideration of the fundamental problem you're trying to solve, is the best way to move a cash-cow product—lucrative but not growing—back to a high-growth industry. After all, if you don't see your customers through naïve eyes, someone else will.

You may be able to innovate and simultaneously involve the customer in the innovation itself, even turning testing and analytics into a marketing campaign. That's what Frito-Lay did when it decided to find a new flavor of chips.

CASE STUDY | Doritos Chooses a Flavor

If you're a big company, it's hard to incorporate customer feedback in real time. Typically, you rely on focus groups and product testing before spending big money on a new product launch. Frito-Lay found a way to mitigate this, and in the process took customer development to new heights. It also generated interesting advertising campaigns.

In 2009, Dachis Group helped Doritos introduce an unnamed flavor, then asked customers to name it.[*] In later years, the company asked customers to choose which flavor it should add to its product line, literally labeling two new flavors A and B, and then testing them.[†] It also asked customers to help write the end of a TV ad that would be

---

* *http://www.dachisgroup.com/case-studies/become-the-doritos-guru/*

† *http://www.packagingdigest.com/article/517188-Doritos_black_and_white_bags_invite_consumers_to_vote_for_new_flavor.php*

broadcast during the Superbowl, giving them access to creative teams at its advertising agency.*

This work required changes to distribution channels, from retail shelf space to the inclusion of temporary inventory. But the campaign worked—the company dominated social media. It had 1.5M visitors to its YouTube channel, and over 500,000 votes were cast by customers. It also found a way to iterate at scale, and do market development alongside brand building.

Summary

- An established distribution system in the consumer packaged-goods industry might seem like a boat anchor that makes it hard to innovate, but Frito-Lay found a way to do so.

- Leveraging social media and the prominence of in-store displays, the company turned its YouTube channel into a giant focus group and increased engagement with its customers.

Analytics Lessons Learned

Another way to revitalize a product is to use a disruptive technology—in this case, ubiquitous social media and two-way interaction—to reconsider how product testing is done in the first place.

Working with an Executive Sponsor

As an intrapreneur, you and your executive sponsor need to be absolutely clear what kind of change you're trying to produce, how you'll measure progress toward that change, what resources you'll have access to, and what rules you'll be subject to. This might seem overly "corporate" for a mercenary looking to blow up the status quo, but in a big organization it's simple reality.

If you don't like it, go start your own company. If you want to work within the system, the change you're after has to dovetail with the change the organization is ready for. This is why executive sponsorship is so important: it's the difference between a "rogue agent" and a "special operative."

---

* http://thenextweb.com/ca/2011/02/05/online-campaign-asks-canadians-to-write-the-end-of-a-commercial/

Existing businesses are different largely because they already exist. Innovators can go rogue asking for forgiveness rather than permission— but the immune system of the host company may reject them. Ultimately, companies need to restructure themselves for a continuous cycle of innovation, but the way to get them to do so may involve baby steps— smaller, more controlled attempts at analytics. That's the approach David Boyle used at EMI Music as he worked to introduce a data-driven culture.

CASE STUDY	## EMI Embraces Data to Understand Its Customers

David Boyle is the Senior Vice President of Insight at EMI Music, one of the major labels in the recording industry. His job is to help EMI make decisions based on data, and to help the company navigate the choppy waters of an industry in transition.

To get the company more focused on data and analytics, and less concerned with anecdotes and opinions, Boyle first had to choose which decisions needed to be made, then find ways to get the right evidence in front of the decision makers.

"The decisions we ultimately focused on were, 'Which types of consumers should I try to connect an artist's music to in which countries?' and 'What kinds of marketing should I do to try to reach those consumers?' Most of that data came from consumer research."

Boyle wasn't short on data. EMI has billions of transaction records from digital services, as well as usage logs from artist websites and applications. "But each of these data sources is very limited in scope and very skewed concerning the types of person that is represented in that data set," Boyle explained. So EMI built its own survey tool. "We found that building our own data set based on asking people questions and playing them music was the way to go." The result was over 1 million detailed interviews, and hundreds of millions of data points.

"Bad data is a pain to sell to people. And even good data is a pain to sell to someone if it doesn't actually help someone, whether that's because it's not in a form that helps them work out what to do or because it doesn't actually answer the questions they are asking," he says. "But when the data's good and it really does help someone, then nobody can refuse it."

Many intrapreneurs talk about the friction they face when trying to create a data-driven culture in their organizations, but Boyle is quick to caution against calling it resistance. "One of the key things we realized early on was that it's not helpful to think of it as resistance. When you realize that the 'resistance' is actually good people who deeply care about the artists and music they are working with, trying to protect them from bad data or bad recommendations, then you see the whole thing differently."

"If you really believe in the data and the recommendations that the data makes, then you focus on why the person doesn't understand the data and you help them to understand it," he explained. "When they understand, then their eyes light up, and they become a bigger fan of the data than I am!"

Despite his success with EMI, Boyle admits there are real differences between a startup and a big company. "In a startup, you have the benefits of starting off as you mean to go on: you can shape the way of thinking and behaving to, for example, incorporate data in decision making right from the start. That's a great advantage over working in a business where the culture is already set." But the startup world isn't perfect, he says. "A startup has another big problem: intense pressure to deliver quickly. I've actually noticed that this can get in the way of things like building the right culture if you're not careful."

To build support and report progress within EMI, Boyle used case studies.

"We got lots of people who'd successfully used our data to help their artists tell their story. They were better and more creative than anything we could have organized centrally to spread the word." EMI's new data helped align particular artists with demographics to whom they'd appeal, allowing the music to reach the most receptive audiences.

Boyle didn't tie the results of research to hard numbers. "We simply said: 'Asking thousands of people what they think about something is better than not asking them, right?' and we showed that we could do so at high quality and low cost, and we went for it. After the first set of data came back, people fell in love with it: it helped them and they loved that."

Initially, the newly acquired research data helped EMI to understand the market and the ecosystem in which artists, music, and digital services exist. But now that the company has that context, it can revisit the billions of transactional records it collected in the past. "If we'd looked at that without first understanding the context in which it sits, we would have taken our artists in the wrong direction," Boyle said.

The project has grown beyond the initial insight team, and now it's owned by the overall business at EMI. In the end, because everyone had access to data, the entire organization bought into the change. But what surprised Boyle the most was how valuable the (relatively small) consumer research continued to be, even though the organization could use the Big Data hoard from billions of transactions. "Good data beats big data," he concludes. "I am constantly surprised at how good it can be when done properly."

Summary

- EMI had a huge amount of data, and little idea of how to use it.

- Rather than mining existing data sets, the company conducted surveys, building a simpler, more specific set of information that executives could get comfortable with.

- Once the value of this smaller interview data was proven, it was easier to sell the value of a broader data-driven culture.

Analytics Lessons Learned

Just because you have a lot of data doesn't mean you're data-driven. Sometimes, starting from scratch with a small set of data collected to solve a specific issue can help make the case for using data elsewhere in the organization. It's also more likely to get executive sponsorship because the problem is bounded and constrained, whereas nobody knows what controversies are lurking in the larger amounts of "data exhaust" the organization has collected over the years.

The Stages of Intrapreneur Lean Analytics

If you're a pioneering intrapreneur, you'll go through a series of stages that maps closely to the stages we've seen in other startup models. But you have a few important steps to consider, as Figure 30-2 illustrates. Note that we've also included a "step zero" for intrapreneurs: get executive buy-in.

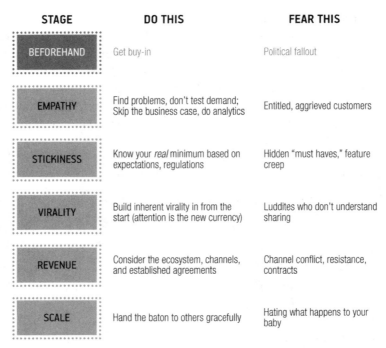

STAGE	DO THIS	FEAR THIS
BEFOREHAND	Get buy-in	Political fallout
EMPATHY	Find problems, don't test demand; Skip the business case, do analytics	Entitled, aggrieved customers
STICKINESS	Know your *real* minimum based on expectations, regulations	Hidden "must haves," feature creep
VIRALITY	Build inherent virality in from the start (attention is the new currency)	Luddites who don't understand sharing
REVENUE	Consider the ecosystem, channels, and established agreements	Channel conflict, resistance, contracts
SCALE	Hand the baton to others gracefully	Hating what happens to your baby

Figure 30-2. Intrapreneurs need an extra step: get an executive sponsor first

Beforehand: Get Buy-in

Before you start doing customer development, you need executive buy-in. This may be implicit if it's your job to try to find new opportunities, but even then, once you think you've found an opportunity, you need explicit approval from an executive. You want to know where you are on the BCG box, and where you're trying to go, and you need to know what metrics your progress will be judged by. You need to know what resources you have, and what rules apply to you. This is like a prenuptial agreement: it's better signed before the wedding.

At this stage, you're defining your analytical strategy, and the lines in the sand against which you'll be judged. These may be goals for the whole company, such as margins, or they may be a growth rate that's considered success. You'll also need to define how you will adjust these metrics based on what you learn.

Empathy: Find Problems, Don't Test Demand

Once you start doing customer development, remember that you're testing problems and solutions—not existing demand. If you're truly disruptive, customers won't tell you what they want, but they *will* tell you why they want it. In 2008, Swiffer creator Gianfranco Zaccai explained, "Successful business innovation isn't about giving consumers what they need now, but about giving them something they'll desire in the future."[*]

Customers weren't telling Netflix they wanted to stream videos, but their patterns of usage, computer adoption, broadband deployment, and browsing told the company a need existed.

This is a place for qualitative interviews. You should talk to existing users and customers, of course. But if you're trying to grow market share, you'll also want to talk to your competitors' customers, to distributors, and to everyone involved in purchasing the product. If you're trying to improve growth rate, you'll talk to adjacent customers. That's what Bombardier did when it expanded from snowmobiles to personal watercraft (despite an initial, failed 1960s foray into the industry that was plagued by mechanical issues).[†]

Skip the Business Case, Do the Analytics

At some point, when it comes time to go beyond interviewing people, you'll need to build a business case. Traditional product managers build profit-and-loss analyses to try to justify their plans: they create a convincing business case, and once someone believes it, they get funding to proceed. But a Lean mindset reverses this: you sell the business model—not the plan—without a lot of prediction, and then rely heavily on analytics to decide whether to kill the product or double-down on it.

This analyze-after rather than predict-before model is possible because many of the costs of innovation can be pushed later in the product development cycle. Just-in-time manufacturing, on-demand printing, services that replace upfront investment with pay-by-the-drink capacity, CAD/CAM design, and mercenary contractors all mean that you don't have to invest heavily up front (and therefore don't have to argue a business case at the outset). Rather, you can ask for a modest budget, build analytics into the product, and launch sooner for less money. You can then use the data and customer feedback you get, which is vanishingly cheap to collect given today's technology, to plead your case based on actual evidence.

Stickiness: Know Your Real Minimum

If you've identified a problem worth solving and a solution that customers will want, it's time to make an MVP. But you need to know the *real* minimum

---

[*]   *http://www.beloblog.com/ProJo_Blogs/newsblog/archives/2008/02/swiffer_invento.html*

[†]   *http://www.oldseadoos.com/*

that you can build. As a big organization, you may have restrictions on data sharing, reliability, or compliance to which smaller organizations (that have less to lose) aren't subject. You also need to identify your unfair advantages.

Consider, for example, the many meal pre-ordering tools on the market today. These mobile applications let you place an order from a food court restaurant, pay, and pick up at an agreed-upon time without waiting. The restaurants like them because they save precious time in the lunchtime rush, and the diners like them because they're simple and buyers can browse the menu at their leisure. It's like Uber for lunch.

Now consider what would happen if McDonalds were to decide to compete by introducing an application. It might have franchise constraints, or regulations for restaurants located in airports, or state laws about disclosing caloric content. All of these would have to be part of the MVP.

Offsetting this, however, is the huge amount of market control the company has. It could promote the app by giving away three hamburgers for free to everyone who installed it. The company would make back the money quickly in saved time at the cash register, and have access to a new marketing channel and untapped analytical insight into its customers.

Intrapreneurs need to factor these kinds of constraints and advantages into their MVP far more than independent startups do.

What's more, as people start using your MVP, you have to manage the beta process carefully. You may be interfering with existing deals in the sales pipeline, or creating more work for customer support. If so, you need to have approval for the rollout and the buy-in of stakeholders. If you're launching an entirely new product line, you may even have to camouflage it so you don't cannibalize existing markets until you know it's successful. This, of course, undermines your ability to use unfair advantages like an existing customer base.

Viral from the Start

If you're trying to move upward in the BCG box, your product should include viral and word-of-mouth elements. In a world where everyone has access to a mobile device, every product needs to have an interactive strategy. There's simply no excuse not to find a viral angle to act as a force multiplier for growth. In fact, adding a viral component is one of the keys to moving dogs and cash cows up into question marks and stars.

Revenue Within the Ecosystem

You'll have less flexibility to set pricing and reinvest revenues in product marketing, because as you grow you'll have to coexist with other marketing efforts by your host company. When Microsoft wanted to test its SaaS-based Office suite, it could do so in a relatively controlled way. But as soon as it wanted to monetize the product, it had to contend with cannibalization and pushback from a channel that depended on license revenue.

Your pricing may have to take into account channels, distributors, and other factors that restrict your freedom to experiment, because changes you make will have an impact on other products in the marketplace. Had Blockbuster entered the streaming video market, it would have had to deal with labor and real estate issues at existing stores.

Scale and the Handoff

In the final stages of intrapreneur innovation, the new product has proven its viability. It's either stolen by a more mainstream part of the organization—which can help it cross the chasm and broaden its appeal—or the team that created it must itself transition to a more traditional, structured model of business and take its place among the other products and divisions of the host organization.

Most of the time, the DNA of a disruptive organization isn't well suited to "boring" management and growth, so you'll need to hand off the product to the rest of the organization and find the next thing to disrupt. That means you really have two customers: the external one buying the product, and the internal one that has to make, sell, and support it.

Ultimately, the intrapreneur must manage the relationship with the host organization as well as the relationship with the target market. Initially, this can be intentionally distant, but as the disruptive product becomes part of the host, the handoff must be graceful.

CHAPTER 31

Conclusion: Beyond Startups

If all goes well, you eventually stop being a startup. You've found product/ market fit, and you're scaling even as your growth slows to that of a big company. But hopefully you're still analytical. Hopefully you're still thinking in terms of learning, and continuous improvement, and demanding that data back up your opinions.

Your startup has succeeded when it's a sustainable, repeatable business that can generate a return to its founders and investors. It might take on additional funding at this point, but the purpose of the funding is no longer to identify and mitigate uncertainties, it's to execute on a proven business model. Data becomes less about optimization and more about accounting. If there are "lean analytics" going on, they're probably in new product or feature discovery, and look more like intrapreneur innovation.

We started by saying that if you can't measure something, you can't manage it. But there's a contrary, perhaps more philosophical, observation we need to consider. It's a line by Lloyd S. Nelson, who worked at Nashua Corporation. "The most important figures that one needs for management are unknown or unknowable, but successful management must nevertheless take account of them." This smacks of Donald Rumsfeld's "unknown unknowns," and as your company grows and achieves a degree of operational consistency, figuring out what you *don't* know becomes a key task of management.

Nelson's point was that we often do things without knowing they'll work. That's called experimentation. But experimentation—for companies of any size—succeeds only if it's part of a process of continuous learning, one we hope to have instilled in you whatever the size or stage of your business.

How to Instill a Culture of Data in Your Company

If you're a leader—the founder of a startup, or a C-level executive in a large enterprise—you can turn analytics into a competitive advantage simply by asking good questions. Earlier in the book we said that a good metric is one that drives decision making. As a leader within your organization, demand proof through data before making decisions.

Data doesn't just lead to better decisions. It also improves organizational efficiency. You can create a flatter, more autonomous organization once everyone buys in to a data-informed approach, because rather than needing to propagate an opinion across the organization, you can let the facts speak for themselves. You can empower employees to make more decisions and take on more responsibility once they've got the data in place to support them. Create a culture of accountability, and then reward those who step up and deliver.

Whether you're in a leadership position or not, you can make your organization more data-centric. Here's how.

Start Small, Pick One Thing, and Show Value

There will always be naysayers in an organization who believe instinct, gut, and "the way we've always done business" are good enough. The best thing you can do is pick a small but significant problem your company faces (take any single metric of importance, be it churn, percent daily active users, website conversions, etc.) and work to improve it through analytics.

Don't go after the most crucial issue your company is facing—that's likely got too many cooks in the kitchen already (or worse, it's mired in politics you don't want to wade into). Instead, pick an ancillary issue, something that can add demonstrable business value but is being overlooked.

This approach, if taken too far, can lead to silos within the company, and that's a bad thing. Once you've demonstrated the benefits with one issue, roll out the process across all departments and product areas.

Make Sure Goals Are Clearly Understood

To prove the value of an analytics-focused company, any project you take on needs to have clear goals. If you don't have a goal in mind (including a line in the sand that you've drawn), you'll fail. Everyone involved in the project needs to be aligned around the goals.

Get Executive Buy-in

Unless you're the CEO and pushing this approach top-down, you'll need executive buy-in. For example, if you want to improve the conversion of website visitors signing up for your free trial software application, make sure the person in charge of marketing is on board. This person's buy-in will be critical in aligning goals, but also in driving the culture up and down the corporate ladder.

Make Things Simple to Digest

A good metric is one that's easy to understand at a glance. Don't overwhelm people with a firehose of numbers. They'll get frustrated, and they're also very likely to start looking at the wrong things, focusing on the wrong numbers, and making decisions without understanding what they're looking at. Metrics can be extremely valuable, but used incorrectly they'll lead down the wrong path.

Remember the One Metric That Matters. Use that principle as a way of easing people into analytics and number crunching.

Ensure Transparency

If you're going to use data to make decisions, it's important that you share the data and the methodologies used to acquire and process it. Decision-making frameworks are needed so that your company can find repeatable strategies for the use of analytics (and lessen the "flying by the seat of our pants" approach that companies often take). Transparency (in both success and failure) is important for breaking down the data silos and people's preconceived notions about analytics.

Don't Eliminate Your Gut

As we've said before, Lean Analytics isn't about eliminating your gut, it's about proving your gut right or wrong. Accenture Chief Scientist Kishore Swaminathan says, "Science is purely empirical and dispassionate, but scientists are not. Science is objective and mechanical, but it also values scientists who are creative, intuitive, and who can take a leap of faith."[*]

You can help push your company's culture by making sure you balance people's notion that instinct and gut are enough with small, data-driven experiments, proving the value of analytics while not completely eliminating the benefits of instinct.

---

[*] *http://www.accenture.com/us-en/outlook/Pages/outlook-journal-2011-edge-csuite-analytics.aspx*

Instilling change in any size organization takes time. You can't expect a company to change the way it does business and makes decisions overnight. Start small, and find experiments you can box in easily and which generate measurable results quickly. Prove the value of analytics in moving your company's KPIs (even a little bit), and you'll be able to make the case for an analytics-focused shift. Use concepts like the One Metric That Matters and tools like the Problem-Solution Canvas to make analytics approachable and understandable for everyone, not just the data scientists. Get people focused on lines in the sand—measurable targets that everyone (including executives) agrees to—so that you can demonstrate results.

Ask Good Questions

There's never been a better time to know your market. Your customers leave a trail of digital breadcrumbs with every click, tweet, vote, like, share, check-in, and purchase, from the first time they hear about you until the day they leave you forever, whether they're online or off. If you know how to collect those breadcrumbs, you have unprecedented insight into their needs, their quirks, and their lives.

This insight is forever changing what it means to be a business leader. Once, a leader convinced others to act in the absence of information. Today, there's simply too much information available. We don't need to guess—we need to know where to focus. We need a disciplined approach to growth that identifies, quantifies, and overcomes risk every step of the way. Today's leader doesn't have all the answers. Instead, today's leader knows what questions to ask.

Go forth and *ask good questions.*

References and Further Reading

The following books were instrumental to us in writing this text, and have informed much of our thinking about startups in general.

The Innovator's Solution, Clayton M. Christensen and Michael E. Raynor

The Rules of Work, Richard Templar

Next, Michael Lewis

Start-up Nation, Dan Senor and Saul Singer

Confronting Reality, Larry Bossidy and Ram Charan

Business Model Generation, Alexander Osterwalder and Yves Pigneur

Growing Pains, Eric G. Flamholtz and Yvonne Randle

High-Tech Ventures, C. Gordon Bell with John E. McNamara

Running Lean, Ash Maurya

The Lean Startup, Eric Ries

Four Steps to the Epiphany, Steven Blank

Don't Just Roll the Dice, Neil Davidson

11 Rules for Creating Value in the Social Era, Nilofer Merchant

Measuring the Networked Nonprofit: Using Data to Change the World, Beth Kanter and Katie Delahaye Paine

The Righteous Mind, Jonathan Haidt

Made to Stick, Dan and Chip Heath

Index

application launch rate metric, 313
app stores
  about, 103–104
  installation volume and, 106
  as two-sided marketplaces, 137
ARPDAU (average revenue per daily
      active user), 315
ARPPU (average revenue per paying
      user), 316–317
ARPU (average revenue per user), 105,
      107–109
artificial virality, 228–229, 287
The Art of Focused Conversation
      (Stanfield), 211
assumptions (Three-Threes Model),
      260–261
Atkinson, Rowan, 203
attention metric, 90
auction marketplaces, 152
audience size metric, 117–118
Automattic hosting company, 274
average days since last visit metric, 127
average revenue per daily active user
      (ARPDAU), 315
average revenue per paying user
      (ARPPU), 316–317
average revenue per user (ARPU), 105,
      107–109

B

BAAN ERP, 358–364
background noise on sites, 122
Backupify case study, 92–95, 256
Baldwin, Ben, 99
Balsamiq application, 94
Barney, Daniel, 303
baselines
  about, 347–349
  enterprise startups and, 366
Bass diffusion curve, 227–228
Bass, Frank, 227
Baymard Institute, 296
BBC study of online engagement,
      334–336
BCG (Boston Consulting Group),
      376–377
Beal, George, 278
Beatport music retailer, 239
Begemann, Jens, 111
benchmarks for metrics, 274–275
bias
  interviewing people and, 166, 215
  in qualitative metrics, 165

Billingsley, Jason
  on mailing list effectiveness, 288
  on search tools, 82
  on shopping cart abandonment,
        297
  on stock availability, 85
blank ads, 122, 322
Blank, Steve, xxi, 16
Blizzard app, 104
BMC Software, 360
Bohlen, Joe, 278
Bossidy, Larry, 373
Boston Consulting Group (BCG),
      376–377
Botton, Alain de, 167
Bouchard, Nicolas, 139–141
Boyle, David, 381–383
breakeven metrics
  CLV-CAC math, 253
  EBITDA, 253
  hibernation, 253
  variable cost, 252–253
Breinlinger, Josh, 143
Brezina, Matt, 311–312
Buffer case study, 257–260
build-measure-learn cycle, xxiii
Business Model Canvas, 32
business models. *See also* specific
        business models
  about, 63–67
  aspects of, 67–69
  categories of, 69–70
  exercise for picking, 70
  flipbooks for, 67–69
  leading indicators tied to, 237
  Scale stage considerations, 256–257
  stages and, 265–269
buyer and seller growth rate, 146–147
buyer and seller ratings, 147, 149
buy-in, executive, 384, 391

C

CAC (customer acquisition cost)
  Backify case study, 92
  determining normal value for met-
        rics, 284–285
  in e-commerce model, 76, 78
  in mobile apps model, 105,
        310–313
  paid engine and, 48
  in Revenue stage, 241, 246–247,
        253
  in SaaS model, 90

M

machine-only optimization, 39
MacLeod, Mark, 305
MailChimp mailing list provider, 287
mailing list click-through rates, 76, 83–84
mailing lists
    answers-at-scale campaign and, 191
    determining normal values of metrics, 287–289
    in e-commerce model, 76, 83–84
Maltz, Jules, 303
managed service provider (MSP), 360–361
marketing definition, 64, 245
Marshall, Alfred, 279
Massive Damage mobile game company, 309, 313
massively multiplayer online (MMO) games, 47, 104
Maurya, Ash
    Lean Canvas, 31, 32, 48–50, 219
    on problem interviews, 169
    Running Lean, 163–164
May, Robert, 92–93
McCallum, Daniel C., 372
McClure, Dave, 45–46
McFadden, Dan, 368
McLuhan, Marshall, 43
Mechanical Turk service, 185–186
media site model
    about, 113
    examples of, 113
    key takeaways, 123
    measuring metrics in, 113–120, 321–330
    stage comparisons in, 267–269
    user flow depicted through, 120–121
    wrinkles in, 122–123
Mehr, Alex, 304
Melinger, Dan, 281–282
Meteor Entertainment Hawken game, 48
metrics. See also OMTM (One Metric That Matters)
    baseline considerations, 347–349
    correlated versus causal, 12, 20–21
    data capture pitfalls to avoid, 40
    in e-commerce model, 75–84, 293–298
    for Empathy stage, 159
    enterprise markets and, 364–370

evaluation exercise, 29
exploratory versus reporting, 12, 15–18
leading versus lagging, 12, 18–20
as Lean Canvas component, 33
in media site model, 113–120, 321–330
in mobile apps model, 105–110, 309–320
moving targets and, 21–23
normal or ideal value for, 273–291
qualitative versus quantitative, 12, 13
for Revenue stage, 241–242
rules of thumb for, 9–13
in SaaS model, 90–98, 299–308
for Scale stage, 256
in two-sided marketplaces model, 142–150, 341–345
in user-generated content model, 127–133, 331–339
vanity versus real/actionable, 12, 13–15
for Virality stage, 230–232, 235
Microsoft, 375, 387
Mine That Data consultancy, 72
Minimum Viable Product. See MVP (Minimum Viable Product)
minimum viable vision, 217–219
MMO (massively multiplayer online) games, 47, 104
mobile apps model
    about, 103–104
    advertising in, 104, 111
    DuProprio/Comfree case study, 141
    key takeaways, 111
    measuring metrics in, 105–110, 309–320
    monetization in, 104, 107–109, 111
    Sincerely Inc. case study, 311–313
    stage comparisons in, 267–269
    user flow depicted through, 110–111
    wrinkles in, 111
mobile download size metric, 310
mobile downloads metric, 309
mode (e-commerce model), 74, 237
monetization
    in media site model, 113–117, 326–330
    minimum viable vision on, 219
    in mobile apps model, 104, 106–109, 107–109

Q

qidiq tool case study, 205–208
QRR (quarterly recurring revenue), 244–245
qualified leads metric, 19
qualitative metrics
  about, 12, 161
  bias in, 165
  in Empathy stage, 159
  MVP process and, 199
  patterns and pattern recognition in, 162
  quantitative versus, 13
  trends and, 165
quantitative metrics
  about, 12
  getting answers at scale, 184–185
  limitations of, 39
  measuring effects of features, 209–210
  qualitative versus, 13
quarterly new product bookings metric, 19
quarterly recurring revenue (QRR), 244–245

R

railroad example, 372–373
Rally Software case study, 211–215, 363
ramen profitability, 258
ranking
  mobile apps, 106
  problems, 173
rates in metrics, 10
ratios in metrics, 10
real/actionable metrics
  about, 12
  vanity versus, 13–15
reality distortion field, 3–8
recency of visits to site, 127
recommendation acceptance rate, 76, 83
reddit site
  advertising on, 122, 125
  case study for, 332–333, 336–337
  content creation and interaction, 128
  leading indicators in, 238–239
  spam and bad content, 338–339
  tiers of engagement, 126, 129
referral element (AARRR), 46

referrals
  enterprise startups and, 363
  traffic from, 323–324
Reichfeld, Frederick F., 231
reporting metrics
  about, 12
  exploratory versus, 15–18
response rate metric, 206–207
retention
  as goal in Stickiness stage, 208–214
  leading indicators for, 236
  sticky engine and, 47
retention element (AARRR), 46
revenue element (AARRR), 46
revenue per customer. *See* CLV (customer lifetime value)
revenue source (business model), 67–68
Revenue stage (Lean Analytics)
  about, 154
  business model comparisons, 269
  depicted, 53
  enterprise startups and, 363–364
  finding revenue groove, 245–246
  goal of, 241
  intrapreneurs and, 387
  market/product fit, 250–252
  metrics for, 241–242
  Parse.ly case study, 247–249
  penny machine example, 242–245
  summary of, 254
  usage example, 155, 156
revenue streams box (Lean Canvas), 33, 50
Ries, Eric
  on engines of growth, 47–48, 55, 64
  on Lean Startup, xxii
  Long Funnel example, 52
The Righteous Mind (Haidt), 168
River Out Of Eden (Dawkins), 38
Rogati, Monica, 39–40
Rogers, Everett, 278
Rose, Kevin, 198
Rubicon Consulting, 128
The Rules of Work (Pearson), 373
Rumsfeld, Donald, 15–16
Running Lean (Maurya), 163–164

Timehop case study, 232–234
  usage example, 155, 156
  ways things spread, 228–229
visit frequency metric, 95

W

Wang, ChenLi, 236
Wardley, Simon, 369
web performance metric, 290–291
Webtrends tool, 139
Wegener, Jonathan, 232–233
WiderFunnel Marketing agency, 79
Widrich, Leo, 257
Wikipedia site
  content creation and interaction,
    128
  user-generated content model and,
    126–127
  value of created content, 131
Williams, Alex, 353
Wilson, Fred, 83, 133, 278
Wilson, Harold, 351
WineExpress.com case study, 79–82
Wong, Benny, 232
Wooga game developer, 111
word-of-mouth virality, 228–229,
    325–330, 363
WP Engine case study, 274–275
Writethat.name site, 66

Y

Yammer site, 336, 358
Y Combinator accelerator, 277, 332
Year One Labs
  minimum viable vision, 217
  MVP as process, 197
  OMTM considerations, 58
  qidiq case study, 205
Yipit site, 65
Young, Indi, 179
YouTube site
  advertising on, 327–328
  content creation and interaction,
    128
  monetizing, 326–330
  tiers of engagement, 126

Z

Zaccai, Gianfranco, 385
Zadeh, Joe, 5
Zappos.com, 74
Zero Overhead Principle, 356
Zoosk dating site, 304
Zyman, Sergio, 64, 245

About the Authors

Alistair Croll has been an entrepreneur, author, and public speaker for nearly 20 years. In that time, he's worked on web performance, big data, cloud computing, and startups. Alistair is the chair of O'Reilly's Strata conference, TechWeb's Cloud Connect, and Interop's Enterprise Cloud Summit. In 2001, he co-founded web performance startup Coradiant, and since that time has also helped launch Rednod, CloudOps, Bitcurrent, Year One Labs, the Bitnorth Conference, the International Startup Festival, and several early-stage companies.

This is Alistair's fourth book on analytics, technology, and entrepreneurship. Alistair lives in Montreal, Canada, and tries to mitigate chronic attention deficit disorder by writing about far too many things at *Solve for Interesting* (*http://www.solveforinteresting.com*). You can find him on Twitter as @acroll, or email him at *alistair@solveforinteresting.com*.

Ben Yoskovitz is an entrepreneur with more than 15 years of experience in web businesses. He started his first company in 1996 while completing university. In 2011, he joined GoInstant as VP Product. The company was acquired in September 2012 by Salesforce.com, and he continues in his role with GoInstant and Salesforce.com.

Ben has been blogging since 2006. His *Instigator Blog* (*http://instigatorblog .com*) is recognized as one of the top blogs on startups and entrepreneurship. Ben is also an active mentor to numerous startups and accelerator programs. He regularly speaks at startup conferences and events, including the Michigan Lean Startup Conference, the Internet Marketing Conference, and the Lean Startup Conference. You can reach him on Twitter as @byosko, or email him at *byosko@gmail.com.*

In 2010, Alistair, Ben, and two other partners co-founded Year One Labs, an early-stage accelerator that provided funding and up to one year of hands-on mentorship to five startups. Year One Labs followed a Lean Startup program, making it the first accelerator to formalize such a structure. Four of those five companies graduated from Year One Labs, and three went on to raise follow-on financing. One of those companies, Localmind, was acquired by Airbnb. A great deal of Alistair and Ben's experience and thinking around Lean Startup and analytics emerged during this time.

Have it your way.

Get even more for your money.

Join the O'Reilly Community, and register the O'Reilly books you own. It's free, and you'll get:

- $4.99 ebook upgrade offer
- 40% upgrade offer on O'Reilly print books
- Membership discounts on books and events
- Free lifetime updates to ebooks and videos
- Multiple ebook formats, DRM FREE
- Participation in the O'Reilly community
- Newsletters
- Account management
- 100% Satisfaction Guarantee

Signing up is easy:

1. **Go to: oreilly.com/go/register**
2. **Create an O'Reilly login.**
3. **Provide your address.**
4. **Register your books.**

Note: English-language books only

To order books online:

oreilly.com/store

For questions about products or an order:

orders@oreilly.com

To sign up to get topic-specific email announcements and/or news about upcoming books, conferences, special offers, and new technologies:

elists@oreilly.com

For technical questions about book content:

booktech@oreilly.com

To submit new book proposals to our editors:

proposals@oreilly.com

O'Reilly books are available in multiple DRM-free ebook formats. For more information:

oreilly.com/ebooks

O'REILLY®

Spreading the knowledge of innovators   oreilly.com